THE HISTORY OF DUNSTER CHURCH AND PRIORY

VOLUME TWO

Joan Jordan

ryelands

MARTE

QUÆ·SITA   TUENDA·ARTE

British Library Cataloguing-in-Publication Data
A CIP record for this title is available from the British Library

ISBN 978 1 906551 11 7

RYELANDS
Halsgrove House,
Ryelands Industrial Estate,
Bagley Road, Wellington, Somerset TA21 9PZ
Tel: 01823 653777   Fax: 01823 216796
email: sales@halsgrove.com

Part of the Halsgrove group of companies
Information on all Halsgrove titles is available at: www.halsgrove.com

Printed and bound by Cromwell Press Group, Trowbridge

CONTENTS

ACKNOWLEDGEMENTS

I am indebted to Mr H.F. Merchant (and to the late J.P. Brooke-Little C.V.O., M.A. F.S.A., FHS, Norroy and Ulster King of Arms, Chairman of the Heraldry Society) for permission to quote from his article on the *Luttrell Hatchments at Dunster*, which first appeared in the *Coat of Arms* published by the Heraldry Society (1985/6).

I am also indebted to the late Col. Sir Walter Luttrell K.C.V.O., M.C., J.P., for his permission to reproduce photographs of the hatchments in St George's Church, Dunster. Sir Walter also kindly gave me permission to reproduce photographs taken of original paintings of his ancestors at Court House, East Quantoxhead. Sir Walter's family retains the copyright of these photographs.

My thanks are due to Mr R. Sherlock for his permission to include his measured drawing of the chandelier in Dunster Church, and to Lt. Colonel N.D. McIntosh, M.B.E., of the Regimental Headquarters, Richmond, Yorkshire, for information concerning the Green Howards Regiment. I thank Mr Caldwell for providing the information about James Thornhill and his 'Brazen Serpent' painting in St George's Church. Mr Dudley Dodd's paper on Anthony Salvin added to my knowledge of the nineteenth-century rebuilding of Dunster Castle. I am also indebted to Lady Money-Coutts, Mr Richard A. Todd and Mr Joseph Newbery for information regarding the family of the Rev. Richard Utten Todd, and to Sir David Money-Coutts for his valuable advice.

From the research angle, my thanks are especially due to Mr D. Bromwich M.A., A.L.A., formerly the Head Librarian of the Local Studies Library, Taunton, who provided continued assistance for many years. I am also grateful to the Heraldry Society, the Royal Society of St George and the staff of Minehead library.

The Parish Council of St George's Church very kindly gave me a grant towards this project. I am also indebted to the Marc Fitch Fund for its generous grant. For the great interest and financial support of my friends, and especially to Manette and John Nelson, and Maureen Tuttle, I also extend my appreciation and gratitude. The photographs were nearly all taken by the late Geoffrey Lancaster; I am also grateful to Michael Hankin and Robin Downes for their photography.

Most importantly, I am grateful to the late Mr Ted Beer for his continued and unvarying patience, interest and considerable expertise. He was entirely responsible for putting my original manuscript of my projected

Volumes III -VI into typeface and storing it on discs, having previously typed up, without remuneration, almost all of my Volumes I and II, now published as the first volume of this book.

Also I have to thank Sue Lloyd, M.Phil., of the Genge Press, Minehead, for her professional gifts as the editor of what would have been an unwieldy tome without her expertise. My thanks also go to Mr Steven Pugsley, of Halsgrove, for his patience and support.

Editor's note

For the purposes of publication this book has had to be severely abridged. This means much interesting material, including private letters, technical estimates, genealogies, reminiscences, etc. has had to be omitted, along with many illustrations. Many of the documents to which the author had access have now become lost or hard to read, others are in private collections. The Somerset Archive & Record Service, which already holds a collection of Dunster Parish Magazines and Church Year Books, has kindly agreed to store the author's full original text, complete with footnotes and original illustrations, at the Somerset Record Office, Taunton, where the public will be able to have access to it.

DEDICATION

To my late husband and all the friends
and organizations who have supported
this project over many years

CHAPTER ONE

DUNSTER LIFE and the LUTTRELL FAMILY in the LATER SEVENTEENTH CENTURY

In 1655 Francis Luttrell succeeded his brother George, who had died without issue, and the same year he married a Cambridgeshire lady, Lucy Symonds, the granddaughter of the renowned parliamentarian, John Pym. Thus the stand taken by the Luttrell family during the Civil War was further buttressed, for Thomas, the grandfather of George and Francis, had married Jane Popham whose family also espoused the Roundhead's cause.

Francis Luttrell had been baptised at Dunster in November 1628, the year which had witnessed the presentation of the Petition of Rights to a reluctant King, a bill 'against arbitrary imprisonment, martial law, forced loans and the billeting of soldiers and sailors'.[1] His career begins with his admission as a Member of Lincoln's Inn in 1646 and it is possible that he was in London in 1658 when on 3 September 'died that arch rebell Oliver Cromwell.'[2]

The Restoration
Since December 1653, England had been governed by Cromwell, who ruled as Lord Protector through his Major-Generals. But Cromwell died in September 1658, to be succeeded by his amiable but weak son Richard, whose lack of character and training foundered over the difficulties which arose between him and the army. On 23 April 1659, Parliament was dissolved and it was evident that the Protectorate was withering away. John Evelyn wrote in his diary three days later:

> April 25. A wonderful & suddaine change in the face of the publique: The new Protector Richard slighted, severall pretenders & parties strive for the Government, allAnarchy and confusion; Lord have mercy upon us...
> October 11...The Armie now turn'd out the parliament.
> October 16. We had now no Government in the Nation, all in Confusion; no Majistrate either own'd or pretended, but the souldiers & they not agreed; God Almighty have mercy on, & settle us...[3]

General discontent at the resultant general lawlessness and anarchy was growing, and many now longed for the peaceful days before the Revolution, when the King and Parliament had ruled the country. The Governor of Scotland (now united with England), General Monck, was the commander of the finest army in Britain and a friend of Parliament, to which he believed it was his duty as a soldier to be obedient. In February 1660 he marched on London and recalled the old Parliament, to general rejoicing. Members previously excluded because they refused to sign an agreement 'to be faithful to a commonwealth without a king or house of lords' [4] were now able to return, including William Prynne, who had been imprisoned at Dunster Castle. [5]

On 31 March, 1660 a general election took place and the country was in a ferment of excitement. Many were the candidates who strove for parliamentary seats. Francis Luttrell was returned for Minehead. He was returned again the following spring and remained a Member of Parliament until his death in 1666.[6]

On 25 April, 1660, the new Parliament met. The lords voted that '"according to the ancient and fundamental laws of this kingdom, this government is, and ought to be, by king, lords, and commons" and the commons promptly agreed.' The proclamation, agreed by both houses, 'emphasised that Charles II, immediately upon the decease of his father, had succeeded, "by inherent birthright, and lawful and undoubted succession" '. [7]

John Evelyn records:

> 29th May. This day, his Majesty, Charles the Second came to London, after a sad and long exile and calamitous suffering, both of the King and Church, being seventeen years. This was also his birth-day, and with a triumph of above 20,000 horse and foot, brandishing their swords, and shouting with inexpressible joy; the ways strewed with flowers, the bells ringing, the streets hung with tapestry, fountains running with wine; the Mayor, Aldermen, and all the Companies, in their liveries, chains of gold and banners; Lords and Nobles, clad in cloth of silver, gold, and velvet; the windows and balconies, all set with ladies; trumpets, music, and myriads of people flocking, even so far as from Rochester, so as they were seven hours in passing the city, even from two in the afternoon till nine at night.[8]

Whilst there was now to be a single figurehead, Charles Stuart acted on the provisions of the Declaration of Breda with caution, and made these provisions 'subject to parliamentary approval'. Parliament now occupied a more prestigious role of authority than it had formerly enjoyed and constitutional rule was ensured.[9]

Charles II, looking back to his former days of defeat at the battle of Worcester and his subsequent romantic escapes, decided to commemorate the Boscobel Oak and institute the Order of the Royal Oak, an award to be bestowed on the loyal supporters of the House of Stuart. County lists were prepared and notable cavaliers were naturally included. Somerset numbered fifteen nominees for this accolade but it is remarkable that Francis Luttrell's name was included for his family were noted parliamentarians. Perhaps, as Lyte suggests, 'the demolition of the greater part of Dunster Castle by order of the Council of State after the Civil War was over, may have caused a change in his politics'.[10]

King Charles II was crowned on 23 April 1661 in the abbey church of Westminster. A short time later, on 8 May, the king announced his intention to marry the Infanta of Portugal, Catherine of Braganza. With this lady in mind, Colonel Francis Luttrell, the second son of Francis (who had died in 1666), caused the balustrade of the oak staircase he had installed in Dunster Castle, to bear a carved representation of a Portuguese coin.[11]

At the Restoration in 1660 all churches were required to display the Royal Coat of Arms by statute. Our Carolean example in St. George's church is a splendid and large example. It is displayed on the Norman north wall of the nave but, since the churchwardens' accounts extant are not earlier than 1670, we have no details. It is known that the hatchments which were erected in the autumn of 1953 were restored before that date and it is possible that the Royal Coat of Arms was similarly restored. One wonders if Francis Luttrell's change of politics, no doubt brought about by the destruction of a large part of the castle by the Parliamentarians, was perhaps outwardly and very visibly affirmed by the purchase of one of the largest and most impressive of examples. These arms seem to have escaped the attentions of those who repainted the Stuart arms with those of Hanover during the 1715 and 1745 Jacobite rebellions. It may be that it was hidden, as at that time it was sometimes the practice to paint a new canvas and fix it over the top of the existing one. Very often these boards were executed by a sign writer or a local artist. The St George's example bears the usual floriated C and the date 1660. The arms are given by Parker as:

> Quarterly: *I. and IV. counter-quartered; 1. and 4. France: 2. and 3. England: II or, a lion rampant within a double tressure flory counter-flory gules, Scotland: III azure, a harp or, stringed argent, Ireland. All within the garter and crowned. Authority: great seal.* Supporters: *a lion gardant imperially crowned or, and a unicorn argent, armed, unguled, crined, and gorged with an imperial crown, having a chain affixed to it, or.* Motto: *DIEV ET MON DROIT.*[12]

Francis Luttrell II and his Wife Mary Tregonwell

Francis Luttrell I died six years after the Restoration of King Charles II and his burial took place at Dunster on 14 March 1666. Lucy, his wife died on Christmas Eve 1718 and was buried at Dunster on 7 January 1719. Their eldest son, Thomas, baptised at Dunster on 19 March 1657, died in 1670. The heir was therefore Francis Luttrell II (b. 1659), their next son, who was baptised at Dunster on 16 July 1659.

When the two little boys were six and four years of age in 1663, their father bought a 'smale great sadle for a child, of pinck coulored plush trimed with silver lace'.[13] It cost him the princely sum of £4. He appears to have indulged his family for he paid £7 10s at another time for 'a box of sweet-meates'.[14]

In 1663, on 20 October, the baptism of Francis and Lucy's third son, Alexander, took place. Three years later the small boys were fatherless and in 1668 their grandmother, Jane Luttrell, also died and was buried at Dunster in November of that year. She obviously cared greatly for the welfare of her youngest grandchild, nicknamed 'Sany', and did not want him to be disadvantaged by his elder brother, Francis. She undertook to provide for him and made a will in his favour. However, as we shall see, Alexander's mother, Lucy, had to fight through the courts to obtain the sizeable sum left to him by his grandmother Jane's will.

In 1676 Francis Luttrell II matriculated at the age of seventeen years at Christ Church, Oxford, but he left the university without a degree. While he was there there was some idea of buying a peerage for him. Anthony Wood, the antiquarian, writing on 26 October 1678 said:

> I was told from Sir Thomas Spencer's house that the King hath given Dr. Fell, Bishop of Oxon, a patent for an Earl (which comes to about 1000 *l*) towards the finishing of the great gate of Christ Church near Pembroke College. He intends to bestow it on Mr. Lutterell, a gentleman commoner of Christ Church, of Somersetshire, having 4000*l* per annum at present.[15]

The ennobled earl was certainly not Francis Luttrell II, whose income was exaggerated by Wood. In February 1679, Francis, aged twenty, became the Member of Parliament for Minehead and would remain the town's parliamentary representative until his death in 1690.

On 15 July 1680, he made a most advantageous marriage to a beautiful and wealthy heiress, Mary Tregonwell of Milton Abbas in the county of Dorset. This striking lady, the owner of fabulous jewels, appears unadorned in her oval portrait in Dunster castle. The twin portrait of her husband, by then Colonel Francis Luttrell, hangs beside it over the fireplace in the former parlour, now the dining room of the castle. He is shown wearing a brown periwig, a lace jabot and a steel gorget with gold rivets. The appointment to the rank of colonel had been made by the Earl of Winchelsea, the Lord-Lieutenant of Somerset. When Charles II's illegitimate son by Lucy Walters, the Duke of Monmouth, landed at Lyme Regis in June 1685, Colonel Luttrell was colonel of a regiment of foot.

When the momentous landing took place, Francis was in need of money. It is said that Mary Luttrell had an independent income of £2,500 derived from capital which she estimated to be £50,000.[16] However, it was from money that Francis had given her that the necessary funds were provided. The story goes that he had been in the habit of presenting her with a guinea, or broad piece of gold, when fines were imposed on his tenants for the renewal of leases. She had hoarded this money at Dunster Castle and had amassed about £500. Out of this she gave him £200 towards his military exploits. Colonel Luttrell's military endeavours in support of King James II did not succeed for he had to evacuate Taunton castle on the approach of

Monmouth and his superior forces. On his arrival at that place, Monmouth assumed the title of King. West Country sympathizers were with him. Indeed there is a fanciful tale which casts Colonel Francis in a very different role and tells of him setting out from Dunster with his forces to fight for Monmouth. Hindered in their progress by heavy cannon and a plentiful supply of beer, they are said to have ambled through the countryside, arriving at the battle of Sedgemoor as the battle was coming to an end. The Royalist forces had counter-attacked and Monmouth and his supporters were overwhelmed. The defeat is said to have caused Colonel Luttrell to rally his forces and to march them back to Dunster with great rapidity where they quickly donned their working smocks and were ready to be surprised by the Royalist victory, news of which was brought to them by James II's forces seeking out the fugitive rebels.

In the latter part of James II's reign, Francis Luttrell withdrew his support for the king and was one of the first men of note to rally to the standard of the Prince of Orange at Exeter in November 1688. He was asked to raise an independent company of foot soldiers and this he promptly did and, it is said, he completed the muster in only three days. The local people charged him the enormous sum of £1,500 for worthless clothes acquired at great speed. Colonel Luttrell maintained this company for a fortnight at his own expense and by February 1689, several companies were amalgamated with a regular regiment of the line stationed at Portsmouth and the Isle of Wight and subsequently at Plymouth. Colonel Francis Luttrell was the first colonel of this regiment, which later became known as the Nineteenth Foot — or more familiarly as the Green Howards. The officers were from notable Somerset families and in 1782 the regiment became associated with the North Riding of Yorkshire. The Devon and Somerset families from which the officers were drawn were those of Northcote, Malet, Bowyer, Wyndham, Coward, Dodington, Prater, Sydenham, Stocker and Hancock.

It is not surprising that Colonel Luttrell was in need of money in 1685 when you consider the accounts rendered by his tailor, William Franklyn of Covent Garden, London.[17] What a wealth of information we have here which gives the reader an authentic insight into the costume of the last quarter of the seventeenth century! The costs are revealing and show, not only the differences in cost of materials, but also how little the tailor and the seamstress gained from their intricate, time-consuming labours when no machine was available and all was executed by human hands. This wonderfully evocative and colourful reflection of the period is quoted in Lyte and is given here in full:

> 1681, August. "Making a rich laced cloath suite, 1*l*.18*s*. Silk and galloone. 5*s*. A pair of scarlett silk stockings with gold, 1*l*.15*s*. Buckles to the britches. 3*s*.6*d*. Silk to line the britches, 10*s*. Pocketts and staying tape, 3*s* 6*d*. A sett of rich gold buttons, 2*l*.14*s*.6*d*. Rich gold brest buttons, 4*s*.6*d*. Fine drawing the suite, 3*s*.6*d*. 2 ½ yards of superfine gray cloth, 2*l*.12*s*.6*d*. Buckram and canvas, 1*s*.3*d*. 5 ½ yards of rich Florence sattin, to line the coate, 4*l*.14*s*. Scarlett plaine ribbon, 1*l*.5*s*. 4 yards rich gold and scarlett

ribbon, 6*l*.5*s*. 18 yards rich gold orar lace for coate and britches, 18*l*, Gold chaine to the suite, 14*s*.9*d*. Rich gold needle for the gloves, 10*l* 5*s*. A pair of gloves, makeing and faceing, 9*s*. A scarlett fether, 1*l*.8*s*. Rich needle gold fring for a scarffe, 35*l*.5*s*. Silk for the scarffe and making itt, 18*s*."

On 24 March 1682, a quite different aspect of life in Dunster is revealed by the following entry in the Churchwardens' Accounts: 'Gave three boyes for goeing up top of Grabist to witness against a parsell of idle people that was there time of Divine Service. 6d.'

In March 1682, Mr. Franklyn the tailor charged for 'a light colloured cloath suite' which was made of 'superfine Spanish cloath att 20s per yard.' This was adorned with '12 dozen of rich gold buttons at 4s 6d per dozen', apart from 'gold buttons for the britches' costing 3s 6d. How was it possible to sew 144 buttons on to one suit apart from those on the breeches? This was, however, not the only instance of this vast number of buttons being used on one suit, for on the same day, Franklyn supplied 'a sad colloured suite', which also had 144 buttons on it but added to these '5 dozen of gold brest—ditto for wast(coat) and britches'. These must have been smaller buttons for they cost 10s for the 5 dozen. The ribbon used cost £2 10s and is referred to as 'sad colloured gold and silver ribbon for shoulder and sword'. 'Rich broad gold orace lace for the wast(coat) and hands of the coate' cost £7.

The costs of the materials were variable but the 'druggitt suite' ordered three weeks later must have been for less auspicious occasions since the material cost only 5s a yard, although considering that 8 yards were required, it must have been of narrow width. Only a month later a 'stuffe suite' was made. This used the same amount of material and the 'fine stuffe' cost 9s 9d a yard and '11 dozen silver and silk buttons' and '3½ dozen of small buttons' cost respectively £1 18s 6d and 4s 6d. 'A sett of figured 10d ribbon for sword, shoulder and hand knotts' for this suit cost £3 4s and '2 dozen of pinck and green 16d ribbon' cost £1 12s.

By November Francis required a riding coat and this was made of a woollen cloth known as 'fine Spanish drabdebery' which cost 20s per yard. The coat was lined with 'blew fine rateene' and the buttons were 'larg silver plate buttons' that cost £3 10s.

The fashion for such a proliferation of buttons seems to have died out by 1685 and the few that were used were less expensive. A 'cloath suite' made in November 1685 had a few 'silke buttons' costing 8s. A coat made the same month was of 'fine French ratteen' at 20*s* a yard and had facings of striped satin to the 'hands', or cuffs. The breeches worn with the coat were to be of 'black fl_oward velvet' and the stockings were now of 'wosted.' On the other hand, the waistcoat was a garment of great elaboration and required '5 ½ yards of blew Florence damask' which cost £3 11s 6d which was to be adorned with five pounds' worth of gold lace on it and on the cuffs of the coat.

The extravagance of Francis Luttrell and, as will be seen later, of his wife Mary, is beyond belief. Colonel Luttrell desired 'to outdo' his brother officers in the splendour of his attire. A uniform supplied by the Government was to be better than the others, and in the same month of April 1689 charges were made for improvements:

> To pay for the lineing of your imbroydered coat, being of richer sattin and much better than the lineing of the other officers 1*l.*6*d.* To pay for blew cloth for your coat, being much better than the other officers, 10*s.*

Tregonwell Luttrell, the eldest child of Colonel and Mrs. Luttrell, was born on 12 February 1683 and was baptised at Dunster a month later, or thereabouts. Lyte has an account of some of the clothes he wore. They are rich garments for an infant. He was just over seven years of age when his father died in 1690 and he himself never lived to inherit the castle. He died at Sheerness in October, 1703 and was buried at Dunster on 31 October 1703.

Tregonwell's sister Mary was born on 25 November 1681 and baptised on 20 December. The items ordered by Mrs. Luttrell that October included: 'a suite of lace childbed linen, mantle and apron, £10; several yards of lace; suits of fine lace linen; a silver porringer and spoone, £1 5s; 18 yards of rich white sattin and gold floured silk for the gowne and pettycoate at 26s per yard [*making the gowne and pettycoate cost 12s.*]; 3¼ yards of rich cherry gold and silver flowred silk for a mantle, at 38s per yard, with Florence sarcenett to line all three mantles', etc. etc. The cradle, bolster, pillow and quilt of white embroidered satin cost £16, with a further satin quilt costing £3 10s. A chest of drawers in 'Prince wood' cost £4 10s.

Expensive purchases continued throughout the 1680s and by July 1688 Mrs. Luttrell's debt to William Franklyn amounted to £819 13s 8d of which £15 10s 6d represented interest on £345 for nine months. As a contrast to this riotous extravagance, the rate levied on Colonel Luttrell for the year 1686 was £1 19s 0d.[18]

In 1423 the livery worn by Sir Hugh Luttrell's servants was green and red; the cost of the green cloth was £4 15s 4d. By 1424, blue cloth (blodii) was used for which 103s 4d was paid for 'Five dozens'. By 1426 the livery colour reverted to red and green. Now over two hundred years later, in 1683 we read: 'Makeing of seven liveries laced, 5*l*'. These were of grey cloth lined with yellow 'padoway' with black and gold buttons, which alone cost £5 10s. From other similar entries it appears that the black and gold buttons cost about 1s 9d per dozen, so that £5 10s would represent about 750 buttons for the seven liveries.[19] How, one asks could each livery have been adorned with 107, at least, buttons, even accounting for a waistcoat, a coat and knee breeches!

The silver plate at Dunster Castle in 1690 was valued at that date at £652. Apart from the plate of silver and silver-gilt, Colonel Francis Luttrell was also the owner of much pewter.[20]

When Colonel Francis Luttrell died in 1690 at the age of 31 years, he is said to have been in debt to the tune of £12,000, not including a further £10,000 which he owed to his brother Colonel Alexander. He died at

Plymouth on the 25th July, and his widow spent £300 on having his body brought back to Dunster for interment. The Overseers' Accounts for 1690[21] show that contrary to the law of 1666,[22] which was made more stringent in 1678, when an affidavit signed by a magistrate was required, Francis Luttrell was buried in linen and not wool.

The untimely death of Colonel Francis Luttrell resulted in much trouble. A contest in the Prerogative Court (Probate Court) at Canterbury between Mary Luttrell, the widow, and her brother-in-law, Alexander ('Sany'), the younger brother of the later Francis, ensued.

Alexander was the guardian of the three surviving children of Mary and Francis[23], namely Tregonwell (b. 12 February 1683, d. October 1703), Mary (b. 25 November 1681) and Frances (b. 17 April 1688). Frances married Edward Harvey about Christmas 1705, and secondly, Edward Ashe of Heytesbury.

Mary married Sir George Rooke, then a widower, on 21 January 1701. Her portrait by Michael Dahl may be seen at Kingston Lacy, Dorset. Rooke was an illustrious connection for the Luttrell family. He was a gentleman sailor from a good family — his father was Sir William Rooke, a Sheriff of Kent. He had volunteered for the second Dutch War (1672) as a young man. By 1691 he was a Vice-Admiral and by 1702 he was Commander-in-Chief of the English fleet off Spain and in the Mediterranean.[24] In 1704 Rooke, along with Admiral Shovell, gained the fortress of Gibraltar for England.

The year her husband became Commander of the English fleet, Mary died in childbirth. She had been married for only eighteen months and was buried at Horton in Kent.[25] The infant, George, survived and had most illustrious god-parents in the persons of Queen Anne and her consort, Prince George of Denmark.

Back in 1693 the full extent of Colonel Francis Luttrell's debts became known. We have already seen the extravagance of the couple's dress. The year after their marriage in 1680 they had installed the elaborate plaster ceiling in the present dining room which displays the Tregonwell arms: *Ar three pellets in fess cotised Sa betw three Cornish choughs ppr.*

It is said that this ceiling 'has affinities with the work of Edward Goudge', one of the most important plasterers of the late seventeenth century who made his own designs. The best kind of plaster, sometimes used for a finishing coat, was obtained by burning gypsum (Plaster of Paris). The usual ingredient for English plasterwork was, however, slaked lime. At Dunster the design includes *putti*, acanthus scrolls, and cavorting animals. The date 1681 is incised in Roman numerals above the chimney piece and the whole work is in an ebullient, full-blooded naturalistic style deriving from France and the Low Countries.

At the peak of their magnificence in the 1680s, Mary and Francis Luttrell had also installed the oak and elm staircase which occupies the space of a former medieval D-shaped tower. The pierced elm panels fashioned from nine-inch planks display lively curving acanthus leaves inhabited by animals and *putti*. All is *mouvementé*; the *putti* abandon their usual classical poses and chase the hunt. Fox-hunting, beagling and stag hunting are represented. The newel posts are surmounted by the ever-popular vases of fruit, but perhaps the unique feature pertaining to Colonel Luttrell is the trophy of arms which commemorates his own military career, described earlier, which culminated in his formation of the famous regiment later known as the Green Howards.

Various coins are carved in the staircase panels: Irish bronze half-pennies with a harp are allusions to Charles II and his Queen, Catherine of Braganza. The royal coins carved in the third panel of the balustrade are, in the foreground, Charles II silver shillings bearing the king's head and interlaced C's. The carver represented the 1683-84 issue, so dating his work.[26] In the background the Portuguese Queen is graciously alluded to by coins displaying the swallow-tailed cross. The staircase has been attributed to Edward Pearce because of the similarities with his documented staircase at Sudbury Hall, Derbyshire (1676).[27]

Although Colonel Francis Luttrell had died in 1690, it was not until March 1693, when their mother Mary and the executrix undertook the administration of the personal estate, that Mary and Frances, his daughters, received the £4,000 each to which they were entitled under his will .[28]

Sir Thomas Wyndham had advanced a loan on the security of the Manor of Beggarnhuish, so lands anciently held by the Luttrells of East Quantoxhead were lost for all time. The bulk of the real estate was strictly entailed and the claims of the creditors could therefore not be met by their sale. Mary Luttrell clung to her jointure of £1,500 a year and, even though she was entitled to a life interest in all the furniture, nevertheless, it is thought that she provided some money to safeguard it from the creditors. For years the servants of the household had not been paid, and the Dyke family, who had a claim on Colonel Francis's personal estate, contended that Mary's jewels should be counted as part of it. The jewels were said to be worth £800 though Lyte considers that this sum was exaggerated. 'Some of the ornaments had come from her mother, the daughter of a former Lord Mayor of London; others were presents from her husband.'[29]

The 1690 inventory of the contents of the castle was meticulously compiled. We know that 'hangings of gilt leather' in Mary Luttrell's closet were later sent to her home, Milton Abbas. It is unknown when the set in the Gallery arrived at the castle. Hardly anything came under the hammer, for Mary Luttrell departed with her jewels, furniture and plate. However, all, except by tradition one diamond ring, was lost in a great conflagration at her London house off Piccadilly. Narcissus Luttrell,[30] the diarist, of the Saunton Court (Devonshire) branch of the family, recorded on 19 November 1696:

> Yesterday morning a sudden fire hapned in Mrs Luttrell's house in St. James's Street, being newly and richly furnished, which burnt to the ground, the lady herself narrowly escaping and 'tis said she lost in plate, jewells, etc, to the value of 10,000*l*.[31]

Mary Luttrell, remembered in Minehead by Tregonwell Road, was, according to a romantic account, rescued from the fire by a gallant Swede,

Captain Jacob Bancks, who held a commission in the English navy. She married her rescuer and lived for another eight years, dying of the smallpox on 2 March 1704. At Milton Abbas there is a large and most impressive monument to her memory. Jacob Bancks did not remarry and Milton Abbas eventually passed to his second son.[32] He did very well for himself and was knighted in 1699. Through Luttrell influence, he became the Parliamentary Representative for Minehead and served in nine successive Parliaments. Bancks Street in Minehead is named after him.

Dunster in the Seventeenth Century

The chronological progression of the Luttrell family leads now to Colonel Alexander Luttrell (1663-1711) but, since the eighteenth century had dawned before he came to reside at Dunster Castle, his history will be dealt with later.

Some family names occur frequently in the history of Dunster and its area: the Everards of Aller in Carhampton, for instance. The Everards are first mentioned in the time of Reynold de Mohun II (d. 1257/58) when William Everard was one of the witnesses to the earliest charter for a market in Dunster.[33] A further charter made between 1269 and 1279 was again witnessed by William Everard.[34] In 1324 a charter of John de Mohun III is witnessed by a Robert Everard. Later, William, John and Robert Everard were in trouble because they were among several persons who had poached hares, coneys (rabbits), partridges and pheasants from Sir John de Mohun V's warrens at Carhampton and Rodhuish. They had also assaulted the schoolmaster Richard who was Sir John's toll collector at the Dunster Fair.[35] In the sixteenth century Thomas Everard the younger paid rent in 1529 to Sir Andrew Luttrell for 'a clotherack caulyd the myddell racke upon Grobfast, with a fullyng myll cauld Frekeford'.[36]

In the seventeenth century this family is again mentioned in the memorandum left by George Luttrell (d. 1629), when during the Rogation week the perambulation of the bounds included the reading of a gospel at Everard's house.[37]

Sir H.C. Maxwell Lyte's family features in the information concerning Hugh Luttrell, who married Jane (d. 1675) the daughter of Thomas Lyte of Lytescary. One of their daughters, Susan, baptised at Carhampton 8 April 1634, married John Everard of Otterhampton and died in 1678.

The history of the Blackford family goes back, at least, to 1630 when Richard Stodden, alias Blackford, is mentioned in connection with land transactions with Francis Fortescue. He may have been Richard Blackford's father.[38] Richard Blackford was a barrister who practised in London and became a Master of Chancery. He lived in a house called 'The Hall', now the 'Castle Hotel', which is of mainly seventeenth-century date, although the façade, at least, was probably rebuilt in the early nineteenth century. Doubtless there was a Pre-Reformation building on this site. The house next to it, now a jewellers, was called 'Le Smyth' and owned by the abbots of Cleeve. 'The Hall' retained its name, at least, until 1887, since it is so named on the Ordnance Survey map of that date. (The Overseers' Accounts refer in

1760 to 'Prowse's house (late Blackford's near ye Cross)'. (The cross was at the end of the High Street outside the castle gates.) There are references to a Mr Prowse and a Thomas Prowse in Hancock's *Dunster Church & Priory,* where Mr Prowse is given as a ratepayer and one of the principal inhabitants of the parish in 1686, and Tho. Prowse signs as a witness to the Overseers' Accounts in 1713.

In 1667 Richard Blackford, Attorney of the King's Bench, acquired one third of the manor of East Luccombe from Sir P. Fortescue, Bart.[39] His daughter, Mary Blackford, died in 1669 aged twelve. The memorial brass to her memory is to be found in St. George's church immediately below the Royal Coat of Arms. This brass was relaid in 1875 in a new stone on the floor of the north side of the nave.

In 1689 Richard Blackford died and the Churchwardens' Accounts show that he was buried in the church: a location reserved for important and locally notable persons.[40] Mr Blackford also paid for his own seat in the church. A brass to his memory, relaid in a new stone in 1876, may be found in the floor of the south aisle, opposite the south porch door and a little to the west of the entrance. The inscription is surmounted by the arms of Blackford within a cartouche: *Gules a chevron Arg between three estoiles Or.* Beneath the arms there is a skull, crossbones and two sprays of laurel. According to A.B.Connor:

> This is a very good example of that charming style of lettering which seems to show forth the irrepressible joy of the writer in fine curves. It is found at its best in this county. Obviously by the same hand in the beautifully-wrought inscription to Thomas Dyke, M.D., 1689 at Kingston St Mary.

Connor also quotes the will of Richard Blackford:

> The will of Richard Blackford of Dunster, Somerset, one of the King's Masters Extraordinary in the Court of Chancery, dated Jan. 8,1688, was proved Apr. 4, 1689, by Elizabeth Blackford, the relict [47.*Ent.*]. He mentions 'My son William. My daughter Sidwell Blackford. My sister Mary Coffin. My sister Christine Blackford. My cousin John Quirck. My cousin Robert Siderfin. My sister Hawkins. My son in law Edward Dyke.'*(Brown's Som. Wills, IV, 78).*[41]

William, Richard Blackford's heir, now took over his father's seat in church, and paid 6d for it. He would also have been the executor of his father's will from which Dunster Church benefited by ten shillings.

The Overseers' Accounts also record:

> "Paid Mr [William] Blackford for a counsellor's advice at London 10s. and his solicitor 3s 4d and posted ye 2s about Ketnors discharge."

Mr Blackford was, it seems, in practice in London as a barrister at this date (1690). Later he became a Master in Chancery. [42]

In 1694 William Blackford bought the manor of Bossington from Sir John Sydenham of Brympton and a little later acquired the Holnicote estate from Mr William Martyn, who had succeeded to the estate through his uncle by marriage, Charles Steyning, the last of the Selworthy family of that name. In 1699 William became an even greater landowner, acquiring from Anthony Stocker and Sarah his wife, the manor of Avill and land in the parishes of Dunster, Carhampton, Crowcombe, Stogumber, Timberscombe and St Decumans. He died in 1728; the history of the Blackfords in the eighteenth century will be told later.

Dunster, far away in the West Country, was remote from the court of Charles II and international affairs. Nevertheless, the birthdays of her monarchs and battle victories in distant lands were heralded by England's church bells throughout the realm, including Dunster, as we can see from the Churchwardens' Accounts.

There are none of these surviving for Dunster before 1670. The extracts used here are from *The Register from 1670 to 1847*, compiled by Rev. G. Barrington Simeon, whose entries are almost indecipherable and muddled (noted 'Barrington Simeon'in the text), and from *Dunster Church and Priory* by Prebendary F. Hancock (noted 'Hancock'). On 29 May 1670, we read:

1670		£	s	d
April 27 {	Paid William Warman...a seate and nailes		1	0
	Killing a seale.			
	Pd for the Book of Articles [43]			6
May 29. For ringing the 29th of May			10	0

The 29th May 1670 was the fortieth birthday of King Charles II and also the tenth anniversary of his re-entry into London at the Restoration.

Two days after the bells had rung to mark the king's birthday, the hugely unpopular Treaty of Dover with the French, was signed on 1 June 1670. The English people abhorred both France, which they closely associated with Catholicism, and the autocracy of their king. (As part of the Treaty, Charles had agreed to announce his conversion to Catholicism.)

Louis XIV declared war on the Dutch in March 1672. By the Treaty of Dover, England was to gain part of the Dutch seaboard and Dutch ports. In the event the expeditionary force which was to land and assist the French was prevented from so doing through the genius and seamanship of the Dutch Admiral.

Following on this historical diversion, the Dunster Churchwardens' Accounts from 1670-1699 continue:

			£	s	d
1670	June 5.	The Goldsmith for mending the challis		2	0
		Midsummer quarter for the hospital		10	7

At the foot of the page of Barrington Simeon's entries appears an undated entry:

			£	s	d
	Constable of the hundred Midsummer				
	quarter for hospital			10	0
June 5.	The Sakson (*Sexton)* for his quarter due				
	the same time.			2	6
June 15	Given to Seamen that lost their ship.			1	6
August 2	Paid Robert Ashford for pointing the Tower	5	0	0
	For 21 sacks of Lime at 1*s* 2*d* per sack	1	4	0
	For washing the Surples [*surplices*]			1	0
	For ringing the fifth of November.			10	0
	[*a strange entry for 2 August*]				
	Constable of the hundred Midsummer				
	quarter for hospital			10	0
1671	February	Paid two sailors that came by pass.			6
		Given two women by pass			6
		Paid for killing seven hedgehogs 2*d* the pees		1	2
		Paid Walter Slocombe for killing			
		3 hoopers [*bullfinches*]			1½
	May 5	given to a poor indigent minister		2	0
	May 29	Paid Robert James one shilling in			
		confidence that he is to keep and maintain the			
		Clapper in good repair [*yearly GBS*]		1	0
	Sept 29	John Atkins for Glassing the Windows		1	0
		For ringing the bell in the evenings and			
		mornings		5	0

In 1672 on April 10, it was noted that Arthur Dennis the Warden delivered: 'two Register books in parchment; two account books; one silver Chalice with a cover; two pewter fflaggons; one standing plate; one Branched Houst Cloth; one Pulpit cloth; one cushion; two blackcloths; one Surples; one Great Bible.One book of Erasmus; One book of Jewell v Harding.[44]One book of Homiles; one little box to keep writtings; one Lining [*linen*] Table Cloth; two little boxes to gather money; one Book of Cannons; two Table Napkins; three Comon Prayer books and one Pewter Bassin'.

Seat rents varying from one shilling to one penny per year were also listed, besides expenses incurred:

	£	s	d
For one pound of Candles for the Clarke			4½
For the ringing of the 4 o clock bell		6	0
For 2 quarts of sack for the Commonyon		4	0
at Mic. Mas.[*Michaelmas*]			
For one thousand Hille Stoanes		10	0
For two thousand Hille Stoanes.	1	0	0

£6 7s 7d was spent this year on church building, hill stones, timber, hooking up 'coppells' in the church.[45]

	£	s	d
Paid John Clements for a poste for the			
hier*(higher)* Church Stille		3	0

'The bishop [Creighton] was at Dunster in this year, and a dinner in his honour cost the parish £1 17s 10d.'

	£	s	d
1673 *(no month)*			
Killing 6 Bulfinches.			6
March 6 Killing 4 Hoops			2
Mr Churchwarden for killing one hedghog		2	0

Before leaving the year 1673, we come to the mystery of the missing Norris brass. The inscription read (in Latin): 'Here lyeth the body of Mary, ye daughter of John Norris, late customer of Minehead, who dyed 22 of March, 1673'.[46] The first we hear of this brass is an account of the *History and Antiquities of Dunster*, published in the *Gentleman's Magazine* of 1808, part II, p. 246.

This brass was still in existence in 1830, as Savage gave the location of the 'Wyther brass', 'in the south-aisle of the present church' and mentions 'another brass' and gives the Latin inscription for Mary Norris.[47] However, in 1905, when Hancock's book was published, he wrote 'this brass does not now exist'.[48] It therefore seems probable that it was lost during the 1876 restoration. The new pedestal provided in 1876 for the font may cover the Mary Norris brass if it was, in fact, near the Wyther brass, as the re-laid brasses were in 1876 put in stone slabs and replaced as near as possible to their original positions.

The Churchwardens' Accounts continue in 1674: For ringing for the joy of a peaxe [*peace*] with the Dutch: 5s.[49]

So, in Dunster weighty events of national importance were marked, along with the sad little entries regarding the killing of small birds and hedgehogs:

	£	s	d
Paid William Crasse and John Clarke for			
killinge10 bullfinches		10	

In the same year (1674) the recurring problem throughout the year was that of church restoration. The Accounts noted stones, flags, and timber bought and 12 score quarrels of glass, at a cost of £1.[50]

	£	s	d
Paid William Warman for mending the			
Rod *(rood)* Loft and for Timber about it.		7	0

	£	s	d
Other entries for 1674 were:			
For stopping ye pigeons out ye church... (no amount stated)			
Pd one years hospital	2	2	4

	£	s	d
Pd Clerk for keeping the Clock and Chimes for one whole year.	1	10	0
Paid Mathew Adams the Sexton his years wages		10	0
Paid Robert Ashford and his men for fitting up the Vane		3	4
For taking down the Vane and for beere for the workmen.		2	0
Given to John Oliver of Mynehead towards his loss by fire		10	0
For … [?*mending*] of a Bixgay			
For Henry Sexton for ½ days work			6
Paid the Clarke for ringing the bell in the morning.		8	5
Paid John Shenton and others for killing hoopes.			2
Paid John Atkins for glazing the windows.	1	9	4

Work continued on the church. Hancock lists:

		£	s	d
1675				
	For (…..) for a Bixgay.			8
	Paid for Timber for the rayles about ye Communion Table	1	10	0
	Paid William Hole for Painting the Church and for beere.	6	13	6
	Mr Start for boords to sett ye ten commandments in.		11	6

There are frequent references in the Churchwardens' Accounts to money being given to those who had suffered at the hands of the Turks:[51]

		£	s	d
1677	By this year Thos. Trevelyan is dead and his heirs hold Knowle.			
	Given to several persons that suffered by an inundation of the sea		1	6
	Given to one redeemed out of Turkish slavery			6

Mr Thomas Dennis, one of the principal inhabitants of the parish by 1686,[52] who in 1667 paid a rate of 1s for the maintenance of the poor of the parish,[53] now emerges from the shadows. He is referred to as 'Thos dennis of ye Ship' (now the 'Luttrell Arms'). The accounts for 1677 show:

	£	s	d
Mr Dennis for wine for the Communion at Christmas and Easter		14	0

23

Another reference to the Turkish invasions occurs in 1678:

	£	s	d

1678

		£	s	d
Given to woman and five children Ann Mason and...Turrell that had lost £17 and their husbands taken by the Turks			1	6
Paid for a Prayer book that was reade when the fast was				6
For a Comon Prayer Book			15	0
Given to men and theare family which had lost ship and goods coming from Virginny going to Plymouth			1	6
Given to one Mr Leigh and 10 Seamen that had lost their ship coming from the West Indies		*no amount given*		
Paid for an act for the Burrying in Wooling				6

This unpopular Act, passed in 1678 and intended to support the ailing woollen industry, directed that all corpses should be shrouded in woollen cloth, or a penalty of £5 would be payable by the executors. [54]

By 1679, 'Frances Luttrell, Esq.; Sir Hugh Stewkley, Heirs of Trevelyan, Dr Handcocke, Francis Pearse, gent., and Mrs Canes' were the chief ratepayers. Mentioned in the accounts for this year:

	£	s	d

1679

	£	s	d
Paid towards the building of a church in London for the Grecians that came into England[55]		1	0
Killinge a polecatt			4
John Briant for killing a polecatt			4
Mendinge the pulpitt cloth and for silke and cloth to amend him		1	4
Recd of Wm. Shenton for breaking the ground in the body of the church for the burying of Will his son		6	8
3 bottles of Sacke.		6	0

1680

	£	s	d
Killing one fox		1	0
6 Seamen that were taken by ye Turks Will Norrish a new doore and doornes for ye drang.		13	0
A poor man escaped out of slavery			6
A poore man that was redeemed out of Turkey	*no amount*		

		£	s	d
1681	John Attkins for glassinge ye Church windowes	2	19	0
	for Ringing when ye Lord Bishop came here.		7	0

Great preparations were made for this visit: 'the surplis was washedand mended', and one shilling was paid for cleaninge the windows.

	£	s	d
1682 Paid for ringing the curfew bell.		6	0

The word curfew comes from the Old French *cuevrefeu*, in modern French *couvrefeu*. There was a regulation which was widespread in medieval Europe, by which fires had to be covered or extinguished at a fixed hour each evening and this was indicated by the ringing of the curfew-bell.

	£	s	d
Nov. 8 Paid William Norrish for Righting the Bear [??*beer*]		1	6

seven shillings and two pence recvd for goods taken from the decenters [*dissenters or Non-Conformists*] by order of law. 'It is agreed that William Pleaseway is to have and enjoy ye shoop under ye Churchgate walle for his natural life after his father'.

[*Barrington Simeon adds in 1684 regarding this 'shoop': 'paying yearly the sum of one shilling a year to the Churchwardens of Dunster'*]

In 1682 the amercements (discretionary penalties for non-attendance at borough meetings) were 6d apiece for free suitors and 3d for other 'resiants', or residents, within the borough. 'The lord's tenants', that is to say, leaseholders, were afterwards subject to a fine of one shilling apiece for similar default.[56]

The year 1684 is devoted both by Hancock and Barrington Simeon to the bells, whose history will form a separate section at the end of this Chapter.

On 6 February 1685, King Charles II died and it is perhaps because of his unspoken refusal on his deathbed to take the Holy Sacrament at the hands of the Anglican Bishop of Bath & Wells, Dr Ken, that this event was not marked by the solemn tolling of the bells of Dunster.

On 10 February 1685, James, Duke of York, was proclaimed King James II, and on 14 February, King Charles II was 'very obscurely buried in a vault under Henry the Seventh's Chapel at Westminster'[57] because both Charles II and James II were avowed Roman Catholics. King James made no attempt to hide his Roman Catholicism. However he promised the Privy Council to endeavour to maintain the Government both in Church and State, 'as by law established'.[58]

The accession was marked at Dunster:

	£	s	d
Gave ye ringers ye day the king came to the throne		13	0

Three months later the Monmouth rebellion, touched on in the previous chapter, took place. The Duke of Monmouth, the eldest illegitimate son of Charles II and Lucy Walters, had been living in exile in the Netherlands.

While the Earl of Argyle, an exiled Scot, attempted to raise a revolt in Scotland, Monmouth, accompanied by about 150 followers landed at Lyme Regis on 11 June 1685. He denounced the Catholic King James as a usurper and claimed the throne for himself.

At first Monmouth must have been optimistic for he was soon joined by around 4,000 foot and 500 horse, so that the Devonshire militia fell back before him. He marched towards Bristol and, having forced the king's forces, including Colonel Luttrell and his regiment, to withdraw from Taunton, was proclaimed king there. But his successes were short-lived: he was cornered at Bridgwater and failed in an attempt to break free by a night attack across the marshes at Sedgemoor. After the rout of his followers, Monmouth was discovered disguised in a ditch. He was beheaded on 6 July, 1685, less than a month after his landing.

There followed the cruel hunting of fugitives by Lord Chief Justice Jeffreys and the holding of the Bloody Assizes. In Dunster, on the day after the battle of Sedgemoor, the churchwardens paid 7s 6d to the ringers, 'upon the rout of Monmouth',[59] but in spite of this show of loyalty to the king, three men were hanged at Dunster and at Stogumber. (A portrait of Bishop Mews, Bishop of Winchester (1684-1706) in the Inner Hall of Dunster Castle shows the bishop wearing a black patch on his cheek to conceal the scar of a wound he received while fighting for James II at the battle of Sedgemoor.)

Sir George Clark observes regarding the social implications of the rebellion:

> ... the most important social fact about Somerset, Devon and Wiltshire, from which his army was drawn, was that this was one of the great industrial regions of England. Most of the towns where his army quartered, Axminster, Taunton, Shepton Mallet, Frome, were clothing towns. ... It cannot be irrelevant to notice that ...the English woollen industry was sinking into a depression with which the parliament was occupied during these very days. Poverty and unemployment among the wage-earners were Monmouth's recruiting agents.[60]

The Churchwardens' Accounts for 1685 include:

	£	s	d
Paid for ringers the 26th of July		16	6
September Tried at Taunton for participation in the Monmouth Rebellion. Henry Luckwell, John Deanes and William Sully. Executed at Dunster.			
Paid for ringin the King's birthday (Oct 15th) [61]		12	0
Paid for a dozen of oupes [bullfinches]			5
Paid for Expenses for presenting the Rebells att Stogumber		2	6

The Bishop of Bath and Wells visited Dunster at the end of 1685. Bishop Ken was known for his benevolence and piety and he was the only person in England known to have interceded for those who suffered from the cruelty of the suppression of Monmouth's rebellion. The Churchwardens' Accounts for that year conclude with the following entries:

	£	s	d
Paid for ringing to the Coming in of the Bishoppe		5	0

The Holy Communion was celebrated at his visitation, and the elements for use at it cost 6s 6d, along with other expenses:

	£	s	d
Paid Mr Grant for Jublycate (duplicate)		1	0
Paid Robert Strong for a table for the Duplicate [62]			4
Ye Catechisme Books at ye Visitation		1	0
Gave ye Ringers ye day the king came to the Crowne		13	0

There appear to be no Churchwardens' Accounts for the year 1686. However, it would seem appropriate to include the Sealy brass under that year. Although the inscriptions thereon range from 1693 to 1788, they all refer to the relations of William Sealy, about whom we first hear in the year 1686 when he is listed as one of the principal inhabitants of the parish of Dunster, in the Rate-book for that year.[63] In 1693 there is an entry in the Overseers' Accounts as follows:

May ye 10th Received of Mr William Sealey, 3s 4d being moneys leveyed by the Justice on Mr Thomas Joanes A minister for being overcome with bear (beer). And give to the poor as ffolloweth [64]

Also from the Overseers' Accounts for the year 1708: 'Henery Eastine to Mr John Sealy for Mr William Sealy's esteat'.[65] (Henry Eastine was one of seven apprentices bound out to various persons.)

In 1713 William Sealy's name again appears in the Overseers' Accounts as a witness to a receipt for Dorothy Luttrell in respect of a bequest of the late Colonel Alexander Luttrell, her husband, to 'ye poor of ye psh'. [66]

The inscription on the brass reads:

Edward, son of William and Mary Sealy, 1693, aged 3; Justine, mother of William Sealy, 1695, aged 81; Elizabeth, dau. of William and Mary Sealy, 1696, aged 3;.Mary, wife of William Sealy, 1702, aged 44; William, son of William and Mary Sealy, 1705, aged 23; Mary, wife of Francis Chaplin, dau. of William and Mary Sealy, 1737 aged 57; Elizabeth, dau of Francis and Mary Chaplin, 1788, aged 80.

The Sealy brass, according to Connor, was re-laid in a new stone on the floor of the North Aisle (actually the north side of the nave), to the east of Mary Blackford's brass, during the Victorian restoration: In Connor's opinion:

The whole composition is crude in execution, but there is a dignity about the design which is characteristic of the period. The lettering in italics shows individuality, that of the first entries, 1693, 1695 and 1696, is good. In subsequent entries the initial letters are Roman capitals, and gradual deterioration sets in until the latest record in 1788 is poor in the extreme. Altogether the inscription is a most interesting example of local workmanship during a period of nearly a hundred years.[67]

The Churchwardens' Accounts for 1687 record:

	£	s	d
Paid at the Court when we presented Rosemond Merrick and Christian House		1	6
Paid John Milton for six Crosses.		1	6
Paid Mr Briant for killing a wild catt		1	0
Paid for ringing of the bell at four of the clock		6	6
Paid for a booke wherein was thanksgiving for the Queen being with child		1	6
Paid John Warman for mending the screen door			6
Paid John Briant for killing a ffox		1	0
Paid for mending of the clock after the weight had fallen on him.		10	0

In 1688 Bishop Ken was one of seven bishops sent to the Tower by James II for refusing to read his Declaration of Indulgence in church on two successive Sundays. This declaration suspended all the penal laws, not only against Roman Catholics but against Non-Conformists: the king was intent on making England a Catholic country again, and had appointed Roman Catholics to positions of authority. After the bishops' request to withdraw the Declarations, the king had them arrested for libel. They were tried but the jury returned the verdict of 'Not Guilty'. The bishops were perceived as heroes. The Churchwarden's Accounts read:

	£	s	d
July 1st Paid the Ringers for Ringing for the Bishops and Prince of Wales for Joy of his birth in meat, drink and money.	2	5	3
[*This was 1688, although given under 1687 by Hancock*]			
2 books of Prayers for ye Prince of Wales		2	6

The bell-ringing for the Prince of Wales refers to the birth of a son, James Edward Stuart (the future 'Old Pretender') on 20 June 1688 to James II's second wife, Mary of Modena, a Roman Catholic princess. (His first wife, Anne Hyde, had given him two daughters, both future queens: Mary, born in 1662, and Anne, born in 1664.)

Up to that time, the heir presumptive to the throne had been William III of Orange, a strict Calvinist, who was the son of William II of Orange and James II's eldest sister Mary, as well as being the great-grandson of James I and the grandson of Charles I. The birth of the Prince of Wales dissipated the Church of England's hope of relief from Catholic succession. Indeed, Bishop

Ken refused to acknowledge the new heir to the throne on the grounds that he would be breaching his Coronation Oath and for his conscientious scruples he was deprived of his bishopric.

However, later this same year, William III and his wife Mary, daughter of James II and Anne, became king and queen, following the Glorious (and bloodless) Revolution of November, 1688. William and his Dutch army were welcomed by the English Protestants, and Colonel Francis Luttrell was one of the first notables in the West Country to join William's standard. After a brief resistance, James II left for France where he would spend the rest of his life in exile. On 13 February 1689, William and Mary formally accepted the offer of the English throne.

The Churchwardens' Accounts for 1689 reflect these events:

	£	s	d
Paid 12 of the Prince of Orange soldiers going to Cornwall		2	0
February 14th Paid, for ringing for joy of the happy arrival of King William and Queen Mary in London		17	6

However old loyalties died hard. Barrington Simeon records:

	£	s	d
Pd the ringers for ringing the 29th May	1	0	0

The 29th of May was the birthday of Charles II who had died four years earlier in 1685. However, the Dunster bells did ring on many occasions for William and Mary, in 1689, for example, for their coronation:

	£	s	d
Paid for beere and ringing when the King and Queen was crowned in Beere and Bonfire		15	0
Paid Sam Chaffin for beer and the ringers at the proclaiming of King William and Queen Mary		15	0
Pd to Robert Venner for Beere when the King and Queen was crowned		3	6
Pd G. Clarke for making 14 doors for the seates at 1s 6d a door	1	1	0
For colloring them at 4d per door 15 doors[68]		5	0

In 1689 the bells of Dunster signalled a victory over the French: 'Gave the ringings in beere at the routing of the French: 2 shillings'. This is perhaps a reference to the relief of Londonderry, which had been besieged by the French in the Irish Wars, aimed at the restoration of James II to the throne. Soon after followed the victory of King William over King James II's forces at the battle of the Boyne. On 11 July, 1690 William gained possession of Dublin and James escaped to France. A solemn thanksgiving was ordered throughout England.

William's return was marked by the bells of Dunster:

	£	s	d
1689/90 Paid for a book of prayers and thanks for William's return from Ireland		1	0
1691 Paid for a prayer-book and proclamation for a fast day		1	6

When Limerick surrendered to the Dutch the bells of Dunster rang out once more, and soon rang again to celebrate the resulting peace treaty:

	£	s	d
Pd for ringing at the Surrendering of Limbricke (Limerick)		6	0
Paid for ringing the feast day at the surrender of Ireland		1	5

Here the Irish question must be abandoned and a return made to the Dunster Churchwardens' Accounts:

	£	s	d
Paid towards the ringing for the coming of the Lord Bishop Kedar (Kidder) to the Towne.	1	0	0

Mem. Collected by briefe for the poor captives in Turkey by the minister and Church wardens two pounds fifteen shillings and three pence three farthings witnesse our hands.

> John Grant Minister
> { John Moffat
> { John Curnell Churchwardens

	£	s	d
Paid for ringing at the King's return out of Flanders and the making of the rate.		6	1

There are more references to the ringing of the 4 o'clock bell costing 6s 6d in 1691, which in 1689, together with 'taking down the desk' had only cost 4s 6d.

With reference to 'the King's return from Flanders', King William, after Ireland had been subdued in 1691, turned again to the great European struggle in which he had been engaged even before he became King of England. English troops fought alongside those of Holland, Spain and the Holy Roman Empire in this struggle against the might of the common enemy, France, which had become, under Louis XIV, the greatest power in Europe.

The next entry in the Dunster Churchwardens' Accounts refers to the intended invasion of England by the French, who assembled an invasion army at Cap la Hogue which was joined by James II:

1692

	£	s	d
Paid for ringing the Thanksgiving day	1	5	8

[i.e. for the destruction of the French fleet which had been fitted out for the invasion of England] May 29. 1692.

	£	s	d
Paid the Clarke for ringing the 4 o'clock bell		6	6
Paid the ringers for ringing the Queen's birthday		1	6
(April 30). [*Barrington Simeon gives this out-of-date order*]			
For a visitation dinner and all the officers there			
being manie	1	3	0
Paid for a large new coman prayer book in folio.		12	0
Paid John Marsh the carier for bringing the			
Prayer Book from Exeter			9

At this date there were 176 ratepayers in the parish of Dunster. Payments listed in 1693 in the Accounts include charity to passing strangers, wounded soldiers and victims of French pirates alongside the usual rewards for killing pests. Church repairs included limewash plaster at 9s 4d, and £8 to some men for three and a half days' work repairing the church.

In 1694, collections were made for the Parish of Maidstone (1s 9½d), Warwick, York and Northumberland. The bells were rung for 5 November and for King William's 43rd birthday. Twenty-four dozen quarrels of glass were bought for the church at 10d per dozen, and John Strong was paid 2s 6d for making a 'joynstule' for the Communion Table. The Clerk was paid 3s for tolling the bell when Queen Mary died on 28 December.

The Dunster Churchwardens' Accounts record that William III returned to England in the autumn of 1695 and they also record his victory at Namur:

1695	£	s	d
Paid for ringing when the King came home Sept. 22 '95		10	0
Paid Robert Adams for a bisgay		2	6
Paid for ribbon to tie the surplice			9
Paid for making the surplice, 10*s*. and washing it 1*s*		11	0
Pd James Masun for glassing the Church Windows	1	8	6
Paid for ringing the morning bell.		6	6
Paid Robert Venner for killing a kite			2
for a prayer book for ye takeing of Namur.		1	6
killing 5 polecats		1	8
11 yeards and ½ of bag Hollond at 3*s* 8*d* per yd.			
and for ribbon to tie the surplice	2	2	9
for making of it.		11	0
Paid for two prayer books and a proclamation of 2nd June	2		6
Paid for a key for the Chancel door			10
Paid for ringing the 4 o'clock bell.		6	6
1696 Paid for a book against cursing and swearing			4
1697 For ringing at the visitation at the Bishop's arrival		5	6[69]

In the peace treaty of Ryswyck between France, England, Holland and Spain, signed on 30 October 1697, King Louis XIV of France was forced to recognize the 'heretic' William as King of England and William's sister-in-law

Anne as heir presumptive. Louis had also to withdraw his support of the Catholic King James. The bells of Dunster marked the treaty of Ryswyck:

			£	s	d
	For ringing when the peace was proclaimed			13	6
1698	July 2.	Paid for visitation dinner		10	0
		Paid Mr Briant for killing varments		2	10
		Paid him for a lock and staple for the Churchyard and mending a bisgee		1	8
		Paid John Strong for a winscott [wainscott] for Mr Grant's seat.		10	8
		Gave to the redemption of a Slave in Turkey		5	0
1699		for 7 polecatts and 1 kites head		2	6
		A Visitation dinner	1	0	0
		Paid for tills [tiles]taken out of ye old Church		1	6

'The tiles were no doubt the original heraldic and otherwise decorated tiles, of which so few remain'.[70] Those which did remain were used in the de Mohun chantry chapel (then called the Sacristy) at the time of the Victorian restoration.

We have deliberately omitted the year 1684. In that year occurred what may be called an hilarious local attempt to cast a bell. It seems appropriate here to trace the history of the bells of Dunster in the later seventeeth century.

Hancock mentions an entry for a new bell rope, costing 4s 6d, in the Churchwardens' Accounts for 1670. For ringing bells evening and morning that year, the bell-ringer was paid 5s.[71] In 1671 'Rich. Dart is paid £1 4s for a new clapper for the fourth bell', and 'one Robert James takes a contract to keep the said clapper in order for a term of seven years for 1s sterling.[72] Accounts for 1672 refers only to the ringing of the four o'clock bell (the angelus) which cost 6s.[73] The next year the cost of ringing this bell had been increased; Andrew Everard was paid 7s.

There are constant allusions to the 4 o'clock bell and the ringing of bells morning and evening. Dunster was a Benedictine foundation and the Rule of St Benedict persisted; traces of it remain in both Protestant and Catholic service books and derive from the medieval tradition.

In St Benedict's day, the ringing of the bells, at night, was a necessity, in order to get everyone out of bed. As the hour for the night office approached, the bells announced the start of the daily routine of worship. The monks' night office started at 2 am, or shortly after in winter and was followed at 3 am with the singing of the office of Vigils or Nocturns, later called Matins. Lauds followed at dawn.

Perhaps in Post-Reformation England, the four-o'clock bell, if it was rung at first light, was a tradition recalling the singing of Lauds by the departed monks of Dunster, but it could have recalled the office of Vigils since 3 am at Monte Cassino would probably approximate to 4 am at Dunster. The evening office of Vespers concluded with the brief service of Compline at sundown.[74]

No mention is made in the Churchwardens' Accounts of the seventeenth century to any specific hour, except the 4 o'clock, for the ringing of the bell. However, we will later find references to the 6 o'clock bell which was rung morning and evening even as late as the twentieth century.

Under the heading of 'Chantry of S. Mary', Hancock refers to the cult of the Blessed Virgin Mary and it is in the Lady Chapel (St Mary's Chantry) – now the vestry, that the traditional recitation of the five 'Hail Marys' and the 'Our Father', would have taken place up to the Reformation.

> The Ladye-Chapel had its own precious vestments and its own golden chalice; wax candles, offered by Mary's clients, living and dead, burnt during the Mass, and before her image; the missals, the graduals, the psalters, were Mary's own, and the lamp that shone there night and day was in the custody of one who was appointed to guard and keep the Chapel. [75]

According to the Churchwardens' Accounts in 1674, if the entry again refers to the four o'clock bell, the charge had yet again increased from 6s to 7s and now to 8s 5d:

	£	s	d
1675			
Pd the Clarke for ringing the bell in the morning		8	5
In 1675:			
Paid for the mending of the bell clapper		3	0
Pd William Warman for taking of him out and putting him in		1	0

In 1677 Robert James, who had a contract from 1671 for seven years to maintain the clapper, was paid 17s for a new clapper for the fourth bell and the same year William Warman and his two sons were working on the third bell; for their work they received £1 7s 10d and eight new bell ropes were installed costing £1 8s.[76]

The momentous year as far as the bells are concerned was 1679, when the Churchwardens' Accounts record:

	£	s	d
Paid when they range all the bells for the first time		1	6 [77]
Again eight bell ropes were purchased at a cost of	1	1	0 [78]

The second bell in Dunster is inscribed 1679.[79]

It is not clear why all the bells were rung in 1679 but on 3 February 1679 the Long Parliament of the Restoration was dissolved and for the first time in eighteen years an election was held.

In 1680 there is an unspecified payment for the ringing of the 'courfew' bell, which in 1682 cost 6s 0d, and Hancock tells us that 'at this period (i.e. 1680), the ring was already one of eight'.[80] The following account concerns a gallant attempt to re-cast the tenor bell here in Dunster which is not without its humorous side.

The story is taken from the Churchwardens' Accounts:

	£	s	d
1684			
Paid Mr Pordie for casting of the bell	£10	0	0
paid for 52 pounds of metell aded to the bell	1	19	0
paid for wood to tast the bell and cole			
and caridge and cleving		14	6

Additional metal is obtained from Bristol, and William Warman and his sons are employed to execute the work at Dunster.

1684 Pd Wm Warman and his sones for taking doune the bell and ffor hanging ofen [of him] up, 11s. Pd for Beare when they took downe the bell 1s.. Pd for draing of Stones to Conegar for the ffornis [furnace] and caridg. 1s. Paid for caring [carrying] of clay and sand for the ffornis 6s 6d. Paid for caring of bricks for the ffornis 2s 6d. Paid for the caring of the bell to loxhol [81] and ffor the bringing ofen to Church againe 2s. Pd for beare when they hung up the bell 2s. Pd for making the fornis 17s 10d. Pd beare for workmen 2s. Pd to sink the hole for ye fornis. 1s. [*According to Barrington Simeon the man who sank the hole was John Clarke. He says that Thomas Holman was paid 2s for stapel [staple] for the bell.*] Pd the expenses in making the bargen [bargain] for the casting the Bell and for making the bonde for ye performance ofen one yeare 13s. 5d".[82]

It would appear that the bell was taken from the church, a furnace built near Loxhall Bridge and an attempt made there to re-cast it there. Hancock continues:

The spirited attempt to do bell casting at home does not appear to have been a success, for when in 1688 the fourth bell required repair, it was sent via Watchet, under care of Jenkin Philpot, to Bristol, whence it was returned by way of Minehead, and rehung by Wm Warman "1688. Pd for carriage of the 4th bell to Bristoll and bringing back.15s"... The repairs to the fourth bell were not satisfactory, and again it is taken down and sent to Bristol. This time it was re-cast. "Pd Mr Purdew the Bell founder for casting the 4th bell the 2nd time with the increase of metall being 54 pounds at 1s per pound £12. 6s."[83]

The bell is inscribed: 'John Clement and Richard Busher, churchwardens, 1688. R.P. (Purdew)'.[84]

ENDNOTES

1   Steinberg, *Historical Tables* 58 BC – AD 1963, 139

2   Evelyn: D.J.E 109 (edited by de la Bédoyère)

3   Ibid. 110-111

4   Davies: E.S 256

5   Ibid. 256. See Volume I, Chapter 12

6   See Lyte: H.D. Part I 201

7   Davies: E.S. 259

8   Evelyn: D.J.E 340/1 (edited by William Bray)

9   I am indebted to Professor Davies for the substance of this account.

10 Lyte: H.D. Part I 201

11 Further details of this staircase are given later

12 Parker: G.T.B.H. 25.

13 Lyte: H.D. Part I, 202.

14 Ibid.

15 Ibid. 204 (Note 2).

16 Ibid. 205.

17 All following details concerning these accounts may be found in Lyte: H.D. Part I, 207/14.

18 Hancock: D.C.P., 145.

19 Lyte: H.D. Part I, 214.

20 Ibid.

21 Hancock, D.C.P., 148

22 First Act ordering Burial in Woollen 1666

23 Jane, the middle sister, was baptized at Milton Abbas on 19 August 1684. She died and was buried at Dunster on 14 November 1688.

24 Mowat: H.G.B., 421/2.

25 Lyte: H.D. Part I, 215 (Note 2).

26 Dodd: G.D.C. 17.

27 Ibid.

28 Lyte: H.D., Part I, 216 (Note 1).

29 Ibid. 215 (Note 1).

30 Narcissus Luttrell, son and heir of Francis Luttrell and Catherine, dau. of Narcissus Mapowder of Holsworthy, Devon. He is remembered as the collator of Prynne's catalogue of the muniments at the castle with original documents.

31 Lyte: H.D. Part I, 217.

32 Ibid. 218

33 Lyte: H. D. Part I 277

34 Ibid. 280

35 Ibid. Part II 343

36 Ibid. Part I 299

37 Ibid. Part II 348

38 Hancock: D.C.P 78 (Note 1)

39 Ibid. (Note 2)

40 'breaking the ground in the church for Mr Richard Blackford's grave: 6s. 8d.'

41 Connor: M.B.S 10

42 Hancock: D.C.P 149

[43] Thirty-Nine Articles. Set of doctrinal formulæ defining the dogmatic position of the Church of England.

[44] John Jewel, Bishop of Salisbury, published in 1562 his treatise aiming to prove that the reformation had been necessary. Thomas Harding defended the papacy. See Cross: O.D.C.C. 726

[45] 'Coppells' may refer to 'couples', or principal rafters, sometimes referred to as 'copylls'.

[46] In the fourteenth and fifteenth centuries and again in the nineteenth century the word 'customer' meant a person who collects customs, a customs officer. Perhaps the term related to the customs officer for the harbour at Minehead.

[47] Savage: H.C. 409/10

[48] Hancock: D.C.P. 77

[49] Charles II was compelled to make a separate peace with the Dutch when the House of Commons refused him the necessary funds to prosecute the war. The treaty was signed on 19 Feb. 1674.

[50] Hancock: D.C.P 170

[51] Fourteen years earlier, Turkey had declared war on Austria. Hostilities continued between the 'infidels' and other European countries until 1699.

[52] See Hancock: D.C.P. 136

[53] Ibid. 146

[54] Ibid. 171/2

[55] A Greek Orthodox church was built in Soho in 1677. Greek Street commemorates the Greek colony.

[56] Lyte: H.D. Part 2 310

[57] Evelyn: D.J.E (ed. by William Bray) ii., 214/5

[58] Ibid. ii., 212.

[59] Lyte: H.D. Part 1, 205

[60] Clark: L.S. 1660-1714, 119/120, Notes 1 and 2

[61] This was his fifty-secondbirthday.

[62] *Jublycate* is likely to mean the *Jubilate*, Psalm100, provided as an alternative to the Benedictus at Morning Prayer in the B.C.P from 1552 onwards. See Cross: O.D.C.C 747.

[63] Hancock: D.C.P. 146

[64] Ibid. 150

[65] Ibid. 153

[66] Ibid. 154

[67] Connor: M.B. 11.

[68] There were box pews in Dunster church. They were apparently painted.

[69] The bishop visited in 1697. The dinner cost 10s. Another Visitation dinner in 1699 cost £1.00

[70] Hancock: D.C.P. 181

[71] Ibid. 168. Many of the following entries also appear in G.B.S. *The Register from 1670-1847.*

[72] Ibid. 68 also G.B.S as before.

[73] Ibid. 169

[74] Much of this information comes from Lawrence: M.M 29

[75] Hancock: D.C.P 18/20

[76] Ibid.68

[77] Ibid. 172

[78] Ibid.69

[79] The list of the bells which hangs in the Bell Chamber gives the date of the second bell as 1679 and says it was cast by Henry Bayley Jnr. Charcombe, Northants.

[80] Hancock: D.C.P. 68/9

[81] Loxhall bridge now carries the A39 across the river Avill near Dunster Park Gate.

[82] Hancock: D.C.P. 69. Also included in G. B. S., *The Register from 1679 - 1847*[83] Ibid. 69/70

[84] Ibid. 67

CHAPTER TWO

DUNSTER LIFE and the LUTTRELL FAMILY in the EARLY EIGHTEENTH CENTURY

The Luttrell Family

When Colonel Francis Luttrell died in 1690, his only son and heir, Tregonwell Luttrell (b. 1683), was just seven years of age. He and his sisters, Mary, Jane and Frances, became the wards of Alexander Luttrell, their father's younger brother. Tregonwell died in 1703, before attaining his majority, and never inherited the Dunster estates, which passed to Alexander Luttrell.

Alexander and Francis Luttrell had had an older brother Thomas, who had been baptized at Dunster on 19 March 1657 but he died at the early age of thirteen and was buried at Dunster on 20 July 1670. Their father, Francis the elder, died in 1666 and until 1680, when Francis, the second son and future Colonel Francis, reached his majority, the Dunster estates were managed by his mother, Lucy, Francis the elder's widow.

Alexander, the youngest son, was baptized at Dunster on 20 October 1663 and was named after Colonel Alexander Popham, his grandmother's brother. His grandmother, Jane Luttrell, doted on the little boy. Unlike most of her contemporaries, she did not invest in land or indeed make any judicious investments, but unwisely hoarded 'a great treasure of gold, silver, etc.' at Marshwood where she lived. Born Jane Popham, Jane Luttrell died in 1668 when Alexander was five years of age and bequeathed him a considerable sum. However, as mentioned earlier, his mother, Lucy Luttrell, had to fight through the courts to obtain it. I am grateful to Mrs Hepper of Marshwood Farm, Blue Anchor, where Jane's treasure was hidden, for in 1995 making papers available to me from which the following account, by Lucy herself, has been taken. (Lucy here refers to her uncle by marriage, Colonel Alexander Popham [1], as 'my uncle Popham'):

> ...after her death my uncle Popham came with her will opened it and read it. Wherein she gave her daughter [*presumably Amy*], £20, Frank [*i.e. Francis Luttrell, Lucy's husband*] £300 and all the rest to Sany [*her grandson Alexander's nickname*]. But when he came to examine the great chest, in the

drawer where he saw [*what had been*] so full of silver was full of writings. And in the house found but £18 in gold and £80 more in silver. And it is concluded to be stolen by my cousin [Amy] that waited on her. And the watchman was apprehended upon suspicion before her death and is now in the gatehouse in Westminster, and the other is sent to Ilchester gaol...[2]

The fortune had been estimated at anything between £6,000 and £30,000 and Lucy subsequently went to enormous lengths and through many lawsuits to try to recover it for her son, accusing her sister-in-law Amy (Jane's daughter and the sister of Lucy's husband Francis) of secretly removing the money. Eventually, Amy and her second husband George Reynell were convicted of theft, and had to pay £6,000 and £200 costs. George was imprisoned in the Marshalsea, from which he escaped, and Lucy sued the Marshal and Keeper of the Gaol and obtained judgement for £6,200.

Alexander's career followed the predictable pattern laid down for the sons of local gentry and, after Oxford, he studied law and then joined the army. He was admitted as a member of the university, or matriculated, just before he reached the age of fourteen and was a gentleman commoner of Christ Church. A gentleman commoner did not receive any financial support from his college but he did receive commons; that is a definite portion of food supplied by the college at a defined price. In 1680, whilst still at Oxford, he was admitted as a student to the Middle Temple and left the university without a degree. Like many young blades of the period, he sometimes indulged in riotous behaviour. He and his friends, Lord Bulkeney, Leopold Finch and five others on one occasion had all been imbibing at the Crown, in Oxford. On emerging from the tavern they espied the dowager Lady Lovelace in her coach and on this June evening they are said 'to have 'plucked her out of the coach,' calling her by opprobrious names and otherwise misconducting themselves in the street.[3]

Alexander's elder brother, Colonel Francis, as we have seen, had raised an independent regiment[4] on the 19th November 1688. On 28th February 1689, Alexander joined the regiment and received a commission as Captain. The regiment was now put on a more regular footing and first saw active service at the Battle of the Boyne in Ireland on 11 July 1690. Colonel Francis died a fortnight later on 25 July and it was quite natural that Alexander should expect to succeed him as Colonel of the Regiment. To his disgust and that of several other officers, a Thomas Erle from another regiment was appointed, so he and a number of other officers resigned:

> Expecting to succeed his brother in ye command of ye Regiment which he justly might, his brother having raised it and laid out great sums of money thereon, but it having then given to another, this Capt. Luttrell with several other officers of ye Regiment quitted ye same.[5]

From the same source we learn that Alexander served in all the wars in Flanders, so he would have served under William of Orange at the battles of Steinkerke and Landen and at the siege of Namur in 1695.

In 1694 Alexander Luttrell had rejoined his former Lieutenant-Colonel, William Northcott, who had been placed at the head of a new regiment of foot.[6]

On 21 September 1697, Alexander went on half-pay.[7]

> The regiment was disbanded in 1697 but, in 1702 he and several of his brother officers accepted commissions in a regiment of Marines [*31st Foot*] under the command of George Villiers. In December 1703, he was promoted to be Colonel of the regiment.[8]

Colonel Alexander was also engaged in local politics and was returned to Parliament by Minehead borough in October 1690, in succession to his elder brother Francis. During the next fifteen years he was re-elected on six occasions but he did not stand in 1705; Sir John Trevelyan and Sir Jacob Bancks were returned in his stead.

The harbour at Minehead was improved by Alexander who spent a good deal of money on the project. It was his ancestor, Sir Hugh Luttrell (d. 1521) who had built a small pier and had enlarged the harbour. This put the little town of Minehead on the map and was of considerable benefit to its trade. This Sir Hugh Luttrell was made Admiral of Minehead. Now, in the eighteenth century, there was according to Lyte:

> ...a project of reviving in [*Alexander's*] favour the office of vice-admiral [*note the demotion*] which had been held by his ancestor the second Sir Hugh Luttrell, and by his brother Francis Luttrell...[9]

In 1703 and 1704 certain events shaped the future direction of Colonel Alexander's life. His nephew, Tregonwell, the heir to the estate, died in 1703 and his sister-in-law, Lady Bancks, died in 1704. Alexander left the army and took up residence at Dunster castle in 1705.[10] On 20 July he married, at Exminster, Dorothy, daughter of Edward Yarde of Churston Ferrers in Devonshire. A marriage portrait by Michael Dahl, showing her attired in primrose satin with blue drapery falling from her head down to her left shoulder, hangs in Dunster Castle. (Whilst Lyte definitely identifies the sitter as Dorothy Luttrell, the National Trust had in the 1980s some reservations on this point.)

On 10 May 1705, Dorothy Luttrell gave birth to the son and heir, named Alexander after his father. Two years later, again on 10 May, Dorothy, named after her mother, was born but she died young. Both children were baptized at Dunster. The third child, Francis arrived on 9 April 1709 and he became known as Francis of Venn. More will be said about this Francis and his wife Ann later.

There are two half-length portraits of Colonel Alexander at Dunster Castle. One shows him wearing a large periwig and dressed in a red coat with a white neckcloth. During his residence at Dunster castle, he re-named many of the rooms, but did not make any important structural changes.[11]

The room on the north side of the Leather Gallery, from some date after 1815 erroneously called 'King Charles's Room', presumably acquired this diversity of names when the colours of the furnishings were changed. It was known as 'the White Chamber' in 1691 and 1705 and as the Yellow Chamber in 1741 and the Red Chamber in 1781. It appears that the misnomer was based on the fact that the room now called 'King Charles's Room' at the northern end of the Gallery, and in 1781 called 'the Red Chamber', had 'a narrow dark closet behind the panelling' which was assumed incorrectly to be one of the Prince of Wales's hiding places.

Dunster in the Eighteenth Century; Queen Anne's Reign

In 1700 when Colonel Alexander Luttrell was pursuing his army career and was acting as guardian of the heir Tregonwell, the two churchwardens at Dunster were John Hossome and Robert Stickland. A rate was levied 'for the repairing of the psh Church of the said psh'. The 167 ratepayers contributed about £44 annually, paying approximately £11 per quarter.

In 1701-2 the Churchwardens' Accounts record:

	£	s	d
Paid for a plate for the Comn Table		2	0 [12]
Pd for Beer for ye Ringers when the Queen[13] was proclaimed		10	0
Paid Ye Ringers when the Queen was crowned		9	0
Paid for Beer when the Parishioners met to consider the Church.		4	0

The final entry for 1701 records:

	£	s	d
John Horman towards ye timber in ye Closter Courte.		20	0 [14]

The most momentous event of 1701 was the passing of the Act of Settlement whereby Parliament decreed that on Queen Anne's death the crown was to pass to Sophia, the daughter of Elizabeth 'the Winter Queen' and Frederick, Elector of the Palatine, 'the Winter King'. Sophia was the granddaughter of King James I on her mother's side. She married Ernest Augustus, Elector of Hanover, duke of Brunswick-Luneborg but since she died the same year as Queen Anne in 1714, it was her son George who established the Hanoverian line in England and became King George I.

Internationally, the outstanding event of 1701 was the opening of the Spanish War of Succession. In that year the French King of Spain, Philip V, entered Madrid and the French also occupied the Spanish Netherlands. Between April and September, Prince Eugene defeated the French in Lombardy and on 17 September, England, Holland and the Emperor allied themselves against France, as the balance of power in Europe was threatened.

The year 1702 includes references in the Churchwardens' Accounts to the future King George I and his wife Sophia Dorothea of Celle:

	£	s	d
Proclamation and a prayer for Prince George.		2	6
Pd for a Booke for the fast and prayer for ye Princess Sophia		2	6
Pd for one yard of Black Ribbon for the Surplice			6
A Common Prayer Book and Carriage		14	0

There are also references to the parish church:

	£	s	d
Paid John Chilcott for bear [*beer*] when the parishioners met and consulted about the Church.		8	0 [15]

John Ellsworthy for carring [*carrying*] tile from the Priory. [*no money is quoted here*].

Hancock comments:

> The references to the priory in the churchwardens' and overseers' books look as if the building, like so many other ancient buildings of the class, was, alas! used as a convenient quarry from which to obtain materials for repairs.[16]

In 1703 another special rate is made 'for the repairing of the Psh Church': 'Lead, tiling, and timber for the church cost this year the substantial sum of £29'.

Neither the Churchwardens' Accounts for this year nor the Registers, as given by Hancock, make any reference to the death of the heir Tregonwell in that year. They record only:

	£	s	d
Paid for bringing the Timber out of the Cloister Court into the Church		1	6
Dec. 24th. Pd George Budd for a Book of Prayer about ye tempest			6

This was the great storm during which Bishop Kidder was killed at Wells.[17] The same year the church was involved in much expenditure on the tenor bell, which needed to be re-cast. Under the heading 'Bells' Hancock records:

> Paid for Casting the Tener bell Eighteen Pounds and paid for new Mettle 2qrs. 20½ lbs. and alowed for waste in melting ye old bell 1 cwt. 0qrs. 8 lbs in all is 1cwt. 3 qrs 0½ lbs at £7. per hundred is Twelve pounds, five shillings seven pence halfe penny in all £30. 5s 7½d.[18]

Barrington Simeon includes further entries:

	£	s	d
March 4 Pd for beer at the casting of the Bell		5	0
Pd Richard Phillips for making the seventh and eighth bell wheels	3	0	0

In 1704, further expense was incurred on this bell:

> Pd the bell founder for new casting the Bell £5. Pd his advance for mettle 3 qrs 22lbs. at 15d per lb £6. 12s 6d.[19]

The total cost of the tenor bell was thus £41 18s. Also noted in the Churchwardens' Accounts for 1704 were these expenses:

	£	s	d
Pd for cleaning the Redlaft [*Rood loft*] ye pillars and windows		2	0
Pd Mr Keymer for his diner when ye Lord Bishop was hear [*sic*]		2	6
Ringing at the victory at hoistat [Hochstaedt]		4	0

There was no reason to ring the bells since this was a French victory in the War of Spanish Succession. In 1704 it was, however, followed by the Allies' great victory at Blenheim.

Two purely parochial entries in the Churchwardens' Accounts intervene before greater issues again creep into the ringers' calendar:

		£	s	d
1704	Making ye Matting Round ye Communion Table		7	0
	Mr Thomas Fry for painting ye Church and ye Pulpit	3	0	0

The year Colonel Alexander Luttrell came to live at Dunster Castle the bells were rung to celebrate the victory of Blenheim:

	£	s	d
Pd for ringing for the Duke of Marlborough's sukses over the French		4	0

The battle of Blenheim, actually Blindheim, near Hochstaedt, was fought on 13 August 1704. Dunster, understandably, was a little late in celebrating this victory in which Marlborough and Prince Eugene crushingly defeated the French army. No doubt news travelled slowly and the distance was great from Bavaria to Somerset.

During this War of the Spanish Succession, Gibraltar, whose rock and harbour could provide England with a naval base, was taken on 4 August 1704 by a combined Dutch and English fleet. It was surrendered to Admiral Rooke, the Commander-in-Chief of the English fleet off Spain. As noted earlier, Rooke's wife, who had died in 1702, was Mary Luttrell, daughter of Colonel Francis and Mary Luttrell.

In an endeavour to assemble the reasons why Minehead boasts so many references to this period, we must firstly remember that George, the son of Mary Rooke née Luttrell and Admiral Rooke, was favoured by illustrious god-parents, Queen Anne and her husband Prince George of Denmark.

His grandmother Mary Luttrell née Tregonwell had married Jacob Bancks, a Swede who had the rank of captain in the English navy, in 1696 He was knighted in 1699 and, no doubt, due to Luttrell backing, he represented Minehead in nine successive parliaments from 1698 to 1713. Today, he is remembered by Bancks Street in Minehead.

In 1714 Sir Jacob commissioned the sculptor Francis Bird (1667-1731), to provide a statue of Queen Anne similar to that which he had carved to celebrate the completion of St Paul's cathedral in 1712. The London statue stood before the west front of the cathedral and had at its four corners figures representing Britannia, Ireland, France and the American colonies. The Minehead statue was originally placed in St Michael's church but when the church was restored in 1880 it was removed. Plans to place the statue in the Town Hall did not materialize and in 1893 the people of Minehead subscribed to pay for a canopy and columns to protect the eighteenth-century effigy.[20]

It is little surprising in view of Colonel Alexander Luttrell's army career during the reigns of William and Mary and Queen Anne, and the latter's favour shewn to Colonel Francis Luttrell's grandson, that to-day we have Blenheim Gardens and Blenheim Road to commemorate the great victory over the French at the battle of Blenheim, and the statue of Queen Anne marking a special connection between the Luttrell family and the Queen.

Four parochial items appear in the Accounts before the bells are rung to celebrate Marlborough's successes:

	£	s	d
1705			
Recd of Wm Blackford, Esq, for healing the ground when Wm. Blackford was buried		6	8

(This Wm. Blackford Esq. was presumably William, the son of Richard Blackford (d. 1689) who died in 1728. The William who was interred is obviously an earlier William.)

	£	s	d
1706			
Wm Pleasway for his shops rent.		1	0
[*The arch under the churchyard wall*]			
Pd John Hyles for killing a Pole Cat			4
Richard World and his man for 2 days worke for paveing ye ground where Missus Blackford was buried and mending ye tile		4	8

(Mrs Blackford was presumably Elizabeth Blackford, the widow of Richard Blackford (d. 1689). She died in 1698 and was buried on 7 January.[21] No doubt the entry for 1706 was in connection with later paving where she had been buried eight years earlier.)

Ye Ringers for ye surrender of Ostend	(no amount given)

This entry relates to Marlborough's defeat of the French at Ramillies and the conquering of the Spanish Netherlands. By the end of 1706 all that remained to France in the Netherlands was Mons, Charleroi, Namur and Luxemburg.

There are no entries in the Churchwardens' Accounts for 1707 or 1709 and the only entry for 1708 refers to:

	£	s	d
Ch. Orchard, Esq., for Knowle			
Pd for Sheaves of Reed for ye Alms House and Clock House		7	0

1708 was the year which saw Marlborough's crushing victory over the French at Oudenarde and on 11 September 1709 he won the battle of Malplaquet, where the regiment founded by Francis Luttrell, later known as the Green Howards, earned its first battle honours.

The Churchwardens' Accounts continue:

	£	s	d
1710			
Pd for a Prayer Book and proclamation for a fast 28 Mch		1	6
For Iron and work about the vane and Thomas Morcombe			
for Setting up the Vane and Tom Wilkins for cullering it.	1	5	0
1711			
For beere when we made bargaine about ye Clock		2	0
for making ye watch part of the Clock.	5	0	0

Colonel Alexander Luttrell died on 22 September, 1711 and was buried at Dunster at 6 o'clock.[22] The chimes, at that time, played the 113th Psalm 'Praise the Lord, ye servants'. (As if this was an instruction to the castle staff!) There is no mention in the Churchwardens' Accounts of the bells being tolled.

The final entries for 1711 read:

	£	s	d
For finishing ye Chimes		16	6
For amending the striking part of the Clock		10	0
For carrying a vagrant woman out of Dunster		4	6
For amending of the quarter clock		1	10
For a translation of the Psalmes to the Clerk.		2	10

The Luttrell Hatchments

The first of a splendid series of hatchments, placed in Dunster Church in 1953, is that of Colonel Alexander Luttrell. Hatchments derive from medieval achievements; the most famous of these in England is that of the Black Prince which hangs over his tomb in Canterbury cathedral. It was usual to hang the hatchment on the front of the house, in this case, the castle, during the period of mourning and to place it in the church after the funeral, although occasionally it was carried in the funeral procession.

According to Mr H.F.Merchant:

> The arms shown on this hatchment are quarterly first and fourth Luttrell and second and third Hadley quartering Durborough, impaling Yarde.[23]

This hatchment which is the only one to display the old punning crest of the Luttrells, an otter, from the French *loutre,* is the middle hatchment on the north wall of the vestry, formerly the Lady Chapel (see chart).

Mr Merchant blazons this hatchment as follows:

for Alexander Luttrell, 1663-1711 (wife Dorothy, née Yarde); -

Arms: -   *quarterly first and fourth –or a bend between six martlets sable for Luttrell; second and third – quarterly first and fourth – gules on a chevron or three crosses crosslet sable for Hadley; second and third – or on a bend cotised sable three Bear's heads argent for Durborough;*[24] *impaling – argent a chevron gules between three water bougets sable for Yarde.*

Crest: on a helm with a wreath *or and sable,* an otter *passant sable.*

Mantling: -   *gules* and *argent*

Supporters: -   *two swans argent, ducally gorged and chained or* [these supporters are held to be derived from the white swan badge of Bohun, the families being linked by marriage – Margaret, daughter of Humphrey de Bohun married Hugh Courtney and female descendants of theirs married into the Luttrell line].[25]

Motto: *Quæsita Marte Tuenda Arte.*[26]

This motto, which might be translated 'Taken by War, Held by Skill', seems hardly appropriate to the manner in which the Luttrells acquired Dunster castle and their estates; one wonders how it came to be adopted and what its significance, if any, might be.

There is no doubt that this first hatchment is that of Colonel Alexander Luttrell since it displays the impalement of the arms of Yarde – Alexander married Dorothy Yarde and he was the only male Luttrell to marry into the Yarde line after the Luttrell/Hadley marriage. But according to Lyte, the series in the church began with the hatchment of Colonel Francis Luttrell. It has been suggested by H.F. Merchant that it is just possible that there was an earlier hatchment on display when Lyte was compiling his history.[27] But according to Colonel Sir Walter Luttrell 'if it ever existed it is certainly not in the Castle nor loaned to the Green Howards'.[28]

The hatchment of Colonel Francis Luttrell, should it ever appear, would have borne an impalement, or more probably an inescutcheon of pretence since his wife Mary Tregonwell was an heiress, showing the arms of Tregonwell. These arms are: *Crest:-Arg three pellets in fess cotised Sa, betw three Cornish choughs ppr. A Cornish chough ppr holding in the beak a chaplet Erm and Sa.*[29] (The plaster frieze in the dining room, formerly the parlour, of Dunster Castle shows two shields. The first displays the arms of Luttrell impaling those of Tregonwell and the second displays the arms of Tregonwell alone. Mary Tregonwell, an heiress, probably provided the money and directed the form of the heraldic decoration. This work bears the date 1681. Before leaving the subject of Colonel Alexander Luttrell's armorials we should mention his seal, which shows the Luttrell arms: *Or a bend betw Six Martlets Sa differenced with a crescent.* The crescent alludes to the fact that he was, up to 1690, when his elder brother died, a younger son. The crest here resembles a fox rather than an otter.

After Colonel Alexander's death in 1711, Dorothy Luttrell, his widow, managed the estate until her own death in 1723, as the heir, Alexander, was only six years old.

Dorothy Luttrell was described by her contemporaries as 'a very prudent and charitable gentlewoman'[30] and as 'the great good lady at the Castle.' [31] In 1720, she met the outstanding debts of her late brother-in-law, Colonel Francis Luttrell, who had died in 1690, thus, in the words of another admirer, further adding to her 'former just, charitable and pious actions'.[32]

In the little market town below Dorothy Luttrell's castle, stray roaming pigs appear to have been a problem and in 1712 an order was issued by the borough court to the street-keepers who appear to have taken advantage of this situation. It stated:

> That the street-keepers shall not exact or receive more than one penny for one pig, and proportionately for any number they shall take up within the burrough, besides the duty to the bayliff for the pound.[33]

The street-keepers' duties were made difficult by 'persons who laid dung on the public thoroughfares, or washed sheepskins in "the Dunster river."' Sometimes those elected to carry out these duties were themselves accused of failing to do so and the lord of the manor also occasionally came under attack for failing to keep the pavement of Market Street (High Street) in proper condition'. Other complaints were that 'he had not repaired the stocks, the pillory and the ducking-stool, "instruments of justice"'. In 1714 'several persons were presented for erecting porches in the street beyond the line of their pent-houses, and for setting up sign-posts before their respective doors.'[34]

The clerks of the market kept a watchful eye over weights and measures. There were bread-weighers and ale-tasters; failure to reach the prescribed standard resulted in the baker who had offended being taken to court. The ale-tasters seem to have succumbed to bribery and demanded either 'a sample quart of beer, or a penny', 'according to the custom of the manor'.[35]

The Peace of Utrecht between France and Britain, Holland, Savoy and Portugal was signed on 11 April 1713. The bells of St George's rang out and the ringers received 12d for beer and 5s. The next year, further celebrations went on in Dunster when on 5 June the ringers received 2s 6d 'for ringing at a thanksgiving day for peace being proclaimed'. It was even better for the ringers on 7 July when they rang 'on the thanksgiving day' and twenty of them attended a dinner, the total cost being £1 2s 9d.[36]

The entry in the Churchwardens' Accounts following this dinner goes back to 8 March 1713, and records that the ringers were paid 'for ringing being the Queens accession day to the Crowne' the sum of 5s.[37]

In the same year a pewter plate 9¼ inches in diameter was presented by F. Bradley and T. Stadden, Churchwardens, who were also Overseers of the Poor. [38] This has the name of the maker, 'Philip Foy', a Bristol pewterer, and four other marks on the rim, with the names of the churchwardens and the date inscribed on the reverse.

In 1714 Wm Strong made a joint stool for the church, recorded in the Churchwardens' Accounts as costing 3s.[39] More importantly a silver salver (a paten) was purchased at great expense:

	£	s	d
"ffor a Salver weighing 19oz. 10 dwt at 6s 6d per oz.			
for graveing 2s 6d	6	11	0

It was made in 1711, the year of Colonel Alexander Luttrell's death, and is inscribed 'James Wilkins, jr., Henry Slocombe, Churchwarden. 1714'. The Overseers' Accounts for 1708 refer to Henry Slocomb as someone who had taken on apprentices.[40] This salver is listed in the Parish Inventory.[41] Hancock describes it as:

a silver dish 10¼in. in diameter, standing on a foot 3¾ in. high, which is boldly splayed and moulded, *Marks*: mark of William Gamble (London, ent. 1697)[42]; 2 offic; date letter for 1711 [*he then gives the inscription*].[43]

Queen Anne died on 1 August 1714. She was succeeded by George of Hanover, the great grandson of King James I. Dunster celebrated, as the Churchwardens' Accounts record: 'August 8th: Ringing at the Proclaiming of King George … 5s.' [44]

On 30 September 1714, the new king (1660-1727) arrived in England. Ostensibly George was welcomed but some felt that James Stuart, if he were indeed the son of James II and Mary of Modena, had a greater claim to the throne. However, as James Stuart resolutely refused to renounce his Catholic faith, this removed any parliamentary support for his cause, and on 6 October 1714, £1 1s was paid to the Dunster ringers for 'Ringing King George's Coronation'.[45]

The final entries for the year 1714 appear out of order in the Church-wardens' Accounts, as follows:

	£	s	d
Oct 6th. Proclamacon against Immorality		1	0
March 29 Pd Mr Escott Lady-day hospital		3	0 [46]

'Lady-day hospital' may refer to the poor-house/workhouse which had been established at the end of the seventeenth century. Lyte records that, 'three small houses… were between 1696 and 1699, let to the overseers of the parish, to serve as a workhouse'.[47] (These houses were near the site of the Wesleyan school which was built in Mill Lane in 1825.) According to Hancock, it was 1699 before the poor were established in a poorhouse.[48] This was actually in Mill Lane, near the corner of West St where two cottages and a garage now stand. Here the poor were constrained to live under strict rules.

As early as 1667 a rate had been levied on the ratepayers of Dunster for the benefit of the poor. Hancock gives details of the names of the principal inhabitants of Dunster who helped to provide 'for ye maintaynance of ye poore of the psh.' [49] Money was also derived from fines, and sometimes the poor and their children were cared for by the villagers:

> 1692   John Clements for keeping Antony Courteney for board for him 2s
> fier in his chamber 2s 4d. = 4s 4d
> For a bottle of Stirtick Water 1s
>
> 1693   Thirty faggots of wood cost 4s., and six "bushells of coles" 3s 6d
> May ye 29th 1693. Received 1s being monies leveyed on Wllm
> Williams by ye Justice for not being to church in time of Service and
> given to the poor as followeth. [Six poor people received 2d each.]

It was an indictable offence not to attend divine service on the sabbath. The Overseers' Accounts for the remainder of the seventeenth century may be found in Prebendary Hancock's *Dunster Church and Priory*, 150-2. Here only those relating to the eighteenth century will be quoted:

> 1700   There is a bill for clothing the poor at this time
> Paid Hugh Matthews for 14 yards of freeze at 2s 4d. per yd £1. 12s 8d
> paid him for 13½ yards Carsey [*Kersey*] at 2s 2d per yd = £1.9s 3d.
>
> 1702   Received of Justice Siderfin 2s., it being Levyed on Tackbeard a smith of
> Luxborough for swearing, and gave it as ffollowes
>
> 1702   May the 1st, of Esq. Siderfin 5s 6d, which was paid by Kensett of
> Winsford for breaking the Saboth and other offences it was given to ye
> persons underwritten.
> Pd. ye Kings Tax for Buring [*burying*] Buckmans Child and Mary
> Bakers Child 8s.
> Mr Hewett his bill for ye cureing Joan Eames thigh £3.

Work was carried out on the almshouses in 1702:

	£	s	d
Gave ye Workmen yt wrought at ye Almshouse in beer 6d			
and pd. for Carriage outt of ye rubble		1	6
Pd George Westlake for Thetching [*thatching*] ye Almshouse		8	0
Pd for Sparrs and watering ye reed		1	3
Also for a hundred of reed		14	0

> 1703   Upon Burying of Sarah the Wife of Heman Ball on the 27th
> November. Ano. Dom. 1703, 50s was paid because she was
> buried in linning and was thus disbursed.

Earlier in 1703 Robert Giles died and his burial was marked by a stone placed in the floor of the nave where he was interred. His wife died two years later and the stone, known to have been still in existence in 1830, was inscribed: 'Robert Giles, March 12, 1703. Elizabeth, his wife, May 5, 1705'.[50] In 1704, Henry Clement died and his death too was marked by an inscribed stone placed over his grave in the nave of the church. [51]

The next entry in the Overseers' Accounts is for 1707:

> 1707   The Clarkes rate is forgiven for his publishing the 2 rates yearly
> High Rent for the Alsmshouse, 1s.
> [Hancock here remarks that 'from this time on there are frequent allusions to this institution'.]
> Geo. Westlake in want in Candles 2½d, in Sugar and brimstone 1½d = 4d.
> Given Anne bello 3 yds. Prest Bays and ½ yd Culld lining to make
> a body [*bodice*] to her gown she being almost naked, 2s 10d.
> ffor sacke [*dry wine*] for....boy in sickness . . . . . . 8d [52]

Regarding apprentices, the accounts note:

> We have bound out 7 apprentices which are as under:
> James Bach alias Wescumbe to Henry Slocumbe of Mash fur Sir Hugh
>   Stukleys esteat.
> Henery Eastine to Mr John Sealy for Mr William Sealy's esteat.
> Thomas Long to John Beaker for Mrs Escote's esteat at Alcum.
> Robert Long to Thomas Mercum, bearers, ffrancis Quirke,
> John Question, George Dolbridge jr. for the Ship [*the Luttrell Arms*] and
>   Robert Court.
> Joane Prole to William Blackwell, bearers, John Andrew for Mrs
> Willicumbes esteat in Alcum and Robert Copp.
> Jane Sagg to Mr John Whitelock Gent. for his estate in Dunster.
> Jone Rawle to Henery Millar-Hopkin Morgin for Elicum, Baldwin Knight,
> bearers. [*£1 is at this time paid for each apprentice.*]

The following appears at the end of the summary of the Overseers' Accounts for this year: 'Note it. In Robert Burts yeare. Pease and Bacon were very deare'.[53] The said Robert Burt died in 1711and left 40s to the poor of Dunster.[54]

In 1712 Baldwin Knight and Robert Dibble were appointed parish officers for the town of Dunster. (The overseers for the country were Robert Drew and Henry Millar.) Money given to their successors in 1713 by Dorothy Luttrell for the benefit of the poor was noted in detail:

> 1713May ye 19th. I recvd by us ffrancis Bradley and Thomas Staddon
> Churchwardens and Overseers of ye poor of ye pish of Dunster by ye approba-
> tion and direction of some of the inhabitants thereof whose names are subscribed
> as Witnefses hereunto, of ye honble Mrs Dorothy Luttrell the sume of Eleven
> pounds, sixteen shillings and sixpence for halfe a years interest ending at Lady-
> day last past for ye sume of 473 *lib*. being as well for money wch Colln ffrancis
> Luttrell had in his lifetime of ye said psh poore stock and ye interest thereof, as
> well as for 50 *lib* given in and by ye last Will and Testamt of ye honble Coll

Alexander Lutterell to ye poor of the psh, we say recvd			
ye said sum of	11	16	6
Principle Money	292	0	0
Interest thereof for 9 years at 5*lib.* percent	131	8	0
Legacy given by Coll. Luttrells Will	50	0	0
	473	8	0
Interest for 473 *lib* 8*s* 0*d* yearly at			
5*lib* per cent	23	13	0
Halfe years interest is	11	16	6

ye 8*s* makes 11 *lib* 16*s* 11*d*.
Wm Sealey, Wm Leigh, Cha. Crockford, Wm Eeston, Tho. Watts Tho.
Griffen, Tho. Prowse were witnefnes".[55]

Many bequests had been made before by the Luttrell family who held the capital, the interest being used for the benefit of the poor. The money was lent out at interest in the form of small loans.

The 1713 Overseers' Accounts continue as follows:

> June ye 6th. Memorandum that there was forfited by George Delbridge Junr for ye use of the poore of Dunster seven shillings and sixpence, for selling of Ale in paints [*pints*] not sealed, and given by Mr Leath Supervisor to Francis Bradley and Thomas Staddon by ye Justices order, and was thus distributed, with a ginna [*guinea*] given by Sr Jacob Banks.
> August 18. Gave Legs Children when they had ye small pox 1*s*.

That year overseers received £1 from one ffry (Fry) of Minehead for swearing; a further £1 from one Lenard, a farmer, 'for ye rent of the psh garden' and 4s from him for a tree in the same garden.

The next entry in the Overseers' Accounts is for 1715:

By Mr Blackfords orders ye Crowners feys [*fees*]	13*s* 4*d*
George Rawle Jorney to Wells	10*s*
Robert Coffen for Waching of the dead Corps.	9*d*

Hancock ends his citations from the Overseers' Accounts for the year 1715 as follows:

> Now follows beautifully written, "An account of the Writings in the Box within the Poors Chest on the North side of the Chauncel in Dunster church viz; 95 Indentures, 62 Discharges, 12 Orders of Sessions, 25 orders of removals, 45 warrants against intruders, 28 Miscellanies, 266 documents in all. October 12, 1715. The keyes to the chests in the middle loft in Dunster Tower is the first as you enter the loft the others in order. [The keys belonged to William Blackford (2), William Question (ye 3rd of that name), and Thomas Chilcot.]

	£	s	d
The apprentice list is as follows:			
John Owen apprentice to John Markham, cordwainer	5	0	0
John Reed apprenticed to Rob. Leigh Weaver	5	0	0
John Baker apprentice to Sam Cowline thatcher	5	0	0
Ann Strickland apprentice to Mary Stride Sempstress	3	0	0
Amy Perkins with her apprentice		16	0
four pairs of indentures.		19	0[6]

These entries appertaining to the year 1715 can be placed in an historical context for in that year, the fourth of Dorothy Luttrell's widowhood, the first Jacobite rising began. On 6 September, at Braemar, the Earl of Mar proclaimed James Stewart, the Old Pretender, as he later became known, as James III. In Scotland, Edinburgh remained loyal to the Hanoverians but the majority of the towns supported the rising. In England riots took place in a good many towns but King George remained unruffled and showed no signs of returning to his beloved Germany.

The Jacobites were seen as a threat to the business interests of England. Although no reference to the Jacobite rebellion appears either in Lyte or Hancock, it would appear that Dunster, manufacturing its local broadcloth, known as 'Dunsters', would have supported the Hanoverians.

The gossip in Dunster in 1716/17 centred round two topics: the building of a gallery at the west end of St George's Church, and the saga of 'Old Blake'.

The Overseers' Account records re 'Old Blake':

	£	s	d
1717 for an old rug [rug] ffor old blake in his sickness		2	6
ffor 4 yards of cotten Tape ffor old blake when his arme was cott off			6
Ye doctor poole ffor cotting off old blakes arme	1	1	6
ffor bare [beer] when old blakes arme was cott off in treating ye Doctor poole			9
ffor sope [soap] for old Blake in washing him			2
ffor a nick [neck] of mooton [mutton] for old blake in his sickness			5
Pd baldwin Ringlet ffor care ye old blake made in his sickness		3	0

A second doctor was now called to old Blake's bedside as the Overseers wanted a second opinion:

	£	s	d
Pd beare in treating of Doctor Cording ffor going to old blake		3	
ffor sope for washing old blaks clothes		1 ¼	

'Bays thread' is procured for him, his daughter is paid for tending him; 'one yard of bays and straw' are purchased for him; Elizabeth

Morgan is called in to help, and yet 'old blake' died and put the parish to fresh expense:

	£	s	d
ffor ye people in stretching fforth of old blake		1	2
Alexander Pitcher for his attending of him			10
for his shroud 4s8d. and a affidavit for him			6

Another death took place this time in the almshouse: Joan Morgan's goods were sold to defray the expenses of her funeral:

> 1 brass pott 9s., one tubb 1s 4d., one curn [churn] 1s., one skillet 1s. Her wood she had left 5s., ffor a bedstead 2s 2d., ffor a frying pane, 3d., ffor a pail 10d., Her coffin cost 6s., her shroud 4s 3d, ye grave 1s. ye bell 1s 6d., stretching forth of her 1s., her affidavit 6d. Her bare [beer] when she was buried 1s 2d, for taking out of ye yood [wood] 6d." [57]

The project for building a gallery at the west end of Dunster Church was afoot in 1716. Presumably the 1717 entry in the Churchwardens' Accounts referring to a payment of £2 2s 6d 'for orders for Building the Gallery', refers to the legal requirements of a 'faculty' (the right to carry out certain ecclesiastical acts) which the churchwardens would have had to obtain from the bishop at Wells before the work could begin. In 1716/17 they met the carpenters to consider the carrying-out of the project:

	£	s	d
1716-17 For beer at Will Pleassways when we met the Carpenter about the gallery.			6

The bishop visited Dunster in 1717, no doubt to approve the scheme:

	£	s	d
Gave to the Ringers when my lord Bishop came		6	8
Ye Clerks dinner same time		1	0
Severall pieces of Oake for ye Gallery	6	2	0

Naturally the parishioners were involved in the discussions. The Churchwardens' Accounts record:

	£	s	d
Spent with Parishioners when they met about the gallery		7	2
64 Deals @ 3s and Carriage	9	12	0
2 Tuns of timber from Madam Luttrell	4	4	6
Oak from Old Cleeve	1	0	3
Wages for the Gallery, etc.	9	7	10 [58]

The gallery would have been where the bell-ringers and the orchestra (perhaps two fiddles and a flute, with a bass viol) sat. It was also the only place in church where the young lads and local farmhands were allowed to sit. It was removed in the nineteenth century.[59]

There is only one entry in the Churchwardens' Accounts for 1718:

	£	s	d
1718 Mʳ Anthony ye Church Bible and parchment	4	4	0 [60]

That year saw the death of Lucy Luttrell and the undertaking of much work on the almshouses. Lucy Luttrell, Dorothy Luttrell's mother-in-law and the widow of Francis Luttrell I, died on Christmas Eve 1718 and was buried at Dunster on 7 January 1719. She was the granddaughter of John Pym, the great parliamentary leader during the Civil War, and had married Francis Luttrell in 1655. She was therefore of an advanced age at the time of her death. Her three sons, Thomas, Colonel Francis and Alexander, had predeceased her.

In 1718 Dorothy Luttrell, Alexander's widow, purchased the advowson of St Michael's church Minehead for her son Alexander and thus had the right to appoint the incumbent.[61]

That year, work on the almshouse was again carried out, on the instructions of the overseers of the parish. The master mason employed was paid 1s 4d per day, while the labourer received 1s per day. The almshouse would appear to have been re-thatched, as a 'hundred of reed' was purchased for 7s. But some of the roof must have been tiled, because 'Mr Samuell Chafyn was paid 4s 2d for tyle stoanes' and Mr Gyles Escott received 15s for 'stoanes'.[62]

The same year Dorothy Luttrell received a bill (sent to her under-age son), presumably for repairs to the Priory Church, 'for new leding [sic] 20 feet of glass in the old church, 3d per foot, 6s 6d; For 5 dozen of new quarrys in the old church, 10d, per dozen, 4s 2d'.[63]

The Overseers' Accounts for 1718 concluded with the following entries:

> Spent upon the parishioners in binding out prentises. 1s.
> Paid for a horse at the Blew Anker and expenses in binding out prentices 2s6d.
> Paid Mrs Thorne for a horse for Andrew Dibble. £3.
> Thos Lang and George Chaplin There bill for caring (carrying, or conveying) of men to Jail £2. 8s 4d.
> Do. Thos Burge and William Coffin bill for caring men to jail £4.[64]

Perhaps the greatest national advance of the year 1718 was that of inoculation against the scourge of smallpox introduced by Lady Mary Wortley Montagu.

1719 saw the re-casting of Dunster's seventh bell. The articles for casting the bell cost 7s 4d.[65] The re-casting was done by Mr Wroth of Wellington and cost £23 4s.[66] Candles at the rate of 6d per pound were allowed to the ringers of the bell at this period at 4.00 am daily. (The stairs were unlit until 1934 when electricity was installed.)

In 1720 the 'New Way' to the castle was completed on the instructions of Dorothy Luttrell. The earlier hazardous approach was a death trap and only the most skilled of coachmen or horsemen would negotiate it safely.

Part of this earlier way is still to be seen; a steep cobbled ramp beside the stairway built to the right of it. Dorothy Luttrell's 'New Way' took a winding road opposite the stables round the eastern side of the Tor, eventually reaching the level of the south-eastern angle of the castle, where it ended in a little platform close to the domestic offices. In 1723 the last small fragments of the medieval castle were removed from the Tor and a bowling-green was laid out, followed by the octagonal summer-house in 1727.

While all this work was proceeding, in the church an inventory was being taken. The Churchwardens' Accounts record the details:

> 1720 An inventory of furniture belonging to the Communion Table and other things in and belonging to the parish Church of Dunster,
> Taken the 26th day of May Año Domi 1720.
> A Silver Chalice and cover for wine.
> A silver Salver for bread.
> A Pewter plate to hold the offerings.
> A Pewter plate heretofore used to hold the Consecrated Bread.
> Two pewter flaggons and a wooden Trencher.
> A large velvet carpet to cover the Communion Table.
> A large Holland table Cloth and two Holland napkins.
> Three long Cushions to place round the railes of the Communion Table.
> A Pewter Bason to hold the water in the vaunt. [*font*]
> A Surplice and a Cushing in the Reading seat.
> A Cuishong for the Pulpit.
> A long purple cloth to cover ye 'Desk for ye Archdeacon'.
> Three purple Cuishons to be used at ye Visitation.
> A large purple cloth to cover the Table for ye Register [*the Archdeacon's official*]
> An old and new Bible.
> A Book of Homilies.
> A Common Prayer Book for the minister and another for the Clerk.
> Three Register Books.
> Two Books chained of the Defence of the Apologie of ye Church of England.
> Tate and Bradys new version of the Psalms.
> A little desk and a large desk.
> Doctor Prideaux's Book of the duty of a Churchwarden in the hands of ye Churchwardens.
>
> Attested by us
> Willm J. Kymer. Minister.
> John Shenton ⎫
> Abraham Allen ⎬ Churchwardens
> Giles Edmonds ⎭
> Willm Hurford Elder-men[67]

For Setting of the 'clapses [*clasps*] of this book. 4*d*.[68]

The final entry for the year 1720 reads:

	£	s	d
Paid Edward Hodge for making of the little Tower door		2	0

In 1721, lead for the church this year cost nearly £17.

		£	s	d
1722	Paid for casting the brasses and putting them in		17	0
	Paid Priory servants for hedgehogs		1	4
	Paid Castles servants for hedgehogs		4	6 [69]

Dorothy Luttrell's New Chapel

In 1722 Dorothy Luttrell employed Sir James Thornhill (1675/6-1734) to design a chapel at the castle 'partly on the site of an ancient semi-circular tower'.[70] where Salvin's drawing-room now stands. This white-walled chapel is depicted in an eighteenth-century painting which hangs in the morning room of the castle.

Sir James Thornhill was not an acknowledged architect but he was a decorator in the grand baroque tradition. He had won the important commission to decorate the 'Great Hall', the lower hall and the vestible of Greenwich Hospital, Wren's masterpiece. Between the years of 1715/17 he painted the cupola of St Paul's Cathedral with scenes from the life of St Paul. Thornhill also painted the fine frescoes in the chapel of Wimpole Hall in Cambridgeshire and in 1715 he excelled himself in the execution of the painted ceiling in Queen Anne's bedroom at Hampton Court.

In 1722, the year Dorothy Luttrell engaged him, Thornhill, now Sergeant Painter to George I, was elected Whig M.P. for Melcombe Regis. The work at Dunster to his designs and under his direction, executed in 1723/4, was estimated to cost £1,300. The actual estimate, 'supposing it were to be done in London where Portland stone is 2s 0d per foot cubical', apparently relates to this chapel. In fact the chapel was built of brick, faced with ashlar, which judging from the painting, was indeed Portland stone. It had four windows, two of which flanked the entrance and faced south and a porch on the north side. The family pew on the mezzanine level was on the longer side of the building. To hang over this pew Thornhill painted 'The Lifting Up of the Brazen Serpent' (*Exodus* VII, 9-25). This was a very popular subject in the eighteenth century and thoroughly in keeping with the chapel. Today, the painting hangs in the Priory Church on the north wall of the Luttrell chapel. In 1956, Prebendary Dunlop, Vicar of Dunster, would make this entry in his *Yearly Notes*: 'There have been some notable gifts to the Church, including Sir James Thornhill's painting of "The Brazen Serpent"...'.[71]

The chapel was demolished during the Salvin restoration in the 1870s to make way for the present drawing-room. The painting was then removed and prior to its removal to the Priory Church, according to Mr Julian Luttrell '[it] hung on the castle staircase when he was a boy'. Lyte refers to 'a silver flagon, salver and cup mentioned in 1744 as belonging to the communion table'.[72] This silver from Dorothy Luttrell's chapel is now at Alcombe (see later chapter).

In the autumn of 1722, William Kymer, vicar at Dunster from 1704-1729, was placed in charge of the two young sons of Dorothy and the late Alexander Luttrell, and accompanied them to Oxford. Alexander, then aged seventeen, followed the family tradition observed by his father and by his uncle, the late Colonel Francis, and went to Oxford, to Christchurch, to matriculate. His brother, Francis, was but thirteen years of age and this must have been an exciting adventure for him. When they reached Oxford, the two young men resided at the Star and went shopping, purchasing wigs which cost the enormous sum of £4 each. £15 was deposited with the bursar as security for their good conduct. After a week they returned home to Somerset stopping on the way at Burford, Cirencester, Sudbury, Bristol and Stowey.[73]

The next year on 19 November their mother Dorothy Luttrell died. She was buried in the family vault of the Priory Church. Her will, made the previous October, provided £350 for the completion of the castle chapel. This was achieved in 1724 and the consecration was most probably carried out by George Hooper, Bishop of Bath and Wells, whose somewhat indifferent portrait hangs on the back oak staircase of the castle.

ENDNOTES

1. Alexander Popham (1605 – 1669) was a Colonel in the Parliamentary army and played a leading role in Cromwell's campaign in the western counties until 1646 when the Civil War in Somerset ended with the surrender of Dunster Castle.
2. Marshwood Papers
3. From Wood's *Life and Times* (vol ii, 542), quoted by Lyte: H.D Part I 219
4. From 1744 nicknamed 'The Green Howards', after its Regimental Colonel, General the Honourable Charles Howard. This nickname became part of the official title of the regiment in 1920.
5. Extract from M.S at Dunster provided by Lt Col. N.D. McIntosh M.B.E. Regimental Headquarters Richmond, North Yorkshire.
6. Lyte says he joined as a Captain but the army records in Yorkshire refer to him as Lieut-Col of Colonel William Northcott's Regiment of Foot, 16 February, 1694.
7. Records of the Green Howards
8. Lyte: H.D Part I 219 (Note 2)
9. Ibid. 132 (Note 3)
10. Ibid. 219
11. Ibid. Part II 372
12. Hancock: D.C.P 181. 'This pewter plate still exists'.
13. Anne, who acceded on the death of King William
14. This garden, now called the Remembrance Garden, is on the north side of the church.
15. Hancock: D.C.P 182
16. Ibid.
17. Ibid.
18. Ibid. 70
19. Ibid.
20. Byford, Enid: *Somerset Curiosities*
21. Hancock: D.C.P. Registers, 112
22. Ibid.
23. Merchant: L.H.D. 175, in his article on the 'Luttrell Hatchments at Dunster' in *The Coat of Arms* (Heraldry Society, Autumn 1985/6)
24. The Hadley/Durborough quartering derives from the marriage of Alexander's great-great-grandfather, Thomas Luttrell (1525-1571), to Margaret Hadley, a remote cousin. She was the daughter, and became the heiress, of Christopher Hadley of Withycombe; one of her ancestors had married the heiress of the Durboroughs of Heathfield and an earlier Durborough had married a co-heiress of the Fitzurses of Williton and Withycombe. Through these connections she brought to her husband the manors of Williton Hadley, Withycombe Hadley and Heathfield, and various other lands in West Somerset (Merchant L.H.D, ibid.)
25. Merchant : L.H.D. Appendix. 186
26. Ibid.
27. Merchant correspondence 12/7/1989.
28. Luttrell correspondence 20/8/1989
29. Burke, Sir B. 1026.

[30] Lyte: H.D. Part I 221
[31] Ibid.
[32] Ibid.
[33] Ibid. Part I 311
[34] Ibid.
[35] Ibid. 310
[36] Hancock: D.C.P 184
[37] Ibid.
[38] Listed in the Inventory in the PCC Minutes (DPB 1920)
[39] Hancock: D.C.P 184
[40] Ibid. 153
[41] D.P.B 1920
[42] 'Maker's mark G.A., with three pellets and crown above; within a circle William Gamble' (Bates: I.C.P 155)
[43] Hancock: D.C.P 115
[44] Ibid. 184
[45] Ibid.
[46] Ibid.
[47] Lyte: H. D. Part II 340
[48] Hancock : D.C.P. 152
[49] Ibid. 133, 145
[50] Ibid. 83. Taken from Savage, *Hundred of Carhampton 1830*
[51] Ibid.
[52] Ibid. 153
[53] Ibid. 150/154
[54] Ibid. 158
[55] Ibid. 154/5
[56] Ibid. 154/6
[57] Ibid. 156/7
[58] Ibid. 127
[59] The faculty for its removal is dated 22 March 1875
[60] Hancock: D.C.P. 185
[61] Lyte: H.D. Part I 221 (Note 3)
[62] Hancock: D.C.P 157/8
[63] Lyte: H.D. Part II 430
[64] Ibid. 158
[65] Barrington Simeon: GBS 1670-1847
[66] Hancock: D.C.P 70
[67] Ibid. 120/1
[68] Barrington Simeon: GBS 1660-1874
[69] Hancock: D.C.P 185/6
[70] Lyte: H.D. Part II 373
[71] In 1970 Mrs Alys Luttrell had the painting cleaned
[72] Lyte: H.D. Part II 373 (Note 1)
[73] Ibid. Part I 222

CHAPTER THREE

DUNSTER LIFE in the EIGHTEENTH CENTURY; HENRY FOWNES LUTTRELL

Alexander Luttrell II

When Dorothy Luttrell died in 1723, Alexander II came into his inheritance, which comprised not only the landed estates but the ready sum of £2,300 which she had deposited in the castle just before she died. Lacking the convenience of a bank she had left a small handwritten note with the information that: 'There is in the writing closett 2,300*l* in money, besides a hundred pound in broad pieces and moyders received by leases.'[1]

In 1726, the year Alexander reached his majority, he married, judiciously, it would appear, Margaret Trevelyan of Nettlecombe. Her father had died the same year as Alexander's father in 1711 and she succeeded to his estates.[2] She seems to have been a stalwart lady for, in spite of being several years older than her husband, she outlived him by twenty-seven years, dying in 1764 in the reign of George III.

Since the couple had only one daughter, Margaret, Alexander was the last male representative of the Luttrell line, seated at Dunster since 1375.

At the first opportunity after his coming-of-age, Alexander was returned as a Tory on his family's interest for Minehead, voting regularly against the Whig government, supreme in England from 1714 to 1760.[3] He was elected as one of the borough's parliamentary members in the parliaments of 1727 and 1734. The expenses involved were later to be clearly apparent to his son-in-law, Henry Fownes Luttrell, who observed on his own election 'I too plainly see the rock my father Luttrell foundered upon to run myself into the same danger'.[4]

It was not only election expenses which beggared Alexander Luttrell but personal indulgence and family commitments. His parents had laid upon him the burden of providing a fortune of ten thousand pounds for Anne Luttrell, the daughter of his younger brother Francis, whose wife Anne Stucley had died in giving birth to Anne in 1731.

The purchase of expensive wigs when he and his brother went up to Oxford in 1722 has already been noted. It appears that the good-looking Alexander, who kept a huntsman and a gamekeeper at Dunster, loved fine clothes and enjoyed having his portrait painted; a prevalent indulgence of the day.[5] The castle inventory of 1744 specifies three portraits of him as being at the castle. One may possibly be identified with a very small canvas representing a boy, bewigged and wearing a red coat, with a sword by his side and a bird on his arm, perhaps by the Swedish miniature painter Boit.[6] Alexander Luttrell II's second portrait was also painted when he was still a boy. This depicts him 'in a light periwig and coat and waistcoat of mouse-coloured velvet'. Again, gorgeously attired, his third portrait was painted when he was a young man and shews him still wearing 'a light periwig & a blue velvet coat lined with white satin'.[7]

More is known about the fourth portrait signed by John Vanderbank and dated 1729, when Alexander was aged 24 and the father of the three-year-old Margaret. Here his taste for fine clothes goes one better: his light periwig is larger and his brown velvet coat is worn over 'a very long waistcoat of a rich material embroidered, or interwoven, with gold'.[8] Vanderbank, who in 1726 had received a commission to paint George I and Queen Caroline, also signed a portrait of Alexander's wife Margaret in 1729.[9]

According to Lyte, there are two further portraits of Alexander II at Nettlecombe Court and Bathealton Court, in both of which he is dressed in red velvet. One may be by another painter of royalty, Enoch Seeman, to whom he paid sixteen guineas in 1733, 'for four pictures'.[10]

The Church and Parish of Dunster

During Alexander II's lordship of the manor of Dunster, the secular and religious affairs of the parish receive some notice in the Overseers' Accounts and those of the Churchwardens.

In 1725, for the first time, the churchwardens were appointed by the minister and inhabitants of the parish. Two years later the public-spirited overseers, Thomas Stadden and John Shenton, who had replaced Francis Bradley, disdained to accept £5 for extending their care beyond their period of office.[11]They also paid for the 'parish treat' (probably a celebration of the accession of George II), which cost 14s.

It was in 1727 that George II ascended the throne, but in the Church-wardens' Accounts under 1728/9 there is an entry as follows: 'June 15 for ringing when the King was proclaimed: five shillings and sixpence.'

The same year a 'faculty' (official permission) was sought for a new altar-piece from John, Bishop of Bath and Wells by the Reverend William Kymer and his churchwardens Robert Allercott and Abraham Allen.[12] On 4 March 1728, authorisation was duly given.[13] The Churchwardens' Accounts note:

	£	s	d
1728-29. Paid Mr Brown for a facelty [sic] at Wells	2	5	0
Pd Ricd Phelps (Painter) for doing up the Altar Piece	40	0	0[14]

In 1808 this painting was referred to in the *Gentleman's Magazine* as 'a large indifferent painting of the Crucifixion by a person formerly resident in Dunster'. Hancock, writing in 1909, mentioned that:

> The chancel of the parish church was disfigured by an unsightly arch, which was filled by a glass screen. Above the altar hung a large picture of the crucifixion, by that very indifferent artist Mr Phelps of Porlock.[15]

In 1728 it would also appear that the poor people of Dunster were hungry, because 'several poor people' had to pay a five-shilling fine 'for corn taken notoriously away'.[16] They seem to have been driven to steal the corn. The same year also saw the embryonic emergence of the councils now known as the Parochial Church Council and the Parish Council. In those early days the church council presided over the affairs of the Overseers of the Parish, whose activities, judging by their accounts, went back at least to 1654.

At a public meeting of the parishioners of Dunster on 29 October 1728, the following resolution was unanimously agreed upon:

> That there be from thence forward a Public meeting of the Parishioners at the usual place in the Parish Church on the first Tuesday in every Month about 3 of the Clock in the Evening duly to consider the affairs of the Parish, to hear the grievances of the Poor, and to View and examine the Overseers' monthly Accounts.

It was also resolved that the Overseers should pay the 'Poor' every Friday morning at the Parish Church. The money would be forfeited if those entitled to it did not attend then without good reason, or if they failed to attend Divine Service (especially on Sundays). The Church Wardens were to 'give directions to the Sexton to place every Sunday in the Middle Isle of the Church two Forms or Benches, one for the Poor men, and the other for the Poor women to sit thereon during Divine Service'.

The Resolutions agreed on were signed by H. Luttrell,[17] Will Keymer Curate, Robert Alercott, Abraham Allon, Thomas Burge, John Bryant, Fr. Bradley, Sam Chaffin, John Hossom, Hugh Mathewes, John Morkham, Robert Strong, Thomas Watts and Baldwin Knight.[18]

The church was indeed the focal point of Dunster life; its officials held sway over the entire village, and the poor, should they fail to fulfil the edicts of the church, were deprived of their very livelihood.

The Overseers' Accounts continue in 1731:

> Pd Dorothy Leigh for beer at 4 Parish Meeting concarning [sic]
> the work-house 9s 1½d

In 1732 the workhouse expenses are fully recorded in those accounts:

	£	s	d
Paid Willm Blake Esq the years rent	7	0	0
Paid Willm Holman his Sallary	10	0	0
Paid Hen. Harrison for 56lbs of cheese		9	0
Paid for 29 Bushells of Wheat	4	6	8
Paid for 17 Bushells of Malt and Grinding	2	18	7
Paid for 20 lb of Hopps	1	3	6
Paid Mr Pearse for 39lb of Beeff		5	8

In 1735, one entry relates to Alexander Luttrell's father-in-law, Sir John Trevelyan, who had to pay £2 10s 'for carrying of a gun by Peter Slape'.[19]

On 22 February the burial is recorded of nineteen soldiers, a boy and two women who had drowned the day before. This mass interment cost the parish the princely sum £9 4s.[20] Only 1s 2½d was found in the drowned soldiers' pockets, according to the Churchwardens' Accounts for 1736. They also record a mystifying entry as follows: 'Recd of Mr Hobhouse for ye taking up 3 rugs which were owned and for a quilt, £2'.[21]

That year 'a black man' was converted to Christianity and, on being baptised, he took the cognomen William Dunster 'in remembrance of his new birth'.[22]

The Visitation of the bishop, to whom hospitality had to be extended that year, was a financial headache for the parishioners and churchwardens. No doubt they were pleased to receive him and they rang the bells to affirm this. At the end of the previous century the ringing for 'Bishop Kedar' (Kidder) 'coming to Towne' had cost £1 although in 1717 the ringers only received 6s 8d for ringing when my lord bishop came. The big expense that year was the visitation dinner, which had cost £1 19s, plus the clerks' dinner, for one shilling. In 1736 the Parishioners decided that the Churchwardens should not pay more than 20s at each visitation dinner, nor should they pay more than 10s each ringing day throughout the whole year. This resolution was agreed on Easter Tuesday, 27April 1736, and signed by Mr Question, Curate.[23]

Death of Alexander Luttrell II; Hatchments

Alexander Luttrell II was only thirty-two years of age when he died on 4 June 1737. His is the second hatchment in the series in St George's Church, the first being that of his father Colonel Alexander Luttrell.

The value of the hereditary property had been reduced either by Colonel Alexander or his son when the manor of Williton Hadley was sold to Sir William Wyndham.[24] Merchant comments:

> ... in his [Alexander Luttrell II's] hatchments the Hadley/Durborough quartering has been dropped from the Luttrell arms so that the shield shows merely Luttrell impaling Trevelyan; ... the ostrich feathers crest has now been adopted in lieu of the otter previously used.[25]

The ostrich feather crest, or panache of feathers, was used by the first Sir Hugh Luttrell (d 1428). It was revived by George Luttrell (1560-1629) in a different form[26] and by the time of Margaret and Henry Fownes Luttrell it would have dwindled into a plume of five stiff feathers.

The arms of Trevelyan depict the half-submerged legendary horse of Lyonesse: the horse which saved its master, the first Trevelyan, from drowning when that mythical land of King Arthur, between Land's End and the Scilly Isles, was submerged 'full forty fathoms under water'.

Burke gives the arms of Trevelyan (Nettlecombe co. Somerset and Wallington co. Northumberland, bart) as follows:

Gu, a demi horse ar. hoofed and maned or, issuing out of water. In base ppr; though it appears by old seals that the arms were once a lion ramp. holding a baton..

Supporters:— *Two dolphins ppr*

Motto:— *Tyme tryeth troth.*[27]

On occasion Alexander Luttrell used his father, Colonel Alexander's seal, but he also had one on which his arms were impaled with those of his wife. A further seal shews the arms of Luttrell only but has swan supporters.

The blazoning of Alexander Luttrell II's hatchment is as follows:

Arms:— *Luttrell (or and sable); impaling per fess wavy in chief gules a demi-horse rampant argent in base barry wavy of four argent and azure for Trevelyan.*

Crest:— *on a helm with a wreath argent and gules out of a ducal coronet or a plume of five ostrich feathers argent* [this crest is thought to derive from the similar one of the Courtney arms but it is difficult to account for the lapse in time between the Luttrell-Courtney marriages and its adoption — some 250 years]

Mantling:— *gules and argent.*

Supporters:— *two swans argent ducally gorged and chained or.*

Motto:— *Quaesita Marte Tuenda Arte.*[28]

Twelve days after Alexander II's death he was buried at Dunster. For some years after his death, a certain Robert Coffin received 5s annually for 'cleaning the seats and monuments in the old church at Dunster belonging to the family of the Luttrells and which had always been allowed by the family'.[29]

It was the custom to distribute among friends and relations mementoes of the departed and, on the occasion of Alexander Luttrell's death in 1737, thirty-nine mourning rings at a guinea a piece and six small ones at ten shillings were purchased and presented to the mourners. This was an extravagance which could ill be afforded for Alexander died in debt.

Anne Luttrell

Six years earlier, Anne Luttrell, Alexander Luttrell II's sister-in-law, wife of his younger brother, Francis of Venn, had died in childbirth on 30 October 1731, aged twenty-one years. Only three months later, Francis himself (b. 9 April 1709 and baptized at Dunster) followed her to the grave on 6 January 1732, aged only twenty-two years.

After Francis and Anne married at Kingswear (Devon) they had gone to live at Venn, a house belonging to Alexander Luttrell situated south of Brompton Regis which took its name from Michael de Venne (1272). The only child of the marriage, also named Anne, survived and more will be said about her later.

The marble mural monument to the memory of Anne Luttrell her mother, who was also the daughter and heiress of Charles Stucley of Plymouth, is to be found on the south wall of the south-east aisle, to the west of the monument erected by George Luttrell in 1621. It was moved to its present position during the Victorian restoration.

The epitaph on this monument is fully recorded by Hancock and in the *Gentleman's Magazine 1808*.[30] This simple mural monument with columns and a pediment is signed by M. Sidnell of Bristol and is surmounted by the arms of Luttrell bearing on an inescutcheon of pretence those of Stucley of Devonshire. It is flanked by flaming urns, the symbol of death. The blazoning of the arms Stucley, or Stuckley (Afton co. Devon) is: *Az three pears pendant Or*.[31] The *Dictionary of British Sculptors (1660-1851)* says of Mr Sidnell:

> Michael Sidnell flourished between 1714 and 1745 and was of Bristol. Sidnell was an architect as well as a statuary, and his monuments are consequently architectural in design; he also makes much use of heraldic shields and coats of arms. [32]

It is interesting when considering this monument to Anne Luttrell nèe Stucley to trace the connection between the Stucleys, the Beaumonts and the Luttrells. In the fifteenth century an Alice Stucley married Thomas Beaumont III (d. 1487). He was the son of Philippa Dinham and Thomas Beaumont II (b. 1400 d. 1450), whose father Sir William Beaumont (b. 1366 d. 1423) was the son of Sir John Beaumont and Joan Stockley, who were also the parents of Catherine Beaumont (d. 1435), the wife of Sir Hugh Luttrell (d. 1428), both of whose effigies lie under a canopy to the north of the Priory Church chancel.

The Question Family

Between 1731 and 1738 the curate of Dunster was the Reverend Thomas Question. In 1645, when Dunster Castle, held by the Royalists, was besieged by Colonel Blake, forty houses belonging to a John Question were destroyed by fire. Lyte recalls that:

> John Question of Dunster, surgeon, was in 1647 subjected to a fine of 100*l* for espousing the Royalist cause, but the amount was eventually reduced to 10*l* in consideration of the gratuitous services which he had rendered for sick and hurt soldiers serving with Colonel Blake in the siege.[33]

In 1658 John Question signs, as Churchwarden, the entry in the Registers in that year recording the burial of his wife, Elizabeth Question: 'Elizabeth, the wife of John Question, Churchwarden, royalist, surgeon, kind to friend and foe, very much to the fore, is buried'.[34] A rate levied for the maintenance of the poor of the parish also includes the name of John Question, who pays 2s. A Mr Question given in the Overseers' Accounts for 1674 as 'curing John

Dowent leedge [*sic*] £1 5s 0d'.[35] Lyte also mentions a further Dr Question in writing about the 1767 parliamentary elections.

A William Question ('ye 3rd of that name') is noted in the Overseers' Accounts for 1715 as one of those having a key to a chest in the church tower.[36]

Although it would appear to be correct that Thomas Question was the curate and John Question the Churchwarden and surgeon, matters were confused by Hancock and Lyte.[37]

There is a marble monument to the Revd Thomas Question 'born 15th September 1702. Buried the 14th October, 1738' on the tower wall. In 1959 this and a second memorial tablet (to the memory of John Williams and his wife Jane) had to be removed and re-erected because the organ was being moved to its present position. These two marble memorial tablets were not replaced at the time, and were found at my suggestion in the stoke hole in November 1990, during the recording of the church by volunteers from the Exmoor II Group of NADFAS, led by myself.[38] There was a legal requirement to replace them but ethical and historical reasons also supported this requirement. Following a letter from the author to the Diocese Chancellor these two memorial tablets are now back as near to their original position as possible.

To return to 1740, the next important event was the purchase of the magnificent Georgian chandelier, as the Churchwardens' Accounts show:

	£	s	d
1740 July 17, Paid Mr Treer's Bills for the Candle Stick	16	5	0
Paid for a box in which the Candle Stick was brought		4	6
Paid Nat Walstone for painting the Iron belonging to the Candle Stick.	1	0	0
Paid Henry Harrison and Hen: Rawle for Carriage of ye Candle Stick from Bristol and to Dunster.		1	6
Paid John Bishop for Ironwork belonging to the Candle Stick.	5	4	0

There is a reference to this chandelier in the *Gentleman's Magazine* article: '....also a brass chandelier of 18 lights, inscribed, "Gaven by Jone Brewer, ten pounds towards this branch."'[39] The chandelier is inscribed *Francis Billo. Bristol. Fecit.*

Professor Nikolaus Pevsner notes: 'chandelier 1740; of brass hanging from some big piece of iron ornament. By Francis Billo of Bristol.' Billo (probably 'Billot') was a French Huguenot.

Mr Robert Sherlock, who has published a study of chandeliers, has made an accurate drawing of our Dunster 'candle stick'. He informed the Rector that there was only one other chandelier known to be signed by Francis Billo of Bristol. It was in the United States, at St Michael's Church, Marblehead, Massachusetts, and was inscribed 'The Gift of John Elbridge Esqr of ye City of Bristol. 1732'. Some of the patterns used by Billo in making this chandelier were used again at Dunster.[40]

According to Mr Sherlock, 'Mr Treer's Bills' could have been a misreading of 'Mr Francis Billo'.[41] The very fine chandelier in St Mary's Church,

Stogumber, is not dissimilar from the one in St George's, Dunster and was made in 1771-2 by Thomas Bayley of Bridgwater, whose firm would re-cast three of the bells at St George's in 1743.

Margaret Luttrell

Margaret Dyke née Trevelyan, the widow of Alexander Luttrell II (d. 1737), for several years brought up her own daughter, Margaret Luttrell (b. 1726), Anne Luttrell (b. 1731), her late husband's niece, and Elizabeth Dyke (b. 1725), the niece of her second husband, Edward Dyke, who was to become Lady Acland in 1745. For these three, all heiresses, she had sole responsibility.

Anne Luttrell's monument in Dunster Church was mentioned above. Her dowry had been a great drain on the resources of her uncle, Alexander Luttrell. In 1751 she married Edward Morton Pleydell of Milbourne St Andrew and Whatcombe House in Dorset. Her portrait by Thomas Hudson hangs in Dunster Castle.

Margaret Luttrell, the only child of Margaret and Alexander Luttrell, was baptized at Dunster after her birth on 7 February 1726. There was therefore no male heir to the Dunster Castle and its estates. At the time of her father's death in 1737 her mother found herself faced with his debts and an eleven-year-old daughter to bring up. The castle was closed and the Dunster estates were thrown into Chancery.

It is therefore no wonder that the widowed Margaret sought security and refuge for herself and her child at Tetton Park under the protection of Edward Dyke of Tetton and Pixton, whom she married in 1741. Edward Dyke's maternal grandmother, Elizabeth Blackford, had died in 1698. The date of her burial, 7 January, is recorded in the Dunster registers, since in the seventeenth century the Blackfords were residents of Dunster and lived in the house then called 'The Hall' now the 'Castle Hotel'.

It would be 1744 before the Master in Chancery made his final report on the accounts. The year before, a three-day sale of Luttrell property was held at the Crown Tavern in Taunton. Although the pictures and furniture were saved, all the silver belonging to the late Alexander Luttrell II and to his father Colonel Alexander Luttrell was sold. Apart from purchases made by a goldsmith, Mr Alexander, who assisted at the sale, and by Lancelot St Albyn, the agent and receiver of the rents for that year of 1743, purchases were made by members and close relations of the family. The names known to us were Sir John Trevelyan, the seventeen-year old Margaret Luttrell's grandfather; George Trevelyan her uncle, and Mrs Margaret Dyke (formerly née Trevelyan), her mother.

The prices ranged from 4s 8d to 6s 6d per ounce. The accounts of the agent included £2 4s 6d for Mr Alexander, goldsmith, for his assistance; £2 1s 5d to a Mr White for the use of a room and expenses in the Crown Tavern, Taunton, and 5s for the cryer or salesman.[42]

'Master Eld's Report in the Chancery suit Kymer v Trevelyan on 23 July 1744', mentions 'a silver flagon, salver, and cup and cover' which belonged to the communion table in Dorothy Luttrell's chapel.[43] William Kymer, Curate at Dunster between 1704 and 1729, would probably have conducted the Holy Communion service in the chapel, built between 1723 and 1724 and completed with the £350 Dorothy Luttrell left for this purpose in her will, dated October 1723. According to Lyte: 'these [*i.e. the flagon, salver and cup and cover*] are now in use at the new chapel of St Michael at Alcombe, having been presented by the present owner of the castle [*Geoffrey Fownes Luttrell*]'.[44]

In 1742, the year after Margaret Luttrell remarried, we hear about the activities arranged for the employment of the occupants of the 'Poor House'. These people were kept diligently at work: from 14 December 1742 to 5 April 1743, over 500 pounds of pinnions (wool) was bought at a cost of £12 3s 11½ d. The resultant yarn brought in £16 8s 3d so the profit made after paying for the 'pinnions' was £4 4s 3½d.' [45]

Church Bells

In 1743 a contract was made with Thomas Bayley of Bridgwater, bell-founder, for the re-casting of three of the Dunster Church bells, including the third and sixth, at a cost of £60.[46] A further expense of £1 11s 6d was incurred in 1747 because after re-hanging the bells the chimes had to be altered.

Between 1703 and 1704 the tenor bell at St George's had been re-cast for £41 18s 0d[47] but by 1767 it gave out. In June 1768 Mr Bayley was paid £14 14s 0d 'for casting the Tennor bell and the Little bell with addition of Metall and repairing the other'.[48]

By 1782 there was again trouble over the tenor bell, also the fifth bell. Both appear to have been cracked and had to be re-cast, this time by George Davis, bell founder, who was paid £57 15s 0d for the re-casting and hanging of both bells.[49]

The 'Articles of Ringing' were painted on the walls of the bell chamber and appended to them were the signatures of 'William Gale, John Withers, Churchwardens 177 [1]'.[50] (The date 1771 is suspect because on Hancock's list of Dunster Churchwardens those for 1771 are Henry Fownes-Luttrell and Thomas Leigh.)[51] The name of John Withers does not appear until 1784 when he was the People's Warden.[52]

The names of 'George Gale, gent., William Clark, church wardens, 1782' appear with that of 'George Davis, Bridgwater,' after the list of inscriptions on the bells.[53]

The Dyke, Acland and Blackford Families

Following on the 1743 contract with Thomas Bayley of Bridgwater, bell founder, the year 1744 shows a reference in the Churchwardens' Accounts to the Aclands: 'Paid Sir T.W. Acland Huntsman for killing a fox in the Parish three shillings and fourpence'.[54]

Margaret Luttrell's second marriage must have improved her financial standing but it lasted for only five years since Edward Dyke died on 14 August 1746; he was buried at Dulverton on 21 August. Margaret was to outlive him by eighteen years. Neither Edward Dyke nor his brother, John Dyke (d. 1732), had provided an heir to inherit the great wealth and landed estates which had been amassed with great rapidity by the much-intermarried Blackford and Dyke families. So Edward Dyke's nephew Edward Smyth inherited his uncle's estates in Bampton and elsewhere, and was directed to take the name and arms of Dyke.

The Blackford estate had been acquired by William Blackford the elder, of Holnicote, the son of Richard Blackford of Dunster (d. 1689) and his wife Elizabeth (d. 1698). (There are brasses to the memory of Richard and his daughter, Mary in St George's Church.) William Blackford purchased the manor of Avill and went on to secure Bossington and Holnicote. He married Elizabeth, the daughter of John Dyke of Pixton, near Dulverton, whilst his two remaining sisters, Sidwell and Elizabeth, married Thomas Dyke and Edward Dyke his elder brother.

This William Blackford died on 22 August 1728 and was buried at Selworthy in the family vault. Only two years later his son William, the younger, also died. He had married Henrietta, the daughter and co-heir of Joseph Collett of Hertford Castle, who had been President of Fort St George. But she pre-deceased her husband and was buried at Selworthy. Their little daughter and only child, also named Henrietta, died at the age of seven years on 16 December 1733. She too was buried at Selworthy, where there is an impressive monument to the Blackford family.

The Blackford estate in Somerset then passed to Elizabeth Dyke, the daughter of Thomas Dyke of Tetton-in-Kingston, near Taunton, and Mary Dyke, his wife and cousin. Elizabeth was the cousin of the young Henrietta and one of the little girl's co-heirs. The other co-heir was her great-aunt Elizabeth (d. 1737), wife of the Edward Dyke (d. 1740) who inherited the Holnicote estate.

Elizabeth Dyke became a very rich heiress since she was named in the wills of her grandfather Edward Dyke (d. 1740) and in that of her uncle Edward Dyke (d. 1746) who had married Margaret Luttrell. On 7 January 1745, she married Sir Thomas Acland at Kingston.

That same summer of 1745, Charles Edward, the 'Young Pretender', the dashing and adventurous twenty-five-year-old son of the 'Old Pretender' (James Stuart, the supposed son of James II and Mary Modena), came to Britain to try to win the throne. He landed on the island of Eriskay on 23 July and initially enjoyed some success. The Stuart standard was raised at Glenfinnan on 19 August 1745; Edinburgh fell to the rebels on 17 September and on 21 September the Jacobites vanquished the King's forces at the battle of Prestonpans.

The Dunster Churchwardens' Accounts read:

	£	s	d
1745 Paid for a Form of Prayer on the account of the Rebellion		1	6

This entry was followed by an item of more local interest:

	£	s	d
May 2nd. Pd for Form of Prayer concerning the Infection of the horned cattle		1	6

The rebels were finally defeated at Culloden on 16 April 1746 by the Duke of Cumberland.[55] The Churchwardens' Accounts record:

	£	s	d
1746 April 27. Gave the Ringers when the News came that ye Duke had overcome the Rebells in the North.		5	0
Paid Mrs Measpe for a new surplice and working and making	5	12	6

Henry Fownes Luttrell

When the younger Margaret Luttrell was twenty-one she fell in love with her second cousin Henry Fownes of Nethway in the parish of Brixham, Devon, the eldest son of John Fownes of Kittery Court, Kingswear and of his second wife Anne. Anne was the daughter of Samuel Maddock of Tamerton Foliott, near Plymouth, and his wife Isabella Mohun, the third daughter of Warwick Mohun, second Baron of Okehampton. Warwick Mohun's ancestry can be traced to Sir Reynold de Mohun, ancestor of the Mohuns of Hall and Boconnoc (Cornwall)[56] and son of that great benefactor of Dunster Priory, Sir John de Mohun III (d. 1330) and his wife Ada Tibetot (d. c1324).

Henry Fownes and Margaret Luttrell shared a common ancestor, Edward Yarde, whose daughter Dorothy married Colonel Alexander Luttrell (d. 1711), Margaret's grandfather. There appears to be a further connection between the Luttrells and the Yardes, since Walthean Yard was the second wife of Sir Hugh Luttrell (d. 1521).

One of the conditions laid down by Margaret's late father Alexander Luttrell (d. 1737), was that on her marriage, her husband should take the additional surname of Luttrell. Another was that he should spend at least six months a year at Dunster Castle. To these requirements Henry Fownes seems readily to have agreed, for one of his first acts was to have a seal of Brazilian pebble engraved with the arms of Luttrell quartered with those of Fownes.

The marriage between Margaret and the twenty-four-year-old Henry took place at Kingston church on 16 February 1747. It was said that 'the union proved exceptionally happy, and her letters to her husband, when parted from him (were) conceived in a spirit of the sincerest affection'.[57] Sometimes she acted as his secretary, which in the great task of restoring the estate must have been very valuable to him. Brought up modestly in the home of her step-father Edward Dyke at Tetton Park, she found herself, as a new bride, released from the control of her guardian and the lawyers. She must have revelled in the adoration and marriage gifts Henry bestowed upon her.

One of the four portraits of Margaret at Dunster Castle portray her most charmingly as a small bare-footed child dressed in white muslin offering cherries to a bird. Later she was painted by Richard Phelps of Porlock, who had painted the altarpiece for the church. In this three-quarter-length portrait she is portrayed with her arm resting on a marble-topped gilded table and dressed in grey and blue satin. Another painting, obviously executed when she was a little older, shows her dressed in a grey lace-trimmed cloak and a blue be-ribboned dress with modestly crossed lace bands across her chest and a lace 'Mary Queen-of-Scots' headdress. Finally, a head and shoulders painting shows her with an open lace collar.[58]

When Henry Fownes Luttrell married Margaret in 1747 the family estates were in serious financial straits, but under his wise administration all was changed and he made serious endeavours to put Margaret's affairs on a firm footing.

> ...he revived the suit in Chancery and obtained the sanction of the Court for the sale of the outlying manors of Heathfield and Kilton. No sufficient offer was, however, forthcoming. After this, he made several vain attempts to sell the manor of Minehead at his own price, which avowedly included a considerable sum for a seat, or perhaps two seats in Parliament....[59]

Henry personally paid off the mortgages on the estate and in 1760 he purchased the reputed manor of Foremarsh in the parish of Dunster and Carhampton. This was an understandable purchase since the fields were intermixed with his own and houses 'under the shadow of the Castle'. The owner, John Poyntz of Gray's Inn, was the last male representative of the Roman Catholic family associated with St George's Church, notably by the fourteenth-century altar slab now at the High Altar in the Priory Church whose probable former position is now remembered by the Victorian Poyntz brass in the north aisle.

Henry Fownes Luttrell was a typical eighteenth-century country squire who rode to hounds and was fond of his horses. This did not preclude him from an addiction to cock fighting. Although it was a condition laid down by his father-in-law that he should spend six months of the year at Dunster, much of his time was taken up in Devonshire where he owned a small pack known as 'the merry Harriers'. His riding whip is displayed at Dunster Castle beneath his portrait which shows him in a short light periwig, drab hunting coat and with the same whip and a dog by his side.[60]

Christmas Day 1747 must have seen great celebrations at the castle for Margaret gave birth to her first child who was baptized the same day. Though always known as 'Peggy' she was christened Margaret after her mother and she was the only daughter to survive infancy. The month of August during the 1750s must have been the saddest month of the year, for Peggy had three sisters, all named Anne, who were baptized at Dunster on 4 July 1750, 30 June 1751 and 4 May 1758 and buried there on 18 August 1750, 1 August 1751 and 12 August 1758 respectively.

When Peggy was three or four years of age Richard Phelps portrayed her in a full-length portrait with a dog beside her. In 1769 her marriage portrait was commissioned from no less a person than Sir Joshua Reynolds; she married on 24 April 1769 in London at St Anne's, Soho, John Henry Southcote of Buckland Toutsaints, and Stoke Fleming in Devonshire. This portrait hangs beside that of her brother Henry (1753-1777) in the former parlour, now the dining-room, of Dunster Castle. The original portrait and a contemporary copy are alike at Dunster Castle. One belonged to successive members of the Southcote family.[61]

Sir Joshua Reynolds was well-known in the homes of well-to-do West-Country families, and painted almost every man and woman of note in the second half of the eighteenth century. Inspection of Peggy Luttrell's painting reveals that the face is deathly pale due to the fact that the carmine has faded out completely. Most of Reynolds's sitters-books still exist. For the month of April 1769 he notes 'Miss Luttrell', and adds 'when Miss Luttrell is finished to write to Mr Luttrell, Dunster Castle, Somersetshire'.

This portrait has been wrongly attributed by Reynolds's biographers to a sister of Ann Luttrell (1753-1809), the Duchess of Cumberland, who had no connection with the Irnham or Dunster line of Luttrells.

Peggy Luttrell had been born in 1747 and we now return to her father's involvement in the affairs of the 1740s and to the Overseers' Accounts of 4 November 1748, as follows:

> Recd. of Henry ffownes Luttrell, Esq., £28, being one years Interest of the £800 of ye parishes money in his hands due ye 18th day of October last". This sum, of which we have had glimpses all through these accounts, was no doubt the nucleus of the fund now called the "Luttrell and Eld Charity." In 1752 the sum again appears as a sum "reported to be due by Francis Eld, Esq., one of the Masters of the High Court of Chancery on behalf of the Luttrell estate, for the use of the poor of Dunster.

> 1749 The doctor, Rob.Cording, had £5.5s per annum "to supply the Poor of the Parish with Surgery and Phisick as need shall require and at any distance within two miles of the same." Mr Lewis Bradley the same amount.

> In 1764 reference is made "to the decree some time since obtained in the High Court of Chancery," at a vestry meeting, and it is agreed to accept Mr H.F. Luttrell's personal bond, in order to "extricate the Dunster Castle estate off and from the payment of the said £800 and interest to which it was subject and charged with by vertue of the said Decree". [62]

On 31 March 1749 the first-born son of Margaret and Henry Fownes Luttrell was born. He was named after his grandfather Alexander and was baptized the next day, but only lived for only three months.

A well-known inhabitant of Dunster died the month Alexander was born. Nathaniel Ingram was probably the owner of the grist mill which was purchased from him by Henry Fownes Luttrell who, in 1765, would turn it into a fulling mill. Ingram must have been regarded as a person of some importance since there was a monumental stone slab to his memory placed in the nave of the church, inscribed 'Nathaniel Ingram, March 7, 1749, aged 65'.[63]

In 1751 the so-called 'Governess' of the Parish workhouse was 'ye Widow Helman', who contracted to maintain for '1s 6d per week every pauper taken in ye workhouse'.[64]

The next year a village wedding took place while at the castle a son and heir was born to Margaret and Henry Fownes Luttrell. The wedding invites speculation, for the entry in the Overseers' Accounts reads:

> 1752   The overseers pay "Willm Snowden of West Anstey to be married to Mary Govier of Dunster parrish", £1. 18s., and in addition 6s 6d for the marriage fees. [They also provided] "6 wodden dishes for Work house." [65]

Did the overseers pay William Snowden to marry Mary Govier? Perhaps it was 'a shot-gun marriage' or perhaps Mary was someone for whom they had responsibility, possibly an inmate of the workhouse.

Margaret and Henry Fownes Luttrell must have been overjoyed at the birth of a son, having lost their first-born son Alexander. John was to survive; he was baptized at Dunster on 24 June 1752.

A little over a year later, on 30 July 1753 Henry Fownes Luttrell, named after his father, was born at Tetton Park. On 29 December that year a letter was written to his grandmother Margaret Luttrell, now Mrs Dyke, by her father Sir John Trevelyan. He sends thanks for a gift of fish and writes:

> Dear Daghtr I am much concernd that your little Harry has been so much out of order. I hope that this will find you both in perfect health the good news will give me great pleasure the little lad is quite well. I have got the Gout in one foot but it has not ben very painfull nor hindered me from dining the Parlour yet. all here joyn in Compliments to you and Miss Haydon. I am your most affectionate Father.[66]

'Little Harry' grew up to be a lieutenant in the Royal Horseguards, and later a captain, but he only lived to be twenty-four. After his death on 4 January 1777, his father on 24 January paid the overseers £5 'for the penalty due on the burial of the late Capt. Luttrell in linnen'.[67]

In 1754, on 30 November, the fourth son of Henry and Margaret was baptized at Dunster and named Alexander after their late first-born son. He was educated at Pembroke College and in 1779 was instituted into the rectory of East Quantoxhead. The next year he became the Prebend of Combe Decima in Wells Cathedral and was instituted to the vicarage of Minehead. He appears not to have resided at East Quantoxhead nor at Minehead.

In 1755 smallpox raged in Dunster. The same year Henry Luttrell decided to 'bring the park home' which meant that the deer were to be removed from Marshwood to Dunster. A deer park was created (which did not include the medieval park to the south). This necessitated the scrubbing up of ferns, whorts and heather and the planting of new trees which did not include the oaks on the higher ground, thought to be as ancient as the forest of Dunster which existed in the reign of Henry III.

The judicious eighteenth-century planting, ever mindful of the vista, necessitated the removal of many hedges. It also became necessary to buy plots of land from various owners and where land was leased, the leases had to be extinguished and compensation paid. The new park comprised three hundred and forty-eight acres, all in the parish of Carhampton. One can image the picture when most of the population turned out to assist in driving the deer to their new home, a direct route having been made by cutting through intervening fences.

We are indebted to this man of considerable taste and refinement who added many eighteenth-century touches of great charm such as the bridge over the river Avill near the Mill Walk. His restrained taste is evident in the Morning Room of the castle where the plaster moulding is of a classical character in the fashion of the period; particularly attractive is the delicate work over the entrance to this room from the staircase. The doors of mahogany with their door-cases, the marble mantelpiece are all redolent of his good taste and provide a contrast to the elaborate and rather florid heavy plasterwork so typical of the earlier seventeenth century, found over the stair-case and in the dining room. On this staircase is a portrait of an unknown Cavalier. This picture and that of Henry, Prince of Wales, the elder brother of Charles I, came from Nethway, Henry Fownes Luttrell's Devonshire home.

In 1756, the year the Seven Years War broke out, Francis Luttrell, the fifth son of Henry and Margaret, was born on 9 February and baptized the next day. Francis was sent to school at Eton, just before his fifteenth birthday: a three-day journey via Bridgewater (on horseback), Wells (in two chaises), and then via Marlborough and Reading.[68]

Following the family pattern, after university, he studied law, having matriculated in 1773 at Queen's College Oxford. He became a doctor of civil law, a DCL, and was called to the bar at the Middle Temple. His eldest brother John, the heir, was the Member of Parliament representing Minehead from 1774 to 1780 but, on the death of their father, John took over the running of the family estate. Francis then became the junior Member for that borough until 1783. He became a Commissioner of Customs in December 1793 and later Chairman of their Board.[69]

Margaret Luttrell produced ten children, the last of whom, Thomas, was born on 10 February 1766. Thomas joined the army in 1782 as an Ensign in the 89th Foot. In 1783 he became a Lieutenant in the 49th Foot and a Captain in 1787. In the same year and until 1800 he was Lieutenant-Colonel of the Somersetshire Fencible Infantry. He did not marry until he was forty-four years of age; his bride was Catherine Cave Browne of Stretton-in-le-fields, Derbyshire. The marriage took place in October 1807 but lasted for less than four years as on 19 January 1811 Thomas died. Unlike his ances-tors, he was not buried in the family vault at Dunster but was interred in Bath Abbey.

Dunster Life in the Later Eighteenth Century

In the year 1760 there is a good deal of information in the Overseers' Accounts regarding the sums of money paid out to persons prepared to take apprentices:

	£	s	d
1760. bound out this Year			
May 16th. To Mr Tho. Escott with John Reed bound to him in respect of late Mr Hugh Escott's Estate with a bearer.	1	0	0
To Mr Robert Leigh with Tho. Philpott bound to him in respect of part of Marsh Estate and the Tythes	1	0	0
To Thomas Rogers with Thos Elsworthy bound to him in respect of Danters Meadow and Bondington House, and his Trade.	1	0	0
Pd for 3 pairs of Indentures for the above 3 apprentices		11	0
Pd Mr Lewis Taylor with Willm Craze bound to him in respect of Duddings with Sevl bearers.	1	0	0
July 18th. To Mr Nathl Edbrooke with Mary Escott, bound to him in respect of lower Staunton Estate with several bearers	1	0	0
Pd for 2 pairs of Indentures for the said two Apprentices		7	4
	5	18	4 [70]

Among the several locations in Dunster mentioned in 1760 there are possibly seven which can be designated as taverns, or alehouses. 'Spears Cross'; 'Phillpotts House now the 3 Marriners'; 'The George Inn in High Street'; 'Courts formerly ye Compass'; 'Swan Alehouse'; 'Whitehorse Alehouse' and 'ye 3 Cupps Inn'.

Other locations mentioned are 'Chesters House by Lower Elm'; 'the Bullock market in High Street'; 'House under Castle Torr', 'ye old nunnery house in Church Street', 'ye Corn market in High Street'; 'ye Cross in High Street, Prowse's house (late Blackford's near ye Cross)', 'Ye Workhouse in West Street'; 'Ye footpath garden' in Water Street;[71] 'House beyond Gallox bridge'; Strong's 'house in High Street near ye cross called ye loge House'; 'Rattle Row'; 'Bondington House', and 'Middle Street by ye Church Yard Gate'.[72]

The Workhouse was in 1762 run by Sarah Reed who had succeeded the widow Helman. She was provided with the same sum of money to maintain one pauper as the previous 'governess': 1s 6d per week, but if the pauper was under ten years of age she was given only one shilling per week. For these sums she was to provide 'meat, drink, washing, lodging and firing', whilst the overseers provided clothing and working tools. The one shilling for children under the age of ten was later increased to 1s 6d, as 'the contract was found to have been rather too low'.[73]

Hancock comments:

> There must have been something very near starvation in the Dunster poor house. In 1766 there were sixteen old people in the poor house and fourteen children. The workhouse appears to have belonged to Mr Thos. Leigh, who received a rent of £10 per year for it.

> 1772 "Beef is now 2¾d per pound, and mutton 3 d, wheat 7s per bushel, cheese 1¾d per pound, wool 7d per pound, a peck of carrots 10d, a peck of "peese" 7d "3 peck and three quarters of taters 3s 9d".[74]

In 1771 a new Parish Clerk was chosen by the parishioners whose prerogative it had been to make this choice from time immemorial. George Rawle the younger, a mason, was their choice and he was engaged for the 'usual salary of three pounds per annum for his trouble'.[75] According to Savage, a memorial stone in the nave still existed in 1905 which bore the inscription: 'George Rawle, Oct. 15, 1799, aged 56; twenty-seven years clerk of this church'.[76]

Dunster Castle and Henry Fownes Luttrell

Perhaps Henry Fownes's most conspicuous, if most frivolous achievement, was the folly known as Conegar Tower. A folly, or alternatively a grotto, was an eighteenth-century 'must' for a cultivated landowner. In 1774 Phelps designed this hollow, cylindrical tower to stand on Conygar Hill. It acted as a landmark for sailors in the Bristol Channel. In the 1980s it was surrounded by 'ruins' hidden in undergrowth and by trees, but a restoration took place in 2000.

A Victorian transcript of the original building accounts follows:

9th September 1775			
Expenses in Building	£76	11	0½
Mason's bill	£41	11	8
320 Hhds [hogsheads] of lime	£17	6	8
3 Hhds of Cider to men	£ 4	2	6
Entertainment to 15 men after the			
work was finished at 3/- £ 2.5. 0d			
Expenses of building the archways			
and Towers at the West End of Conegar			
including £6. 6. 0d for Haulage	£18	14	10
	£160	11	8 ½

This information was copied from some unknown source in the time of George Fownes Luttrell (1826-1910). It misleadingly states that the owner of the estate at the time was John Fownes Luttrell Esq., rather than Henry

Fownes Luttrell. It also wrongly states that John Fownes was the first M.P for Minehead.

As far back as 1559, Minehead had received a royal charter of incorporation and in 1563 it sent two Members to Parliament: Thomas Luttrell (1525-71) was one of them.[77] Henry Fownes Luttrell and his son John were the first of the Fownes Luttrells to be elected to Parliament, though Henry's father-in-law, Alexander Luttrell II (1705-37) had been elected one of the Members for Minehead in the parliaments of 1727 and 1734.

Parliamentary Elections

From letters included in Lyte's *History of Dunster*, we gain a vivid picture of the shenanigans of eighteenth-century general elections. It is a tale of bribery and corruption; of 'buck feasts' and balls; of guns and huzzas, mounted horsemen, constables and sheriffs and candidates in post chaises. The scene of corrupt political practices, of ever-open hands ready to accept bribes proffered is well illustrated by William Hogarth's caustic pictures of an election, painted during the years 1754-5.

In the second half of the eighteenth century the electoral register was a cause of agitation among the people. The American War of Independence, which had broken out in 1775, and the French Revolution in 1789, established the idea of liberty and democracy, further encouraged at the beginning of the nineteenth century by the Industrial Revolution. This unrest would eventually lead to the Reform Act of 1832.

Before 1832, the franchise was unjust. In order to vote, one had to be male, and either (a) a freeman of the borough; (b) the member of a corporate borough; (c) rated to the church and poor rate; or (d) the holder of a burgage tenure. The chief scandals were bribery of voters, and the existence of 'rotten boroughs', where representatives were nominated by the Crown, or by some person to whom it had granted the right of nomination. Minehead was one of these. Seats were bought and sold as a matter of course. Until the Ballot Act of 1872, the nomination of candidates for election to the House of Commons took place at the hustings. Nominations were frequently accompanied by grave disorder and much intimidation took place.

In the eighteenth century at Minehead, personal and local issues were foremost in the minds of the electorate. Beyond their limited horizons, questions of national policy, of Whig and Tory interests, were scarcely regarded. The Minehead franchise was extended to those parishioners of Minehead and Dunster who were 'pot-boilers', that is to say resident householders who lived in the borough of Minehead, which was comprised of the three tithings of Minehead, Alcombe and Staunton, the receipt of alms of any sort being almost the only disqualification.[78]

After the death of Alexander Luttrell in 1737 four persons successively occupied the two seats: Sir William Codrington and Thomas Carew of Crowcombe who represented the interests of Dunster Castle in the House of Commons; Francis Whitworth of Leyborne in Kent, a property owner at Blackford, near Minehead, and John Periam, a local squire.

In 1747, when Henry Fownes married Margaret Luttrell, the two MPs were Thomas Carew and John Periam. Just a month after the marriage Francis Whitworth died and his son Charles wrote to Henry on 19 March 1747 that he planned to stand for election and suggesting that he and the Luttrell interests would be best served if they stood together.[79]

Henry Fownes refused this offer. Lyte comments: 'Believing himself able to command one seat, he does not seem to have cared who received the other.'[80]

No doubt preoccupied with country pursuits, Henry does not appear to have been keen to pursue the command of his seat with any energy. His agent John St Albyn wanted to know if he definitely intended to stand for parliament. He advised that some expense would be incurred to secure his election; a point which would not have been lost on Mr Luttrell since he was acutely aware of the fact that electoral expenses had partly been the cause of his father-in-law dying in debt. St Albyn told him that he had been told that Whitworth was prepared to 'risque his whole fortune'and that there was another candidate who was determined 'to get everything that money could provide'.[81]

This other candidate was the M.P for Taunton, Percy Wyndham O'Brien, the brother of Charles Wyndham of Orchard (Williton), Second Earl of Egremont who became Secretary of State between 1761 and 1763.

On 16 May Henry Fownes Luttrell's anxious agent wrote that 'as lord of the manor you do not appear to be sure of more than about one quarter of the votes'.[82] Henry lost little time in putting before the inhabitants of Minehead his unequivocal intention. He wrote to them on 24 May:

> ... My anxiety for being a representative is not so very great as even now to make me determine either to offer myself or support a friend at the ensuing election, but only ask the free voice of the constituents for one or the other, clear of all expence to myself ... I too plainly see the rock my father Luttrell foundered upon to run myself headlong into the same danger.
> [83]

He was not really interested in politics and if he did decide to stand it would be 'entirely on the Castle interest.'[84]

Thomas Carew, who with Sir William Codrington had represented the Castle interest in Parliament in 1737, in June 1747, announced his willingness to stand again for the Castle in the possible absence of Henry Fownes Luttrell.[85] But still concerned about the financial burden the election would have entailed, Henry Luttrell explained in his reply that he had thought himself 'justly entitled to the Natural Interest in the borough' and likely to be returned 'with little or no expense'. He also felt obliged to support John Periam, who, after the late Francis Whitworth, had occupied the second seat representing the borough.[86]

But after an unsatisfactory meeting with his principal supporters at Blue Anchor, John Periam withdrew his candidature in favour of Thomas Carew. However, after a conference at Somerton attended by Sir Thomas Acland,

Henry Fownes Luttrell, John Periam and Thomas Carew, Thomas Carew retired and John Periam was re-instated. He received the support, as always, of Henry Fownes Luttrell, but the Blue Anchor incident had caused some of his erstwhile partisans to desert him for Whitworth, and Periam once again withdrew.

The Castle interest collapsed. Luttrell, at the critical point, and no doubt, frustrated by Periam's vacillation, sought solace with his hounds in Devon at Nethway. Minehead lost interest in the Castle's nomination and on 30 June 1747 Whitworth and O'Brien were returned to Parliament without any more opposition.

At the time of the General Election of 1754 Henry Fownes Luttrell was intent on disposing of the troublesome manor of Minehead. He was asked in the February to give his support to a possible purchaser, Henry Shiffner, 'a wealthy Russian merchant'. On 8 May Mr Luttrell wrote from Nethway to assure Mr Shiffner that he would not propose any other person.[87]

Others standing for election were Charles Whitworth, who was happy to join forces with Shiffner, and a new candidate, Daniel Boone, Percy O'Brien's brother, whose candidature was supported by the influential Earl of Egremont.

Henry Fownes Luttrell was determined to get Shiffner elected but was somewhat hampered by the fact that he was High Sheriff for that year. Nevertheless, he wrote to the electors of the borough of Minehead recommending Shiffner.

Of these electors, one hundred and eighty-one declared their allegiance, although sixty-four of these were illiterate and one hundred and seventeen were not fully literate. Shiffner was thus assured of one of the seats.[88]

However, an incident of some kind aroused the resentment of the voters and the result of the poll was that Whitworth won, gaining 283 votes. Boone came second with 178 votes and Shiffner came last with 145 votes.

Mr Shiffner was a very angry man. In a letter to Henry Luttrell on 2 May, he complained ' I did not give a shilling to buy votes, and was only at the expence [sic] of treating, etc. 1,200l does not clear my expences [sic].'[89]

It was January 1757, before Henry Fownes Luttrell decided that it would be a wiser policy to appease the voters. He distributed half a bushel of wheat to each of the two hundred and two Minehead voters without differentiating between those who had voted for Boone against Shiffner. On occasion, the Lord of the Manor further invited the principal inhabitants of the borough of Minehead to venison feasts at the castle.

By November 1757, Henry Fownes Luttrell and Lord Egremont came to an agreement whereby, at the new election, each of them would chose a candidate and together they would oppose any third rival.

So in 1761 Lord Egremont proposed his brother Percy Wyndham O'Brien, Earl of Thomond. O'Brien had been one of the members for Minehead in the 1747 election, but had not competed in the 1754 election. This time Shiffner came first in the polls, held on 28 March 1761, gaining 287 votes. O'Brien came second with 226 votes and thirdly came Lord Clanbrasill with 69 votes. Out of the two hundred and ninety-one electors

who recorded their votes, only four failed to give one to Shiffner but his
success had not been achieved without personal expense and the monetary
support of Mr Luttrell. Lyte writes:

> There is in Luttrell's handwriting a very significant "List of voters at
> Minehead that refused taking the 3 guineas, 1761," the number of electors
> who disdained such a reward being exactly thirty. Their names are repeated
> in a "List of voters in Minehead asked to dine at Dunster Castle, 8
> September 1763, having not taken the 3 guineas after the election," and
> they were invited again in August 1764.[90]

The relationship between Mr Luttrell and his victorious candidate
blossomed into a close friendship and the letters Shiffner wrote gave the
squire of Dunster a window on the world of Westminster and the politics of
his time. This included Parliament's attitude to the Peace which in December
1762 ended the Seven Years War (1756-63) between Prussia allied with
England against a coalition of Austria, France, Russia, Sweden and
Saxony. [91]

During the term of the 1761 Parliament, support for the Luttrell interest
was kept alive by the provision of venison feasts which, together with supper
at local hostelries and the distribution of small amounts of money acted as
sweeteners to tempt the Minehead voters.

As early as September 1766, preparations for the 1768 election were
under way. 'Sixteen "gentlemen of the Bowling Green Club had half a buck
sent 'em and Sir Jacob's bowl of punch"'. Likewise around twenty non-
members of this club received half a buck to be 'dressed at the Plume of
Feathers with Sir Jacob's bowl of punch'.[92]

For Henry Fownes Luttrell all was overshadowed by the death on 13
August 1766 of his beloved wife, Margaret. She was 40 years of age and had
borne her husband ten children. Her health had never been robust but it is
said that she and Henry had conducted their relationship on an exceptionally affectionate and happy plane.

There is no visible memorial to Margaret in Dunster Church but she was
buried there with her ancestors, in the family vault beneath the Priory
Church where on the north wall of the chancel her hatchment may still be
seen. This third hatchment in the series for Margaret Luttrell (1726-66) is
blazoned: *Arms:— quarterly first and fourth –Azure two eagles displayed
and in base a mulletArgent for Fownes; second and third – Luttrell; (or and
sable); impaling-Luttrell; overall-an inescutcheon of Luttrell.*[93] (The arms of
Luttrell are, of course, *Or a bend between six Martlets Sable.*)

Mr Merchant observes:

> Margaret Luttrell's hatchment is particularly interesting on account of the
> unusual form of marshalling adopted. In addition to her husband's arms of
> Fownes quartering Luttrell, her own arms of Luttrell are shown not only as
> an impalement but also as an inescutcheon of preference.[94]

Henry Fownes Luttrell remained a widower for five years until in 1771 he married Frances, the daughter of Samuel Bradley of Dunster, who claimed descent from the Luttrells through her mother. Frances outlived her husband by twenty-three years. During her widowhood she resided at Taunton but she was interred at Dunster in November 1803.

In 1766, Henry Fownes Luttrell, devastated by the loss of his beloved Margaret, decided to stand for Parliament himself. However that November a Dr Richard Brocklesby, a London-based doctor of Somerset origin, decided to liberate the borough of Minehead, in which he had been born, from the all-pervading influence of powerful local landowners. His aim was to find at least one representative whose character was beyond reproach and in this endeavour he was joined by some of the most eminent inhabitants of his birthplace. They decided to approach the newly appointed Chancellor of the Exchequer, Charles Townshend. This alarmed Percy Wyndham O'Brien, Earl of Thomond, who had come second in the 1761 election. He endeavoured to join forces with Henry Fownes Luttrell against their common adversary. Henry wrote to the Rev. Leonard Herring, vicar of Minehead, that:

> The late severe loss I have sustained has made home become very dull and insipid to me, and therefore I have some thoughts of changing the scene and going into Parliament. ... I purpose to communicate this intended scheme of mine soon to Mr Shiffner, that he may look out for some other borough in case I should carry it into execution.[95]

Charles Whitworth, the MP elected in the 1754 election, now announced his candidature in a 'round robin' dated 29 January 1767. John Short wrote to Henry Fownes Luttrell from Minehead:

> I have just time to tell you that Mr Whitworth has declared himself a candidate for this borough and that Dr Question have [sic] received a letter from him referring him to one which Mr Warren has, wherein he promises to give the poor fellows ten guineas a man, and that Stroude and Powell have been amongst them. The bells have been ringing this evening, I suppose upon that occasion.[96]

Luttrell was not one whit abashed, replying:

> His promise of ten guineas a man who will give him both votes may be thought by some an alluring bait, but when the generality of the town come seriously to consider that places, as well as a little temporary cash, will be wanted, I presume they will think of some other person to serve them, who will be more capable of doing it than, I apprehend, is in Mr Whitworth's or any merchant's power to do.[97]

Henry Luttrell seems now to have decided quite firmly on his course, for by 1767 he had appointed Richard Cox as his political agent. Cox had known Luttrell since at least 1762, when he had been invited to a dinner at the castle. He was involved in the cider trade but had become a citizen of some importance in Minehead. His new political role necessitated a suitable dwelling and in 1768 we read in Douglas Stevens's *A History of Townsend House, Minehead*: 'there is a bill for repairs to "the Houses of Townsend" from a certain John Sully for the sum of three pounds, two shillings and one penny...'.[98] Richard Cox would live here for nineteen years.

On 14 March Luttrell issued his address to the electorate of Minehead, declaring himself 'unconnected with Mr Shiffner and every other person'.[99]

Money and corn had been offered as a bribe but various people in the town made their own demands in exchange for their votes. They wanted jobs and wished to be offered posts as excise men and 'tide waiters', etc.

A week after Luttrell's address to the electorate on 14 March, the Vicar of Minehead, the Rev. Leonard Herring, wrote to his patron:

> We shall all make a point of carrying this election, notwithstanding the strong opposition that is talked off; and if you'll send down 200*l.* to be distributed as we see necessary, I'll return you by the following post a fixed majority, in defiance of all their efforts. 'Tis the opinion of us all that something of this kind must be immediately done. To save every expense in our power, we have entered into an agreement never to have one public dinner, and if you expect our company in the evening, we shall insist on having nothing but a welch rabbit.[100]

But Mr Shiffner, who had won the 1761 election and had formed, it appeared, a warm friendship with Henry Fownes Luttrell, was not easily shaken off. On 24 April he announced to the voters of the borough that he would stand at the next election.

Lord Thomond disappeared from the scene and Charles Townshend died. But the idea of an independent candidate was not entirely dropped: the Duke of Grafton was invited to send a purely ministerial candidate to Minehead. The idea of a Whig government selecting a representative was, of course, abhorrent to Luttrell, the Tory country squire whose local interests would thereby be threatened. Power and influence largely resided with the parliamentary representatives of this pocket borough. Therefore, leaving country pursuits behind, Luttrell took himself off to the seat of government to oppose any such scheme. Here his success was gained, presumably subject to a promise of support in the next House of Commons.[101] In exchange the government gave him 'immediate patronage of all offices in Minehead' and thus he wrested Minehead from the Whigs and firmly established Tory family dominance as Lords of the Manor.

The Vicar of Minehead wrote to him on 2 October 1767:

> "Luttrell for ever" is now the general cry to serve both high and low. You never had a more favourable opportunity of putting in another member than at present...[102]

Parliament was dissolved on 11 March 1768 and on 18 March, Minehead entered the contest for the selection of its members. Soon after 9 a.m. the proclamation was made at the cross, or market-place, of Minehead. This was followed by the precept, or rules of action, and the bribery oath was read aloud. The three candidates, Mr Luttrell, Mr Shiffner and Mr Whitworth, were then proposed, and the poll began about ten a.m.[103]

It was common knowledge that the majority of the electors would give one vote to Luttrell and the fight therefore devolved on the other two. The contest was fierce and for many hours the contestants ran neck and neck. The result was a triumph for Henry Fownes Luttrell who polled 301 votes, whilst Whitworth came second with 197 votes. Shiffner came last with 167 votes.

The victory for Luttrell was a costly one, for between April 1767 and October 1768 he incurred expenses amounting in total to £1,868 5s 9d, even though to avoid falling foul of the law, he had not exacted promises by overt bribery. Nevertheless he sailed as 'near to the wind' as he dared and in 1767 he voluntarily sold wheat to the poor of Minehead at a reduced price and gave over £300 to necessitous voters. (There were, however, fifty-five incorruptible citizens who were separately listed as, 'gentlemen who will not take money'.)[104]

Apart from tacit bribery, much of the money expended by Luttrell went on outward displays and inducements. As soon as Parliament had been dissolved, canvassing had commenced and fifty-five pounds of gunpowder had been used. (This resulted in compensation which had to be paid for new window panes, as the guns had shattered the windows of hoped-for supporters.) A few days before the election, sports had been conducted 'in a field behind a house on the quay'. There are hilarious accounts of 'sailors in sacks' who had run for 'a pair of handsome trowsers' and 'landmen in sacks' who had 'run for a hat'. Women had run for 'a handsome pair of stays [corsets]', and 'a handsome shift', while girls 'tied back to back' had to run for 'a pair of pumps that cost 3s'.[105] On election day the maids at the castle were bedecked with ribbons while £12 was spent on the usual fees paid to the Crier, to eight constables, and eight chairmen. Two drummers and a fiddler were also engaged. Naturally, primary attention was paid to the supply of food, beef, bread and cheese, ale, wine and rum and this accounts for a large proportion of the expenditure.

Those who had cast their vote for Luttrell were now rewarded, and on 22 March 1768 on Minehead Quay, Richard Cox handed every sailor four guineas and the landmen, who had not received Luttrell's guinea in 1767, received a reward of five guineas for their support. These hand-outs came to the considerable sum of nearly £1,000.

Spurred on by his success, Henry Luttrell determined to secure full control of Minehead and to this end prepared to nominate both seats at the next election.

Sir Thomas Acland of Holnicote reserved his support, writing to Luttrell on 16 April 1768:

I am persuaded that your weight and property in the borough, properly managed, would with little trouble secure to you the nomination of both members. It would not be consistent with that candour which ought to be observed, were I not to say that I ca'nt (as matters are at present circumstanced) think of serving Mr Shiffner, or of opposing Mr Whitworth, for whom I have some regard.[106]

At the beginning of August 1774, three days were allocated to carrying out a carefully organized and systematic canvas of the Minehead electorate on behalf of Mr Luttrell and his 'friend' who turned out to be none other than his second son, and heir, John Fownes Luttrell.

However, Shiffner was still the favourite second choice of some of the electors; they preferred to vote for him rather than for Luttrell's son. They were intent on maintaining a fairer balance of power, and of not over-weighing the castle interest.

Mr Luttrell seems not to have been altogether happy about the legality of the blandishments being offered to the Minehead people and he sought legal advice from John Heath, K.C. who advised:

It is most prudent to avoid giving any extraordinary entertainment, but no law prohibits you from entertaining your friends at your house, before the issuing or ordering of the writts of election, tho' such friends should be voters, or even afterwards, if it be not in great numbers, or in an extraordinary way.[107]

Sir Charles Whitworth withdrew his candidature after being offered a safe seat at East Looe in Cornwall. Another candidate retired gracefully on perceiving he had little support. So the final canvassing before the General Election of 1774 was simply on behalf of Henry Fownes Luttrell and his son John, on 4th October. On the 5th and 7th there was 'nothing doing in Minehead', which is not surprising when one reads of the explosive eruption of sound and entertainment which followed on the 8th.

It took only the votes of ten electors and the two constables who each voted twice, once for Mr Luttrell and once for his son John, to ensure the overall dominance of the Luttrells over the electorate of Minehead. (Richard Cox must have resigned his office for Lyte refers to the election agent as George Gale.)[108]

Although, according to Lyte, George Gale claimed to have spent not one penny on the voters, less than four months later he was distributing gold pieces among the electors of Minehead. Voters who would have been against Mr Luttrell received nothing. In the accounts '635*l.* 5' are entered as 'gratuities given to the poor voters'. 118 of 'the common voters' were entertained at different public houses on the 20th of October at a charge of 5s a head. On the same day 'the principal voters' received 'a treat' or 'general feast' at the 'Plume of Feathers' inn.[109]

Henry Fownes Luttrell resigned his seat within a few weeks of the General Election. He had never really wanted to pursue a parliamentary career and his only desire had been to maintain the Castle interest, which could now be ensured by his son John holding the second seat. Thomas Pownall, recommended by Lord North of Dillington House, Somerset, was chosen to take Henry's place on 31 December 1774. The expenses of this by-election were less than £50.

A parochial detail of interest arises in 1776 when Henry Fownes Luttrell paid for seat money in St George's Church. The Churchwardens' Accounts record that he paid for four seats in the 'Isle', as well as:

> Mr Thomas Leighs seat in the north Isle, for the lives of John Fownes Luttrell, Alexander Fownes Luttrell, and Francis Fownes Luttrell and Thomas Fownes Luttrell and his sons.   4. 0. [110]

At the beginning of the year 1777 Henry, the third son of Margaret and Henry Fownes Luttrell, died and was buried at Dunster on 4 January 1777. Again, the five pounds penanlty was paid for burying him in linen.[111]

That year Mr Luttrell addressed himself to more local affairs and he purchased various tenements in Dunster and also acquired the manor of Staunton Fry for £5,500. This enhanced his 'interest' in the parliamentary borough of Minehead. He also purchased tenements in Dunster and significantly Lyte tells us that he 'extinguished the rights of most of the commoners on the Marsh'.[112] These rights went back to the days of John de Mohun III: a few years after his charter of 1301, in an undated charter, he declared:

> To all the faithful of Christ who shall see or hear the present writing, John de Mohun, lord of Dunsterre, greetings in the Lord. Know ye all that I have granted and confirmed for ever for me and my heirs to all my burgesses of my town of Dunsterre and their heirs and all who hold a whole burgage that they shall freely dig and at their pleasure carry away slime (*slyman*) for improving their lands, in the whole of my marsh between the road that leads to the sea-port of Dunsterre and the marsh of Richard of Avele; and that they shall have common of pasture with all their plough-cattle (*averiis*) at every time of the year, except in my several marsh which is called Estmersh, [so] that they shall neither dig there and carry away, nor have common there with their plough cattle... [113]

However, the ancient right specified in the same lord's charter seems not to have been withdrawn by Henry Fownes Luttrell in 1779:

> ... I have furthermore granted to the same burgesses and their heirs for ever, on account of the love which I bear to the said burgesses, that they shall have furze (*jaones*), whorts, (*moritas*), turves (*turbas*), ferns (*fugeras*) and heath (*brueras*), sufficient for their fuel on my hill Croudon, for ever ... [114]

In 1779, 'the firing for the poor house was principally supplied by heath pulled and cut on the hill.[115] The same year the overseers laid out some money, perhaps for an inmate of the poorhouse: 'A pare of britches 3s 6d and a skinn to mend ye britches 1s 9d'. The vestry appear to have occasionally dined together at the expense of the poor rate: 'March 24. For a rump of beef 39 lbs., and a loyne of Veal for Easter Meeting ' (no cost given).[116]

The General Election of 1780 saw Henry Fownes Luttrell unwaveringly pursuing the successful policy he had followed in the 1774 election. He again announced his interest would be exercised in favour of two candidates bearing the name of Luttrell. They were his sons John and Francis, who were duly elected unopposed. On 30 October 1780, their father Henry Fownes Luttrell died and was buried at Dunster in the family vault.

His hatchment, the fourth in the series, hangs on the south wall of the Priory Church to the west of and next to that of AlexanderLuttrell (1705-37). It is blazoned thus:

Arms: *quarterly first and fourth – Luttrell (or and sable); second and third – Azure two Eagles displayed and in base a mullet Argent for Fownes; impaling – per pale – on the dexter – Luttrell; on the sinister – Or a chevron between three boar's heads erased Gules for Bradley; overall – an inescutcheon of Luttrell;*
Crest:-   *on a helm with a wreath Or and Sable out of a ducal coronet. Or a plume offive ostrich feathers Argent.*
Mantling:-   *Gules and Argent.*
Motto:-   *Quaesita Marte Tuenda Arte.*[117]

Dunster Parish

Minor parochial matters occupy the Churchwardens' Accounts in the last years of the eighteenth century. In 1782, for instance, '12¾ yards of fine Holland for a new surplice' cost £2 4s 7½d. There was trouble with the Dunster Church bells: the tenor and the fifth bells were again found to be cracked; a rate was passed to defray the expense of re-casting. In 1799 the clerk elected in 1771, George Rawle the younger, died. A new clerk, whose name is not given, was elected. In the same year, or possibly in 1800, the Churchwardens' Accounts also record that the vicar of the parish, the Rev G.H. Leigh, was chosen as one of the churchwardens.[118] He was again chosen in 1802/3/4.

The Overseers' Accounts for the years 1791 to 1799 note that in 1791 allowances were made for twenty-two houses which are recorded as having fallen or been pulled down, including 'a house over Gallox bridge'. Other items are as follows:

Item 1793. The title deeds belonging to the parish of Dunster are now in the custody of Mr John Hole Innkeeper of the said parish.
Pd. Wm. Hitchcock by order of ye Commanding officers of the Militia his son for sarveing [sic] for Mr George Beadon £3. 0s. 0d.
John Collards wife 45 weeks and a child 3 weeks he sarveing in the militia for Wm Staddon. £2 8s.

(By 1795 wheat had risen to 11s per bushel, beef to 4d, pork to 3½d., cheese to 3½d per pound.)

Total expenses for Richard ffry to serve in the Navy £25. 2s. 4d.

Paid to the wife Nicholas Collard he sarveing in the Militia for William Moody £1 15s.

David Sellicks wife he sarveing in the Militia for William Webber £1. 15s.

John Collards wife he sarveing in the Militia for William Staddon £2. 18s.

Paid Mr Sanders for enoculating [sic] 30 of ye poore £7. 10s. [119]

sarveing [sic] for Mr George Beadon £3. 0s. 0d.

John Collards wife 45 weeks and a child 3 weeks he sarveing in the militia for Wm Staddon. £2 8s.

(By 1795 wheat had risen to 11s per bushel, beef to 4d, pork to 3½d., cheese to 3½d per pound.)

Total expenses for Richard ffry to serve in the Navy £25. 2s. 4d.

Paid to the wife Nicholas Collard he sarveing in the Militia for William Moody £1 15s.

David Sellicks wife he sarveing in the Militia for William Webber £1. 15s.

John Collards wife he sarveing in the Militia for William Staddon £2. 18s.

Paid Mr Sanders for enoculating [sic] 30 of ye poore £7. 10s. [120]

ENDNOTES

1 Lyte: H.D. Part I 221
2 Lyte remarks, 'a post-nuptial settlement of his estate was made in 1729 (H.D. Part I 222)
3 Sedgwick: H of C 1715-1754 231
4 Lyte: H.D. Part I 233
5 Ibid. 222
6 Ibid. 223 This portrait is now at East Quantoxhead.
7 Ibid.
8 Ibid. This portrait is at East Quantoxhead.
9 An early portrait of her, in blue and white satin, also survives
10 Lyte: H.D. Part I 223
11 Hancock: D.C.P 158
12 Abraham Allen was one of five who attested an inventory of church property in 1720.
13 Somerset Archives and Record Office, Ref. O/D/du 6/1/1
14 Hancock: D.C.P 186
15 Ibid. 127/9. This painting was removed during the Victorian Restoration.
16 Ibid. 159
17 Surely this would have been Alexander Luttrell (1705-1737).
18 Hancock: D.C.P 190/1/2.
19 Ibid. 159
20 Ibid. 112
21 Ibid 187
22 Ibid. 112
23 Lyte: H.D. Part I 187
24 Ibid. 222/3
25 Merchant: L.H.D
26 See Seal 18 in Lyte: H.D. Part II 544/5
27 Burke: G.A 1029
28 The blazoning of all hatchments has been taken with the author's permission from F. Merchant's article: LHD
29 The eastern part of the church, the Priory Church was used for a number of years after 1737 but by 1791, or a little before, it is described by Collinson as 'stripped of all its furniture and totally neglected and by 1830 Savage reported a more lamentable situation.
30 Hancock: D.P.C 83/4; Hamper: HAD 878
31 Burke: B.G.A 984
32 Gunnis: D.B.S
33 Lyte: H.D Part I 195
34 Hancock: D.C.P. 103/4
35 Ibid. 140
36 Ibid. 156
37 Hancock in his list of Incumbents of Dunster gives John Question, 1730, and Lyte quoting 'The Vicars and Curates of Dunster' also misleadingly gives John Question 1731-1738. Lyte also mentions a further Dr Question in writing about the 1767 parliamentary elections.

38   NADFAS: National Association of Decorative and Fine Arts Societies

39   H.A.D 878.

40   PRORG4/ 4619 (corr: 6/12/1995 from Mr Robert Sherlock.)

41   Or Mr Treer may have been the carrier or other intermediary. Treer of Bristol is
      erroneously listed as the maker in the list of valuable items owned by the church,
      pasted in the front of the *Dunster Minute Book* (1920).

42   Lyte: H.D Part I 226

43   Ibid.   Part II 373

44   Lyte: H.D Part II 373

45   Hancock: D.C.P. 159/60.

46   Ibid. 71

47   For full details see Hancock: D.C.P 70

48   Ibid. 71

49   Ibid.

50   Ibid. 71/2

51   Ibid. 198

52   Ibid. 67

53   However, neither William nor George Gale appear in Hancock's list. William
      Clark appears in that list for the years 1780/1/2.

54   Hancock: D.C.P 187

55   He married an Anne Luttrell who was not of the Dunster or Irnham line of
      Luttrells.

56   See Lyte: H. D. Part II 477/488

57   Lyte: H.D. Part I 226/7

58   'There is a fifth portrait of Margaret Luttrell at Bathealton Court painted some
      time after her marriage'. Lyte: H.D. Part I 227

59   Lyte: H.D. Part I 228

60   Ibid. 229

61   Ibid. Part I 261

62   Hancock: D.C.P 160/1

63   Savage: H.H.C. via Hancock: D.C.P. 83

64   Hancock: D.C.P 162.

65   Ibid.

66   *Trevelyan Letters to 1840*, edited by Mary Siraut

67   Hancock: D.C.P 164

68   Lyte: H.D. Part I 535.

69   Ibid.

70   Hancock: D.C.P 162/3

71   Water Street, now called Park St., was known as 'la Waterstret' in 1323 and as
      Gallokystret in 1342. In 1800 it is referred to as Gallox Street, otherwise called
      Water Street, but by this time the southern part beyond the river was commonly
      called by the former name and the northern part, in the present Park, as Water
      Street.

72   Hancock: 163

73   Ibid. 163/4.

74   Ibid. 164

75   Ibid. 188

76   Savage: HHC, via Hancock DCP 83

[77] Lyte: H.D. Part I 169
[78] Ibid. 230
[79] Ibid. 230/1
[80] Ibid. 231/2
[81] Ibid. 232
[82] Ibid.
[83] Ibid. 233
[84] Ibid.
[85] Ibid. 234/5
[86] Ibid. 235
[87] Ibid. 236/7
[88] Ibid. 238
[89] Ibid. 239
[90] Ibid. 242
[91] Ibid. 243-4
[92] Ibid. 244
[93] Merchant: L.H.D. 186
[94] See Merchant: L.H.D 178
[95] Lyte: H.D. Part I 245/6 . Charles Townshend died the next year, 1767.
[96] Ibid.
[97] Ibid. 246/7
[98] Stevens : H.T.H 6
[99] Lyte: H.D. Part I 247.
[100] Ibid. 248
[101] Ibid. 249
[102] Ibid.
[103] Ibid. 250
[104] Ibid. 251
[105] Ibid. 250/1
[106] Ibid. 251/2
[107] Ibid. 252/3
[108] Richard Cox's health may already have been deteriorating. See Stevens: H.T.H. 7
[109] Lyte: H.D.Part I 255
[110] Hancock: D.C.P 188
[111] Ibid. 164
[112] Lyte: H.D. Part I 229
[113] Ibid. 282
[114] Ibid. 281
[115] Hancock: D.C.P 164
[116] Ibid.
[117] Merchant: L.D.H., 186. On page 178 he adds: 'in 1780 Henry predeceased her [i.e. Frances Bradley] and as his hatchment (4) shows, by this time in his quartered arms he had transposed Fownes and Luttrell and henceforth Luttrell occupied the first and fourth quarters... etc'.
[118] Hancock: D.C.P. 188
[119] Ibid. 164/5
[120] Ibid. 164/5

DUNSTER LIFE from the LATER EIGHTEENTH CENTURY to VICTORIAN TIMES; GEORGE FOWNES LUTTRELL

In 1780 John Fownes Luttrell, born at Dunster in June 1752, became Lord of the Manor. His marriage to Mary Drewe (d. 1829), and the marriage of Margaret and Henry Fownes Luttrell, his parents, accounts for the arms depicted on the hanging sign outside the 'Luttrell Arms', owned by the Luttrell family. They may be blazoned thus: *Arms: Quarterly first and fourth – Or a bend between six Martlets Sa; second and third: Az two Eagles displayed and in base a mullet Arg for Fownes; impaling Ermine a Lion passant Gu for Drewe.*

Five stylised ostrich feathers rise from the strawberry leaves of the ducal crest-coronet of the Luttrells. (The inclusion of such a coronet in a crest does not imply rank but is integral to the crest.)[1] The helm is a barriers helm for a baronet and knights and, like the mantling which flows from beneath the crest, the tinctures used are *Az* and *Or*. These are the Fownes colours, used for the mantling of only one hatchment in the church, that of John Fownes; usually the colours employed are *Gu* and *Arg*. The swan supporters, which are certainly an indication of illustrious ancestry, shew only a minimal version of the chains at the base of the tails.

Public Life in Dunster in the Eighteenth Century

The known history of the 'Luttrell Arms' up to the seventeenth century has already been given. In the eighteenth century, in the time of Alexander Luttrell (1705-1737), there was trouble in Dunster over the inn sign, a large new sign-post made of timber and iron set up at the beginning of 1736 in front of the house and painted by Richard Phelps.[2]

We know the names of some of the numerous hostelries which existed in Dunster in 1760. There was 'Spears Cross' in West Street; 'Phillpotts House', now the 'Three Marriners'; 'The George Inn' in High Street; 'Courts', formerly 'ye Compass'; 'ye Three Cupps Inn' and two alehouses, the 'Swan Alehouse' and the 'Whitehorse Alehouse'.[3] In 1736 the new sign for what was then known as the 'Ship Inn' aroused the animosity of the tavern and inn-keepers who may have regarded it as a threat to their trade. One Philip

Harrrison took the law into his own hands and demolished it. He was fined £5 as we know from the Borough Court records for October, 1736.[4]

'The Ship' fell into a state of serious disrepair and by 1777 the ruins of the old 'Ship Inn' and garden yielded no rent. James Stowey, of Stowey and Jones, surveyors, submitted a plan and elevation of the 'Ship Inn' which cost £1 11s 6d. The required work proceeded and the restored inn became the 'Luttrell Arms'. John Mountstephen was chosen as the new landlord.

Stowey and Jones had been employed in about 1773 by Henry Fownes Luttrell to work at the castle, replacing two former entrances from the stair-case into the Inner Hall with three arches.[5] Luckily for posterity, the gallery above the staircase remains as remodelled in 1773. However, the mock-medievalising hand of Salvin in 1869 would deprive us of the grace of the eighteenth century by substituting the heavy arches we have today.

Earlier, in 1763, the yearly rents of the Cornhouse, Markethouse or Yarn Market, Tubhouse and Shambles were fixed at a so-called survey conducted at the old 'Ship Inn'. It appears that this survey was in the nature of an auction where various would-be tenants bid against each other for the lease of these buildings. The bids rose from £47 to £60 and at this time it was George Gale, the Luttrell election agent, who paid £60 per annum and was granted the lease.[6]

Up to 1825 Dunster retained to a greater extent the appearance and functions of a working market town. The shambles divided the street unequally; the eastern side being much wider than the western side. These parallel ways extended south from the Market House, or Yarn Market. In the seventeenth century the rents received by the Lord of Dunster for 'shops inclosed' was greater than that for 'standings', where butchers, shoemakers and others plied their trades. A new and convenient market-house was erected by John Fownes Luttrell on the eastern side of the street.[7]

Although Elizabethan work remains in Dunster, particularly within houses, many changes took place in the late eighteenth and early nineteenth centuries. For example, 'the Cage House' was rebuilt by Dr Abrahams after he had purchased the old timber-framed building, resembling a cage, from John Fownes Luttrell. Here only the ancient cellars remain. The 'Castle Hotel', originally built by Richard Blackford in the seventeenth century as a private dwelling, and in 1760 known as 'Prowse's house (late Blackford's near ye Cross)' also undoubtedly underwent a change to its façade in the early nineteenth century. There are many other examples.

The references to a Cornhouse in the survey may have been to a building in the Wheat Market. Lyte tells us that 'a little to the south of the Ball stood the Corn Cross, mentioned in 1705 as close to the Wheat market'. Also: 'to the east of it was a building known as the Tub House'.[8] The shambles would have been placed right up to the cobbles on either side. These cobbles provided means of access and egress and belonged, as they do today, to the properties bounding the High Street.

It was customary for the members of the Court Leet and the Court Baron to meet, until 1825, in the Town Hall. The meetings were held annually at this time; the principal business was to impose fines of 4d a piece on all male residents in Dunster between the ages of fourteen and seventy who had failed to present themselves at the Borough Court. 'The collector was usually satisfied if he could levy 1d to maintain the principle that suit was due'.[9] The Court Baron levied greater fines on non-attenders; freeholders who offended were fined 2s 6d and leaseholders 1s. Afterwards the court members adjourned to the 'Luttrell Arms' to regale themselves at the lord's expense.

The Luttrell Family

To return to John Fownes Luttrell, the new Lord of the Manor. He matriculated at Queen's College Oxford in 1770 but like many previous Luttrells did not proceed to a degree. He married Mary Drewe on 2 August 1782. In Tudor times the Drewes had lived at Killerton; when they sold up to the Aclands they established themselves at Broadhembury. Francis Drewe, Mary's father, was of Grange and Broadhembury.

Between the years 1789 and 1793 John Luttrell purchased from Lord Stawell the entire Stewkley inheritance at Dunster which comprised 'the rectorial tithes, the advowson and several burgages and fields in Marsh'.[10] (The advowson, or right to appoint the incumbent, is today in the hands of the bishop of the diocese.)[11] In 1796 John Luttrell paid £8,000 to Juliana, Lady Langham for the rectory and advowson of Withycombe. Fifteen years later he bought the manor of Sandhill in the parish of Carhampton from Hugh Escott.[12]

Seeking to concentrate his interests, he set off against these purchases the sale of the outlying manor of Heathfield Durborough to John Perring of Combe Florey. This sale took place in 1803 and brought him £22,000.[13]

John Luttrell was keen on racing and won silver cups at Lingfield in 1781 and at Totnes in 1789. (These are today on display at Dunster Castle.) True to form, he had his portrait painted on various occasions, notably by Opie. For this portrait he paid four guineas in 1782 when he was thirty years of age. At this time Opie was only twenty-one years of age and was on the verge of the fame which he afterwards enjoyed. John Fownes Luttrell was also painted in miniature, the work being set in diamonds.

His wife Mary Drewe and her sister Charlotte are also charmingly portrayed by John Downman in pastel, the works being set in oval frames. Downman specialised in these small portraits. Examples of his work may be found at the Tate Gallery and Wallace Collection. These three portraits are all at Court House, East Quantoxhead.

Much is known about John Fownes Luttrell's parliamentary activities.[14] As has already been stated, he was elected an MP with his brother Francis in the 1774 election. In 1780, when their father Henry Fownes Luttrell died and John succeeded to the estates, he rather belatedly rewarded the Minehead electors who had supported the two Luttrells in the 1774 election with a gift of four guineas each. Lyte tells us that:

> In an "alphabetical list of voters", there is a note by George Gale— "those marked 'Gent' do not take money and are invited to the annual treats".

Among these 'gentlemen' were the local surgeons, the captains of several
ships, a farmer, a butcher, a glazier and a roper.[15]

Three years after their father Henry Fownes's death, Francis Fownes
Luttrell left politics. Without reference to the electorate of Minehead, John
replaced his brother with the non-elected Henry Beaufoy from Shropshire,
who doubtless had to pay for his seat at Minehead.

Between the dissolution of Parliament in 1784 and the General Election
of 1790, Minehead saw three changes in its junior members. Henry Beaufoy
was re-elected but he had also been returned for Great Yarmouth, which he
chose to represent. Charles Phipps of Mulgrave Hall (Yorks) was chosen to
replace Beaufoy but he died in 1786. Robert Wood of 'Lyme Grove in Surrey'
succeeded him but in 1790 George, Viscount Parker was returned with John
Fownes Luttrell and served for five years.

There seems not to have been a suitable candidate willing to purchase
the junior seat for Minehead in 1795 and so John Fownes Luttrell, ever
mindful of maintaining the castle interest, put forward his thirty-two-year-
old brother Thomas. Thomas was appointed as a stopgap, but became
Commissioner of Customs in December 1793 and later became Chairman of
the Board.

John and Thomas Fownes Luttrell served together for only one year,
1795-6, when the family interests were severely challenged by two contestants who persuaded the electorate that they should be freed from 'tyrannic
sway'. They were John Langston of Sarsden House (Oxon) and Rear-
Admiral Charles Morice Pole. The poll of 28-30 May saw a weakening of
the castle interest, as John Fownes Luttrell and John Langston were the
successful candidates.[16]

John Langston, the new MP, wished to secure his interest in the borough
and bought land on which he built houses. This sounded an alarm among the
'principal inhabitants' and twenty-four of them set out to strengthen John
Luttrell's position. They met at the 'Plume of Feathers' in November and
recommended two inducements, namely that Mr Luttrell 'should repair 'the
common houses' and erect temporary shambles for the butchers.[17] The third
resolution was that:

> That Mr Luttrell be recommended to dispossess all such persons of their
> houses, grounds, etc. as were inimical to his interest at the last election [18]

Further, those gathered at the *Plume of Feathers* 'bound themselves to
give a preference in the employment of labourers to all such as had supported
Mr Luttrell at the recent election'.[19]

The next Minehead election was in 1802. John Langston again offered
himself as one of the candidates and was now joined by James Woodbridge.
John Fownes Luttrell began canvassing on his own behalf and on behalf of
a John Patteson.

It was an election which fermented a great deal of ill-feeling and a public
enquiry regarding infractions of the laws against bribery was narrowly

averted. Langston's influence was curtailed when he agreed to sell his Minehead properties. These properties cost Luttrell £7,000 but cleared the area of his opponents.

The next General Election took place on 1 November 1806. John Fownes Luttrell, acutely aware he was unpopular, withdrew at the last moment. Perhaps the 'rough list of inhabitants of Minehead likely to vote for Mr Luttrell and his friend' which had been completed on 22 October 1806 was a sparse one. Again there is a list of voters treated in different public houses in Minehead for a supper and drink on 24 October.[20]

Four days after Sir John Lethbridge and Lord Rancliffe, almost certainly Luttrell's nominees, had been returned as MPs for Minehead, that is on 5 November 1806, seventy-two gentlemen were invited to dine at the 'Plume of Feathers' in Minehead. Luttrell was determined to get in by hook or by crook and when Sir John resigned within only a few weeks of the election on 14 January 1807, John Fownes Luttrell stepped into his shoes.

This parliament was of short duration for George III desired a House of Commons that would support the ministry formed by the Prime Minister, Lord Bentinck. Following the dissolution of the 1806 Parliament a concerted attempt was made to overthrow the supremacy of the castle interest in the borough of Minehead.

In spite of two days of intense propaganda directed against John Fownes Luttrell by the Hon. Thomas Bowes, he was again elected. Bowes had urged voters to exercise their 'freedom of suffrage' and expressed his desire to defend them and to offer his protection 'from the shackles and abuses of tyranny and corruption.' This message was strengthened by a ballad:

Shall Britons bold be bought and sold
Slave-like-more traffic in a fair?

Voting began on 8 May and after 7.00 pm, poor Bowes, overcome by Luttrell who had polled 123 votes against his 64 (108 votes going to a John Denison), sent a letter to Mr William Leigh in which he informed him that '...he would not give Mr Luttrell any further trouble'. [21]

In 1812 John Fownes Luttrell and his eldest son and heir John (b. 1787) were elected 'by acclamation and with the most cordial demonstration of regard'.[22] Their election was celebrated by a ball held in November where all the hundred and fifty guests were drawn from the professional and commercial classes.

Four years later, in February 1816, John Fownes Luttrell died. He was buried at Dunster. Mary, his widow, lived on until March 1829. In Dunster Church, his hatchment, the fifth in the series, hangs on the south wall of the vestry, to the east of the later hatchment for his wife Mary Luttrell née Drewe. John Fownes Luttrell's hatchment may be blazoned thus:

Arms: quarterly first and fourth Luttrell (Or and Sable); second and third Az two Eagles displayed and in base a mullet Arg for Fownes; impaling Ermine a Lion passant Gu for Drewe.

Crest:-   *Out of a ducal coronet Or a plume of five ostrich feathers Arg.*

Supporters:-   *two Swans Arg, ducally gorged and chained Or.*

Motto:-   *Quaesita Marte Tuenda Arte.*

            [There is no mantling in this hatchment.]

There were nine children of the marriage, five sons and four daughters, all baptized at Dunster. The sons were: John, his heir, b. 26 Aug 1787; Henry, successor to his brother, b. 7 Feb 1790; Francis, b. 10 Feb; Alexander, b.1793 d. 1888, Rector of East Quantoxhead, and Thomas, b. 11 Sept 1794, Vicar of Dunster. The daughters, all buried at Dunster, were Mary Anne, b.27 July 1783, buried May 1835; Margaret, b. 8 Oct 1784; buried June 1858; Charlotte, b. 23 Mar 1786, buried Mar 1791 and Harriet, b. 21 Oct 1788, buried April 1870.

John Fownes Luttrell the Younger

The new heir, John Fownes Luttrell the younger (b. 1787), educated at Eton and Oriel College, Oxford, where he took the degree of M.A., succeeded in 1816. True to form he increased the family estate by purchasing more land, acquiring the manor of Eastbury and Briddicot Farm in Carhampton, which had been in the ownership of the Perceval family. As we have seen, John Fownes Luttrell had been elected with his father as one of the Members for Minehead in the 1812 election and was re-elected in 1818. He served on four more occasions, always nominating who would stand for the second seat. However this situation was about to change, with the advent of the great Reform Bill of 1832, which aimed to reform the whole electoral system. Large numbers of decayed or 'rotten' boroughs would be disenfranchised, including Minehead.

The first Reform Bill was introduced to the Commons on 1 March 1831.The bill disfranchised sixty boroughs of less than 2000 inhabitants, and returning 119 members. Minehead had only 215 voters. These were for the most part tenants of John Fownes Luttrell, and he did not give up without a fight. He and his agent set to work to prepare a detailed case supporting the threatened constituency with facts and statistics of a favourable nature. The historic importance of Dunster was alluded to and it was pointed out that, far from being just a 'pocket-borough' of the Luttrells, there had been within the past three decades two contested elections. It was proposed that Carhampton, Withycombe, Wootton Courtenay and Timberscombe should be included in the parliamentary borough. All to no avail: with the passing of the Bill in 1832, Minehead lost the right of sending up representatives to Westminster. John Fownes Luttrell later stood for the western division of the county in the Tory interest, but he was not successful.[23]

John Fownes Luttrell died unmarried and was buried with his forebears at Dunster on 21 January 1857.[24] He was succeeded by his brother, Henry (b. 1790). Like John, Henry was educated at Eton but then went on to

Brasenose College, Oxford, where he gained his B.A. In 1816 he was elected to succeed his father as one of the two members for Minehead. He was successful in the 1818 and 1820 elections but on becoming one of the Commissioners for auditing the public accounts, he resigned his duties as a Member of Parliament. He spent twenty-seven years of his life as a Commissioner and resided for many of them in London. He died unmarried in October 1867.

Hatchments for both brothers hang in Dunster Church, after the sixth hatchment in the series, which probably relates to their mother Mary Fownes Luttrell (d. 1829) but H.F. Merchant maintains that 'an element of doubt must be attached to these attributions' to her and to her sons John and Henry.[25] Mary Luttrell's hatchment hangs on the south wall of the vestry, west of the hatchment to her husband John Fownes Luttrell (d 1816). It may be blazoned thus: *Arms: quarterly first and fourth – Luttrell; second and third – Fownes, impaling Ermine a Lion passant Gu for Drewe.*

The seventh hatchment for John Fownes Luttrell, 1787-1857 (or perhaps Henry Fownes Luttrell) may be found at the west end of the vestry. It may be blazoned thus:

Arms:	*quarterly first and fourth – Luttrell (Or and Sable); second and third – Fownes.*
Crest:	*on a helm with a wreath Or and Az out of a ducal coronet Or a plume of five ostrich feathers Arg.*
Mantling:	*Or and Az.*
Supporters:	*two Swans Arg gorged [not ducally] and chained Or.*
Motto:-	*Quaesita Marte Arte*

The eighth hatchment for Henry, 1790-1867 (or John Fownes Luttrell) may be found on the north wall of the vestry and is the most westerly of the three hanging there:

Arms:	*quarterly first and fourth – Luttrell (Or and Sable); second and third – Fownes.*
Crest:-	*out of a ducal coronet Or a plume of five ostrich feathers Arg. [there is no helm or wreath]*
Supporters:	*two Swans Arg ducally gorged and chained Or.*
Motto:-	*Quaesita Marte Arte* *[There is no mantling on this hatchment]*

Mr Merchant observes:

It will be noticed that hatchment (7) is the only one to have mantling in the or and azure field colours of the Luttrell/Fownes quartering; in all other cases where the mantling occurs it is gules and argent – following the general custom of the time. Hatchment (7) also has a wreath or and azure, all other wreaths are in the or and sable colours of the Luttrell arms except

$(2)^{26}$ where, unusually, the wreath is in gules and argent colours of the mantling.[27]

The next brother of John Fownes Luttrell (1787-185) and Henry Fownes Luttrell (1790-1867) was Lt. Col. Francis Fownes Luttrell (1792-1862). His portrait hangs in the library of the castle he never inherited. His brothers were batchelors who died childless but Francis died five years before Henry. So it was Francis's son, George Fownes Luttrell who succeeded to the title of Lord of the Manor in 1867.

Francis Fownes Luttrell

Francis Fownes Luttrell is specially commemorated in St George's Church, not only by the last hatchment in the series (see below), but also by the three-stepped lancet windows by Clayton and Bell over the High Altar, in the Luttrell Chapel, formerly the Priory Church.

Francis was named after his uncle Francis (d. 1823). He had been born on 10 February 1792 and as was customary, baptized at Dunster. He had matriculated at Christ Church, Oxford in 1810 but left without a degree. In March 1813 he became an officer in the Grenadier Guards and he was staying at Dunster Castle when the news of Napoleon's escape from Elba was announced. Francis journeyed to London to join his battalion and fought at the battle of Waterloo on 18 June, receiving a wound to his hand. Wellington's army defeated Napoleon, who was banished to St. Helena, where he later died.

On 21 February 1824, Lt Col. Francis Fownes Luttrell married his cousin Emma Louisa, the daughter of Samuel Drewe. The wedding took place at Kensington and in the April of the next year the thirty-three year old Francis decided to leave army life. He sold his commission, settled at Kilve Court and pursued the role of a country squire. He was Master of the West Somerset Fox-Hounds, the first Chairman of the Williton Board of Governors and in 1839 he became Lieutenant Colonel of the Second Regiment of Somerset Militia. He and Louisa, who appears not to have used her first Christian name, had nine children.

Apart from the heir, George, their other sons were: Edward, of Kilve Court, born 1831 and educated at Eton and Christ Church, Oxford (d. 3 July 1865); Arthur John (b. 1832), who entered the Royal Navy and died in 1847 at Penang; Francis (b. 1836), educated at Eton and Oriel College, Oxford, who died in 1880 in Natal. This Francis left two daughters by Helena, his wife, daughter of Stephanus Maritz of Natal: Helena Louisa (Nina) and Margery. The final son was Reginald (b. 1839), educated at Eton and Oriel College, Oxford, who died in 1866 at Torquay.

The daughters of Francis and Louisa Fownes Luttrell were: Augusta Margaret (b. May 1825), baptized at Kilve, who died in 1880; Charlotte (b. 1828), d 1842; Caroline (b. 1829), who was accidentally burned to death at Kilve Court in 1856, and Mary Anne (for whom we have no dates), afterwards of Clanville, Minehead, who married Henry Anstey Bosanquet, barrister-at-law, in 1861.

The hatchment for Lt. Col. Francis Fownes Luttrell (1792-1862) is the ninth and the most easterly hatchment on the north wall of the vestry. It may be blazoned thus:

Arms: *quarterly first and fourth – Az a bend between six Martlets Arg for Luttrell [these are correctly used for the arms of the Luttrells of Irnham, as the Luttrells of Dunster's arms are Or a bend between six Martlets Sa]; second and third – Fownes, impaling Ermine a Lion passant Gu for Drewe;*

Crest: *out of a ducal coronet – Or a plume of five ostrich feathers Arg [there is no helm or wreath];*

Supporters:- *two Swans Arg ducally gorged and chained Or;*

Motto:- *Quaesita Marte Tuenda Arte.*
[There is no mantling on this hatchment].

Mr Merchant says of this hatchment:

Although Francis never held the castle the remaining hatchment number (9) would seem to relate to him since it displays an impalement of Drewe and he married Emma Louisa Drewe (obit. 1818). This hatchment appears to be somewhat weak in design and construction, is poorly drawn, and, remarkably, shows the azure and argent version of the Luttrell arms in the Luttrell/Fownes quartering.[28]

Lt. Colonel Francis Luttrell had, apart from his two elder brothers John (d. 1857) and Henry (d.1867), a younger brother, Alexander, rector of East Quantoxhead, and Thomas, born 11 Sept 1794 and baptized at Dunster. Thomas, like his four elder brothers, was educated at Eton and then proceeded to Exeter College, Oxford in 1814. He returned to Somerset and in 1821 he became Vicar of Dunster, having first served as a curate.

Dunster Parish in the Early Nineteenth Century

The preceding vicar was the Rev. G. H. Leigh, mentioned in a legal letter written in January 1799 regarding 'Sir John Trevelyan's title to the Manor of Golsoncott and Roadwater, a part whereof is agreed to be purchased by the Rev. Mr Leigh for the Augmentation of the Vicarage of Dunster...'.[29] Leigh was also chosen to be one of the churchwardens that year, an office he again filled in 1801. The Leigh family had featured prominently in the history of the parish. In 1667 a John Leigh was one of the churchwardens who paid a rate of 2s 8d for 'ye maytaynance of ye poore of the psh'.[30] He and William Leigh were named among the 'principal inhabitants' of the parish in 1686, and in 1713 William was one of the witnesses to a document concerning money left by members of the Luttrell family for the benefit of the poor of the parish.[31] In 1744 a Robert Leigh assumed the office of churchwarden and in the Overseers' Accounts this entry appears: To Robert Leigh with Tho. Philpot bound to him in respect of part of Marsh Estate and the Tythes ... £1. 0. 0. [32]

A Thomas Leigh owned the workhouse in 1766 and rented it to the Overseers of the Poor for £10 per year. [33] An inventory of the beds and bedding, held by the 'Parish Workhouse or Poor's House, Dunster' was compiled on 11 March 1805. The Overseers concluded that:

> ... the Bedding of the House (the Beds only excepted) appears to us very scanty. The Sheets are not sufficient for cleanliness. There are no blankets — at which we were surprised, — nor are the Rugs sufficient of themselves to keep the elderly people warm. We are of the opinion that several new Mats are immediately wanted, as well as some sheets, and that Blankets or Rugs, or both, ought to be provided before another Winter, and that these Articles ought to be more frequently examined and reported, and the Inventories regularly handed down from one set of Overseers to the next.[34]

Hancock observes that:

> There appears to have been thirty-eight inmates of the poor house at this time. As in the similar case of Minehead (*vide* author's *Minehead*), the overcrowding must have been of a most shocking description.

In 1807, thirty-six 'neat' rates were levied, which amounted to £453. 15s 6d., and the overseers paid out:

	£	s	d
Weekly pay.	200	11	3
Paid in sickness.	11	16	0
Disbursement in the house.	99	10	1
Extra disbursements.	130	10	11
	442	8.	3

Hancock comments:

> An expensive year. The poor in the house now spun yarn under the direction of one Thomas Pulman of Doniford who took 20 per cent profit on their work. The system seemed to have been a remunerative one, and it was no doubt an excellent plan that all capable of work in the house should have employment. The traces of the struggle the nation was passing through are seen in the rise of the price of food stuffs.[35] In 1805 bacon is 10d per pound, suet 8d., potatoes 4s. per bag, wheat 9s per bushel, beef 6d. per pound, cheese 4d.[36]

To return to the Rev. G.H. Leigh: in 1808 he was the curate of Dunster and lived at Ellicombe.[37] From 1817-1821 Thomas Fownes Luttrell served as the Rev. Leigh's curate. The Churchwardens' Accounts record:

		£	s	d
1817	Paid Mr Parfitt for a decree granted by the Bishop for the Revd T.F.Luttrell to serve the Church (as Curate) G.H. Leigh being Vicar.			
1818	Paid Mr Bakers bill for ancient chest	5	6	0 [38]

The Rev. Leigh died in 1821. The brass to his memory is mentioned by Lyte and Hancock, who also mentions the brass plate below it, in memory of the Rev. Leigh's wife Ann, who died 11 August 1831.[39]

Thomas Luttrell, who succeeded him, was formally presented to the Bishop by the Luttrell trustees, a procedure which had lapsed for nearly three centuries. Apart from being vicar of Dunster, Thomas was for some years vicar of Minehead and from 1832 also vicar of Carhampton. At Dunster he presided over a church in a very sad state of decay, as will be seen later.

In 1820 King George III died and the first year of the Rev. Thomas Luttrell's incumbency saw the coronation of the former Prince Regent as King George IV in 1821 at Westminster Abbey. The coronation was marked at Dunster by the ringing of the bells; the ringers were paid £2 for their services. That year, perhaps to mark the occasion, a violoncello costing £8 was purchased. This augmented the two flutes and bass viol which played in the west gallery and provided the musical accompaniment to the church services until 1868, when the Rev. Thomas Luttrell presented St. George's Church with the Bryceson organ.

The Functions of Local Authorities

Before quoting from the Churchwardens' Account of 1822-1825, a word about the functions of local authorities in the second part of the eighteenth century. The parish was of great importance locally. It was 'the only surviving unit of government with popular meetings; its vestry meeting took action as a public body, putting the wishes of the justices into effect...the vestry had the power of raising taxes for local purposes and for the poor in the form of a rate. Though the main administrative officers of the parish were not elected but were compulsorily appointed by the justices, a lively vestry could at least examine their spending... The vicar, if he cared to attend, was usually chairman of the vestry...'[40]

It was through the parish units that the commission of peace and justice operated effectively. The Luttrells as Lord-Lieutenants held positions of honour and were leading men of the justices and the heads of the militia. As squires of Dunster they occupied a position of paternal supervision and had much local knowledge. However, the duties of Lord-Lieutenant 'rarely amounted to more than nominating the clerk of the peace and keeping the king informed of the views of the county society whenever a justice's place had to be filled'.[41] A justice could mete out summary justice for minor offences such as poaching. At petty sessions two or three magistrates would deal with a variety of matters and at the quarter sessions they heard appeals and so, exercising supervision over the entire working practices of county government, they became *ipso facto* the government of the county.

The Churchwardens' Accounts provide the information that:

> In the years 1822 to 1825 the parish of Dunster by order of the Parishioners and Vestry assembled was surveyed by William Collard Cox and Robert Pinn Pursey of Carhampton and valued by John Tyler of Wiveliscombe for

the purpose of equalising the Poor's Rate. The parishioners of which Survey and Valuation were written in a book and deposited in the Parish Chest, from that book the following Church Rate was made by order of John F. Luttrell, Esq., and Thos Abraham, Gent., Churchwardens.[42]

Thomas Abraham died aged 62 in 1828. According to the brass to his memory on the north side of the nave, he had practised in Dunster for nearly forty years.[43]

On 26 June 1830, George IV died and was succeeded by his brother William IV. A curious entry appears in the Churchwardens' Accounts for 1831: 'Pd for a prayer for the receiving of his late Majesty King George IV: 2. 6.' This is followed by the entry: 'Prayer for King William and Queen Adelaide' 2. 6. [44] In 1831 there is also an entry: 'Prayer for the troubled state of part of the United Kingdom… 2s 6d'.

As we have seen, 1831 was the year of the Reform Bill, which disfranchised a large number of rotten boroughs of which as we know Minehead was one. Before this bill was passed, great excitement mounted in the country and when the Lords first rejected it demonstrations took place. In the West Country a mob sacked the Mansion House in Bristol, attacked the Tory M.P. and burned down the Bishop's Palace.

The Reform Bill became law in June 1832. The same year, King William was crowned. The Churchwardens' Accounts record the advent of the new king:

	£	s	d
1832. Ringers at Coronation of King William IV	1	1	1

In the early 1830s, epidemics of cholera, quite as horrifying as the plague, spread through the towns. The Churchwardens' Accounts record:

	£	s	d
Form of Prayer against the Pestilence now spreading in some parts of England		2	6

In 1833 two deaths are marked by memorials in the church. One is to John Williams. The Harvey brass to John Harvey died 6 October 1833 aged 77 and his wife Mary, who had died 29 July 1806 aged 40 years, bears an almost indecipherable verse which is fully recorded by Hancock.[45]

Victoria Accedes to the Throne

The accession of Queen Victoria in 1837 was not apparently marked by the ringers of Dunster and the next, more mundane entry is for 1839 when the church rate for that year was 7½d in the pound.

Likewise Queen Victoria's marriage to Albert is not mentioned in the Churchwardens' Accounts, but in 1841, after the birth of their first child, Victoria, the Princess Royal, in 1840, a son, Albert Edward, Prince of Wales, the future King Edward VII, was born and the Churchwardens' Accounts record:

	£	s	d
1841 A Prayer for Prince Albert		2	6
1842 For an order for inserting Albert Prince of Wales [no amount given.][46]			

In 1847 the Dunster Burial Board's Table of Fees was as follows:

	£	s	d
For the Interment of a Still-born child		2	0
For every interment at the expense of any Parish or Union		3	0
For the interment of a Mechanic or Laborer receiving weekly wages of his Wife or Widow or Son or Daughter either wholly or in part dependent on his or her Parents or Parent for maintenance.		3	0
For the interment of a Tradesman occupying a Cottage rated at less than £5 a year or his Wife or Widow Son or Daughter either wholly or in part dependent on his or her Parents or Parent for maintenance.		4	0
For every other Interment		7	6
For every other Interment in a Brick Grave over and above the cost of Masonry		7	6
For the purchase of exclusive rights of Burial in perpetuity in a Common Grave space over and above all other fees and payments.	2	2	0
For every bricked grave for one Coffin a further fee of	1	1	0
Ground for a family Vault to contain six coffins not exceeding 10 feet in depth by 8 feet in width and 12 feet in length.	10	10	0
For each additional Interment in a Bricked Grave or Vault.	1	1	0

A Clerk and Registrar for Grant of purchase for each Grave
Space entry of same in Register and Stamp Five shillings.
Non-parishioners will be charged double for Interment and for the purchase of Grave Spaces and Vaults.

There was also a detailed list of the cost of erecting stone or metal memorials.

A new parish clerk was appointed in 1847 whose name may be Palsway, Falsey or Halsey. Hancock refers to one named Palsway[47] and in other Churchwardens' Accounts the name is given as Falsey. Other Church-wardens' Accounts, not given by Hancock, refer to the appointment of George Falsey /Halsey as Parish Clerk on 5 April 1847. He would be paid £3 per year, plus £3 extra each year for attending to the church clock, the chimes, and for ringing the 6 o'clock bell. The appointment was signed by Thomas Luttrell, the Minister, by Thomas Abraham and Martin Langdon, Churchwardens, and by Thomas Oatway, John Rose Harvey, John Paul and Giles Edmonds.[48]

In April 1848/49/50 and possibly 1851, while Thomas Abraham continued as Vicar's Warden, the parishioners appointed Mr Thomas

Oatway as their Churchwarden. On 12 April 1852, John Rose Harvey was appointed a churchwarden. The same appointments of Abraham and Harvey were made in March 1853 and April 1854. In 1858 from the Church-wardens' Accounts we learn that there is a new Parish Clerk, one Jonah Stenner, appointed at the same wage as before. The signatories, all payers to the church rate, were:

Thomas Abraham	Wm Hole
John Edwards	Geo Risdon
James Slater	James Staddon
Robt Withycombe Senr	John Jones
Thos Oatway	William Thomas
Robt Withycombe Jnr	Richard Groves
John Hole	Thos Burge
William Withycombe	Thomas Baker

In 1859 on 25 April Thomas Abraham was again appointed the Vicar's Warden for the ensuing year, but the parishioners and ratepayers appointed Robert Withycombe Senior to be the People's Warden in place of John Rose Harvey. The signatories were: Thomas Abraham, Thos Oatway, Rob't Hole, Geo Risdon and James Slater.

In 1861 the Churchwardens' Accounts refer to the churchwardens' salary:

> With reference to the Order of 27th April 1861 relative to the appointment
> of the officers for that year, ordered that the same persons at the same rate
> of Salary be continued for the ensuing year.[49]

T.F. Luttrell
Thomas Abraham
Thos Oatway
Thos Gurdon
Robert Withycombe.

Mr Robert Withycombe Senior had again been appointed churchwarden at this 27.4.1861 meeting. In 1862 Mr Abraham was again nominated as Vicar's Warden, an office he had held for fifteen years.

One of Rev. Thomas Luttrell's last acts was to provide funds for the erection of the school in St. George's Street. This was designed by Piers St Aubyn. (In 1909 it was let to the Somerset County Council.) On 17 December 1871, the Rev. Thomas Luttrell died. The next vicar, appointed on 8 April 1872, was the Rev. Richard Utten Todd, for whom George Fownes Luttrell, Thomas's nephew, would build the Priory, now called Priory Court.

A splendid window was later erected at the east end of the south-east aisle of St George's Church to commemorate the Rev. Thomas Fownes Luttrell and his sisters Margaret and Harriet.

George Fownes Luttrell and the Renovation of the Castle

Dunster Castle had been successively in the possession of two bachelor brothers, John Fownes Luttrell (1787-1857) and Henry Fownes Luttrell (1790-1867). These sons of John Fownes Luttrell senior (1752-1816) had a third brother, Lieutenant Colonel Francis Fownes Luttrell who predeceased Henry, dying in 1862. It was therefore George, the son of Francis, who in 1867 succeeded his uncle and assumed the mantle of Lord of Dunster and local squire. George must have been possessed of great wealth much of which he seems to have expended on alterations to the castle and on the church restoration. He is mentioned in Bateman's *Great Landowners* of 1883 as receiving a gross rental of £22,000 from his Dunster estates. However, the sum reserved for the re-building of the castle was constrained to £20,000, less than a twelfth of that which the chosen architect, Salvin, was allowed for the restoration of Alnwick castle.

Since medieval times it had always been the aim of landowners to consolidate their estates around their main holding and George was no exception. He had inherited, through the marriage of his great-grandfather Henry Fownes to Margaret Luttrell, 1,852 acres in Devonshire and in 1874 he took the decision to sell the greater part of this estate. However, he had materially increased his holdings nearer home and four years earlier had purchased the manor of Old Cleeve and the remains of Cleeve Abbey.

The Pre-Reformation abbey of Cleeve was dedicated to St Mary and was known as the Abbey of St Mary in the Flowery Vale. Apart from their religious rites, the Cistercians were important agricultural pioneers who played a notable part in English sheep farming, though care of their lands was undertaken by lay brothers under less severe rules. After the Reformation Cleeve Abbey became a farm. The ruins were used as farm buildings and the pigs occupied pigsties housed in the cloisters.

George Fownes Luttrell had an eye for good land and he also followed his instinct for medieval buildings. He bestowed much care on the monastic buildings of the abbey and started excavations which were not finally completed until the task was taken on by the Department of the Environment in the 1950s. George also purchased the dependent chapel of St Mary, a little to the north of the abbey, and a Jacobean house called Binham.

In 1870, still endeavouring to centralize the estate, he exchanged lands with Sir Thomas Dyke and gained Avill in exchange for land between Minehead and Selworthy. In 1891 he purchased Aller in Carhampton, the former home of the Everards.

By the autumn of 1868 plans were afoot for the alteration of the castle. George Luttrell must have been possessed of enormous drive and energy. Not only did he carry out sweeping changes at the castle but between 1872 and 1874 he built the first permanent residence for the incumbent, the Rectory, followed between 1874 and 1876 with the church restoration. At Minehead he restored the parish church and devoted much attention to the development of the town as a resort and port. He was the prime mover in the scheme to bring the railway to the town. He financed this and was also responsible for work regarding improvements in the sewerage scheme.

Dunster Castle Renovations

George Luttrell's choice to undertake the difficult task of extending and modernizing the castle was Salvin, the domestic architect. The plan of the castle in 1867 is given by Lyte.

Anthony Salvin (1799-1881) had gained a reputation as an authority on the restoration and improvement of castles. He worked on Rockingham Castle, the Tower of London, Windsor, Caernarvon, Durham and Alnwick castles. However, he was not one-eyed in his appreciation and practice of the medieval period and was a truly eclectic Victorian. He could turn his hand to any style and this led to the Tudor style at Mamhead (Devon) in 1828; the approval of, but not the design of, the lush Italian Renaissance interiors at Alnwick, and elaborate references to the Jacobean style at Thorseby in Nottinghamshire between 1864 and 1875. The builder employed to carry out the work at Dunster was George Smith and Co. of London, known to Salvin for work at Thoresby and Windsor.

Most people alter their houses in accordance with the latest ideas and conveniences. Dunster Castle was no exception. Hugh Luttrell (d. 1428) had erected the Gatehouse in the 1420s; an earlier George Luttrell (d. 1629) had turned the castle into a Jacobean manor house. The Civil War saw much destruction to the outer defences and today all we see are the remains of the curtain wall and bastion towers. Then came the grand flourish of the Restoration. Mary Luttrell's great wealth was expended on the Grand Staircase, the Great Parlour (now the Dining Room), and the room which leads from it. In the nineteenth century, Victorian rebuilding laid its heavy hand on Dunster Castle which externally acquired a more 'picturesque' and castellated outline.

It must be said however, that George Luttrell's Jacobean part of the castle was respected, except that the northern tower of the façade was replaced by a more massive structure in whose western angle rose a conically stone-capped staircase turret with medieval arrow-slits. The fenestration of the tower itself lacks the solid symmetry of all the other windows on the northern front, the windows being randomly placed in vague diagonals either side of and below the enormous chimney which rises above the castellation. This tower provided additional accommodation and this, together with a desire for greater comfort and more social amenities, was the pre-eminent requirement of George Fownes Luttrell.

The domestic offices had been in the west wing. Now they were removed to the north-east and housed in the basement of the new north tower, called the Kitchen Tower, and in a rather questionable position in a low range extending from the tower in a northerly direction towards Sir Reynold de Mohun's thirteenth-century gateway. This building, rising only slightly above the Green Court, took advantage of the drop in ground level and had windows on its eastern side. It housed a still-room, a scullery and store rooms, while in the south tower of the gateway there were larders for fish and game. These new arrangements were, however, labour-intensive and far from practical. The servants were summoned by bells, and the food must have arrived in the dining-room in a tepid condition. A hot-water central system was installed by H.C. Price and Company of London and the kitchen was equipped by Stuart and Smith of Sheffield.[50]

George also wanted a gun-room, a muniment room, an office, a library and a billiard room. These were housed on the ground floor of the west wing. This must have been a somewhat daunting task for Salvin, for the site was difficult and there was little ground for extension.

A drawing room to which dinner guests could withdraw was a social requirement. As a consequence Dorothy Luttrell's chapel of 1722 was demolished[51] and in its stead rose the imposing south tower; perhaps envisaged by Salvin as a loose reference to a military keep. This tower dictated the proportions of the drawing-room which was to be on its ground floor. These are ill-balanced as far as fenestration is concerned, with a large bay on the south side and a small obliquely placed window facing south-east. The ceiling echoes that of the library but differs in the treatment of the frieze.[52]

Between the drawing room and the library, a conservatory affording spectacular views and access to the terrace was built. Beyond this, on the site of three small rooms with a mezzanine floor over them, the lofty library was built. Although drawing on styles of previous ages and countries, it is essentially a Victorian room, a room where one could relax and doze before the fire or read with the aid of the newly-introduced gas lighting. Its ceiling harks back to Jacobean plasterwork, formally compartmentalized into geometrical shapes and outlined with a rib pattern. The friezes, however, have burst the bounds of the ceiling's rigidity and display flowing designs reminiscent of late Renaissance, French and Italian styles of ornament. The nineteenth-century wallpaper is noteworthy and imitates Spanish leather. The bookcases of oak were designed by Salvin.

The porch tower over the main entrance was rebuilt on a larger scale and a passage ingeniously constructed under the roof.[53] Two earlier steeper approaches to this main entrance had been accomplished when Dorothy Luttrell's New Way of 1720 had been further extended by Henry Fownes Luttrell in 1750: an extension 'round the western and northern sides of the hill to the Jacobean façade.'[54] A visitor arriving by carriage up George Fownes Luttrell's new drive would have enjoyed both the visual delights of the existing drive and been conveyed more comfortably, for the gradient had been made less steep and the sweep of the drive wider as it wound its way round the Tor.

On descending from the carriage, or alighting from a horse, the entrance to the castle, before the advent of Salvin, would have been made through a doorway with a classically-conceived surround: an arched entrance with a keystone, flanked by columns over which an entablature supported a rectangular tablet. This probably bore a coat of arms and appears to have been flanked by heraldic devices; perhaps the chained swans of the Bohuns. This in turn was surmounted by a triangular pediment. To-day one sees Salvin's arched entrance surmounted by the arms of Fownes Luttrell and Periam, a far more pedestrian entrance than its predecessor.

The Outer Hall, reached by a flight of stone steps, was the result of Salvin's removal of rooms known as the Little Parlour, the Steward's Room and various passages on different levels. To achieve this lofty hall, partition walls and a mezzanine floor above were taken down. Here the ceiling, coved on its narrow side, displays within its heavily-constructed rectangular compartments a nineteenth-century version of a Jacobean plasterwork design. The wall dividing this hall from the Inner Hall is pierced either side by two arches each the width of the intervening wall.

Before the advent of George Fownes Luttrell, the last Luttrell to make significant changes to the property had been Henry Fownes Luttrell (d. 1780). Henry Fownes was influenced by Neo-Palladianism and by Strawberry Hill Gothic, but nevertheless he retained the important elements of earlier years. For example, he retained George Luttrell's spider-web ceiling in the Inner Hall, and the seventeenth-century staircase, as would George Fownes Luttrell in the nineteenth century. Henry had also retained the Restoration doors, door-cases, entablatures, orders and segmental pediments of Francis and Mary Luttrell's doorways. His additions included a graceful eighteenth-century triple arcade whose columns echoed those of the eastern doorway. Salvin replaced this arcade with heavy-handed so-called medievalism and built a double arcade of ponderous solidity with a centre pier.

He also removed the bolection moulding which happily survives in the dining-room. To-day, the only survivors of the seventeenth century in this Inner Hall are the ceiling and the heraldic overmantel of 1589. This surmounts Salvin's 'feudal' chimney piece which he based loosely on a thirteenth-century design.

Henry Fownes Luttrell had followed the fashions of his time and was quite prepared to amalgamate styles, so that the Stuart glory of the castle, the Grand Staircase, received a window in the eighteenth-century Gothic-Revival taste. It was unforgivable that George Luttrell's Salvin saw fit, or was directed, to remove the Stuart doors and door-cases and the Corinthian columns from the Great Parlour and Inner Hall to an ignominious position down in the Billiard room, which had formerly been a kitchen. This woodwork was designed to create, with the exuberant plaster-work of the ceiling, a whole statement of the period. They were replaced with the fashion of the time: good-quality Victorian doors which sadly lacked the swagger of the Carolean period.

The small room leading from the Great Parlour, Salvin made into a serving room to cater for the requirements of those dining in the newly-named Dining Room. The ceiling of this room shared the same bold plaster-work and had originally been used as a room to which guests withdrew to play cards and no doubt wager large sums of money. By the second half of the eighteenth century this small room had become a library.

Salvin constructed a new range of offices between the north tower and the gateway of the Lower Ward. This gateway was the only survivor of the Mohun's castle and was erected in the thirteenth century by Reynold de Mohun. Now, in the nineteenth century, its massive doors, closed since 1761, were re-opened and a staircase was made behind it to give access to the Green Court.

Here the story of George Fownes Luttrell comes full circle with that of the first Luttrell, Sir Hugh Luttrell (d. 1428), who came to Dunster to celebrate Christmas in 1404. It was this Sir Hugh who built the Gatehouse, completed in 1425. It was then divided into two distinct parts by a transverse wall with apparently no communication between the parts, and had upper rooms. In 1765, Henry Fownes Luttrell had had these rooms remodelled and employed Thomas Hall, his surveyor, to carry out the work. Hall also renewed the roof line and built two polygonal towers to flank the entrance which contained a Late Perpendicular doorway. Finally, George, needing a Tenant's Hall, had the floors levelled and the transverse walls and upper rooms removed.

ENDNOTES

1   Friar: N.D.H. 12; Merchant: L.H.D. 178
2   Lyte: H.D. Part I 333/4
3   Hancock: P.C.P. 163. In 1805 there was an 'Old Castle Inn' in Dunster. In 1802, and probably earlier, there were 13 inns in the borough. (see Lyte: H.D. Part I, 265)
4   Lyte: H.D. Part I 334
5   Ibid. 377
6   Ibid. 293
7   Ibid. Part II 332 Notes 3 and 4
8   Ibid. 331
9   Ibid. 311
10 Ibid. Part I 269
11 The right of this gift passed to him when the benefice composed of the parishes of Dunster, Carhampton and Withycombe was created in the 1980s.
12 Lyte: H.D. Part I 269
13 Ibid.
14 Ibid. 262/268
15 Ibid. 262
16 Ibid. 264
17 The temporary shambles must have been for Minehead since those of Dunster were retained continuously until 1825.
18 Lyte H.D. Part I 264
19 Ibid. 266
20 Ibid.
21 Ibid. 268
22 Ibid.
23 Ibid. 272/3 Note 1 273
24 In 1857 'the Board of Trade explicitly admitted the title of the late John Fownes Luttrell to an unclaimed wreck washed ashore between the eastern boundary of the parish of Lillstock and the stream dividing the counties of Devon and Somerset…See Lyte: H.D. Part I, 295 for more details of 'right of wreck'.
25 Merchant: L.H.D. 178
26 The second hatchment is that of Alexander Luttrell (1705-1737).
27 Merchant: L.H.D. 178.
28 Ibid. 181
29 Letter from Mr G.W. Charter to Edward Chalinor of 5 Brick Court, Middle Temple.
30 Hancock: D.C.P 133/5
31 Ibid. 155
32 Ibid. 164
33 Ibid.
34 Ibid. 165/6/7

35   i.e. the outbreak of the Napoleonic War (1805-1814) and the resultant rise in food prices

36   Hancock D.C.P. 167

37   cf. a letter from Mr William Hamper, sent to Mr Urban, the editor of *Gentleman's Magazine*, 6th June 1808, which mentions 'my friend , Rev. George Henry Leigh of Ellicombe, the worthy curator of Dunster.

38   Hancock: D.C.P. 189

39   Lyte: H.D. Part II 418/19; Hancock: D.C.P. 82

40   Watson: R of G III (1760-1815) 44

41   Ibid.43

42   Hancock: D.C.P. 189

43   Ibid.77

44   Ibid.190

45   Ibid.

46   Ibid. Presumably by this is meant his inclusion in the prayers for the Royal family.

47   Ibid.

48   Somerset Record Office. D/P/DU.4/1/1. 1847–61.

49   Churchwardens' fees appear as 10*s* in the 1858.9 and 1861/2 accounts.

50   Dodd: S. D.C.   92

51   This demolition may have taken place prior to Salvin's arrival since neither his plans nor his correspondence with George Fownes Luttrell allude to it. A letter dated 19 September 1868, from Sir Peregrine Palmer Acland refers to 'where the old chapel stood'. See Dodd: S.D.G., 99 (Note 30).

52   Dodd: D.C.G. 28. I am indebted to Dudley Dodd for information from his extensive paper 'Salvin at Dunster Castle' supplied by the Somerset Local Studies Library, Taunton.

53   Lyte: H.D. Part II 381

54   Ibid. 378/9

CHAPTER FIVE

THE VICTORIAN RESTORATION
of ST GEORGE'S CHURCH I

The Benefice of Dunster in the Late Nineteenth Century

The Rev. R. Utten Todd, who was to play a major role in the Victorian restoration of the church, had been appointed 'Curate and chaplain of the Old Priory of Dunster', on 8 April 1872. Prebendary Hancock provides some details regarding the benefice at this time:

> The benefice received small augmentations in land from time to time; and the late Mr Todd found, on his induction to the living, that a part of his income was drawn from lands lying in no less than five parishes, viz., Old Cleeve, Treborough, East Anstey in Devon, Glastonbury and Meare. The diocesan surveyor of the time, Mr Whitehead, endeavoured to survey these lands in 1872, but found it almost impossible to determine the boundaries of the portions of land in Glastonbury and Meare. The farms of Blackwell, in Treborough and Carhampton, consisted of a farmhouse and one cottage, about forty-five acres of meadow and arable, and three acres of wood. It was purchased in 1762, and the purchase money was made up as follows: Q.A.B. £400, Mrs Sara Townsend £100, Pyncombe Charity £100. The inconvenience of such scattered holdings was of course very great.[1]

With regard to Treborough, it is interesting that a barn situated at Golsoncott, sheds and linhays near the barn; a small cottage on the Blackwell Farm lands at Treborough, and a barn and cattle stalls were all occupied by Amos Tudball: the name so much associated with St George's Church, as the family of Tudball served as churchwardens and bell-ringers for many years. (Peter Tudball is still a bell-ringer).

Taxes were payable on the parishes of Meare and Glastonbury amounting to £1 13s 9d. Hancock also refers to the stipend of the vicar. 'The owner of Dunster Castle for the time being pays the vicar of Dunster in the February of each year the sum of £20.' He observes that ' the origin of the payment, which appears to be of great antiquity, is unknown.'[2]

In 1871-2 the Luttrells built a house for the vicar and his family near the dovecote of the former priory, to the design of P.J. St Aubyn, who was the architect responsible later for many of the fine Edwardian villas in Minehead.

The schools erected in 1871 were also to the designs of Piers St Aubyn. This family had ancient connections with Dunster. A Reynold de Mohun, an ancestor of the Mohuns of Cornwall and a younger brother of the last male de Mohun of Dunster, John de Mohun V (d. 1322), had married a Joan St Aubyn.[3] In the eighteenth century, Lancelot St Albyn/Aubyn, was in 1743 receiver of the rents and in 1747, a John St Aubyn was the agent for the Luttrell estate.[4]

Work on the erection of the residence for the vicar, the Priory (now Priory Court), started in 1872, and the property, valued at £3,000 in March 1873, was handed over by George Fownes Luttrell to the Ecclesiastical Commissioners in 1874. In consideration of the increased value of the benefice, they arranged to pay, 'a perpetual annuity of £50 to the incumbent of the living of Dunster and to his successors to meet the benefaction of the house and premises which had been offered in favour of the cure'.

The history of the benefice from the early eighteenth century is as follows. In 1717 the patron of the benefice was Sir Hugh Stewkley, a descendant of the Hugh Stewkley who was the first lay rector of Dunster after the Dissolution of the Monasteries. The benefice then passed into the hands of the Lords Stawel of Cothelstone and Wootton Courtenay. On the death of the last Lord Stawel in 1825, the advowson, or right to appoint the vicar, became invested in his only daughter and heiress, Lady Sherborne. It was sold by her trustees to John Fownes Luttrell who died in 1857.[5]

The Priory, known from Feb. 1879 as the Rectory, included the glebelands to the north-east; the orchard and kitchen garden to the west of the glebe-lands, and the site of the present rectory and garden. The houses which bear the inscription 'Vine Cottage 1833' are shewn on the 1874 plan as Area Cottage. Behind this cottage and on the south side of the present rectory drive were a coach house, harness room, stalls, loose boxes and a large coach house.

In the conveyance of the necessary land, dated 12.1.1874, George Fownes Luttrell Esq. undertook to grant the Ecclesiastical Commissioners:

> All that piece of land containing 1a 1r 20p[6] or thereabouts situate in the Parish of Dunster in the County of Somerset being part of two closes of land called respectively "The Priory Orchard" and "The Priory Green" and numbered respectively 276 and 266 on the Tithe Commutation Map of the said Parish of Dunster Together with the Dwellinghouse standing thereon or on some part thereof known as "Priory House" Which said piece of land expressed to be hereby conveyed is bounded on the East and South East by a public road called the Priory Road, and on all other sides by other property belonging to me ...

All this land was given to be the site for a parsonage or house of residence with garden and glebe and road leading to it for the Vicar or Incumbent for the time being of the Parish of Dunster. The deed conveying the land was duly sent to the Registry of the Diocese of Bath and Wells by 20 January 1874.

George Luttrell now turned his attention to the problem of the scattered church holdings, instructing his solicitor T. Ponsford to enquire of the Inclosure Commissioners whether his proposal of taking over the various pieces of land, and transferring to the benefice some of his own tithes in exchange, would be allowed by the regulations.

The Inclosure Office replied on 6 December 1877, two days later, that there was 'no objection in principle to the proposed Exchange of the Tithe Rent Charge for land belonging to the living of Dunster and the case is not affected by the fact that Mr Luttrell is the Patron of the Living'. So an arrangement was made between the patron of the benefice of Dunster, i.e. George Fownes Luttrell, and the incumbent, the Rev. R.U.Todd, an arrangement sanctioned by the bishop of the diocese and the Ecclesiastical Commissioners.

The great tithes were handed over to the benefice in exchange for glebe lands. The effect of this was that the benefice became a Rectory instead of a Perpetual Curacy, which it had been up to this date. The incumbent became Rector instead of Vicar (by courtesy). The great tithes were valued at £180 a year, and there was also an annual grant of £50 a year from the Ecclesiastical Commissioners which was made from 1874 when Mr Luttrell had presented the Priory House and grounds to the Benefice.

The gross annual value of the living of Dunster became £30 a year, with a Rectory house and grounds. (Five years earlier, in 1874, the gross value had been £120 with no house.) This was a change of great importance and meant much had been done by Mr Luttrell to improve the temporal position of the Church. (Up to this time Dunster had been one of the 4,000 Beneficies of less value than £200 a year.) The Rev. R. Utten Todd announced in the Parish Magazine for February 1879, that in future the house hitherto known as The Priory would bear its proper name of Rectory.

The Condition of the Church of St George in 1872

When he became vicar of Dunster in 1872, the Rev. R. Utten Todd had inherited a church in great need of repair. J.C.Buckler, a well-known architect, visited Dunster in 1838. He had been called in to examine the fabric of the church and to submit a report on its condition. He found that:

> With regard to the eastern part, or "old church"...the walls were "shattered and infirm in places" that the roof was very defective and covered with, "a thick coat of moss", that the mullions and the tracery of the windows were "dilapidated and ruinous", and that the floor, "stripped of its pavement", was "strewn with relics of canopied monuments and various kinds of rubbish". In rainy weather, water lay in a pool in the northern transept. Proceeding westward, he found that "the recessed arch at the back of the altar" was a "resceptacle of rubbish". The windows in the north aisle were decayed. The piers in the nave although structurally safe were far from upright. The gallery at the west end blocked out the light and gave to that part of the church, "the gloomiest of a crypt". All the doors admitted "intolerable draughts". The pavement, composed of fragments of stone, bricks and tiles, was "in the worst possible condition", dangerous by reason of its unevenness. Many ancient oaken seats "elabo-

rately and finely ornamented "were concealed by later wood work" the most promiscuous unseemly and uncomfortable assemblage of pews that can be met with".

The priory church had fallen victim to the degeneracy of this age of drunken debauchery and bawdiness strewn as it was with fragments of fallen masonry and broken windows it was ever open to moss-inducing elements. Shut off from the parish church by walls, its only use was the subterranean vault which received the remains of the deceased Luttrells.[7]

Buckler's vigorous language had its effect. Many of his recommendations were followed. The communion-table seems to have been set back a little, although not moved under the eastern end of the tower, as he had proposed. A large screen with glass panels was put up immediately behind it, with similar screens put up to separate the aisles from the transepts. A rather pointless arch was built to connect the two Norman jambs at the western pier of the tower, while a small vestry was formed from the external turret which formerly gave access to the loft over the main screen. But in the 'old church' (i.e. the Priory Church) only the most necessary repairs were undertaken.

The still appalling state of St George's Church, Dunster in 1842 was recorded in the *Ecclesiologist*:[8]

> The fine Cross church of St George, Dunster, Somerset has been treated in the most wicked manner. The nave is screened off for weekly service. The Chancel [*of the Priory Church*] has no pavement whatever and it is used only as a burial ground for the family at the neighbouring Castle. Within a few years lime used to be burned in the Transept. But, as the garrulous person who keeps the keys of the church informed visitors with infinite satisfaction, a very great deal of good has been done lately: the flooring of the Nave has been raised; and the area fitted throughout with deal pues; the open oak seats, said to be finely carved, having been sent up to the Castle: a new nave arch has been introduced, apparently for the purpose of being blocked up. A painting said to be good, which stood in the former arch, was sent up to the Castle.
>
> Lime is no longer burned in the Lantern, and the Font, before painted, has been covered with a fine sort of rough caste, and now looks something like sandstone; except on the side next to the wall, where the red and white colouring still remains. There are still in this church two particularly rich Roodscreens, and it would appear from the one which forms a division in the nave, that for a very long time this part only has been used for public service.

A Decision to Restore the Church is Taken

In 1875 a complete restoration of the church, with Mr G.E. Street as the architect, was instigated by George Fownes Luttrell and the vicar, the Rev. Utten Todd. The final cost of the restoration would be £11,063. 3s, of which Mr George Fownes Luttrell contributed £9,295. 14s.

The previous year, in August 1874, the Rev. Utten Todd had informed his parishioners that a fund would be started to pay for the proposed restoration. Besides paying for the repairs to the Priory Church at the east end, Mr George Fownes Luttrell would also bear the greater portion of that required for the Parish Church.[9] However, the vicar hoped that all the members of the parish would contribute what money they could. He proposed a monthly offertory in aid of the restoration fund on the 3rd Sunday of every month. By March 1875 the total sum in the Fund amounted to £794 7s 6d, including two anonymous donations of £100 and £50 from parishioners.

On 23 April 1875, St George's Day, the first public meeting of the Parishioners to consider the proposal for extending the work of restoration was held. The meeting took place in the Reading Room and was well attended. These resolutions were unanimously agreed:

> It was proposed by G.F.Luttrell, Esq.and seconded by J.Gatchell, Esq. that this meeting deems it expedient that the Parish Church be restored according to the plans prepared by Mr Street.
>
> It was proposed by Mr George Risdon and seconded by Mr James Staddon, that a subscription list be opened for such as are disposed to assist in the work.

The vicar warned that:

> The total cost of the restoration is estimated at £6,600 but this includes the warming of the church throughout. Of this sum £4,600 goes to the restoration of the old church, or Monk's Chapel, and the transepts, and all that part of the Parish Church westwards as far as the Skreen. The remaining £2,000 is reserved for what has to be done between the Skreen and the west door. This part of the work comprises chiefly the restoration of the roof, the straightening of the pillars and the substitution of low and open seats for the present high and uncomfortable pews.

By April 1875, a long list of subscribers had been drawn up. Gifts noted ranged from £1 to two donations of £400, from George Luttrell and from the vicar's brother, the Rev. J. Utten Todd. The amount raised in the church collections amounted to £107 13s 2d, with a further £3 6s 7¼d from a box in the church porch.

Preparations for work on the western, parish portion of the church began in May 1875. In June 1875, the Rev. R. Utten Todd reported in the Parish Magazine:

> On Sunday, May 9th, the Sunday after Ascension Day, Divine Service was held for the last time in the Parish Church, as we have all known it. It now presents a strangely altered appearance. The Skreen has been carefully boarded up, the organ removed, the high deals which covered the old pews have been taken away and much of the roof on the inside has been laid bare.

Gifts for specific items from non-parishioners had also been received, to the value of £70 50s 0d. The Parish School Room had been licensed by the Bishop of the Diocese for the administration of the Holy Sacrament, the Solemnization of Matrimony and other rites of the Church.

In August 1875 the Rev. R. Utten Todd was able to report that the work on the western part of the church had begun:

> Before this meets the eyes of most of our readers, they will have seen for themselves the work of restoration has begun. The contractors are Hale and Sons of Salisbury; the sum mentioned in the contract is £3,310[10] and the time agreed upon for the completion of the work is 'on or before August 31. 1876'.

This was a remarkable accurate forecast, since the church would reopen on 13 September 1876. The Rev. Todd explained that restoring the parish church would cost more than the £2,000. As yet, they had little more than £1,640, including the sums promised as well as received. It was reported in September 1875 that a further £103 8s 0d had been contributed. R.J.S.Todd Esq. gave a second donation of £100, which it was proposed to devote some portion to a special object.

The Work of Restoration Begins

The Faculty (official permission) to restore and improve the parish church of Dunster, headed 'Diocese of Bath and Wells from the Lord Bishop of Bath and Wells to the Churchwardens of Dunster', is dated 11 May 1875 and is a most impressive parchment document which can be seen at the Somerset Record Office, Taunton.

It permits Joseph Gatchell and Charles Henry Samson, the Church-wardens 'to restore and improve the said Parish Church and for that purpose to make and perform the several alterations improvements and other works particularly specified and described in the said Schedule'. The Schedule detailed the extensive alterations and repairs necessary, and was signed by the Registrar, William Doré.

The architect chosen by George Fownes Luttrell to oversee the church restoration was George Edmund Street. R.A. The actual work was done by men regularly employed on the manor under the able supervision of Mr C.H. Samson, the churchwarden.

G.E.Street was one of the most eminent architects of his day. While working on Dunster Church, he was also working on numerous other projects both great and small, such as designing an altar cloth for St Paul's, Rome; planning new churches as far apart as Lausanne and Barnsley; and restoring many other medieval churches like that at Dunster. He later expended much loving care on the nave of Bristol cathedral where he also built the western towers (1877) and was also involved in the 'restoration' of the south transept of York Minster (1875-80). His most celebrated secular work is the Law Courts in London, begun in 1866.

The principal craftsmen involved in the restoration were listed in the detailed report on the re-opening of the church in the *West Somerset Free Press* of 13 September 1876:

Messrs Clayton and Bell of London. Windows and Triptych.

Mr Fred Drake of Exeter. Windows.

Mr W. Godwin of Lugwardine Works, near Hereford. Tiles and floor covering.

Messrs Haden of Trowbridge. Heating apparatus.

Messrs Hales and Sons, builders of Salisbury (work in parish church).

Mr Harry Hems of Exeter (Principal parts of carving, i.e. bench ends, stone carving of pulpit and restoration of monuments.

Messrs Robinson of London. Screens and stalls in Priory Church.

Messrs John Warner and Sons. Bells.

The churchwarden, Mr C.H. Samson, arranged the medieval tiles in the chapel now known as the Mohun Chantry Chapel, and a Mr Hill laid them. Messrs Gillett and Bland of West Croydon replaced the old Parish Clock and Chimes. Mr J.B. Webber of Dunster carried out the repair of the main screen.

The cost of the restoration was about £12,000, of which Mr George Luttrell contributed nearly £10,000. Other generous gifts were received from Rev. J.U. Todd, the vicar's brother, and from people connected in some way with the Luttrell family, such as Mr Gatchell, whose daughter Lucy had married Alexander Fownes Luttrell (b. 1754, d 1816). Lady Hood, George Luttrell's mother-in-law, was also generous, as were Mr and Mrs Bosanquet (George Luttrell's sister Mary Anne had married Henry Anstey Bosanquet).

Roofs in the Parish Church

The general instructions for the roofs specified: 'Roofs to be stripped and carefully cleaned of all whitewash, nails, paint etc. All firring up to be removed. Decayed and defective timbers to be made good with new oak of same shape and scantling as the old work. New plates to be inserted wherever old are decayed or not of Oak.' Only the finest oak and fir were to be used.

Before the 1875/6 restoration the nave roof, like the Priory Church roof, was plastered and only the ridge rib, the purlins and the main braces were exposed; the common brace being covered with plaster, as can be seen in John Buckler's drawing of 1842. When the roof was repaired, traces were found of the fire that had occurred some eighty years earlier, started by workmen repairing the lead work. The contractor was told to 'take his own dimensions of the several Works and to make his new Works fit the old Work in every respect'. All decayed timber would have to be replaced, and towards the east end in particular, many of the rafters would have to be renewed and properly fastened with oak pins.

Regarding the West Gable and the gable crosses, the workers had to reset the coping and make all good with copper cramps, and fix new crosses and new saddlestones of approved wrought stone, carefully preserving the Gable Cross on the West Gable.

The south aisle was to be restored to its original flat-roofed design, while new battlements were to be added to the restored west end of the aisle. This flat roof must have been in existence before 1780, as the south aisle is shown with a pitched roof in contemporary illustrations.

Internally the south-aisle roof received special attention: the carpenter and joiner were specifically enjoined to treat the interior coffered roof of c. 1450 with great care. (In about 1850, the plastered roof of the south aisle in the Priory Church had begun to fall in. So Thomas Hole of Dunster had 'carved many of the existing bosses in the roof, which he copied from the old and decayed ones which had been taken down'.)[11] Between the chancel and the south aisle a new plate, supported on masonry from the walls, was to be introduced to take the feet of the chancel rafters above the aisle rafters. The north aisle was said to be 'in fair condition' but a new oak plate, properly supported from the wall, was to be inserted to receive the end rafters.

Porch; Doors ; Stonewalling

Work on the porch appears to have been completed by July 1876, as the Vicar, the Rev. R. Utten Todd then noted in the Parish Magazine: 'another great improvement will be found in the Porch on the south side of the church which has had a new oak roof and two new stone benches'.[12]

Throughout the church new oak doors were to be provided, copied from old models and preserving all the locks and furniture on the present doors for re-use.

As for the interior walls, the Masons, Bricklayers and Wallers were instructed to: 'remove all defective stones and carefully substituting others. Rake out joints and repoint with care where necessary ... the face of the stone to be preserved & not plastered over with mortar'.

The original building had been built with the knowledge that the stonework would be plastered and therefore it was not necessary to attain a high standard. Now the Victorians in their desire to uphold the 'truth to nature' theory revealed poor work which had to be raked out and pointed. Before Victorian times rubble stone walls inside a church – and sometimes outside too – were always rendered. In earlier times lime had been burnt in the church for making mortar.

The removal of the plaster in 1876/7 revealed a Norman doorway in the west wall of the nave. The Rev. R. Utten Todd wrote in October 1875 in the Parish Magazine: 'It is a fragment of the church built some 800 years ago by William de Mohun, the great lord of Dunster, in the reign of William, the Conqueror'. (In fact, since the first specific reference to a religious house at Dunster occurs in 1177, it is more likely that the actual work started in the reign of Henry II (1154-89).) The Rev. Todd continued:

> It must have been built into the wall ... about 400 years ago when a small west doorway[13] the one now in existence [*i.e 1875*] was made and when the church was in all points altered and re-built [*c. 1500*].

By April 1876, the vicar was able to report that the Norman doorway had been 'capitally restored'.

The Organ

The organ presented to the church by the Rev. Thomas Fownes Luttrell in 1868 had stood in front of the west door. It had to be moved as part of the restoration. In August 1876 Messrs Bryceson set up the organ in North Transept. Water power (50 lbs. to the square inch) would be used to work the bellows. In 1878 the instrument was insured for £300.

The Tower

Not a great deal appears to have been done to the tower itself. No work was needed on the exterior at this time, though it would have to be repointed in 1884. Inside, the steps were repaired and the piers of the tower and the western end were faced with wrought sandstone ashlar. The 'Skeleton Arch', which used to rise over the Norman shafts in the western part of the Tower, was removed, as it was not part of the building. Under the belfry a foundation 2½ feet high was made to receive the tile pavement for the floor of the sanctuary.

Celure;[14] Flooring of Ringing Chamber and Belfry

Looking up from the sanctuary of the parish altar one sees the carved celure, worked by Mr John Webber to the design of Mr G.E. Street, whose personal involvement in every detail was a hallmark of his work. New floors were installed in the belfry and ringing chamber.

Partitions And Screens

After Buckler's damning report of 1838, a large screen with glass panels was put up immediately behind the communion table. Similar screens were put up to separate the aisles from the transepts, which became cut off.[15] At the eastern end of the transepts, both north and south, there were brick walls, as Samson's working plan, made prior to the 1875/6 restoration, showed.

The specification for restoration instructed the builders to 'remove and clear away partitions between chancel and tower and transepts at W. end of chancel aisles'. All the old fragments of these screens were to be carefully preserved and re-used. Open wooden screens were made by Robinson of London to divide the chancel of the priory church from the lateral chapels north and south. Stalls, like those of a private chapel, were set up in the chancel, and open screens were made to divide it from the lateral chapels, that on the north being converted into a vestry.[16] A partly closed screen was to be set up between the tower and the chancel, behind the choir stalls. One of the partitions which was removed from its former position between the eastern piers of the crossing tower was the ancient choir screen. It was placed, after the removal of the wall, under the 'shouldered arch' in the south transept and received a nineteenth-century cresting. This partition, and the screen between the north transept and the vestry, act to-day as parclose screens to the pre-Reformation chantry chapel of St Lawrence and to the Lady Chapel, making clear the demarcation between the Priory Church of the Luttrell family and the Parish Church.

The Rev. Todd wrote in the Parish Magazine for February 1877:

> Since Christmas last, Mr Robinson's workmen have been busy putting up the Skreen in the Priory Church, and fixing the stalls at the western end of it ... The skreens are of the same design as those at the sides of the sanctuary, and are very light and graceful. The stalls are twelve in number; four on the north side , and four are on the south: the four at the western end are canopied, and are divided by one of considerable dimensions, intended for the Priest who says the service.

This feature was explained by Dr Eeles: 'Owing to lack of space between the parish altar and the western end of these stalls it was impossible to make a doorway in the centre of the stalls at the west end in the usual way, and Street adopted the Spanish use of a central bishop's throne in this position making it the stall for the principal officiant.'[17]

The main rood screen, which stretches across the whole width of the nave and aisles, also received attention. When it was made in 1498/9, the main rood screen was an open screen as we see it today. However, some time before 1875/6, it had been filled in, for in 1808 William Hamper had written, 'the upper part is painted white and yellow, and has a very good general effect'.[18] The specification reads:

> Open out the Rood screen by clearing away all the filling in between tracery and uprights, removing all whitewash stains and guarding with great care any indications of old painting that may be discovered ... repair the ancient screen between the west portion of the nave and the Chancel and Chancel aisles in the eastern portion of it.

The repairs to the eastern face are very evident in the tracery which includes a representation of St. James. This is Victorian work, a copy by Mr J. B. Webber of Dunster, of an earlier head. In 1878 the restored screen was insured for £300. It is described by Preb. Hancock as follows:

> This screen is 11ft high and of fourteen bays. The canopy which supported the rood is of a very rich description. We find the Altar of the Cross in Dunster Church mentioned in a will as early as the time of Edward II (r. 1307-27) and in various later wills. This altar no doubt stood in the customary position, viz. on the right hand side of the chancel arch.

The Lucy mass[19] had been celebrated daily since 1276 'at the altar of the Holy Cross ... commonly called the Roodloft'. The broad roodloft was between the western piers of the crossing tower; the altar of the Holy Cross, was on top of it and approached by the still existing door. In 1498/9 a new roodloft was erected to the west, in its present position, thus forming a parish chancel, following a dispute between the parishioners of Dunster and the Prior. The chancel or presbytery was handed over to the prior and monks to form a separate and distinct church for their private use ('the Priory Church'). The high altar of the parishioners was moved westwards, to stand on or near the site occupied by the altar of St James.[20]

The medieval altar of St James was against the south pier of the crossing tower and its exact position is marked by a cross and a bracket in stone. However, although a site had now been found for their high altar, the parish priest and the laity of Dunster were left without a chancel. The patrons of the benefice, as the Benedictine order had done in other places, decided to shut off a portion of the nave to form one. 'So the beautiful screen, so singularly perfect, was erected across the nave, and the newel staircase to reach its loft built'.[21] (This staircase was later blocked off.) The screen must have been finished by 1533/38, when the parishioners sought the appointment of a secular priest to say the Lucy mass from the new roodloft.

The choir screen had remained between the eastern piers of the crossing until 1875/6. The earlier rood screen between the western piers of the tower and the choir screen had marked the division between the monk's chancel, their stalls and their high altar, the altar of St George. Today's main screen does not therefore, as is sometimes thought, divide the priory church from the parish church but was merely placed twenty-five feet to the west in order to form a parish chancel.

During the Restoration this screen was thoroughly cleaned, with four or five coats of later paint besides varnish removed. At 54 feet long, the rood screen is likely to be one of the longest of any church. Dr Eeles believed it to be of a local variety chiefly associated with Devonshire.[22] Professor Pevsner agreed with this diagnosis:

> The best rood screens of wood are in the W [of Somerset], and they belong to the Devon series, with both the varieties of tracery represented which are usual there, that where in each division a middle mullion runs up into the apex of the arch and that where two sub-arches divide the main arch. The best examples are at and round Dunster (Dunster 1498, Minehead, Bicknoller, Carhampton, etc). What is in other parts of the county cannot compare with them...[23]

Kenneth Wickham, in *Churches of Somerset*, agreed that the Dunster screen was of the Devonshire type, and thought it 'the greatest of them all'.[24]

The Priory Church

In view of the fact that the Priory Church had been re-built in the thirteenth century in the Early English style, it was perhaps, the happiest of choices to have employed the services of George Edmund Street R.A., that devotee of early thirteenth-century architecture, which he considered one of the very best periods of national architecture. The present Priory Church had formed the chancel of the original Norman church, probably once terminated by an apse. During the Early English period this portion of the church appears to have been entirely remodelled, and further changes were made during the Perpendicular Period.[25]

The specification for restoration included taking down and rebuilding the whole of the east wall and parts of the north and south walls, re-using the existing stones as far as possible and returning them to their original places. Other work included levelling the ground and underpinning the old walls; cleaning and repairing windows, arches, etc.; restoring the sedilia and the piscina; lowering the east gable to its old line, and preparing the chancel floor and steps for new tiles. The Perpendicular east window was to be removed and the Early English lancet windows, of which traces still remained, to be reinstated instead.

According to the report of the church restoration in the *West Somerset Free Press,* the the Priory chancel was completely renovated: 'nearly the whole of the walls have been pulled down and re-built with sandstone from the Lodge-rocks quarry ...the roof is of oak, and the greater part is new'.[26]

During the restoration the stone altar now in the Priory Church was discovered. In the Parish Magazine for October 1875, the rector wrote that:

> ... the stone used to lie in the north aisle of the Parish Church bearing on it the inscription relating to the burial of members of the Poyntz family, with a date 1583; it was originally an altar slab. ... in the reign of Edward VI an order was issued for removing stone altars. [and another] in the second year of Queen Elizabeth (1559). ... These altar slabs were then frequently used in the pavement of the church and as monumental stones. This appears to have been the case with the slab taken up in the north aisle with the inscription relating to the Poyntz family upon it. From the fact that it is bevelled on only three sides and has the usual five crosses on its surface, there can be little doubt that it was originally one of the altar slabs in the Church.

By April 1876 the rector was able to report that the altar slab had been restored to its original use as an altar in the Priory Church. The inscription was copied onto a brass plate set up in the north aisle where the slab had marked the burial of Edward Poyntz, who died in 1583, and his family. The altar slab was placed on five columns of Blue Anchor alabaster worked by John Long.[27] The altar steps, also of alabaster, had been added by August 1876, though some more work in the same material remained to be done.

Unfortunately the Victorians, as the author discovered when she clambered under this altar to read the inscription, had plastered over it: the neat rectangular *mensa* now bears only the crosses on its upper surface.

According to the *West Somerset Free Press* report, the new altar also had an alabaster super altar and reredos. The latter is not visible today, but the specification does say 'provide the sum of £125 for chancel, altar and reredos'. Also, in a copy of the insurance policy dated 26.11.1878, the reredos in the Priory Church is insured for £100.

The altar slab was likely to have been the altar slab of the chantry of the Holy Trinity at the west end of the north aisle, the aisle in which Edward Poyntz was buried. Edward Poyntz was a Roman Catholic. It is therefore possible that the altar slab was reversed to hide its give-away dedicatory crosses and used as a monumental slab in 1583 when Edward died. A second possibility is that when side altars were demolished in the first year of Edward VI's reign (r. 1547-53), the altar of the Holy Trinity was saved, reversed and set in the floor and when Edward Poyntz died thirty-five years later, the stone was inscribed.

Parish Altar, Triptych, Frontals for Parish and Priory Altars

The Victorians, including G.E. Street, placed enormous emphasis on the importance of the altar, thanks partly to the influence of the Ecclesiological Society (formed for the study of church architecture), which believed that the one fundamental need in any church was to find the most dynamic context in which to present the body of Christ (i.e., the sacrament of the Eucharist).

This 'most dynamic context' was achieved at Dunster by the raising of the parish altar steps (of Babbacombe marble); by rich altar frontals, and above all by the very fine triptych behind the altar. The altar was also moved under the eastern arch of the tower, sixteen feet to the east of its former position. As required by the schedule 'a moveable Communion Table of wood in the Chancel to be formed under the Central Tower' was provided. The altar table would be covered by richly-embroidered altar frontals (see below).

The Triptych

Concerning the triptych, Dr Eeles felt it was among the few really good nineteenth-century reredoses in existence. The central subject, the Transfiguration of Our Lord, was comparatively rare in Western Christendom.[28]

The triptych is indeed fine and is unusual in that the two outer wings are themselves divided into two hinged panels, the inner one rectangular and the outer one arched, flanking the inner central panel. In 1878 this triptych was insured for £100.

£150 was provided for the choir, altar and reredos. The firm of Clayton and Bell was responsible for not only the triptych, but also for many of the Victorian windows in Dunster Church. John Richard Clayton (1827-1913) was an illustrator who became closely associated with Rossetti, John Ruskin, and the Pre-Raphaelites. In 1848/9 he worked under Anthony Salvin, the architect who was responsible for the 1870 alterations at Dunster Castle. In this role he was Clerk of the Works at Wells Cathedral and it was there that he first became interested in medieval glass. Through Salvin, Clayton most probably met Sir George Gilbert Scott, who took him on as an assistant to be engaged in architectural drawing & figurative designs.

Clayton became the partner of Alfred Bell (1832-95) in his successful stained-glass studio in Regent St. Alfred Bell had been introduced to Sir George Gilbert Scott, who invited Bell to come to London, and like Clayton, to join him as an assistant in his London firm. Bell was soon encouraged by Scott to give up his architectural interest and to devote his talents to the design of stained glass windows. Here the meeting of three of the great names associated with Dunster Church took place, for in Scott's office around 1848 George Edmund Street was also a pupil assistant there.

The actual design of the triptych in St George's church could have been Clayton's idea, since early on in his career he had designed and carved St George and the Dragon atop the Westminster School Memorial, and on the Dunster triptych the patron saint, St George with his dragon also appears.

The Altar Frontals

To return to the importance of the altar frontals in Victorian architecture: from the *Memoirs of G.E. Street*, it is clear that Street agreed with this view, as his son writes:

> From the very commencement of his career as an as an architect or a student of architecture, he had taken a special interest in old church embroidery and had devoted himself with a remarkable success to designing embroidery patterns, aided greatly by the exertions of his sister whose skill in reproducing his designs was well known and did much to make them appreciated.[29]

Imagine then the author's excitement when she discovered that Mr Street had apparently designed an altar cloth for our parish church at Dunster. In a letter dated 18 July 1876 to the Rev. R. Utten Todd, written from Mr Street's office in Cavendish Square, the measurements of the planned altar under the tower were given, along with the remark that '*He is designing an altar cloth* [*my italics*] for this (the parish) altar.' Hoping to identify this altar frontal, I was able to find two amongst our church collection which were undoubtedly Victorian and of the highest quality.

The one used at the parish altar was in a good condition, still retaining its original super (upper) frontal of purplish/red-coloured velvet. It is of a lighter colour than the super frontal and is of ribbed silk.

The second altar frontal was presumably intended for the high altar, the altar of St George, in the Priory Church. It was of the same purplish/red-coloured velvet as the parish super frontal. (This was a colour much admired by the Victorians.) It had splendid orphreys (bands of rich embroidery) and fringing. The matching super frontal was embroidered with appliquéd motifs in silk and metal threads.

Both, in my opinion, could be Street embroideries, so I sent a photograph to the Victoria and Albert Museum. Mrs Parry, Research Assistant at the

Department of Textile Furnishings and Dress, agreed that they were particularly fine embroideries:

> Both the Keeper of the Department, Santina Levey and I believe that they could all have been designed by G.E. Street. However, without specific evidence, such as a signed design, this cannot be proved indisputably.

Mrs Parry suggested that the woven orphreys on the high altar frontal were not original but a later addition. Referring to the parish altar frontal, she added: 'it is a pity that one of the frontals has been re-mounted on a plain fabric [*this would probably have been on a velvet ground*]'. A close inspection of the clearly original silk and metal appliquéd embroidery does not apparently reveal that it was re-instated on a new ground and there is no record of when, or if, the embroidery was re-mounted on the ribbed silk which appeared to the museum from the photograph to be 'a plain fabric'. If the original embroidery was re-instated on the ribbed silk, it was done to the highest degree of excellence. However, it is evident that the fringe is not Victorian and, in my opinion, is of 1930 vintage.

The Vicar's Warden, Mr Julian Luttrell, whose family had paid £60 for the altar frontal during the restoration, very kindly took both frontals to London and obtained a report from textile conservators.[30] In trying to definitely ascribe these altar frontals to G.E.Street, I wrote to Philippa Bassett, Senior Archivist of Birmingham Library Services, which, I had recently learnt, held archives of three firms which supplied furnishings and fittings to churches during the Victorian period, including the catalogues & pattern books of Jones and Willis, in some of which the photographs and drawings are identified with specific churches. (Street's son had noted in his *Memoirs of G.E.Street*, that some of his father's altar cloth designs still figured in the Jones and Willis catalogue.) The archivist replied that:

> The Jones & Willis collection includes four volumes described as catalogues of embroidery. They contain photographs almost exclusively of altar frontals, but there is no reference to Dunster, moreover, none of the photographs give any information about the designers of the item.[31]

The author believes both the parish and priory altar frontals were designed by the same person and thought it important to try to conserve the Priory Church frontal. (The Parish Church altar frontal did not need to be conserved and since it was thought not to be entirely Victorian, it would not attract a grant.)

In order to raise the necessary money, a Victorian Garden Party was held in the grounds of Priory Court on Saturday 30 June 1990. This, though sadly rained off, included a Victorian costume parade, stalls, croquet, and cream teas enjoyed to the accompaniment of the Watchet Town Band. The Exmoor II NADFAS Church Recorders' Group, the Mothers' Union, the bell-ringers, the Parochial Church Council and the parishioners generally are to be thanked for this great endeavour which resulted in a net profit of over £960, which was invested.

A grant of £500 was awarded by the Council for the Care of the Churches through the generosity of the Pilgrim Trust. The conditions attached to this award were that 'after conservation, the textiles should be stored in a suitable case to preserve them from damage caused by dust and light, and their use restricted to special occasions perhaps once or twice a year'. The colour, the Rector said, was liturgially appropriate to Lent and Advent, and it was my hope that the embroideries would be displayed on those occasions.

The cost of the work was estimated by the conservators[32] on 26.3.1990 to be £1,120. But a suitable display case had to be made first. An Architect's plan would be required before a Faculty for both the conservation and the display case could be considered. It was thought at the time that the additional cost of a proper Architect's plan and a display case would preclude the acceptance of the grant, especially as the cost of the conservation work was increased in January 1991. However, the Rector was able to negotiate the receipt of the grant from the Pilgrim Trust, so the work of conservation was able to proceed.

In May 1992, I wrote in the Parish Newsletter of how the money raised was being spent:

> ...the total receipts from the Victorian Garden Party were £960. 77 which, with the interest accumulated over the two years, reached the sum of £1,055. 71*p* of which £976.27 was contributed towards the cost of the conservation. Thus with the £500 [grant] the total cost was £1,476.27 and £75 has been reserved for the wooden supports in the Altar Frontal Box. The estimate in 1990 was £1,120 and, at that time there was therefore £340.77 available for a display case [*but this was never made*].

The author had been promised that the Frontal would be displayed on the Priory altar for Lent 1992 but it could not be fixed. It was taken back to the conservators and collected again in May 1992. In July 1992, it was discovered to be far too short. However, I had had had the entire specification copied and framed[33] and this was displayed, with the history of the embroidery illustrated by Mr Lancaster's photographs.[34]

Increased costs eventually precluded the purchase of a case. Thus the frontal and the super frontal will be housed in a wooden box and seen only on special occasions. The work was finally completed on 29 August 1992 and the Altar Frontal was finally placed on the Priory Altar for the first time during Advent 1992.[35]

Monuments

It was a remarkable feat that the Jacobean monument to Thomas and Margaret Luttrell and Joan Luttrell née Stewkley, now to be seen between the west and east windows in the south aisle was moved during the Victorian restoration. It was originally on the south wall of the Priory Church where it marked the burials in the family vault below of the Luttrells whose effigies lie upon it. To make room for it, the mural monument to Anne Luttrell, the wife of Francis Luttrell of Venn, had to be moved to its present position on the wall, west of the tomb. The restorers were instructed to carefully clean and re-polish the alabaster, and refix the repainted old iron railing round it. (These railings were probably those I discovered in the stoke hole, which were later disposed of.) Our illustration shows this monument in its original position, enclosed within the iron-railing.

Of the monument of Sir Hugh Luttrell (d 1428) and his wife Catherine Luttrell née Beaumont (d 1435) Lyte writes in 1909:

> A monument in memory of Sir Hugh Luttrell and his wife seems to have been erected, or commenced, on the north side of the chancel of Dunster church. Both these effigies …have been sadly mutilated in the course of the centuries, and it is very doubtful whether they occupy their original position. They now lie under a canopy carved in stone in an arched opening between the chancel and the little projecting sacristy [*now called the de Mohun Chantry Chapel*] which was almost rebuilt in the nineteenth century.
>
> The shields below them, likewise carved in stone, bear no arms; there is no inscription; and the whole structure, except the figures, may be an Easter Sepulchre of the time of Henry the Seventh.[36]

This monument was long thought to be that of Sir John Mohun and his wife, thanks to the antiquary John Leland, who tentatively suggested this was because of the garland round the knight's helmet.[37] This explains why the specification refers to the monument as 'the Mohun tomb':

> The old Mohun Monument North of Chancel to be taken down to the level of string under the East Window, and the stones of Canopy to be most carefully re-fixed in their old positions with a new parapet to detail of wrought stone … The Mohun Tomb to have the figures raised, and a new moulded and carved slab (similar to fragment still visible in Sacristy) to be provided and fixed. The sides of the Tomb below this slab to have tracery with shields to drawing somewhat like the remains of the panelling visible in the Sacristy.

There is one panel on the north side of the tomb chest which is obviously original. Finally specified is 'a new battlemented parapet to be fixed to the Canopy of this Tomb from details to be provided by the Architect'. This is another instance of Street's personal involvement with detail. The so-called 'battlemented parapet' is more correctly referred to by Lyte in *Dunster and its Lords* where he writes of 'open cresting' copied from a fragment found nearby. One of the carved cusps, c.1500, was found in the Priory Garden, the others were new.

In the 1808 illustration of the tomb chest in the *Gentleman's Magazine* there is no parapet to the canopy; the roof of the chapel is sloping and the

Mary Luttrell née Tregonwell Dunster Castle, N.T. By kind permission of the National Trust. G Lancaster

Colonel Francis Luttrell (d. 1690) Dunster Castle, N.T. By kind permission of the National Trust. G Lancaster

(Previous page) **Mary Luttrell, Lady Rooke,** probably by Michael Dahl
Kingston Lacy, N.T.
By kind permission of the National Trust. The Bankes Collection

(Left) **Dorothy Luttrell née Yard/Yarde** Dunster Castle, N.T.
By kind permission of the National Trust, Dunster Castle.
G. Lancaster

(Left) **Colonel Alexander Luttrell (d. 1711)** Dunster Castle, N.T.
By kind permission of the National Trust.
G. Lancaster

Alexander Luttrell (d. 1737) by Boit Court House, East Quantoxhead. By kind permission of the late Col. Sir Walter Luttrell. M. St J Hankin

Margaret Luttrell née Trevelyan Dunster Castle, N.T. By kind permission of the National Trust. G Lancaster

Hatchment for Colonel Alexander Luttrell (d. 1711) and his wife Dorothy Yarde
St George's Church.
By kind permission of the late Col. Sir Walter Luttrell
G. Lancaster

Hatchment for Alexander Luttrell (d. 1737) and his wife Margaret Trevelyan
St George's Church.
By kind permission of the late Col. Sir Walter Luttrell.
G. Lancaster

**Margaret Fownes
Luttrell née Luttrell**
Dunster Castle, N.T.
By kind permission
of the National
Trust.
G Lancaster

**Henry Fownes
Luttrell (d. 1780)**
Dunster Castle, N.T.
By kind permission
of the National
Trust.
G. Lancaster

**Hatchment for
Margaret Fownes
Luttrell**
St George's Church.
By kind permission of
the late Col. Sir
Walter Luttrell.
G Lancaster

**Hatchment for
Henry Fownes
Luttrell (d. 1780)**
St George's
Church.
By kind
permission of the
late Col. Sir
Walter Luttrell.
G. Lancaster

John Fownes
Luttrell (d. 1816)
by Opie
Court House,
East
Quantoxhead.
By kind
permission of the
late Col. Sir
Walter Luttrell.
M. St J. Hankin

Hatchment for
John Fownes
Luttrell (d.1816)
St George's
Church.
By kind
permission of the
late Col. Sir
Walter Luttrell.
G. Lancaster

QUÆSITA ARTE
MARTE TUENDA

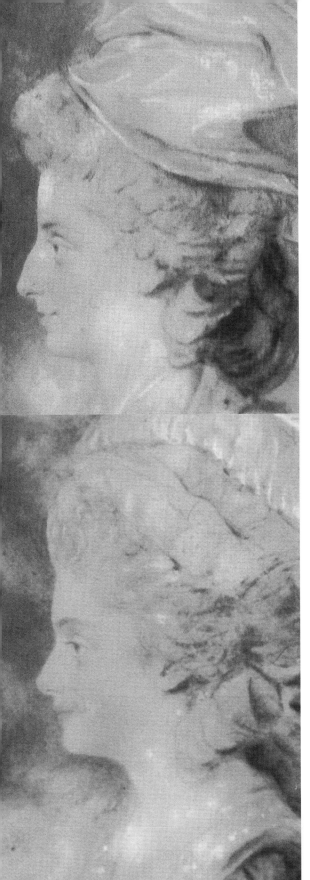

**Mary Fownes Luttrell née
Drewe,** by Downman
Court House, East
Quantoxhead.
By kind permission of the late
Colonel Sir Walter Luttrell.
M. St J. Hankin

**Charlotte Fownes Luttrell née
Drewe,** by Downman
Court House, East Quantoxhead
By kind permission of the late
Col. Sir Walter Luttrell.
M. St J. Hankin

Armorial sign hanging outside the Luttrell Arms, Dunster.
R. Downes

Probable Hatchment for Mary Fownes Luttrell (d. 1829) St George's Church. By kind permission of the late Col. Sir Walter Luttrell.
G. Lancaster

Hatchment for John Fownes Luttrell (d. 1857) (or for Henry Fownes Luttrell (d. 1867) St George's Church. By kind permission of the late Col. Sir Walter Luttrell. G. Lancaster

Hatchment for Henry Fownes Luttrell (d. 1867) (or for John Fownes Luttrell (d 1857) St George's Church. By kind permission of the late Col. Sir Walter Luttrell. G. Lancaster

Lieut. Colonel Francis Fownes Luttrell (d. 1862)
Dunster Castle N. T.
By kind permission of the National Trust.
G. Lancaster

Hatchment for Lieut. Colonel Francis Fownes Luttrell (d. 1862)
St George's Church.
By kind permission of the late Col. Sir Walter Luttrell.
G. Lancaster

North Front of Dunster Castle 1839 from a watercolour drawing by John Buckler (Pigott Colln).
By kind permission of the Somerset Archaeological and Natural History Society. D. Bromwich

Inner Hall, Dunster Castle, *c.* 1860
By kind permission of the Somerset Archæological and Natural History Society.
D. Bromwich

'Gothick' plasterwork, eighteenth century staircase in Dunster Castle
By kind permission of the Somerset Archæological and Natural History Society.
D. Bromwich

Interior of Dunster Church, 1842, showing box pews. By John Buckler (Pigott Collection). By kind permission of the Somerset Archæological and Natural History Society. D. Bromwich

The Priory House, later known as the Rectory, designed by Piers St Aubyn and built 1871-2 as a residence for the vicar. Now called Priory Court. [Source unknown]

South view of Dunster Church, 1780, showing former almshouses. *Gentleman's Magazine* 1808. By kind permission of the Somerset Archaeological and Natural History Society. G. Lancaster

**Font, c. 1530, with
eighteenth century cover**
St George's Church, Dunster.
Taken from drawing of 6.7.1860
in Benefice papers.
G. Lancaster

**Fan vaulting of main screen:
detail showing head of St James**
Victorian, copied from
original fifteenth century screen,
St George's Church.
G. Lancaster

Victorian altar frontal, designed by G.E. Street for the Parish Church.
G. Lancaster

Victorian altar frontal, possibly designed by G.E. Street for the Priory Church.
G. Lancaster

Tomb chest of Hugh (d.1428) and Catherine (d.1435) Luttrell, showing remains of original cresting and Jacobean monument in the Priory Church before its removal to the south aisle during the Victorian restoration. Prob. by G. Stovey, 1843-4; Braikenridge Collection. By kind permission of the Somerset Archæological and Natural History Society. D. Bromwich

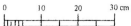

(Left) **Standard of thirteen lights,** one of a pair. The gift of Lady Hood to St George's Church.
By kind permission of Mr K. Astell who holds the original photograph.
G. Lancaster

(Right) **Measured drawing of eighteenth century chandelier,** St George's Church.
By kind permission Robert Sherlock.
Robert Sherlock

0   10   20   30 cm

Detail of window dedicated to Rev. Richard Utten Todd
St George's Church, south aisle.
G. Lancaster

Portrait of Magdalena Todd,
wife of Rev. Richard Utten Todd.
By kind permission of Mr Joseph
Newbery.
G. Lancaster

**Presentation portrait of Rev.
Richard Utten Todd**
By kind permission of his
grandson, Mr Richard Todd.
G. Lancaster

Victorian bench ends in St George's Church, Dunster:

(Above left) Arms of the Luttrell family.
G. Lancaster

(Above right) Arms of the diocese of Bath and Wells impaling the arms of Lord Arthur C. Hervey, Bishop of Bath and Wells.
G. Lancaster

(Bottom right) Bench end showing Victorian carving copied from the medieval bench end shown opposite.
G. Lancaster

Portion of oak-carved bench ends found under boarded floors in nave, used as joist. (From Hancock, *Dunster Church and Priory.*) G. Lancaster

(Bottom left) Birds. G. Lancaster

(Bottom right) Unicorn (in Priory Church). G. Lancaster

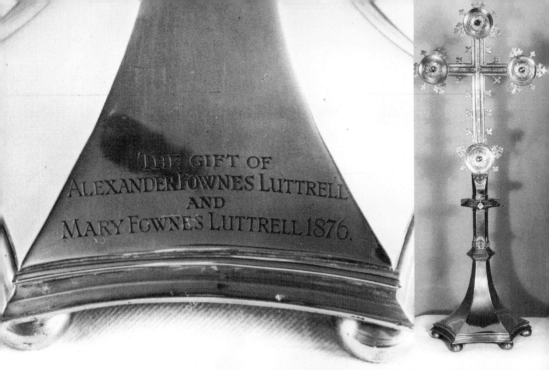

Priory Church Altar Cross showing inscription. G. Lancaster

Portrait of Alexander Fownes Luttrell (1855-1944) By kind permission of the National Trust, Dunster. G. Lancaster

Silvergilt chalice showing the crucifixion in enamels
St Michael the Archangel, Alcombe.
By kind permission of Rev. Alan Mills,
former rector at Alcombe.
G. Lancaster

Glass flask with silver-gilt mounts
St George's Church.
G. Lancaster

(Previous page) **Portrait of George Fownes Luttrell (1826 – 1910)** Reproduced from Lyte H.D., *A History of Dunster*, Part I. G. Lancaster

(Left) **Photograph of George Edmund Street (d. 1881)** Reproduced from A. E. Street, *The Memoirs of George Edmund Street R.A.* G. Lancaster

(Bottom) **War Veteran Bill Dainton with tulips donated to mark the millennium** by the Dutch village of Elst, adopted by the parish of Dunster in 1944 By kind permission of the *West Somerset Free Press.* Steve Guscott

North Transept, St George's Church, before installation of the organ in 1960, taken from photo by Conrad Lewis, 1959.
G. Lancaster

Drawing by the late Ann Rochester of the projected new organ, 1959
G. Lancaster

The Dovecote : the roof being repaired during its restoration in 1987.
J. Jordan

state of dilapidation is all too apparent. In a drawing, probably by G.S. Tovey, done in 1844, railings are shown composed of alternating fleur-de-lys and spear-headed uprights connected by a horizontal rail surmounting the canopy and entrance to the chapel. Those were presumably of seventeenth-century date since they are the same as those which formerly surrounded the Jacobean tomb.

In the Parish Magazine for April 1876, the Rev. R. Utten Todd refers to two tombs in the Priory Church as 'the Mohun and Everard monuments', i.e. firstly the tomb-chest on which now lie the effigies of Sir Hugh and Lady Catherine Luttrell, and on which, the author believes, originally lay the full effigy of Sir John de Mohun III, fragments of which she found in the stoke hole (see earlier), and secondly, the tomb chest on which, in the author's opinion, lies the effigy of Christian de Mohun, widow of Sir John de Mohun IV, who lived in the early fourteenth century. Harry Hems carried out the work and also re-cut the heads, doubtless also 'in exact accordance with the old outline'.

In 1876 the tomb slab of Lady Elizabeth Luttrell of Powderham was also taken up, and placed against the east wall of the south-east aisle. At her death in 1493 she had been buried before the high altar in the Priory Church.

The Replacement or Reglazing of the Windows

Some of the most important changes to Dunster Church during the Victorian restoration were made to the windows, most of which were reglazed. But there were also more far-reaching changes. In the Priory Church one large east window in the Perpendicular style had, in the fifteenth century, replaced a set of three Early English lancet windows. This was now dilapidated and partially blocked up. Other windows of Early English period in the north and south chancel aisles of the Priory Church had also been blocked up. Fragments of the Early English mouldings were found in the walls when G.E. Street undertook the restoration. He decided to reinstate the Early English windows, including the former east window.

Work began in the Priory Church in August 1874; church services, meanwhile, were held in the Parish Church, the western part of the church. The Rev. Utten Todd described the plans for the restoration of the eastern portion in the Parish Magazine:

> ... in the north wall - over the canopied tomb of the Mohuns [*i.e. the tomb with the effigies of the Luttrells*] we shall see two lancet windows, while in the south wall ... there will be three and in the east will be a three-light window of the same date of architecture.... The two windows in the north aisle, which have hitherto been walled up will be replaced and the monument referred to above will be removed into the south aisle, and placed between the two windows there.

The east window of the north chancel, and the two in the north wall of the north aisle are those in the present vestry, the Pre-Reformation Lady

Chapel. They are filled with stained glass incorporating the abbot's crozier and manufactured by Fred Drake of Exeter. Clayton and Bell were responsible for the main east window, the side windows and the east window of the south aisle. The windows were to be re-glazed with glass cut to patterns. The old glass was to be carefully preserved and introduced as directed in the designs. The new glazing was to be 'in quarry glazing with lead strong in the core constructed by an approved manufacturer, and tied with copper wire to the saddle and stancheon bars'.

Christmas 1875 saw the stepped lancet east windows in position in all their glory, described by the vicar in the Parish Magazine as 'a very beautiful work of art'. The window was dedicated to Francis Fownes Luttrell (d. 1862) by his widow and children.

Professor Pevsner noted that 'Miss J.J. Scott points out the similarity of this window to one at St Mary Abbot's, Kensington'.[38] One wonders if Colonel Francis Fownes Luttrell and Louisa Drewe were married there. These windows, shafted on the inside, employ the reduced palette which harks back to thirteenth-century glass. This window was insured for £200 on 29 September 1878. In July 1972, it was damaged, but repaired and cleaned in 1973.[39]

Dr Joanna Cox, an expert on stained glass, said of this window:

> ... [by] London-based firm of Clayton and Bell, both of whom were artists in their own right. Here conventional colour range of red, blue and yellow. Competent leading used effectively. Text in Lombardic script – letters separated by dots. Masonry type of ashlar stonework, yellow hair and wonderful drawing.[40]

As we have seen in the previous chapter, Clayton and Bell were also responsible for the new triptych. Alfred Bell was the Gothic enthusiast. As Marta Galicki wrote:

> [he was] immensely influenced by Pugin and of course Scott; architectural canopy work was his speciality. By the early 1860s he was producing his finest work and had fully developed a mature Gothic Revival style which was essentially mediæval but original in manner, design & colour. This was particularly evident when he collaborated with G.E. Street.[41]

Clayton's forte was figure work. He made simple drawings which were completed by others. He was also imbued with a love of colour. The Pre-Raphaelites used 'dominant primaries...in numerous subtly translucent variations, and relieved by tints new to the High Victorians' repertoire such as cobalt greens, umber and violet'.[42] By 1862 the range was less extensive and at the end of the decade they had 'reverted to standard red, blue and white and the tones became harder and more metallic'.[43] In the 1870s, according to Galicki, 'their colours became heavier and deeper and the effect much more sombre'[44] although I would not say that this was true of the three lancet windows.

In the *Memories of G.E. Street,* A.E. Street noted his father's beliefs about the rights and wrongs of glass painting:

> No shading in glass can be good which is not transparent and that glass is best which trusts more to outline and least to shading... The absence of shading involves not only the loss of ordinary pictorial effect, or chiaroscuro, but also the absence of perspective and this on grounds additional to the incompatibility of perspective with the straight lines of the constructional parts of the window. If you have linear you must have aerial perspective.

At the east end of the south-east aisle (the probable site of the former Chantry Chapel of St Lawrence) is one of the most beautiful windows in the church. It is by Clayton and Bell and was erected to the memory of Thomas Fownes Luttrell, former vicar of Dunster and his sisters Margaret and Harriet. Thomas was the youngest brother of Lt. Colonel Francis Fownes Luttrell. He had presented the Bryceson organ to the church in 1868 and was responsible for building the village school in St George's Street. The subjects treated are the burial of Christ, His Resurrection and His meeting with Mary in the garden, with the Ascension above. This window cost £90 and was insured in 1878 for £200.

Regarding the other windows in this aisle, the Rev R. Utten Todd wrote in the Parish Magazine for April 1876 that:

> In the Luttrell chancel [the south-east aisle], the stained glass windows furnished by Mr Drake of Exeter, have been fixed and the principal parts of the design have been reproduced from old examples, the border of each window being copied from the old lights in the North Aisle of the parish Church. These windows are of an heraldic nature and are on the south wall to the east and west of the tomb erected by George Luttrell in 1621.

The window to the east shows:

(1) The arms of Luttrell impaling those of Courtenay. *Or a bend between six Martlets Sa impaling Or three torteaux in pile a label of three points Az.*

(2) The arms of Luttrell impaling those of Beaumont of Devonshire. *Or a bend between six Martlets Sa impaling Gu and Vairé.*[45]

(3) The achievement of Luttrell.
On a shield couché Or a bend between six Martlets Sa surmounted by a Tilting Helm Az mantled Or doubled Arg. [The mantling is in the form of foliage and is *veined Or.* The helm is encircled by a torse *Or and Sa* which is surmounted by an *otter courant facing dexter.*]
Motto: *Quæsita Marte Tuenda Arte* transposed here to *Arte Marte Tuenda Quæsita.*

(4) The arms of Luttrell impaling the arms of Audley.
Or a bend between six Martlets Sa impaling Gu fretty Or.[46]

(5)   The arms of Luttrell impaling those of Powderham.
      *Or a bend between six Martlets Sa impaling three torteaux in pile a
      label of three points each charged with as many plates.*[47]

The arms shown in this window to the east of the tomb may also be
found over the Gatehouse of Dunster Castle. The first four shields over the
gateway shew the arms of Luttrell impaling the arms of Courtenay,
Beaumont, Audley and Courtenay of Powderham.

The arms of Courtenay refer to Elizabeth Courtenay I (d 1395) who was
the widow of Sir John de Vere. She married as her second husband Sir
Andrew Luttrell of Chilton (Devon). It was she who purchased from Lady
Joan de Mohun, widow of Sir John de Mohun V of Dunster, the reversion
of the castle and its estates. Her son Sir Hugh Luttrell was the first Luttrell
to live at Dunster Castle.

The arms of Beaumont refer to Catherine Beaumont (d 1435), the
daughter of Sir John Beaumont of Shirwill (Devonshire) who married as
her second husband Sir Hugh Luttrell (d 1428). She and Sir Hugh lie in
effigy between the De Mohun Chantry Chapel and the Sanctuary of the
Priory Church.

The arms of Audley refer to the first mother-in-law and second husband
of Elizabeth Courtenay II (d 1.9.1493) whose tomb slab is now in the south-
east aisle. She married Sir James Luttrell (d 1461) and secondly Sir
Humphrey Audley who was taken prisoner at the Battle of Tewkesbury and
beheaded. Sir James Luttrell also had a connection with the Audleys for he
was the son of Sir John Luttrell (d 1430) and Margaret Tuchet, daughter of
Sir John Tuchet, Lord Tuchet or Audley of Nether Stowey Castle.

The arms of Courtenay of Powderham are those of Elizabeth Courtenay
II herself. Her marriage to Sir James Luttrell took place in the chapel of
Powderham Castle since she was the daughter of Sir Philip Courtenay of
Powderham. Sir James was one of those who murdered the Duke of York.
As a result, Dunster castle was forfeit to Edward IV.

The window to the west of the tomb shows the arms of Luttrell impaling
the arms of Hill.[48] These arms are also displayed on the first shield in the
second row over the Gatehouse at Dunster castle. They are:

(1)   *Or a bend between six Martlets Sa impaling Gu a saltire vair between
      four mullets Arg.*
(2)   The arms of Luttrell impaling the arms of Wyndham.
      *Or a bend between six Martlets Sa impaling Az a chevron between
      three 'Leopards' (or 'Lions')*[49] *heads erased Or langued Gu.*
(3)   The achievement of Luttrell.
      *On a shield couché Or a bend between six Martlets Sa surmounted
      by a Tilting Helm Az mantled Or doubled Arg.* The helm is encir-
      cled by a ducal coronet from which issue a plume of feathers. [The
      fine panache crest used by Sir Hugh Luttrell (d 1428) has here
      dwindled into five stiff feathers and the crest of the otter has been
      abandoned.]

(4) The arms of Luttrell on an escutcheon of pretence.[50] Hadley quartering Durborough.

Or a bend between six Martlets Sa impaling Gu on a chevron Or three cross-crosslets Sa for Hadley. Or a bend cotised Sa three Bears' Heads Ar bridled Gu for Durborough.

(5) The arms of Luttrell impaling the arms of Stukeley of Somerset.[51]

Or a bend between six Martlets Sa impaling chequy Arg and Sa a fess Gu all within a bordure Az.

With regard to (1) and (2): the arms of Hill also appear on the tomb of Sir Andrew Luttrell (d. 1538) at East Quantoxhead. Sir Andrew (b. c. 1498) was the son of Sir Hugh (d.1521) and his first wife Margaret Hill the daughter of Robert Hill of Houndston, near Yeovil, a military tenant of the honour of Dunster, and Alice, his wife, the widow of William Daubeney of Barrington. Robert Hill was buried in Dunster Church. Both Sir Hugh (d. 1 Feb.1521) and Sir Andrew were buried at East Quantoxhead, the latter's usual residence. The shields displayed on their tomb are not only of Luttrell impaling Hill but of Luttrell impaling Wyndham. Sir Andrew's wife was Margaret Wyndham of Felbrigg, Norfolk who died in 1580. Lady Margaret née Wyndham's great claim to fame is that she bought the Priory of Dunster from the Crown at the Dissolution of the Monasteries. Her brother-in-law, John, the younger brother of Sir Andrew, was the rector of Dunster and Kilton.

With regard to details (4) and (5) of the window west of the tomb: the Luttrell and Hadley arms can also be seen at Dunster castle on the overmantle in the Inner Hall and at Marshwood. Margaret Hadley (d 1607) married Thomas Luttrell (1525-71). Both lie recumbent in effigy on the tomb to the east of this window, the tomb erected by their son George after the death of his wife Joan Stewkeley in 1621. The Stewkley connection is that Joan Luttrell, the sister of Sir Hugh Luttrell (d 1521) married George Stewkley (d.1508). Their grandson was Hugh Stewkley, Lay Rector of Dunster after the Dissolution of the Monasteries. He married Elizabeth Chamberlayne and their daughter Joan Stewkley (d. 1621) married George Luttrell (1560-1629). The brass at the base of the tomb is to Elizabeth Stewkley and the tomb includes a recumbent effigy of Joan Luttrell née Stewkley. The Stewkley /Stukeley arms do not appear on the tomb but they appear in the Victorian window.

In this window we have therefore successive generations of the Luttrell family. Sir Hugh Luttrell (d 1521) and Margaret Luttrell née Hill were the parents of Sir Andrew Luttrell who married Margaret Wyndham who, in turn, were the parents of Thomas Luttrell who married Margaret Hadley. They were the parents of George Luttrell whose first wife was Joan Stewkley. These two armorial windows were erected in April 1876 and in 1891 were insured for £50 each.

The three windows between the turret, which housed the spiral staircase leading to the rood screen, and the west wall of the south transept, differ from each other in size, design and date. According to Dr Eeles, one at least was in place before the major rebuilding of about 1500: the small window in the south choir aisle immediately west of the large south transept Perpendicular window (it was repaired in 1956).[52] Both are of 'cathedral glass' (i.e. plain glass).

When Dr Eeles was writing his guide of 1940, the rood-loft staircase must still have been accessible from the rood-loft door at the south end of the rood screen. This staircase was later walled up, making the little cubicle known colloquially as 'the broom cupboard', which was provided with a Victorian fireplace from the late nineteenth century for the use of the verger.

In his guide, Dr Eeles indicates that 'the chapel of St Leonard seems to have been the south choir aisle, that of St Lawrence was on the south side of the nave, the aisle between it and the tower being the south transept.'[53] The chapel of St Leonard was therefore in the vicinity of these three windows, and may well have been rebuilt, as in the 1357 agreement made between the Prior and the monks on the one side and the parishioners on the other, 'the parishioners shall for ever maintain the chapel of St Leonard and the aisle between the chapel of St Lawrence and the tower'.[54]

Regarding the south aisle, west of the main screen, Lyte noted an inscription on one of the outer stones above the western window: 'God Save The King. 1624. July XX'. He suggested this might have marked the date of completion of important repairs, of which there was some evidence.[55] There is also an entry in the Churchwardens' Accounts for 1671: ' Sept. 29th. John Atkins for Glassing the Windows. 1. 0.[56] And again in 1681: 'John Atkins for glassinge ye Church windowes: 2. 19. 0.'[57]

Other Victorian glass in the church postdates the restoration but will be dealt with here. The next window west of the window 'of earlier date' in the south choir was erected in 1882 to the memory of Emma Louisa Fownes Luttrell (1798-1881), widow of Francis Fownes Luttrell, and her daughter Augusta Margaret (1825-1880). This window had recently been inserted on the south side of the choir and was manufactured, according to Preb. Hancock, by Clayton and Bell. This was queried by Dr Joanna Cox who expressed the opinion that it might be by Fred Drake of Exeter because of the canopy work and the purplish-grey colouring indicative of that particular maker. This window was insured for £100 in 1891.

The last window before the 1499 screen is simply of 'cathedral' glass. Proceeding clockwise round the church, east of the south porch door the next window was erected after 1883 to the memory of Amelia Anne Hood, the widow of Sir Alexander Hood of Wootton in Surrey, who died on 31. 1. 1883 at Dunster Castle, aged 84 years. She was the mother of Anne Elizabeth Periam Fownes Luttrell, who dedicated the window to her. Anne Elizabeth, who died in 1917, was the wife of George Fownes Luttrell (1826-1910) and to this couple must be given the credit of placing the plans for the restoration of the church in the hands of G.E. Street and those for the reconstruction of the castle in the hands of Anthony Salvin. It is strange that St George's holds no memorial to either of them except that the whole restoration was a tribute to George Luttrell's generosity, of which the existing Victorian work is a constant reminder.

The window to the memory of Lady Hood is by Heaton, Butler and Bayne. (The arms of Hood appear on the sinister side of the shield over the entrance to Dunster Castle. They may be blazoned thus: *Az a fret Arg on a chief Sa three crescents Or.*) This window was insured for £100 on 25 December 1891. It was regarded by Dr Cox as 'undistinguished' and not designed by Robert Turnill Bayne, the highly acclaimed chief designer and partner in the firm of Heaton, Butler and Bayne. (Clement Heaton had discovered the 'flux' used by mediæval glassmakers in 1880. The firm sold their own 'indestructible' colours which were adopted by all the leading firms.)[58]

The next window, west of the south porch, is dedicated by his wife, brothers and sisters to the memory of the Rev. Richard Utten Todd, M.A., rector of Dunster between 1872 and 1886, who died 23 June 1886.[59] This west window was attributed to Clayton and Bell by Hancock. It contains a portrait head of the Rev. Richard, a truly Victorian face with side whiskers. A brass plate beneath the window has the inscription: 'To the Glory of God and in loving memory of Richard Utten Todd, for 15 years Rector of Dunster, the stained glass west window was placed in this Church by his parishioners and friends, 1886.' The main subject is Christ blessing little children, with the text 'Blessed are the pure in heart for they shall see God'. This window was insured for £100 in 1878.

The Rev. Richard Utten Todd (b. 18 March 1838) was the second son of Richard and Mary Ann Todd (1809-1872) to whom the next window to the west is dedicated. I am told by Lady Money-Coutts, the great-grand-daughter of the rector, that family gossip recounts that Richard the father of the rector, her great-great-grandfather, was the illegitimate son of George IV by Penelope Fentham after whom Lady Money-Coutts is named.[60]

Richard and Mary Ann Todd had twelve children; their seventh son was James Utten Todd, M. A., (b 1.10.1847), priest-in-charge at Alcombe which was, until 1953, part of the parish of Dunster. He is also referred to as curate of Dunster. He served the parishes of Dunster, Minehead and Alcombe for forty years and died on 6 July 1913.

The Rev. Richard Utten Todd; his brother the Rev. James; Richard's wife, Magdalena and their second son Killingworth Arthur Utten Todd (d. April 1916), also in Holy Orders, are all buried at Dunster in the churchyard behind the village school, by a large reddish granite cross which also commemorates their eldest daughter, Magdalena Ellen Todd (d.1898 at Brussels). Her three sisters, Isabelle, Margaret and Catherine, lived in the former Vicarage at Withypool and are buried at Withypool.

The Parish Magazine for 11 October 1883 contains a letter from the Rev. Richard Utten Todd to his parishioners, thanking them for their gifts of 'a portrait of myself and ... a silver inkstand'.

After Rev Todd's death in June 1886, his widow Magdalena went to live at Alcombe Lodge, later returning to Dunster to live at 'Sea View', now called the 'High House' (the correct name for the 'Nunnery'). She died on 26 September 1928. Mr Joe Newbery, the grandson of Magdalena's sister, remembers when the Newberys and the Utten Todds enjoyed family picnics near Dunster:

… you needed two people to prawn, one to hold the net, and one to tickle the prawns from under the rocks. My father, Dick and Aunty Cathy were experts. We used to catch lots of prawns and collect piles of winkles and then build a fire from driftwood and had scrumptious teas with lovely fresh bread and butter.

At high tides there were often surplus prawns, in which case Aunt Cathy used to pot them, and eels and other little fish, which I used to catch and cook; but the grown-ups were only interested in prawns and winkles.

Mr Richard A. Todd, the son of Killingworth Arthur, the second son of the Rev. Richard Utten Todd and his wife Magdalena, told me about his great-grandmother Mary Ann Todd, to whom the next window is dedicated. She was the mother of the Rev. Richard and the Rev. James Utten Todd. She was born Mary Ann Hedges and mothered twelve children of whom eight attained adulthood.

This window dedicated to Mary Ann Todd (b. 1809, d. 1872) represents Christ's Baptism. It is ascribed by Hancock to Clayton and Bell. According to Dr Joanna Cox, this window 'is of high quality with well-drawn figures which are wonderfully balanced'. In 1878 the window was insured for £100.

In the Parish magazine for July 1876, the Rev. Utten Todd was able to report that all the windows in the Parish Church had been reglazed with 'cathedral glass', apart from the two close to the font, which were to be filled with stained glass by Messrs Clayton and Bell, 'one of them containing a Representation of the Nativity, the other the Baptism of Our Lord' (the one just described).

The window containing the representation of the Nativity is on the west wall of the south aisle. Dr Cox referred to the 'unusual blue of the Virgin's robe, expensive jewelling all separately leaded' but she thought the canopy work 'crude' and noted that 'the heads were stylistically different'. This window is to the memory of of Charles Edward Ledward, of Hill Park, Frankby, Cheshire (b. 1846, d. 1875) and inscribed 'erected by a fellow student of Tri. Coll., Cambridge, and Theological Coll., Wells'. The fellow student was the Rev. James Utten Todd, the brother of the Rev. Richard Utten Todd; the window was insured for £100 in 1878.

ENDNOTES

1   Hancock: D.C.P. 125
2   Ibid. 125/6
3   Lyte: H.D. Part II 479
4   Ibid. Part I 226
5   Hancock: D.C.P. 124/5.
6   *a* = acre   *r* = rood   *p* = perch.
7   Lyte: H.D. Part II 431/2
8   Published by the Cambridge Camden Society on 17 November 1842.
9   The Priory Church was the responsibility of the Luttrell family as Lay Rectors (following the Stewkleys), after the Reformation.
10 The sum actually came to £3,571 (see Mr Luttrell's account later)
11 Hancock: D.C.P. 127
12 The Parish magazines have been a useful resource. They are now being stored at the Somerset Record Office.
13 This small 16c. Perpendicular door was sent to Alcombe church.
14 A canopy above e.g. an altar.
15 Lyte: H.D. Part II 431
16 Ibid.
17 Eeles: C of St G. 13
18 Hamper: G.M. (H.A.D.) 878
19 Instituted in 1276 in accordance with a bequest from the Lucy family (see Volume One, p 49).
20 Hancock: D.C.P. 7/8
21 Ibid. 10/11. See Volume One, V, 149
22 Eeles: C of St G 13
23 Pevsner: S.W.S 155
24 Wickham: C of S 53/4
·25 Hancock: D.C.P. 22/3
26 13 Sept. 1876
27 This was the same John Long who discovered the coffin lid of Adam de Cheddar (c.1350) in Dunster Post Office. Parish Clerk like his father William before him, John Long was the father of Walter Long, Churchwarden from April 1929 until 27 April 1949.
28 Eeles: C St G (1940), 12/13
29 in *Memoirs of George Edmund Street R.A. 1824-1881* (1882).
30 See letter dated 11 Sept. 1877 from Mr George Fownes Luttrell to the Rev. R. Utten Todd.
31 In a letter dated 28 Oct. 1991.
32 Miss Fiona Hutton and Miss Frances Lennard, at Highbridge, Somerset, recommended by top textile conservator Ksynia Marko to undertake the conservation work.
33 Through the kindness of Mrs Elma Trickett.
34 On a stand kindly made by Group Captain Beamish.
35 During the incumbencies of the Rev. Michael McCormick and the Rev. Christopher Alderson no altar frontals were used at the priory altar.

36 Lyte: H.D. Part I 104. In his 1940 church guide, Dr Eeles also refers to this tomb as probably an Easter Sepulchre of about 1500.

37 Ibid.

38 *South and West Somerset.* Miss Scott, secretary to Dr. Eeles of the C.C.C., informed the author in the summer of 1991 that she thought they were from the same cartoon.

39 P.C.C. Minutes 17. 7. 1972; 11. 9. 1972; 13. 11. 1972.

40 On a visit to St George's Church in the 1980s.

41 Galicki: V.E.S.G. 10

42 Ibid. 11

43 Ibid.

44 Ibid.

45 *Barry of six vair and gu. (*another gu and vair). Beaumont (Devonshire). Burke's General Armory
Vairé Az and Arg overall two bars Gu quartering Gu a saltire vairé Az and Arg. Beaumont of Gittisham. Visitation of the County of Devon.
Az semée de lis a *Lion rampant Or.* Visitation of the County of Devon.
(for the old baronial family of Beaumont)
The first name given in the pedigree is Thomas de Bello of Yolston, Lord of Sherwill (see also Visitation of the County of Devon). *Vair* is a fur (*varus*, Latin for squirrel).This squirrel fur was popular in the Middle Ages as a lining for the garments of those not entitled to wear ermine. Cinderella's 'glass' slipper may have been a fur slipper, since the pronunciation of *verre*, or glass, is the same as *vair* or fur.

46 The arms of Audley have been inaccurately shown in this window light where the 'fretty' is composed of twelve pieces one way and five the other. Correctly the arms of Audley are: *Gu a fret Or.* This means that the armorial charge should shew a *mascle*, or voided lozenge, interlaced with a *bendlet sinister* but many Medieval fretty fields are shown, like the Victorian rendering of the arms of Audley in the tiles in Dunster church, as three pieces in each direction or, in heraldic terms, a *fret* throughout.

47 Burke's *General Armory* uses the term 'bezants' and Vivian's *Visitation of Devon* (1895) the term 'plates'. I have chosen to use the term 'plates' here because they are shewn in the window as representing the tincture *Arg* (silver), ie. the glass is plain. The plate is a silver disc which probably originated as the coin of ancient Barbary and Spain. The bezant is a gold disc, derived from the coins of Byzantium.

48 Hill (Heligan, co. Cornwall) visit 1620; Hill's Court, co. Devon, cos. Hants, Lincoln and Somerset, the Hills of Heligan descended from Sir John Hill, of Kenston, co. Somerset

49 In early armory any lion that was not rampant was a *lion leopardé.* The term leopard was later applied to the *lion passant guardant,* hence the expression ' the leopards of England'. 'In current practice, the term leopard is properly applied only to the zoological creature'. Friar: N.D.H. 213

50 Escutcheon of pretence: 'A small shield charged with the arms of an heraldic heiress and placed in the centre of her husband's arms where it is said to be in pretence'. Friar: N.D.H. 139

51   Stukeley Henton co. Hants bart., extinct 1719 descended from George Stewkeley Esq., of Marsh, co. Somerset, temp Henry VII; Hugh Stukeley, Esq., of Hinton (Hinton Ampner) was created a baronet. 1627; the second bart. d.s.p.m. Burke's G.A. 984.

52   Eeles: C of St G 10 (Note 3).

53   Ibid. 9 (Note 1)

54   Lyte: H.D. Part I 395

55   Ibid. Part II, 426.

56   Hancock: D.C.P. 168

57   Ibid. 172

58   Galicki, 13

59   The statement in the *Dunster Newsletter* of August 1990, that Mr Street dealt with the placing of a portrait of a former Rector of the parish in the window on the north side of the Nave (actually the south side of the south aisle) is incorrect. G.E. Street died in 1881, five years before the Rev. Todd.

60   Lady Money-Coutts's grandfather was the eldest son of the Rev. Richard Utten Todd and his wife Magdalena Todd née Whitehead . He also bore the family name of Richard and was an Anglican minister. Her father, yet another Richard (his son was also called Richard), died when Lady Penelope was a child.

CHAPTER SIX

THE VICTORIAN RESTORATION
of ST GEORGE'S CHURCH II

The Font and Font Jug

The font probably belongs to the first half of the sixteenth century. In his article 'The History and Antiquities of Dunster',[1] Mr Hamper describes it as being decorated with double roses alternating with other symbols. He suggests this may be connected with the successful petition presented by Hugh Luttrell (d. 1521) to Henry VII for the return of the Luttrell lands. (During the Wars of the Roses (1460 – 71) Hugh's father, Sir James Luttrell, who like all the Luttrells supported the Lancastrian cause, had been attainted for treason.) After Henry VII's coronation in 1485 the double rose was used. However it is more probable that Dr Francis Eeles, in his guide to Dunster Parish Church,[2] is correct in dating the font to the subsequent reign of Henry VIII, for he dates it to c.1530, the date he also gives to the west window (but not to its glazing).

According to *The Ecclesiologist* for 17 November 1842: 'The font, before painted, has been covered with a fine sort of rough cast and now looks something like sandstone, except on the side next to the wall, where the red and white colouring still remains.' During the restoration, the old font was to be 'carefully cleaned and restored with a new base moulded and wrought as directed, a new 8lb lead lining laid to shape with outlet and plug complete ...[with] a 6" step to Font of approved Portland stone rubbed.'

It can be seen from a drawing dated July 6 1860 that before the Restoration an ogee-shaped segmental cover was in use. This undoubtedly dates from the eighteenth century and has a very classical and graceful finial. But the Victorians, following the dictates of Ruskin, favoured Northern Gothic taste and regarded the language of the classical southern world as pagan or, worst of all, Roman Catholic. So this cover was removed in 1876 when a new Gothic-style canopy was installed.

The faculty of 22 March 1875 refers to this canopy, but there is no direct reference to the name of the designer or to the carver of the canopy. The restored font was moved in 1876 to a more prominent position at the end of the south aisle and raised upon a double pedestal.

Mr H. Baganel F.R.I.B.A. suggested in 1946 that the font should be moved into the south transept which should become a baptistery. This became an abiding wish of the Rev. G. D. Dunlop who mentions the subject frequently in his *Yearly Notes*. Preceding the use of the nineteenth-century brass ewer, there was in Dunster Church a pewter basin for use at the font, listed in an inventory dated 1720 in the Churchwardens' Accounts.[3]

The present font jug is not inscribed but may be the ewer which the Rev. R. Utten Todd hoped would be purchased with the children's contribution to the restoration of 1876.

The Bells

In the Parish Magazine for May 1875, under the heading ' The Belfry', the Rev. R. Utten Todd reported that a thorough inspection of the bells had been made by a representative of the eminent bell-founders, Messrs Warner & Sons. The Treble Bell was found to be cracked and should be recast, at a cost of about £15, including the carriage to and from London. The Frame was also in a very bad state:

> ... the Ringers should be content for the present with chiming the Bells, as whenever they were rung the wedges which were placed between the Frame and the Wall exercised so much pressure that they tended to make the wall bulge out and injure the masonry of the Tower.

An entirely new frame and Bells, re-hung and re-arranged for Change-ringing, would cost at least £180. Messrs Warner were given the contract to do this, and by December 1875 the vicar was able to report in the Parish Magazine that the magnificent ring of bells had been put in thorough order by this leading firm of bell-founders. The work had been carried out under the immediate superintendence of Mr Henry Boswell, which was 'sufficient guarantee that it was thoroughly well done'. The cost of the re-hanging of the bells was entirely borne by Mr George Luttrell.

Rev. Hancock listed the bells in 1909:

Treble	Cast by John Warner and Sons, London, 1875
Second	1679
Third	Robert Allercott, Robert Leigh, churchwardens. Thomas Bayley, Bridgwater, me Fecit, 1744.
Fourth	John Clement and Richard Busher, churchwardens, 1688. R.P (Purdew).
Fifth	Jefferies and Price, Bristol, 1853.
Sixth	Robert Allercott, Robert Leigh, churchwardens. Jeremias Davies, clericus. Thomas Bayley, Fecit 1744.
Seventh	Mr William Kimer, curat God Save the Church, 1719. Mr Giles Escott, Mr John Seals, churchwardens.
Tenor	I to the church the living call. and to the grave do sommon all. George Gale, gent., William Clark, churchwardens, 1782. George Davis, Bridgwater.[4]

In fact, although these bells date from between 1679 and 1875, there were bells at Dunster from a much earlier date, as we have seen already.

Notes on the bells gathered from ancient records were compiled by the vicar and published between December 1875 and February 1876 in the Parish Magazines. Regarding the tenor bell he wrote:

The tenor was one of the three which required re-casting in 1743, as the following entries show:- 'December 6th 1744. When ye great bell was cast spent 1s' 'George Rawle and two more for straining tenor bell rope 6d'. 'Mr Brown for tenor bell rope weighing 20 lbs., 10 s.' and 'February 22nd 1745, Edmund Williams of Porlock, for mending and cleaning the clock and turning ye hammer from ye 7th to ye 8th bell, £1. 1s'.

However, in 1767 it seems to have met with an accident and once more required to be re-cast; this time the metal was weighed before being sent to the foundry and was found to be 20cwt 3 qrs., and 23lbs. But the unlucky bell did not long remain in working order. In 1782, 'a meeting was called about tenor and fifth bells being re-cast, being both cracked', This time the founder was George Davis of Bridgwater, who returned the bell in the condition in which we now have her.

In January, he wrote about the seventh bell:

This has been more fortunate than her big neighbour, and she has met with no accident since she was cast in 1719 [re-cast by a Mr Wroth]. The only notice to be found of her is that she was taken down and re-hung in 1782, on which occasion 3 shillings were spent on her … There are impressions of several coins and the Luttrell arms (showing, no doubt, that she was given by that family), also T.W. and the initials of the founder.

The year 1743 was an eventful one in the history of the bells:

Mr Thomas Bailey of Bridgwater was to cast three bells belonging to the Parish Church of Dunster for £60. The bells thus recast were the 3rd, the 6th, and the tenor. The tenor, as we have seen, required to be recast on two subsequent occasions. The two former, however, are still in the condition in which they were returned by Mr Bailey. The 6th has impressions of three half-pennies and one penny of Queen Anne. The fifth was cracked at the same time as the tenor, in 1782, and was recast by George Davis of Bridgwater. She again required recasting as lately as 1853.

The fourth bell is the oldest in the Tower, inscribed with the date 1688 when it was recast, but dating back to 1668. The vicar concluded his account by noting that the second bell, originally cast in 1679, was re-cast at the same time as the tenor, in 1766 by T. Bailey.

The bells were rehung and rung for the first time on Saturday 4 December 1875. The Parish Magazine for January 1876 reported on the occasion:

On Saturday, December 4th, our Church Bells were opened, after being re-hung by the Huntsham Change Ringers. The hearty thanks of the parish are due to C.A. W. Troyte Esq., who brought his men here at his own expense, for giving us so great a treat. The ringers ascended the belfry on Friday evening and rang four touches of triples (ie seven bells changing, the tenor being always behind) by the Grandsire method. The number of changes in each touch was as follows:- 168, 336, 504 & 168.

On the following morning, before Mattins, a touch of 670 changes was rung, and the bells were afterwards 'fired' and struck all together. This was followed by a short touch of 76 changes, at about eleven o'clock the ringing of the day commenced. After two preliminary touches of 168 each, the large number of 1000 changes was rung, this would have been increased to the half peal, or 2520, but in consequence of the sun shining full in the face of the man ringing the third bell, there being no blinds in the belfry, this was rendered impossible. However, when a temporary blind had been fixed up, two other touches of 400 and 500 were rung without stopping, and this completed the opening, which was most successful and must have afforded the greatest pleasure to all who heard it ... They are all a ring of bells of which the parishioners may indeed be proud.

The vicar's brother, the Rev. James Utten Todd, later vicar of Alcombe, was curate of Dunster between 1873 and 1877. An enthusiastic bell-ringer, he had refurbished the belfry at his own expense. Now the conductor of the Dunster Guild of Change Ringers, he was keen to introduce change-ringing to Dunster. After a visit to Mr Troyte at Huntsham Court, Tiverton, he returned full of enthusiasm. As a result, in March 1876, it was recorded in the Parish Magazine that:

...on Tuesday, January 30th, the junior members of the Guild met as usual for practice in the Church Tower and at 8 pm proceeded to the Luttrell Arms, where Miss Cruwys had provided an abundant and well served supper ... After Grace had been said, some short touches were given upon the handbells and all went merrily until the Luttrell Arms could no longer legally extend its hospitality ... Considerable progress has been lately been made in change-ringing. We can now ring the 120 changes of Grandsire Doubles upon the handbells, and this is proof that the ringers are mastering the method and that more rapid progress may be confidently looked for in the future.

The publication *Church Bells* reported the same month on the spread of change-ringing in the locality as opposed to round-ringing:

Two years ago our noble science was absolutely unknown, and even unheard of, and now we can boast of five guilds, all in a more or less prosperous condition. It started about Easter 1874, at Porlock ... It was then taken up by Dunster, and the result has been the re-hanging by Messrs Warner of their noble ring; and under the superintendence of the far-famed Mr H. Boswell, their ring of eight is as fine and ringable a one as there is in Somersetshire, while their proficiency is steadily advancing.[5]

By April 1876, it was reported in the Parish Magazine that change-ringing as opposed to round-ringing had taken over during the previous eighteen months. The first 'peal' (five thousand changes) would be rung on the bells of St George's Church on Wednesday August 22nd 1883, as was reported in the Parish Magazine for that September:

> The Guild has lately had the benefit of some instruction from Mr J. Field, of Oxford. After a few days preliminary practice, a touch of about 1,700 was rung on the occasion of the return of Mr Luttrell and family to Dunster Castle, on Wednesday, August 22nd.
>
> Encouraged by success on this occasion, it was determined to try for the whole peal of Grandsire Triples, consisting of 5,040 different changes. Accordingly on Thursday evening, shortly after 7 PM., a start was made by the following side:- 1. J. Field (conductor); 2. W Thorne; 3.J. Grabham; 4.W Thrush, 5. C.B. Craze; 6. R. Hole; 7.J. Utten Todd; 8. J. Payne; and after ringing three hours and eight minutes the bells were successfully brought round. The striking during the first half of the peal was especially good – as good, the conductor remarked, as ever he had heard.
>
> We chronicle this event, as it is undoubtedly the first "peal" which has ever been rung on the Dunster bells.

In the Parish Magazine for February 1879 the death of a Dunster ringer, Joseph Bailey, aged thirty-five, was reported: 'His body was carried to the grave by his fellow-members of the band who afterwards rang a short time with muffled clappers'. In the same issue appears an account of the Ringers' Supper, at which money collected from parishioners was shared out, about 32 shillings each. The Magazine records:

> The old year was rung out with a muffled peal, and the new year welcomed by the young band of change-ringers with three six-score of grandsire doubles. The names of the ringers are as follows:- Frederick Griffith, (steward), John Escott (conductor), George Newberry (belfry-keeper), John Pain, Stephen Willis, Frederick Griffith, Henry Mitchell, William Thrush.

On 31 May 1890 the Bath & Wells Diocesan Association of Change Ringers was formed. To mark this the bells of the diocese were rung in as many towers as possible. A service was held in Wells cathedral and two Dunster ringers were present.

The Tower Clock

In the *Gentleman's Magazine* for 1808, it is noted that:

> The Tower is 90 feet high, embattled at the top with low broken Pinnacles at the corners, and contains a clock, chimes (which play the 113th Psalm-tune at the hours of 1, 5 and 9) and eight bells.

In September 1876 the *West Somerset Free Press*, announcing that the bells had been re-hung, also reported that the parish clock and chimes were completely worn out and that a subscription had been raised among the parishioners to purchase a new clock, while Mr Luttrell had offered to pay the cost of a new set of chimes.

The clock is mentioned in the Churchwardens' Accounts for 1711: 'For beere when we made bargaine about ye Clock 2. 0.; for making ye watch part of Clock 5. 0. 0; For amending the striking part of the Clock 10. 0.;For amending of the quarter clock 1. 10. 0'.[6]

The appeal was launched by the vicar in February 1876:

> In November of last year the old Parish Clock and Chimes were inspected by one of the foremen of Messrs Gillett and Bland of West Croydon. He reported that both were "completely worn out and not worth restoring; and that it would, in fact, be throwing the money away to patch them up". Under these circumstances it is thought desirable that there should be a new clock for the Parish and a new set of chimes for the Church.

The estimate for a new clock was £121, while the estimate for a new set of chimes, for which Mr Luttrell was willing to pay, was £230.

The vicar was able to write in the March 1876 Parish Magazine that more than £100 had already been raised, and from two concerts given recently he hoped to obtain at least £20. So he had felt able to give Messrs Gillett and Bland an order for the clock, and for the chimes 'for chiming the quarters on four bells, after the manner of the clocks at Great St Mary's Church, Cambridge, and at the Palace, Westminster'. The cost of the chimes was estimated to be about £37 10s, to be defrayed out of the donations of £100 given by R.J.S. Todd Esq., for the Parish Church. A further fifteen contributors were listed.

In November 1876, the Reverend R. Utten Todd hoped that work would soon commence and the clock and chimes would be in place by the New Year. However this proved too optimistic, and it was not until May 1877 that the vicar was able to head his article: 'At Last'! and to continue 'the clock has come!'

In July 1877 the Rev. R. Utten Todd wrote in the Parish Magazine:

> The new clock was first set in motion at noon on Saturday, June 2nd, by Mrs Todd, in the presence of Mrs Whitehead, of Kilve court, the Vicar, and J.V. Newbery Esq. The clock having been so arranged by the clock-maker in charge, that upon gently moving the massive pendulum, in two seconds the sweet-toned quarters commenced striking, and afterwards the deep-toned hour blow on the tenor …
>
> … The striking can be distinctly heard on a still night three miles off. The clock has been carefully regulated by the correct time as obtained from Greenwich by telegraph, and its going is at present, about two five-tenth seconds slow *per diem*.

On 1 October 1877, a meeting of the subscribers to the Parish clock had been held at the Luttrell Arms Hotel, with the Vicar in the chair. Because there was a deficiency of £73 7s 11d in the expenses incurred in procuring and fixing the Clock, due to the extra expense incurred in having four new dials instead of the two old ones, it was proposed that a Bazaar should be held.

The result of the bazaar was most satisfactory and the Rector reported that 'we have a balance in hand which will enable us to meet any incidental expenses connected with the clock for some little time to come'. The bazaar in itself is worthy of record. It is a real period piece, a picture of a Victorian country endeavour that has its place in history.

Having thanked Mr Luttrell for permitting the bazaar to be held in front of the castle and for throwing open the Castle Grounds to visitors, the Rev. Utten Todd gives an account of the activities which ensued:

> The stalls, six in number, were erected in a special tent which was pitched in the drive in front of the Castle, and were presided over by Mrs Luttrell, Mrs Hole, & Mrs Clark, Mrs Delacombe, Miss Risdon, Miss Davys, and Miss Wake, each of whom was attended by a most efficient band of assistants. They – meaning of course the stalls – were very tastefully draped, and when filled with all the tempting articles which had been provided for them, looked exceedingly pretty, and we do not wonder that they were so well patronised.

Refreshments, supervised by Mrs Todd and Mrs Maitland, were available in the hall over the castle gateway, with music from Mr Dudeney (the new organist) at the piano, with two companions playing the flute and the cornet. On the Thursday the band from Nether Stowey played in the open air.

Other attractions included Dr Clark's exhibition entitled 'Captain and Mrs Webb crossing the Channel': two mechanical swimming dolls going round and round a slipper bath. In a room below the Hall, the Reverend J. U. Todd was showing Professor Edison's Phonograph – 'one of the most wonderful inventions of this wonderful age'. Unfortunately 'the instrument sent down from London was not, perhaps, the best of its kind – as it required so much exertion on the part of the exhibitor to show it off satisfactorily; but still it worked fairly well ... and was a cause of much astonishment and amusement'. There was also a weighing machine, in the charge of Mr George Cook.

Further work was done on the clock and carillon by C.E. Price of 1, Spencer Street, London in October 1881, while the same firm was called in again in 1884 to overhaul and clean the clock, to cut teeth and to fit a new collet, etc etc. The carillon was also overhauled and cleaned and the cost was £24 5s 0d.

Chiming Machine & Carillon

There had been a Carillon at Dunster by at least 1711, when the Churchwardens' Accounts record: 'For finishing ye Chimes. 16. 6.'[7] This was a new carillon in 1877. The eighteenth-century chimes had played psalms only. In August 1877 the Parish Magazine announced that the new chimes, made by Messrs Gillett and Bland, would soon be in working order. The vicar announced that seven tunes would be played during the week, one on each day, at the hours of one, five, and nine; the change of tune would be made by the machine at midnight. The tunes chosen were as follows: Sunday: 'O rest in the Lord'; Monday: 'Drink to me only with thine eyes'; Tuesday: 'Home, Sweet Home'; Wednesday: 'Hymn 431'; Thursday: 'Blue Bells of Scotland'; Friday: 'Hymn 171 (new edition)' and Saturday: 'Hymn 223'.

The chiming machine is in the same chamber as the clock, and was the gift of Mr G.F. Luttrell Esq. The apparatus by which the quarters are struck was presented to the Parish by R.J.S. Todd Esq. On the 11th of August, all the work of fixing was completed and Mr and Mrs Luttrell, Lady Westbury, and Mr and Mrs Bosanquet and others assembled in the Clock Chamber to hear the seven tunes played through, each being started by Mrs Luttrell. In the September Parish Magazine, which gave the above report, the vicar explained how the new machine worked:

> In the old chiming machine the tune barrel had to perform the heavy work of lifting the bell-hammers. Now, seeing that the hammers varied very considerably in weight according to the size of the bell to be struck, the result was that when a heavy hammer had to be raised a much longer time was required than when a light one had to be lifted. This was the reason of the jerky irregular way in which the old tune used to be played, the high notes being too quick and the low notes on the old bells too slow.
>
> In the present machine the bell-hammers are lifted and kept in suspension by a separate piece of mechanism, viz., a Cam roller, which revolves continually while a tune is being played, and picks up and restores to its place each hammer after it has been released by the tune-barrel and has struck the bell ... the power of the Cam arrangement ensures regularity and precision at every stroke, whether on a large or small bell.

Pews and Bench-ends

In the Parish Magazine of July 1895, in its 'Hints to Worshippers', the vicar reminded the congregation that the proper posture in church was either kneeling or standing. Seats could of course be used during the reading of the lessons and during the sermon. But unless members of the congregation were old or infirm, they should not be used at other times.

Up to the end of the Middle Ages, seats round pillars or against walls were the only ones generally found in churches in England, and these were for the aged and infirm. The earliest pews, of a rough and primitive kind, uncarved and solid, are not earlier than the fourteenth century. By the end of the second half of the fifteenth century, fixed seats had arrived and in the early sixteenth century the idea of pews in the nave, and of pulpits and sermons, became more frequent.

Before the Reformation, parishioners were eager to leave money and goods for the enhancement of the parish church. The various Guilds also played a large part in the maintenance of their local churches. Following the Reformation, gifts and bequests became fewer, so other sources of income and support were sought by churchwardens. Tariffs for seats were fixed, and around 1694 the seats in Dunster Church were let:

> ... at fixed rates of 1s. and 6d. per seat according to their position, thus Mr Peter Mead paid this year for "a plase in the fore seate of the great Alley [nave] 1s., while Mr Corden paid for a plase for his wife in the fore seate of the North Alley [aisle] 6d".[8]

These tariffs do not appear to have changed for over twenty years, for in 1672 Hancock refers to '... a list of seat rents varying from 1s to 1d per year'.[9]

People who obtained parish relief were obliged by the Overseers 'to frequent the Public Worship of Almighty God in the Church, as in duty bound'. Sinful omission and neglect to attend, unless through sickness, meant withdrawal of benefits. Special benches were placed in the church for the poor, one for men the other for women.[10]

References to box pews occur in the Churchwardens' Accounts in the seventeenth century:

		£	s	d
1689	Pd G Clarke for making 14 doors for the seates at 1s 6d per door		1	10
	For colouring them at 4d per door. 15 doors		5	0[11]
1698	Paid John Strong for a winscott for Mr Grant's seat	1	0	8[12]

It was the custom for families who rented pews in the Parish Church to bury their dead beneath the floor of those pews in shallow brick graves. Hancock paints a gruesome picture: 'These graves when opened were frequently found to be full of black and horribly foetid water, in which the coffins floated or had turned over.'[13]

In 1838, when J.C.Buckler reported on the state of Dunster Church, he wrote:

> Many ancient oaken seats "elaborately and finely ornamented" were concealed by later woodwork, the most promiscuous, unseemly and uncomfortable assemblage of pews that can be met with.[14]

And the *Ecclesiologist* of 17 November 1842 reported that:

> The Flooring of the Nave has been raised, and the area filled throughout with uniform deal pues, the open oak seats, said to be finely carved, having been sent up to the castle...[15]

Presumably these were required for Dorothy Luttrell's chapel, but it appears that they did not all go up to the castle, for portions of oak-carved bench-ends were found under boarded floors in the nave during the 1874/6 restoration – they had been used as joists. One of these was re-instated during the restoration.[16] In 1984 it was discovered that portions of the oak pews were in Exeter Museum; these were exhibited at the Dunster Church Flower Festival that year, when the chosen theme was 'The Building of the Church'.

The 'uniform pews' referred to by the *Ecclesiologist* were the box pews which can be seen in John Buckler's drawing of 1842, in the Piggott Collection. 'The parish church was filled with great square pews, both within and without the chancel'.[17]

The schedule of work detailed in the faculty for the restoration of 1875 included the following tasks:

> To take down and Remove ... the whole of the Pews and Seats in the Church and Chancel ... and to erect and set up ... Prayer Desks and Choir stalls, Bible Desks or Lectern, Litany Desk, Credence Table, Organ, Pews or Seats in said Church, Tower and Transepts.

The specification required the masons, bricklayers and wallers to:

> Remove the whole of the modern pews throughout the church and clear away and allow for same in Contract and preserving all old seat ends etc. as models for the new and all traceried panelled work which must all be preserved and reused where directed in the Nave.

Later in the same specification we read: 'New Oak Benches throughout the Church after old models new Oak Stalls to details'. The term 'benches' is used for pews, and 'stalls' refers to those at the west end of the Priory Church. In referring to the pews, new oaken seats, carved by Harry Hems of Exeter, were provided for the nave and aisle, while stalls like those of a private chapel were set up in the chancel.

In June 1875, the Rev. R. Utten Todd, reporting the progress of the restoration, noted that 'the new work has been designed by the architect in striking keeping with the old'. This is typical of G.E.Street, who liked to design every small detail of a church and thus give coherence to the whole.

The vicar wrote that by a happy chance, in taking down the modern pews several old ends were found buried beneath. These, though rotten, were perfect enough to give a clue about how to construct the new pews.

> The fronts and backs are richly moulded, but the mass of work has been thrown into the bench ends. Of these there are upward of one hundred, every one differing from the other, and all alike interesting. The carving has been entrusted to Mr Harry Hems of Exeter (who also did the stone carving upon the church, as well as on the pulpit, and the Luttrell, Mohun and Everard monuments).

At the suggestion of Mr Luttrell and the architect, Mr Hems had visited most of the churches in the county where really good old carved work may be found, and taken plans, casts and impressions. In this way, commented the Vicar, 'Somersetshire work is stamped indelibly upon every item of detail'. He continued:

> Being strictly perpendicular work most carving is of the conventional type; but many of the [bench] ends have forms of local or scriptural interest introduced. Thus there are the arms and monograms of the Luttrell family and of the bishops of the diocese; St George, the Patron Saint is splendidly carved ... One of the old ends has been patched up with the old oak from the building, and it now appears likely to stand as long as any of the new ones. ... The chancel stalls, parclose screens, and the altar table are excellent in their way, and for woodwork, St George's Dunster has certainly attained a high place among the churches of the west.

On one bench end the arms of the See of Bath and Wells are shown on the *dexter* side of the shield: *Azure a saltire per saltire and quarterly Or and Argent*. These were originally the arms of Wells, which became a bishopric on the division of the old See of Sherborne in 990 AD. In 1088, Bishop John de Tours moved his seat to Bath, but it has been at Wells since about the twelfth century, and in 1242 became known as the See of Bath and Wells. On the *sinister* side of the shield, the arms shewn are the basic arms used by various members of the Hervey family: *Gules on a bend Argent three trefoils slipped Vert*. (Lord Arthur Charles Hervey was Bishop of Bath and Wells at the time of the church restoration.[18]) Behind the shield on the Dunster bench-end are the arms of Bath Abbey, rather inexactly rendered by the Devon craftsman.

The old bench-end which was patched up (the third from the west end of the nave on the north side), shows the Victorian work in the top row, left-hand side. The plain moulding is also Victorian but the remainder of the carved inner panel is medieval.

Another bench-end was copied from one found under the floor of the nave, being used as a joist. This and other fragments are illustrated in Preb. Hancock's *Dunster Church and Priory*. The Victorian copy shows three heads at the top, all wearing stylised ruffs executed in the form of semi-circles. In all bench-ends, the central designs are enclosed within a plain moulding beyond which are examples of a great variety of carved borders, each one being different.

The bench-end depicting two confronted birds is of particular interest, since it is obviously copied from a bench-end at East Quantoxhead, a more ancient seat of the Luttrell family than Dunster Castle. The very detailed plumage extends from the head to the body and upper portions of the tail, and ends with the sharply-delineated parallel carving of the tail and lower wing feathers. Another pew end, now in the Priory Church (but originally designed to be in the Parish Church) displays a unicorn. This mythical animal with the neck, head and body of a horse, the legs of a deer, and the tail of a lion, bears a single straight horn growing from its forehead.

The Choir of the Parish Church: Its Tiles And Stalls

In February 1876 the *West Somerset Free Press* wrote of the choir of the parish church: 'The choir will be paved with encaustic tiles, and oak stalls have been placed there.' It added:

> All the columns were found to be out of the perpendicular, and they have been set upright. The tiles laid in the body of the church are of three colours, black, red and buff, and the high and unconventional seats have been removed, new oak ones with carved ends having been sustituted.

The 'new oak ones' were not in use until 1877. Perhaps the tiles were not yet set enough for people to tread on them, for the Parish Magazine for February reported: 'the floors of the church will be furnished with chairs and we hope to be able with the beginning of Lent to meet there for morning prayers on four days of the week.'

Pulpit, Pulpit Desk, Book Rest, Parish and Priory Altar Crosses

The Ham-hill stone pulpit in Dunster Church was placed against the north aisle during the Victorian restoration. In 1946 Mr H. Baganel, FRIBA, an authority on acoustics, recommended to the then vicar, Rev. Dunlop, that a tester be placed over the pulpit, but this was never done. It replaced a rather plain one of the eighteenth century which was sent to St Michael the Archangel at Alcombe but has now been returned.[19]

This pulpit had a brass pulpit desk when it was erected. We have the original black-edged letter, with sketch attached, dated 18 July 1876, written to the Rev. R. Utten Todd from Mr Street's office in Cavendish Square:

> The size of pulpit desk which he [Mr Street] can order of Messrs Potter, S. Molton St. London. W. when required is 15" long and 9 ½" to the rest for the book and it would be in brass.

In the summer of 1988, the author found this brass pulpit desk, blackened and discarded, in the stoke hole of the church. It had been there since 1955, when new arrangements were made for the pulpit. The plain side of the desk would have faced the preacher, whose notes would have covered it, while the decorated side would have been viewed by the congregation looking up to the pulpit.

There was also a beautiful bookrest in a similar style of Victorian brass-work. It must have been designed to stand on the altar of either the Priory Church or the Parish Church. It is an object evocative of the spirit of the age with its air of solid assurance: a very well-made and worthy piece standing firmly on its curvilinear feet. The pierced design includes a cross entwined and surrounded by a flowing floriated design which displays the Victorian love of abundant flowers. It is more than probable that this, like the pulpit desk, came from the same ecclesiastical furnishers, and that Messrs Potter also made the altar crosses.

Floors, Heating and Tiles

The schedule of work regarding the floors was as follows:

> To take up and remove the floors of the Church, Chancel, Tower, Transepts and Porch carefully and preserving any Memorial Inscriptions now lying in such floors and replacing them in or near their present postions.

The floors had to be made level inside, and the level of the churchyard lowered to bring it lower than the floor level inside. Great care had to be taken when disturbing graves and monuments. The floors were to be covered with concrete as a base for tiles.

Heating was also to be installed:

> Warming to be Haden's combined hot air and water in chamber found under N.Aisle, with a chimney to the West of Western window in North Wall finishing above roof as will be directed...

The flues were being installed by November 1875, and by July 1876 the heating system had been completed and most of the floor tiles laid, as the vicar was able to report:

> These tiles ... of three colours black, red and buff ... together form a simple but effective pattern. It may interest some of our readers to know that no less than 24,000 tiles are required for the floor west of the skreen and for the side aisles of the chancel [of the Parish Church]. The chancel itself will be laid with other tiles, and in a different pattern specially designed by Mr Street. These are not yet ready, as they have to be made to order; but meanwhile the oak floor for the chancel stalls is fixed in position, as also the steps leading to the altar which are of Devonshire marble.

Regarding the tiles, the *West Somerset Free Press* wrote in September 1876:

> A number of tiles representing the arms of various families were found among the rubbish under the floor and these designs have been copied in making new ones with which the whole has been paved. They are of a very rich appearance and are laid on the same plan as a pavement which has lately been discovered at Cleeve Abbey. There are no less than forty-five different varieties ... the paving has been executed by Mr W.Godwin of the Lugwardine Works, near Hereford.

The tiling was not completed until December 1876, three months after the opening of the church. The arms of the following families are among those represented in the Victorian tiles:

Audley   *Gules a fret Or*
Beauchamp of Hatch *Vair*[20]

Clare	Or three chevrons Gu
Despenser	Quarterly Arg and Gu in second and third a fret Or overall a bend Sa.
Luttrell	Or a bend between six Martlets Sa.
Martin	Gu a chevron between three crescents Arg.
Mohun	Or a cross engrailed Sa (arms adopted after 1300)
Trivet	Arg a trivet Sa.

When an armorial shield was required, G.E. Street's office would provide a tracing for Godwins. The medieval tiles in the Mohun Chantry Chapel were arranged by Mr C.H. Samsom, the churchwarden and assistant to Mr Street, and laid by Mr Hill.[21]

The firm of Godwin was known for its church tiles:

Random indentations on the tile surfaces gave an antique look which blended in with the medieval surroundings [part of Hereford cathedral] and this effect, with their size of 4 ¼" [108mm], which was nearer to the old dimensions, at once commended them to the ecclesiologists. By 1860 the randomly dented surface had standardised to a texture like orange peel which henceforth was the standard finish and makes Godwin's tiles easily identifiable. Gilbert Scott and G.E.Street especially favoured Godwin tiles.[22]

At Dunster the plain black, red and buff tiles are 4¼" square but the decorated inlaid tiles in the Mohun Chantry Chapel are 5" square.[23]

The Luttrell Vault and the South Entrance to the Churchyard

Under the chancel and transepts of the Priory Church is the Luttrell vault. This was to be extended 14 feet to the west. The walls were to be lined with brick or stone, and the sides were to each have a stone landing built in and supported at ends of brick work of such length and size as to admit of two tiers of coffins on each side. The vault was to be covered with a nine-inch brick arch and an archway was to be formed at the east end in the chancel wall to admit coffins. The vault has not apparently been used since it was enlarged.

The Luttrell burial-ground extends on three sides of the Priory Church. Before the Reformation, it had been part of the Priory garden, but it came into the possession of the Luttrell family, presumably when Dame Margaret Luttrell bought the Priory. In the time of Henry Fownes Luttrell we can see from the estate map, made before 1771, that this land was leased to John Thomas, who lived in the sixteenth-century timber-framed house south of the church.

This house was also restored at this time, by Mr Sansom, directed by G.E. Street. It was to be used as a caretaker's cottage. A gateway of Doulting stone in the Perpendicular style was erected at the south entrance to the churchyard.[24] The wall which formerly ran from the cottage up to the Priory Church was pulled down.[25]

Not everyone approved of the way the cottage was restored. Lyte wrote:

> This [cottage] was described in 1588 as "the stone-healed howse", a fact of
> which the late Mr Street was unaware, when he covered the roof with tiles
> and rebuilt the chimneys in a style suggestive of Sussex rather than
> Somerset.[26]

We now reach the climax of the great operation. The Rev. Todd reported
in the Parish Magazine for August 1976:

> ... now that the work is finished and the scaffolding necessary for it
> removed, the Church looks in a more forward state towards completion
> that it has done as yet. It only remains now to lay down the tiles in the
> chancel, the Sanctuary and the Priory Church; this Mr Godwin has
> promised to do for us this month.

He continued:

> When this has been accomplished, when the seats (some of which have
> already arrived) have been put in their places and the side skreens for the
> chancel and the sanctuary have been fixed, the Church will be ready for
> the re-opening and there is every hope now that this joyful event will take
> place in the third week of September. The 13th has been fixed upon as the
> day and we hope to be able in our next number to give full details of the
> proceedings.

The Church Reopens after Restoration

The church was to be re-opened on 13 September 1876. However, another
important occasion preceded the re-opening of the church. Alexander
Fownes Luttrell had reached his majority on 1 June 1876, but the official
parish celebrations took place in the autumn. As the vicar wrote on 1
September:

> The month we begin today promises to be famous in the annals of Dunster.
> Rarely can it have happened in any quiet country place that two such events
> as the coming-of-age and the re-opening of the Parish Church should take
> place in succeeding weeks. Yet this is what we are all looking forward to
> this month ... Thursday the 7th is the day when the Parish generally will
> be invited to join in the coming-of-age of the "young squire" and we are
> sure we shall all join heartily in wishing him those good things which make
> life truly happy.

Alexander and his sister Mary, the elder of his two sisters, presented a
cross to be placed on the priory altar. It is inscribed with their names and
the date 1876 and is very similar to the parish altar cross. The festivities
began on Monday, 4 September and lasted until the Friday, as the vicar

reported in the October Parish Magazine. Every household in the parish could take part in some event. On Thursday, the 7th, about 320 sat down in the old Priory Barn to a 'right good dinner';

> It was then that the presentation to Mr A. Luttrell, of a silver Tea and Coffee Service, took place; the parishioners having joined together to offer it to him as some token of their goodwill: and loud and hearty were the cheers which greeted him when the presentation was made, and when the toast of his health was proposed.

Unfortunately rain prevented the planned sports afterwards, and the schoolchildren's tea had to be given in the Barn. But on the Friday evening the Castle was illuminated with coloured lights, and there was a beautiful display of fireworks, followed by a ball given by the tenantry.

The completion of the church restoration was a truly joyous period. The church was re-opened by the heir, Alexander Fownes Luttrell. The village was en fête. The choir was wearing purple cassocks, the bells rang out and floral arches still spanned the streets to celebrate Alexander's birthday. The *West Somerset Free Press* records that the auspicious day of the church's reopening on 13 September 1876 opened with a series of changes on the church bells, rung by Mr Troyte and his band of bell-ringers from Tiverton.

The first of the services took place at 8.30 a.m. Well before the next service at half-past eleven,the church was 'literally crammed with people, who were principally of the upper and middle classes; indeed from 800 to 1000 must have been present, and the churchwardens found some difficulty in providing all with seats'. Numerous local clergy were present and some took part in the service. The Right Rev. Lord Hervey, Bishop of Bath and Wells, gave the sermon. (He was a descendant of the famously eccentric Hervey family, of whom Lady Wortley Montagu is alleged to have said: 'When God created the human race he created men, women, and the Herveys'.)[27]

The organist was the newly-appointed Mr T.J. Dudeney, later of Hatch Beauchamp. The offertory on behalf of the restoration fund amounted to £56 10s 2¾d.

The Communion Set

When the Bishop, Lord Arthur Hervey celebrated Holy Communion on the first service of the day, 'there was used for the first time a new set of vessels in silver-gilt — the gift of an anonymous donor of £50 who wished well to our Church and Parish'.[28]

Of this 'new set of silver-gilt', only the original flagon, with its silver-gilt mounts bearing the London assay mark for 1876, remains today in St George's Church.

This communion set is also mentioned in the Parish Magazine and by a variety of people at different dates. The Rev. E.H. Bates, writing in 1900 about the silver in Somerset churches, remarks of Dunster 'there is also a handsome modern set consisting of chalice, paten and flagon, silver-gilt of the present reign'.[29]

Preb. F. Hancock discusses this set and here mentions Clewer:

> There is a handsome set of silver-gilt modern communion plate. The cup is 8ins. high. The bowl is goblet-shaped, and 4½ in. in diameter. It is quite plain. The stem is reeded and knobbed. The knob is decorated with deep panels of moulding and foliage alternately. The foot is 5¼ in. in diameter. It has a band of bold cross-hatching within the filleted edge, and is decorated with four enamelled medallions. (1) The crucifixion in silver on blue ground; (2) S. Peter, all silver. (3) Virgin and child, silver on red ground; (4) S. George, all silver.
>
> The plate belonging to this set is 7ins. in diameter and gilt. It is of a plain pattern shape with a moulded edge. The marks on both cup and paten are Victorian.
>
> The flagon is of silver-gilt and crystal, of a Gothic design to match above. This set was presented to the parish church of Dunster *by the sisters of Clewer* [*my italics*].

Finally, this set is mentioned in the P.C.C. Minutes Book which contains entries from 1920-1985. Pasted inside the book is an undated inventory. It records 'Inventory of valuable Church Property' and mentions:

> ...modern set silver-gilt Victorian chalice 8" in height, 4½" in diameter. Decorated foot. Paten 7" in diameter. Flagon silver-gilt and crystal. N.B. It is absolutely illegal to sell or exchange Church Plate without obtaining a Faculty [*sic*].

To investigate Preb. Hancock's reference to this gift from 'the Sisters of Clewer', the author wrote in December 1989 to the Sisters, who, I learnt from the Vicar of Alcombe, the Rev. Alan Mills, reside at the Convent of St John the Baptist, at Windsor. They replied that the Sisters of Clewer had no official connection with Dunster Parish Church and there was no reference to our set in their archives.

In October 1990 the author discovered that the chalice and paten were actually in use at St Michael's the Archangel at Alcombe, and was invited to inspect them. I identified the chalice and paten as the missing parts of the Communion set given to Dunster in 1876 both by the descriptions I had and by the London assay mark of 1876. The chalice with its enamelled figures was of great beauty. It is distressing to think that this thoughtfully chosen Victorian 'Gothic' Communion set which like the 'icing on the cake', was a final touch to Street's Early English Gothic restoration, is now divorced from its background. This chalice and paten were, I understand, insured for £9,000.[30]

We have much evidence to substantiate our ownership of the chalice and paten and there was no legal conveyance of these objects from Dunster to Alcombe. I believe it was merely by default that when Alcombe became a separate parish in 1953 (see later chapter), they were not returned to Dunster to join the flagon we still hold. Prior to 1953, at some date which cannot be precisely stated, I imagine the chalice and paten were quite informally taken to what was, before 1903, 'the chapel at Alcombe'. In 1903 the present church was built at Alcombe. The priest-in-charge at that time was the Reverend James Utten Todd (d 1913), the younger brother of the Rector of Dunster. The communion vessels could have been taken to Alcombe during the Rev. James Utten Todd's ministry. Or perhaps they were taken there after the Alcombe church was extended in 1937.

Reverting to the celebrations on the day of the re-opening of St George's, Dunster on 13 September 1876: after the church service, at 2.00 o'clock, the 'Luttrell Arms' provided a meal. The party was presided over by George Fownes Luttrell. In a full account in the Parish Magazine, the rector gives the names of those present, who included members of the Luttrell family and the Acland family and many others. Toasts were drunk to the Queen, then to the Bishop, who in his reply declared that:

> Dunster was a place *sui generis* ... there was something in the whole atmosphere of the place which aroused all their feelings. They might look at the castle and the town beneath, and they almost saw the history of England spread before them; and, which was a grand feature, where in all England could they see such a charming blending of the old and the new?

The Bishop continued:

> Among the many things which made Dunster a place *sui generis*, and one which a bishop of the diocese liked to come to, was a happy union between the squire and the parson, and where there was that union, where the squire used his great influence and the means at his disposal in promoting the good work of the parson, as was the case there, an additional charm was given in the place (applause).

The bishop concluded by proposing a toast to 'the landlord of the Luttrell Arms', which caused much laughter and applause, as the landlord was of course George Fownes Luttrell.

In Mr Luttrell's reply, he noted the happy coincidence of the church re-opening when they had just finished celebrating the coming of age of the eldest son, and he begged to join with the toast to himself the health of that son. Cheers greeted this proposal. Then followed a toast to the Venerable Archdeacon Denison, who asked leave to add to this toast the health of his brethren the clergy. He recalled that:

> ... it was now twenty-five years ago ... that he first became Archdeacon of Taunton, and one of the things which had been always nearest to his heart was to see that noble church [*Dunster*] restored as, thank God, it was now. In his wildest dreams about its restoration he never contemplated anything so beautiful in all its parts as he had seen that day.

At 6.30 pm the same day there was a further service attended by numerous people. The preacher was the Ven. Alfred Earle, Archdeacon of Totnes, whose text was 'The fear of the Lord is the beginning of wisdom'.

It was the hope of the Rev. R.Utten Todd, expressed in the September 1876 Parish Magazine, that 'the re-opening of our Church will be the beginning of a fresh stage in the religious life of our Parish'. The vicar detailed various changes he proposed to make and his reasons for doing so. The choir should from now on wear white surplices, as white was 'the colour of holiness'. Evening Prayer would be said daily in church as well as Morning Prayer, and on the evening of Saints' Days a short sermon would be given as well. Various minor changes were made to the order of service, and the hymn books used in future would be the Revised and Enlarged Edition of Hymns Ancient and Modern, 'because the number of Hymns is much greater, and ... in the musical editions of the revised book the marks of expression are attached to each verse, which will be an immense help both to the choir and to the congregation'.

Three months after the church was re-opened, in December 1876, the vicar noted a further gift by Lady Hood: 'two handsome standards of thirteen lights, each the work of Messrs Potter of South Molton Street. London'. These standards are no longer in the church.

At the beginning of 1877 Mr Gladstone was a guest at Dunster Castle and on the afternoon of January 20th, he paid a visit to the church. Afterwards he expressed his admiration for the way in which the restoration had been carried out. The vicar wrote about this auspicious visit in the Parish Magazine for February:

> From what he said we gathered that he was particularly struck with the combination which our church presents of grandeur with simplicity, and with evident signs it displays of a desire that everything connected with it should be of the best and at the same time in accordance with that quiet and reverent tone of feeling which characterises our worship.

Regarding the Restoration Fund, it was not until May 1877 that the Rev. Todd was able to write in the Parish Magazine that they had now closed the account, of which he appended a summary:

Receipts	£	s	d
Subscriptions and donations	743	14	6
Offertories	193	13	8 ¾
Dividends and Interest	43	4	8
Church Box	5	11	8 ¼
Collections at the re-opening	86	17	1
of the church Carpets etc for Altar	10	3	3
Sale of chairs (Roadwater Mission Room)	5	0	0
	£10,078	1	8

Expenditure	£	s	d
Cheque April 6th 1876	500	0	0
" " June 26th 1876	450	0	0
Chairs & carriage	40	7	11
Lamps	16	2	6
Carpets etc for Altar steps	10	3	3
Hassocks for choir	3	8	6
India Rubber mats	6	4	2
Other expenses	17	3	5
Cheque for balance	34	11	11
	£10,078	1	8

In a letter from Dunster Castle dated 11 September 1877, George Fownes Luttrell sent the Rev. R. Utten Todd a full account of what he had received and paid towards the restoration of the church. The costs to him were made up as follows:

	£	s	d
Messrs Hare Contractors	£3,571	0	0
Street	475	0	0
Godwin	247	10	0
Hems	97	10	0
Robinson	1,037	2	0
Clayton & Bell	385	10	0
Drake	118	3	0
Warner	219	1	0
Gillet & Bland, Chimes only.	232	17	6
Bryceson	143	6	0
Bankentein	28	4	0
Altar cloth	60	0	0
Potter	90	15	0
Sundries	41	16	0
By Ponsford and charged to my State Acct	4,115	8	0
Outstanding say	200	0	0
Total Cost	11,063	3	0
In addition to this —			
South aisle East Window about	90	0	0

Received	£	s	d
From Mr and Mrs Bosanquet	468	5	0
Mrs Luttrell	50	0	0
Miss A Luttrell	150	0	0
Lady Hood	100	0	0
Lady Pilkington	10	0	0
Messrs Todd and Gatchell	989	4	0
	1,767	9	0
By G.F. Luttrell	9,295	14	0
	£11,063	3	0

In 1878 the screens, desks, stalls, altar cloths, pews, printed books, furniture and fittings in the Priory Church were insured for £2,700 and those in the Parish Church for £2,500.

It is a matter of opinion whether the Victorian restoration at St George's church was a good or bad thing. Certainly, due to the munificence of Mr George Luttrell, it was possible to carry out the plans of that eminent architect George Edmund Street. R.A. In the surrounding countryside, the parish churches escaped the almost total eradication of their history since neither the money nor the influence was available. The tombs remain in their original places, the brasses are undisturbed, the box pews, or even more delectably, the medieval benchends and tomb slabs all remain undisturbed. It is nevertheless, a fact that something had to be done about Dunster Church, whose east end was cut off and in total ruin.

Perhaps, today, a more sympathetic approach would have been made with due regard and gentler understanding of the beliefs and feelings of the past generations. The Victorians, so confident of the rightness of all their actions and truly motivated by a desire to use the best materials, to work to the highest standards of craftsmanship, swept all before them. This was true in a literal sense too, for floor levels were changed and graves, albeit most reverently, were disturbed. All this has already been explained. But when all is said and done it was accomplished with sincerity and according to the Victorian Christian ethic.

Street's son said of him that his religion was intimately bound up with his work.[31] George Street possessed an ability to read the history of the growth of a building and to come to a correct solution regarding its structural parts. All his works were under his immediate superintendence: he executed all the necessary drawings personally and he liked to involve himself in the design of all the furnishings. This is very apparent in Dunster where we know he designed the carved ceiling over the parish altar and the tiles in the Priory chancel and sacrarium. He carefully inspected all his works and also made friends with his clients: he was a Victorian 'Renaissance man'.

Dr Francis Eeles, in his church guide, *The Church of St George, Dunster* (1940), wrote:

> In 1875 the late Mr G.F. Luttrell spent some £10,000 on a complete scheme of restoration directed by Mr G.E. Street, one of the most distinguished architects of the day. Very great care was taken of every detail, and Mr Street's new fittings are marked by dignity and restraint. More drastic renewals were carried out than would be permitted now.

Professor Edward Freeman M.A. was disappointed that one of the best examples of a divided church had been so drastically altered:

> The church is a cross church with a central tower. Westward of the tower was a perfect church, with chancel and rood-screen, the latter reaching, according to local custom, right across the church, and approached by a turret in the outer wall of the south aisle. East of the tower was a second

choir, fenced off by a second screen. To this the transepts and crossing formed a kind of ante-chapel. Nowhere in short were the arrangements of the class of churches so easily studied as at Dunster, up to the time of a very recent 'restoration'. The two churches, parochial and monastic, west and east of the tower, were absolutely perfect.

He continued:

'Restoration' has had its usual effect of wiping out history. … the ancient arrangement has been altogether confused by taking the neutral space under the tower into the parish choir, and removing the parish high altar to the eastern arch of the tower instead of the western. There is thus no space left between the two choirs.[32]

It is a fitting conclusion to the account of the 1875/6 restoration to record the visit of HRH the Prince of Wales, later King Edward VII, to Dunster Church in September 1879. This followed a private visit to Dunster Castle in August. A full account of this visit appeared in the Parish Magazine, which noted the warm welcome given to to the prince, with the town decorated and illuminated, and the streets lined with crowds. Particular mention was made by the rector of 'the loyalty of Alcombe [which] found vent in the erection of two arches, one of which with the original and happy inscription, "Our green hills greet thee", won golden opinions.'

Alexander Fownes Luttrell

Alexander Fownes Luttrell, whose coming-of-age so happily coincided with the re-opening of Dunster Church, lived to the ripe old age of eighty-nine, having been born in 1855 and dying in 1944. He was the eldest son of George and Anne Fownes Luttrell, was educated at Eton and for a short while served in the Rifle Brigade. In 1867 he received a commission in the Grenadier Guards. He had three brothers, Hugh Courtenay, Edward and Claude Mohun who were at that time nineteen, eighteen and nine years of age respectively.

Later in his life, at the age of thirty, Alexander was involved as a Captain in the Sudan campaign at Suakim. In April 1886 Captain Alexander Luttrell married a Scottish lady, Alice Edwina, the daughter of Colonel Munro Ferguson of Raith and Novar. They had two sons: Geoffrey, born 20 May 1887 and Ralph Paganel, born 20 May 1889.

Alexander's brother Hugh Courtenay (born 10 February 1857) also served for a period in the Rifle Brigade. He was educated at Cheltenham and was Aide-de-Camp to Earls Cowper and Spencer successively when they were Lord Lieutenants of Ireland. He also served as a Member of Parliament, representing Tavistock from 1892 to 1900 and again in 1906. In 1904 he married Dorothy Hope, the daughter of Sir William Wedderburn, Bt., and they had three daughters: Mary, Louisa and Elizabeth, and later a son, William, born in December 1908.

Alexander's brother Edward (born 24 September 1858) was, like Alexander, educated at Eton, as was his third brother, Claude Mohun (born 9 September 1867), who went on to Magdalen College, Oxford and later became a director of Stuckey's Banking Co. His sisters Mary and Beatrice later took an active role in the life of the church in Dunster.

ENDNOTES

1. *Gentleman's Magazine* 1808
2. *The Church of St George* (1934,1940)
3. Hancock: D.C.P. 185
4. Ibid. 67
5. Under the heading of *Belfry Notes* in March 1876 the difference between a peal or ring of bells is explained: 'the term "a Ring of Bells" ... is only properly applied to the entire number of changes, which can be produced on a given number of Bells, as for example, 120 changes on five bells, 720 on six, 5040 on seven. Any number of changes above 5000 may rightly claim the term; a less number is styled a "touch" or "flourish"'.
6. Hancock D.C.P. 183/4
7. Ibid. 184
8. Ibid. 180
9. Ibid. 169
10. Ibid. 191/2
11. Ibid. 176
12. Ibid. 181
13. Ibid. 128
14. Lyte: H.D. Part II 431
15. EC.C. No. XVIII 64
16. See *West Somerset Free Press*, 13. 9. 1876, and Dr Eeles's: C of St G (1940) 13
17. Hancock: D.C.P. 127
18. His full arms are illustrated in A.F.Jewers, *Wells cathedral; its Monumental Inscriptions and Heraldry* (1892).
19. Eeles: C of St G 13. It was returned in 2002.
20. Not a reference, as one would expect, to Beaumont (Devonshire). These arms referring to Catherine Beaumont (d 1435), wife of Hugh Luttrell (d 1428) appear over the gatehouse at Dunster Castle where *vair* is divided by lines of partition known as *barry*. (See earlier chapter.) Correctly these arms are *Barry of six vair and Gu. Vair* alone refers to Beauchamp of Hatch.
21. Parish Magazine, Feb. 1877. In August 1954, the verger, Mr Haydon, told the Parochial Church Council that 'there were some tiles that once belonged to the church stored in the Tithe Barn and that they could be returned to the church'. Nothing further is recorded concerning them in the PCC Minutes.
22. Beaulah: C.T. 19c. 15
23. In 1876 this chapel was renamed the Sacristy.
24. *West Somerset Free Press*, 13.9.76
25. Hancock: D.C.P. 3
26. Lyte: H.D. Part II 337
27. Foreman: G.D. of D. 98-9. Before becoming Bishop of Bath and Wells, Lord Arthur Hervey (1808 – 1894) was Archdeacon of Sudbury, Suffolk. His grandfather was Frederick, Fourth Earl of Bristol and Bishop of Derry, remembered as the builder of Ickworth, Suffolk, and after whom the Hôtels Bristol were named.
28. *West Somerset Free Press,* 13. 9. 1876
29. Bates: I.C.P Proc. S.A.N.H.S. (1900)
   4 In 1900 the Elizabethan silver Communion Cup belonging to Dunster was in use at Alcombe. This is now in the possession of St George's. It is of a type frequently found in the West Country and bears the I.P. mark.
30. Street: M.G.E.S. (1882).
31. Freeman: E.T.D (1883).

CHAPTER SEVEN

DUNSTER CHURCH and PARISH from the LATER NINETEENTH CENTURY to the FIRST WORLD WAR

The Parish Magazines are rich in comments on Victorian social attitudes and religious observances. They are also a valuable source of information about the life led in this lively little town in the second half of the nineteenth century. Many magazines were illustrated with delightful pictures of wildlife. The cost was 2d; but 'cottagers might obtain the Magazine through the District Visitor for 1d'.[1]

They also record touching stories about the inhabitants of Dunster. One such concerned five-year-old Lois Craze, who in 1873, on 29 September, tried unsuccessfully to save her sister Ethelreda from drowning, and in doing so nearly lost her own life. The following April, seventy parishioners presented her with an inscribed set of six silver Apostle spoons to mark her bravery.

In contrast a report under the heading 'Manners of the 19th century' appeared in the August 1877 Parish Magazine. It concerned the escapades of four visitors, two adults and two children, who behaved with less than Victorian rectitude in the parish church and seem to have deliberately flaunted accepted standards or were crassly ignorant of them.

> On Tuesday, 21st August, between the hours of two and three o'clock, two women, well-dressed, and two little girls, apparently about the ages of ten or eleven, were found sitting in the choir stalls of our Parish Church, the women with their bonnets off, laughing and talking loudly, and enjoying themselves .....over a meal! On finding they were observed they departed, and the floor where they had been was afterwards found to be strewn with crumbs and currants, while close by were traces of other acts on the part of the children too disgraceful to be mentioned in these pages.

'Must the church then, be kept locked up at all times, except when service is going on, that it may be protected from desecration?' asked the vicar. Surely not. But 'it would almost seem that some steps must be taken to prevent any recurrence of such godless behaviour as that which we have thought it right to mention'.

Bad behaviour however, was not only ascribed to strangers, for the local youth also became unruly at times and received severe censure from the vicar who wrote in January 1879 that 'several complaints have reached us lately of the bad behaviour of a few younger members of the congregation on Sunday evenings'. The Rev. Todd reminded such offenders of the 1860 Act of Parliament: they were liable to a penalty of up to £5 or up to two months in prison.

Harvest Homes 1877/8

Some relief for high spirits was provided by the events associated with the Harvest Thanksgiving celebrations. Details exist for the 1877 and 1878 Harvest Homes (a custom revived in 1992 as the 'Tithe Barn Supper'). The three parishes of Dunster, Carhampton and Withycombe met annually to celebrate and give thanks for the harvest. In 1877 the Thanksgiving Service in Dunster Church was followed by dinner at the 'Luttrell Arms'. If the weather was fine, games and dancing followed on the Castle Lawns, with the Minehead Band providing the music. The vicar wrote in the Parish Magazine of the proposed proceedings:

> ... among the games there will be a trial of strength between the respective Parishes in the game of rope, but it was resolved at the meeting that only those should be allowed to contest in this game who have engaged in harvesting, and who have taken part in the dinner at the *Luttrell Arms*. It was also resolved that the leg of mutton prize should be discontinued.

In the Parish Magazine for June 1878, harvest drinks were the subject of an article. There was a strict injunction that the drinks were only to be taken between meals. One recipe suggested: 'oatmeal made as thin as gruel, a little salt and sugar to taste: a small portion of nutmeg grated, and an egg or two well shaken up and mixed in while warm'. It was also advised that:

> If beer be used in the hay or harvest-field, it should be the weakest kind of table beer, not containing more than one to one-and-a half per cent of alcohol...the habit of taking large quantities of liquor – even water – at any time is a harmful one, and, when indulged in, is sure to mislead.

The Seventh Harvest Home was held on Saturday 7th September 1878. As was customary, the three parishes combined and the arrangements differ little from preceding years. The Thanksgiving Service began at 12.30 and was fully choral, and the harvest hymn 382 'Come, ye thankful people come /Raise the song of harvest home /All is safely gathered in /Ere the winter-storms begin' rang forth.

The article in the October 1878 Parish Magazine continues:

> The preacher (Rev. W.P. Michell), after alluding to the hopes and disap-pointments attending the harvest of 1878, pointed out the special causes

for thankfulness which there are this year, and dwelt upon the lesson of patience and perseverance which we are taught at harvest time. The church was very tastefully decorated and the Sanctuary was adorned with plants of variegated foliage. On the Altar-table were dishes of choice grapes, pears and peaches.

'We are sorry, however', commented the vicar, 'to hear some preferred to go to the public-house during the hour of worship and thanksgiving rather than to the House of God.' However, everyone assembled for the meal after the service:

> ... about 220 sat down at 2 o'clock to one of those liberally-provided meals for which Miss Cruwys is famous, and ample justice they did to the good cheer.
>
> Mr Luttrell presided, and after dinner, in proposing prosperity to Dunster Harvest-home, he referred to the change for the better which is taking place among the agricultural labourers, the more intelligent of whom are following in the wake of the other classes, and learning to see that enjoyment does not consist of drinking to excess. He also recommended to the attention of those who wished to make the best of the food they had to cook, the course of Lectures on Cooking which was to be given the following week.

Afterwards the Minehead band was waiting to escort the company to the Lawns, where various amusements and competitions soon got under way. However:

> The tug of war was not a success, as the Withycombe men declined to enter the contest, and Carhampton was not represented in its full strength. Dunster accordingly came off easy winner, but the victory was not satisfactory and as the game seems in danger of being abused, and made a source of bad feeling among those who ought to be friends, it would be better, perhaps, to let it drop out of the programme for future occasions. We must thank Dr Clark for introducing a more peaceful entertainment in the shape of the Telephone, which secured a great deal of attention, and was much appreciated.

Another novelty was a tea stall, where a large cup of tea and a roll and butter could be purchased for two pence. Holders of ale-tickets could also exchange them here for tea, an arrangement which proved very successful:

> £1. 2s. 6d was taken in money – the charge– and fifty-six ale-tickets were exchanged so that our venture may be said to have met with sufficient success to encourage us to repeat it.
>
> At 7 o'clock the band marched off the ground followed by the greater number of the company: of these the more respectable were no doubt glad to go back quietly to their houses, and verify the truth of Mr Luttrell's state-

ment that as people get more intelligent they get more temperate at the same time.

The next year, 1879, there was no Harvest Home, chiefly because 'the present year is not one for the kind of rejoicing which belongs to a Harvest Home', due to:

> ... the state of depression in trade and agriculture generally, and the many cases for anxiety which there are, whether we look at home or abroad, seem to show us that our Harvest joy should be accompanied with some searchings of the heart... [this year] should lead us to think whether we have not been guilty of unthankfulness for the mercies vouchsafed us in past years, and whether, as a nation, we have not been too forgetful of the truth that, "both riches and honour come of God", and not just our cleverness and activity.

It was decided instead to offer Harvest Thanksgivings in the course of Sunday Services on October 4th. Special Psalms and Lessons and suitable hymns were chosen in an endeavour to combine the spirit of thankfulness with a spirit of humility.

Sunday School Treat 1880

One of the annual Christmas festivities was the Sunday School Treat. In 1880, 138 children belonging to the Sunday Schools at Dunster and Alcombe took part but others had to be refused on account of the irregularity of their attendance. The Rev. Utten Todd reported that the children seemed to enjoy their tea, expressing their satisfaction 'in the usual vociferous manner'. After tea they were entertained by the vicar's brother, the Rev. James Utten Todd, with his Magic Lantern 'by in which he illustrated the adventures of a mischievous boy, called Jack Holiday, and the history of Dick Whittington, along with some contrasts between good and naughty children, and some laughable scenes which caused great applause'.

Care of the Church

The church was cleaned from top to bottom at regular intervals. For example, in May 1884, it was reported in the Parish Magazine that it was agreed to give the inside of the church a thorough cleaning, from the roof downwards and this had already been carried out.

In May 1881, the Easter decorations were reported upon in the Parish Magazine. Flowering plants from Dunster Castle decorated the Sanctuary; the Font was decorated with beautiful cut flowers, the gift of R. Treolar Esq.; the wreathed Cross upon the Rood Screen 'showed to great advantage'. A kneeling stool had been made for the Litany Desk by Miss Martin and a white frontal worked by Mrs Todd adorned the altar for the Easter festival in 1883.

Hand Hearse

In May 1884 a 'bier upon wheels' was provided for the use of the Parish. According to the account in the Parish Magazine, it was intended to reduce the number of bearers required at a funeral.

The cost of the Bier was £21, and the cost of its carriage to Dunster 17s 10d. This hand hearse survived into the twentieth century (it was kept in Priory Green) but it was said in 1935 that the Parishioners would not use it.

Exterior of the Tower

Nothing had been done to the exterior of the tower during the 1876 restoration and by 1884 it was in great need of being re-pointed. In the May magazine, the Rev. R. Utten Todd reported that the estimated cost was £65 and the Churchwardens would ask for voluntary subscriptions to provide funds.

By October 1884, the tower had been re-pointed and the rector took the opportunity of giving a little of the history of the tower which he had extracted from Maxwell Lyte's book *'Dunster and its Lords'* (1882). He noted that: 'Some alterations must have been made to the [medieval] contract afterwards, for the present tower does not attain to the full height of an hundred feet, nor do the windows quite correspond to the specification of 1443'.[2]

Cottage Hospital and Trained Nurse

There had been a Cottage Hospital in Dunster 'a little above the street' (i.e. West Street) on the north side since 1867 and here provision was made for nine patients. However in 1899 the need was for a trained nurse and Mr J.E. Surridge, B.A., L.Th. offered in a letter published in the Parish Magazine to give five pounds to provide such a nurse, if nineteen others would give the same by Trinity Sunday. With a hundred pounds in hand there should be no difficulty in carrying out the arrangements for providing a Trained Nurse for the Parish. He had ministered to the Parish for four months and regarded the provision as an obvious want in the practical working of the Parish.

New Reading Room 1874

The establishment of a Reading Room and Social Club for the parishioners of Dunster was announced in the Parish Magazine in January 1874. The want of something of the kind had been felt for some time, but it was not until the evening of 29 November 1874 that a meeting was called in the Parish Schoolroom. A committee including Rev. R.U. Todd, Mr John Webber, Mr Thomas Hole, Mr Thomas Burge, Mr James Webber, Mr C. Samson and Mr George Geen was appointed to draw up some provisional rules. These were discussed and unanimously adopted at a subsequent meeting held on 7 December at the old Reading-room in High Street. The First Rule stated:

That the object of the Dunster Reading-room be generally to afford the inhabitants opportunity for reading the publications of the day, and for passing their spare time in quiet and rational amusements.

That to this end, besides newspapers and periodicals, games be provided, but gambling not allowed; that smoking be permitted, and that refreshments such as tea and coffee be supplied at a moderate charge (Sundays excepted); and that a Lending Library be established for the use of the parish.

Only men and boys over the age of fiften were eligible to use the Reading-room, on payment of one shilling per quarter. Honorary members were to pay not less than 10s per annum. The Reading-room would be open from ten to ten on week-days, and from five pm to ten pm on Sundays. It would be managed by a Committee, to be elected annually at the general meeting (the first Tuesday in December), which would meet quarterly. Thirty-one members joined immediately.

Mr Luttrell had kindly offered the use of two excellent rooms 'above the Market-house'. He had also ordered certain alterations to be made 'to the greater comfort of the members'. This building was not the present Yarn Market, which was often called the Market House.[3] Various pictures and plans made in the early part of the nineteenth century show the Shambles, erected in the Market Street of Dunster in 1423, extending some distance southward from this Market House, dividing the street into two uneven parallel ways.[4]

When the Shambles and the old Town Hall, which had formerly stood in the middle of the street, were demolished in 1825, the former 'Market House' became known as the Yarn Market, for the name of Market House was given to a 'new and convenient market house ... erected by John Fownes Luttrell on the eastern side of the street'.The building bears the initials of John Fownes Luttrell and an unexplained date of 1895.[5] I am told by one of the present occupants that this building had been used as a school and he confirms that it was a Market House.[6] He says it was used as a meat market but in the early twentieth century it was also used for promoting a liberal candidate.[7]

The new Reading Room and Social Club was established in two upstairs rooms of this building, provided by George Fownes Luttrell at a nominal rent.

It was opened on the evening of Wednesday January 14th, 1874. Mr Luttrell was duly thanked for his kindness in permitting the use of the rooms and putting them in order for the use of the members. The *Times* was loaned daily by T. Abrahams Esq.; a present of magazines came from Mrs Abrahams, and the papers taken in daily were the *Standard* and the *Daily Telegraph* and weekly, the *Field, Public Opinion,* the *County Gazette* and the *Illustrated Paper.* One friend presented a carpet, another a couple of easy chairs and Mr Bonnor of Alcombe a bagatelle board.

There was already a parish library, which according to the March 1874 issue of the Parish Magazine would now be housed in the Reading-room, but the books would be available to all parishioners, though sitting in the Library and Reading Room was confined to members. The books were to be given out and exchanged every Monday after the club money had been received.

In August 1876 it was reported that because of 'improper use' of the Library by some of the younger parishioners, a separate School-library would be set up in the School-room. Apart from the Reading Room there were many more institutions in Dunster which are mentioned in the Parish Magazines. Those institutions included the Dunster Branch of the Church of England Temperance Society, a Village Hospital, a Dunster Orphanage, a Dunster Clothing Club, the Luttrell and Eld Charity and the Girls' Friendly Society. Articles also appear in these magazines about the Dunster Cottage Garden Show, the Street Lighting in Dunster, the Dunster Park Cricket Club, and the Churchyard and Cemetery.

Music in Dunster at the End of the Nineteenth Century

Music in particular was well catered for. On 23 November 1874, for instance, a concert was given in the large room at the 'Luttrell Arms' by some members of the Dunster Glee Club, assisted by some lady friends, with Dr Ollerhead, Mr Moss and the pupil teachers of the school. The Rev. R. Utten Todd wrote of this concert in the January 1875 issue of the Parish Magazine:

> The music for the most part, was somewhat of an high order (we may call especial attention to the Madrigal "Down in the Flowery Vale", by Festa AD 1541 and to the song by Sir Henry Bishop so well sung by Mrs Windsor, "Bid me discourse") and possibly may not afforded such pleasure to all present as music of the Christy-minstrel kind: but all lovers of the comical element must have been delighted with the singing of Dr Ollerhead, whose performance of "the Swiss girl" was most amusing and will not soon be forgotten. The proceeds of the Concert enabled us to hand over the sum of £5. 5s. 0d to the Treasurer of the Reading-room Committee.

There is only a brief reference in the Parish Magazine to the first Choir Concert held in July 1874 in St George's Church. The proceeds of this successful concert, £8, was divided among the choir members according to their attendance at Friday-night choir practice. The local Choral Festival which took place at Porlock on 11 August 1875 received more coverage:

> The Choirs which took part were those from the parishes of Porlock, Winsford and Dunster; and numbered together between sixty and seventy voices, which were found amply sufficient to fill the small Church of S. Dubritius [sic]...

After the service the choirs sat down to tea in the School-room, and later many played rounders and cricket in the rectory grounds, in spite of the rather wet weather.

The devotion of these choirs was considerable. There were no cars and even attendance at choir practice must have engendered much walking for any of the members coming from outlying farms. No doubt they also used small horse-drawn conveyances and indeed the bus engaged to take home the Dunster contingent from Porlock would have been horse-drawn. Inclement winter weather must have been a severe test of their fortitude and sense of duty.

After the church restoration was accomplished, a Choral Union was formed in Dunster. The first festival was held in the summer of 1877. On 19 July 1877 the rector reported that the twelve choirs met for rehearsal in the morning. At one o'clock, the choirs stopped for lunch. They re-assembled at 3 o'clock, when the singers wearing surplices joined with members of the clergy to process into the church, where the other singers were assembled.

> The number in surplices, including the 15 clergy, was 79, and it comprised members of the six choirs. The hymn was a little unsteady on reaching the Church owing to the distance of the treble singers who were at the head from the basses who were at the end of the procession; but on being taken up by the choirs in Church, it was nicely finished.

The vicar's brother, the Rev. J. Utten Todd, conducted the choirs. Mr Dudeney played the organ 'with great taste and feeling.' As for the anthem:

> It sounded grandly on this occasion, and the quiet devotional way in which Dr Clark sang the solo part in it added to the impressive character of this portion of the Service.

The Choral Union concerts became an annual event. The fourth concert, held on 29 July 1880, was provided by ten choirs from neighbouring parishes. The year before, the total number of voices had been 150 but by 1880 the number had risen to 182, consisting of 119 trebles, 20 altos, 17 tenors and 26 basses, and of these 100 wore surplices:

> The Service commenced at 3.30, shortly before the surpliced Choirs and Clergy, who had assembled in the School-room, walked through the Church-yard in procession singing some of the gradual Psalms. Four members of the Porlock Band walked in the middle of the procession and kept the voices together. The success was thought to have been due to the skilful playing of these musicians. On reaching the west door the surpliced choirs ceased singing and a fresh Psalm was taken up by the Choirs in the Church accompanied by the organ, in which the voices in procession joined as soon as they entered. The organist was Mr C.W. Lavington of Wells Cathedral.

According to the Rev. R. Utten Todd, 'the weakest point in the Service was the chanting of the responses... It would also be well if some of the younger members of the Choirs could be impressed with the fact that they come to sing and not to stare about them'.

There was also a Philharmonic Association, which met for its first practice on 19 August 1877. The inaugural concert, was held on 29 November 1877 at the 'Luttrell Arms'.

As usual the Vicar recorded the proceedings in the Parish Magazine:

> The room was full to overflowing, and many who had neglected to purchase tickets beforehand were unable to obtain admission. The performers, to the number of forty, were seated upon a platform made after a design by Mr Samson, and the concert commenced with the singing of the National Anthem in full chorus with orchestral accompaniment. The instrumentalists then performed Beethoven's celebrated piece "Adelaide", and then followed the chief performance of the evening, Dr Macfarren's cantata, "May Day". Mrs F. Slade, of Minehead, skilfully executed the trying solo assigned to the May Queen. ... taking into consideration the many hindrances in the way of some of the members from a distance attending practice regularly, and the short time that the society had existed, the performance was very creditable, and received hearty applause for the audience.

The second part began with more music from the small orchestra: piano, one flute, three violins, one violoncello, and one double bass. (The vicar passed on a plea for another flute, and a viola, or tenor fiddle, to join them.) The solos were sung by Fraulein Hunderwadel, Miss Sharland, Miss Thristle and Mrs Windsor. Mrs Samson presided at the piano.

The Philharmonic Association's Concerts were thenceforth held at Christmas time and in March. The vicar, the Rev. R. Utten Todd, and his brother the Rev. James Utten Todd were among the soloists and Dr. Clark sang some of the recitatives.

In December 1880 a Mr Moss arranged a concert on behalf of the Schoolmasters and School-mistresses Benevolent Institution. This was a great success, somewhat marred, however, by the antics of a young trouble-maker. According to the Parish Magazine:

> The programme was a long and varied one, and gave evident satisfaction to a large audience. The only thing that at all marred the pleasure was behaviour of an empty-pated youth, who tried to be funny and failed. In one respect he succeeded, and that was in making himself a nuisance ...

Recitations were given including Mr B. Waite's recitation of 'The Jackdaw of Rheims'. Mr Waite also sang 'Doctor Quack', 'in perfect style', and Mr H. Davis gave a spirited recitation of 'Lord Ullin's Daughter'. Miss E.R. Geen sang a Beethoven song; she and Miss Jane Uppington also 'charmed the audience with one of Mendelsohn's sweet duets'.

In April 1881, the rector and choir of Porlock undertook to perform a Mozart Mass in St George's Church. It was included as part of a shortened form of Evensong, being sung instead of the anthem.

There was also a Dunster Band, which in July 1899 sought engagements for the season. Mr C. Thrust was the Bandmaster. According to the rector, 'the Band played very nicely, and look very smart in their uniforms. They would prove a great addition to any local Entertainment'.

In July 1899 it was also reported in the Parish Magazine that the Rev. James Utten Todd, who had played such a significant part in the musical life of Dunster as a curate, was to take up a post in Alcombe, so remaining in the parish:

> Our old friend Mr James Todd will have once more begun work in the parish which he served in the old days so faithfully and for so long. We congratulate Alcombe very sincerely on having secured his assistance. There, no doubt, he will be warmly welcomed, and we hope that Mr Todd will also now be frequently in Dunster itself, where we can assure him his welcome will be just as hearty.

The Boer Wars

The first Boer War (1880-1) between the British and the Dutch in South Africa was fought over the independence of the Transvaal, originally a state founded by the Boers who had emigrated from British South Africa. After the Boer victory at Majuba Hill in 1881, the Boers secured the independence of the Transvaal subject to British suzerainty.

Prebendary Hancock was appointed vicar of Dunster in 1898. The folowing year, the second Boer War of 1899-1902 broke out. This was to bring great sadness to the vicar, his family and the little town of Dunster, as the vicar's son was killed. Calverley Trevelyan Hancock's memorial brass is to be found on the north wall of the north aisle.

Three months after Calverley Hancock died, the Transvaal and the Orange Free State were annexed by Lord Roberts, the British Commander-in-Chief. The Boers gave up the struggle in 1902 and became British subjects.

I imagine, as I sit in the former study of the rectory in Dunster not only the anguish which must have been felt in this very building, then less than thirty years old, but also the multiplicity of events which took place under this roof. Only twelve years after the Boer War, the Great War 1914-18 took place, and Dunster was only one of the small towns and villages profoundly affected.

The vicar must have immersed himself, soon after this tragic loss, in writing his book *Dunster Church and Priory*, which was published in 1905. He included a list of 'early and interesting inscriptions [in the churchyard] alas! rapidly perishing', copied by Mr Walter Ludlow.

Mr Ludlow was a lay-reader at Alcombe and a sidesman at Dunster in February 1895. He continued to fulfil those roles until May 1899, when he was made churchwarden at Alcombe whilst remaining also a lay-reader. In May, 1902, he was churchwarden and lay-reader at Dunster. In the same year he is referred to as the 'painstaking secretary of the Reading Room'. He died in 1909. This prominent participant in the religious life of Alcombe and Dunster was later remembered by a window to his memory and by an alabaster memorial tablet put on the 'north wall of the chancel of the Parish Church of Dunster in memory of the late Mr Walter Ludlow of Dunster'. (This tablet is not to be found in the church to-day. Presumably it would have been placed on the north wall near the memorial window.) The window was erected as a result of a resolution passed at a vestry meeting on 16 April 1909. The window was to be paid for by public subscriptions and dedicated to the memory of 'Mr Walter Ludlow, b 28.1.1850, d 9.1.1909'.[8]

Dr Joanna Cox, the expert on stained glass observes that:

> ... if, as is thought to be the case, this window is by Clayton and Bell, it is very late. Further it has a lovely blue background but is of a style reminiscent of the 1880/90 period which would have been old-fashioned in 1909 also the glass is matt and not transparent.

The Rev. James Utten Todd, brother of the Rev. Richard Utten Todd, died on 6 July 1913. An enthusiastic bell-ringer, he had been assistant priest to his brother at Dunster between 1873 and 1887, and later became assistant priest at Minehead and subsequently curate-in-charge at Alcombe. A petition for a faculty for the erection of a memorial brass to his memory was made by the Rev. Hancock and by Mary Fownes Luttrell, the elder daughter of George Fownes Luttrell, and Edward Cantle, respectively Vicar and People's Wardens. The resolution to apply for this faculty was passed at a vestry meeting convened on 21 June 1915, and the faculty was granted on 7 July 1915. The estimated cost of the proposed work was £15 2s 0d which was defrayed by Messrs Inchedon and Newbery, solicitors, of Minehead.

It is perhaps of interest to record the exact procedure which preceded the granting of this faculty. Greetings were sent by Francis Henry Lancelot Errington, Master of Arts, Official Principal of the Episcopal Consistorial Court of Wells[9] and he charged and commanded Frederick Hancock and the churchwardens to meet the following requirements:

> ...on Sunday next, immediately following the receipt hereof, by fixing or causing to be affixed these Presents on the Principal Door or Notice Board of the said Church of Dunster aforesaid before Ten o'clock in the forenoon, there to remain until after the hour of Five in the afternoon on Sunday the 4th day of July 1915 Cite all Persons having or pretending to have any objections to the granting of a Licence and Faculty for the purposes aforesaid that they do within Seven days from the day of these Presents being so affixed, enter or cause to be entered an appearance in the Registry of our Consistorial Court in the City of Wells and duly proceed thereon to propound their objections accordingly etc etc.

The First World War; Memorials

During the period of the First World War (1914-1918), on the fourth day of July 1915, another notice was posted on the 'Principal Door of the Church' in respect of a memorial brass to the memory of Lieutenant D'Arcy Frank

Blofeld, a 2nd Lieutenant in the Second Life Guards, who died at Ypres, Flanders, on 12 May 1915, aged 26.

The vestry had approved the erection of this memorial on 21 June 1915. The estimated cost was £18, defrayed by Mr Francis Blofeld of Dunster Lodge, Alcombe. Lt. Blofeld was born on 21 April 1890 and was the only son of Frank and Leslie Blofeld. A Mr Blofeld, presumably Frank Blofeld, was later a sidesman during the incumbency of the Rev. Reeder who retired in 1935. A second faculty was requested for the erection of a tablet in the Parish Church to the memory of the late Gunner Henry Patteson Strong. The 'humble petition' was made by Frederick Hancock of Dunster Priory, Dunster. The estimated cost was £23, defrayed by James Beaver Strong of Court House, Banstead, Surrey. Gunner Strong was the son of James and Elizabeth Patteson Strong; he was a gunner of the 14th Siege Battery, R.G.A, a veteran of the H.A.C. He was killed on active service on 29.10. 1917, at Ypres, aged 41 years. The inscription reads, 'He died for freedom and honour'. This memorial is to be found on the north wall of the nave.

Other memorial brasses on the same wall include those to Calverley Trevelyan Hancock (see above), and to the vicar, his father, Prebendary Frederick Hancock. This reads as follows:

> In loving memory of
> Frederick Hancock. M.A: SCL: FSA.
> Treasurer of Wells Cathedral and
> Prebendary Rector of Meshaw 1879-84
> Rector of Selworthy 1884-99. Vicar of
> Dunster 1899- 1920. Born 30 August
> Died 7 January 1920.

His entry in *Who's Who* also tells us that Prebendary Frederick Hancock had married Baptista J. Woodhouse, the daughter of Rev. John Woodhouse of Huish Champflower, Somerset. They had had four sons and two daughters. In 1896 he had become a J.P. for Somerset and county councillor for Minehead division of Somerset in 1896 (re-elected in 1898 and 1901). Besides *Dunster Church and Priory* Prebendary Hancock had written histories of Selworthy, Minehead and Wiveliscombe. I should perhaps also add that the Hancock family was renowned for the brewery at Wiveliscombe.

At the Easter Vestry meeting in 1920:

> Mr Cantle - People's Warden, proffered and Mr Blofeld – sidesman seconded a vote of condolence to Mrs Hancock and her family in the great loss they had sustained by the death of Prebendary Hancock who had been vicar of the parish for the past 20 years. This was carried in upstanding silence by the Churchwardens.

The new vicar, the Reverend Prebendary W.T. Reeder was instituted on 3 June 1920.

The question of fixing a War Memorial in the church was first discussed at the Easter Vestry of 1921. In October, a meeting was held by the Parochial Church Council (P.C.C.), to consider the erection of this memorial and it was agreed to accept the design for a bronze tablet submitted by Messrs I.W. Singer and Co Ltd of Frome.

The estimated cost of this proposed work was £45 to be defrayed by donations. The bronze tablet was to be fixed to the north wall, midway between the Coat of Arms and the end of the north aisle. It would be dedicated to the memory of the men of the Parish who gave their lives in the Great War 1914-1918.

The faculty for the tablet was granted on 12 November 1921 by the newly appointed Bishop of Bath and Wells, St John Basil Wynne. The names of those commemorated are as follows:

Reginald Burroughs.
Edwin Court.
Rupert Edmunds.
William Greenway.
Alan Ladd.
Herbert Moggridge.
William F. Piddington.
John Thomas.
Robert Webber.
Robert C. Webber.
Richard Wedlake.

The inscription reads: 'their name liveth for evermore'. The Churchwardens' Accounts for 1921 record that £56 16s was collected for this memorial which, according to the 1922 accounts, cost £47 9s 6d.

In 1926 it was reported at the P.C.C. meeting that a proposal to ask for a faculty for the erection of a brass tablet in the church to the memory of the late Colonel Bryant be approved. The cost, estimated at £20, was to be defrayed by Mr G.R. Bryant of Stockbridge, Hants. The work was carried out by Wippell & Co. The inscription on the tablet (on the north side of the nave) reads: 'In loving memory of Lieut. Colonel Alan Bryant D.S.O. of the Gloucestershire Regiment who was killed in action at Ypres, 17th October, 1917 whilst in command of the 9th Batt. Northumberland Fusiliers'.

A further brass on the north wall of the north aisle is to the memory of Elizabeth Howard Hodgkin, the youngest daughter of John Eliot Hodgkin F.S.A., 'a tribute from her devoted sister Janet Harrison'. It was not until December 1927 that the application to fix a brass to the memory of the late Prebendary Hancock in Dunster Church was received from Mrs Hancock. This brass had to be removed when the organ was moved in 1960. It was only replaced, in a slightly different place, after a complaint from his daughter, Baptista Maryon and her husband Arthur Willoughby Trevelyan Channell.

ENDNOTES

1 The Dunster Parish Magazines for 1874-84 and 1896-99 are now stored at the Somerset Record Office, Taunton.

2 See Volume One, pp 139-140 for the contract for building the tower in 1443.

3 When it was built in 1629 by George Luttrell, it was referred to in a document quoted by Lyte as the 'New Hall'. Lyte: H.D. Part I 292/3

4 Ibid. Part II, 331.

5 Ibid. These intials and the date have since been removed.

6 The site of the school is also said to have been where Lock's Restaurant now stands.

7 I was told by the late Sir Walter Luttrell that the Reading Room 'was on the present site of the Memorial Hall'. This hall, erected in 1921 on the western side of the High Street may itself have housed a re-located Reading Room. This site was previously the malthouse of the public house 'The Horse and Crook' next door, and later a builder's yard or premises.

8 A Mary Ann Ludlow of Alcombe, died 23.12.1916 aged 79 years and an Ellen Elizabeth Ludlow of Hawkechurch, Axminster died 21.9.1945 aged 94 years.

9 Francis Errington was a distinguished lawyer, the senior chancellor in England, the Bishop's Vicar General and also the Archbishop of Canterbury's Commissary General.

CHAPTER EIGHT

DUNSTER CHURCH and PARISH in the FIRST PART of the TWENTIETH CENTURY; The SECOND WORLD WAR

Lighting in the Church

It was reported in the Parish Magazine for March 1900 that:

> A long felt want has at length been supplied in the church. The lamps put up some twenty years ago,[1] as it was thought then only to serve a temporary purpose, have done good work but, of late, it has been acknowledged by all that better lamps were sorely needed. Through the assistance of a former neighbour, Mr Lutley, twelve lamps, each of a hundred candle-power and of an handsome pattern, have been procured from a well-known Birmingham firm. The lamps not only look well, but give an excellent light. A handsome lamp from Messrs Wipple and Co., of Exeter, has also been placed in the choir vestry.

In the twentieth century the new lights were required to provide for the very practical necessity of being able to read the service of the Church of England, its hymns and psalms. The lamps were all gifts from various members of the congregation.

However, we first hear about the provision of lights in the 1357 agreement between the Lord of Dunster, Sir John de Mohun, and Prior Richard de Childeston. Later in the sixteenth century there are references to bequests made by various Dunster inhabitants to the lights of devotion in the church (see Volume One). In three wills executed between 1509 and 1517, the dedication of these lights is specifically given as the Light of St George, the Light of Our Lady, the Light of the Holy Rood, also known as the Light of the High Cross, and the Dead Light, or Light of Devotion. In 1510 Robert Loty left money to the Light of St Leonard and to the Lights of St George and Our Lady. Just a few years before the royal injunction of 1538 banning images and all devotional lights except those of the Holy Rood, the light which burned before the sacrament at the altar and the light about the Easter Sepulchre, nine Dunster inhabitants bore witness to their Catholic faith and between 1531 and 1574 left legacies to 'the four lights' in their church.

Electric light came to St George's Church in the 1920s. At the Easter Vestry Meeting in 1921:

> A discussion took place on the lighting of the Church and on the proposition of Miss Luttrell [Mary Fownes Luttrell, O.B.E., the Vicar's Warden], the Vestry recommended that the Church should be lit by Electric light.

This proposition was seconded by Mr Blofeld but by 1922 the lighting was still in a transitional stage as the accounts show £4 5s 8d was spent on oil and candles, and only £4 0s 9d on electric light.

In 1923 the cost of the installation of electricity was £119 13s. This was defrayed from the Free Will Offering, an offering administered by the People's Warden, Mr Cantle and his wife.

On 10 October 1934, Mr Hunt of Minehead presented an estimate for £9 17s 6d for the provision of lighting on the belfry stairs, the ringing chamber, and the belfry and clock chambers and this was accepted. Minor details such as the replacement of a suspended light over the organ by a strip light and the provision of additional lighting in the vestry received attention in 1935 and 1936 respectively.

The Minehead Electric Company on 5 September 1938 carried out an inspection of the church lights and fittings, and later carried out the renewals and cleaning they had recommended. A lamp more conventionally placed was desired over the choir stalls and 100-watt lamps were installed at the vicar's instruction.

The lighting of the Sanctuary and the Altar was of paramount importance to the vicar of the time, Preb. Dunlop, who eight years later in his *Yearly Notes* for 1946 wrote: 'the Daily Offices have been said and a week-day Communion established every Thursday. The lighting of the Sanctuary and Altar have become central to the picture'. The entry in his account of the years 1946-1956 enlarges upon this:

> A method of Sanctuary lighting has been introduced whereby the Altar and the Great Arch behind are most effectively illuminated. Curtains have been put up to provide a screen between the Sanctuary and the Transept.

In 1952 the electricity was in a parlous state.[2] Preb. Dunlop's Yearly Notes for this year reveal that anxiety was felt over its safety and insurance cover. He wrote:

> I have also had a report on the Electric Lighting Installation in the Church both from the South West Electricity Board and from Harold Rogers and there is no doubt that it is in a very bad way. Almost outside the range of insurance. I understand that Prebendary Reeder, introduced it some 25 years ago doing much of the work with his own hands – but giving 15 years as the limit of its endurance. Something just must be done and a report has come in from Mr Rogers for our consideration. It will need fairly extensive re-construction and possible expense. These things are what we must

try and effect during the year 1953. The completion and dedication of the Cloister Garden and the installation of a good lighting system.

Mr Harold Rogers was a well-known architect from Oxford who had been called in by Preb. Dunlop. He confirmed the adverse report submitted by the Electricity Board and 'went so far as to say that he did not think that any insurance company would be willing to carry the risk'. Preb. Dunlop further added, 'we really need a completely new installation'.

On 5 May 1953 a sub-committee convened to examine the problem, and announced that the best form of lighting would be pendant lights between the arches with brackets on the north wall.

Major Marsden, the Consulting Church Architect of Messrs Aston and Marsden of Minehead, submitted his report in June and the outcome was that it was decided to postpone the lighting of the Priory Church but to put the lighting of the Parish Church in hand as soon as possible with a firm of repute in this type of work. The cost of the work was estimated at £500. In fact the work carried out in Sept/Oct 1953 cost £560.

Preb. Dunlop wrote about the result of this work and said:

> The Globes may not be ideal but they were the best we could secure – and there was some difficulty in securing them. At any rate the lights no longer hang down the middle of the church but are fixed between the arches and on the walls.

A little later he wrote:

> We have nearly exhausted our reserves over the Electric Lighting System but perhaps that's all to the good – for Dunster people always seem to think we have larger reserves and that checks the Spirit of Giving ... the material used was the best obtainable, and should last for very many years to come. The lighting itself is good and simple and on the right lines and there is much advantage in having got rid of the disused chains which used to hang from the roof of the Church like a spider's web.

Although Preb. Dunlop said that the work was carried out in Sept/Oct 1953, he reported to the P.C.C. on 16 February 1954 that:

> The installation of the lighting of the Church was practically completed. The Architect's Certificate, together with a bill from Messrs Furze for £450 had been received. No Architect's fee had as yet been produced.

Presumably, if the total cost £560, the Architect's fee when eventually presented must have been £110.

In April 1954 'lighting for the pulpit and the lectern was still under consideration'. In the same year concern was being shown over the lighting in the Priory Church. The vicar thought it was not good but said ' we cannot face another £300 bill, especially as the Priory Church does not belong to us'.

A compromise seems to have been reached, for in the Annual Review it was reported that by Easter 1959:

> The Priory Church was lit, not by lights which used to hang somewhat dangerously from the roof and obstruct most disconcertingly, the view of the beautiful lancet windows, but from metal brackets made by a former vicar, Mr Reeder [*Vicar 1920-1935*] in his workshop at the Priory.

Norman Font

It was during the incumbency of the Rev. Reeder that Dunster Church acquired the tub font now in the south transept. He bought it from Thomas Kent Ridler, who had a builder's yard in North Road, Minehead in the 1920s.

The story of the font came to light in November 1989, when the Rev. Doré received a letter from Mr J. K. Ridler of Wootton Courtenay. It concerned the 'crude old stone vessel' to which Mr Ridler drew the rector's attention after the evening in the church devoted to a talk on the restoration of the dovecot. He wrote:

> ... during the 1920's my cousin Thomas Kent Ridler (1880-1946) had a yard in North Road, Minehead in which he carried on, *inter alia*, the business of a builder's merchant, in succession to his father, T.K.R. (1847-1900) and our grandfather, John Ridler (1801-76).
>
> One day I was in the yard with Kent and noticed this article. He said he had been told it was an ancient font from a local church which had been "restored" by a Minehead builder, John Pearse.
>
> I understand Pearse was in debt to the firm when my grandfather died and I expect his business petered out, so that the contents of his yard came to my uncle as a creditor.
>
> In the 1920's few took any interest in local history, but I mentioned this to Preb. W.T. Reeder, Vicar of Dunster, who I knew well when he was Rector of Selworthy.
>
> Kent told me Mr Reeder came in and bought it from him, but I heard nothing more until I recognised it many years later in Dunster Church. It must have deteriorated by lying in an open yard for probably 60 years.
>
> I cannot think of any local church without an ancient font, with the possible exception of Wootton Courtenay where the fine octagonal font might be in too good condition to be really ancient. A tablet states that the Reverend Russell Richards had the chancel rebuilt before he died in 1863 and I wonder if he could have given a new font, employing John Pearse to do the rebuilding.
>
> This may be only a wild guess, but I should be interested if you are able to get an opinion.

Did the Rev. Reeder have some information, now lost to us, that this font belonged to Dunster? If not, why did he buy it and place it in that church whose charter goes back to between 1090 and 1100 AD? The present font is probably sixteenth century and Dr Bettey says that the ancient font was always preserved:

> The font was an important symbol of the pastoral authority of the parish church. It was, for this reason, that in countless country churches the ancient font was preserved when all the rest of the church was rebuilt in the Middle Ages so that, to-day, the font often provides a clearer indicator of the age of the church than almost any other surviving part of the building.[3]

The font in question is an example of the earliest unmounted round ones in a form which is a continuation of Saxon tub fonts. Other Norman fonts of bowl, square, cup or chalice shape may be mounted or unmounted. It is usually apparent that Norman fonts are of a better shape and are more competently decorated than Saxon ones but the round ring of the Dunster font is a continuation of Saxon culture. It is possible that it originally bore decorations synonymous with Norman architecture, i.e. chevrons; arcading either plain or intersecting; cable moulding and even figures, but exposure took its toll. It is indeed possible that this font pre-dates the original church and is Saxon and belonged to an earlier Saxon foundation. It is significant that Mr Kent in his letter speaks of the font's exposure for sixty years in the 1920s, that is from 1860. It could indeed have been discarded at the time of the Victorian restoration of 1874-6 since Mr Kent was only approximating. It was at this time that the Victorian 'Gothic' canopy was placed over the sixteenth-century font.

Church Accounts

It is perhaps not inappropriate, since the tub font was acquired in the 1920s, to include the accounts for 1919-20. They provide an interesting insight and have been transcribed from the *Year Book* for 1920:

Receipts				Expenses			
To collections viz.				Choir Expenses viz.			
Church Expenses	153	1	5	Organist	52	0	0
To Charities viz.				Choir Boys	3	12	10
Dunster Hospital[4]	7	0	0	Washing Surplices	1	1	6
Nursing Assn.	7	3	0	Choir Outing	14	15	0
Viennese Fund	3	10	0	Organ Blower	3	18	0
Alms Box	11	17	8	Tuning Organ	5	0	0
Alcombe Donation to	5	0	0	Repairing Cassocks	1	6	0
Diocesan Quota					81	13	6
A.F. Luttrell Esq.				Charities as per contra	17	13	0
Donation from				Clock and Chimes	5	16	0
Castle Grounds Receipts	10	0	0	Ringing of six o'clock bell	3	0	0
ditto for Clock Fund	5	0	0	Lighting and Cleaning			
Rev. W.T. Reeder	8	8	0	Mr Walton	18	17	6

Voluntary contributions				Mrs Gollop	13	6	0
Admiral Acland	2	2	0	Belfry		12	0
Mrs Tudway	1	11	6	Heating	32	15	6
Donations from				Fuel	16	14	2
Freewill Offering Fund	3	11	9	Stoking	3	3	0
	£218	5	4		19	17	2
				Insurances	7	6	0
Audited and found correct G.E. Flack				Cutting churchyard Grass	3	12	6
7 April 1920				Communion Wine	2	2	0
				Ringing 8.15am Bell		6	6
				Diocesan Quote	15	0	0
				Visitation fees		8	6
				Cheque Book		8	4
				Transferred to Clock Fund	5	0	0
				Repairs	10	13	10
				Sequestration Fees	2	5	0
				Rent of Curate's Rooms	8	8	0
				Postage and Sundries	1	19	8
					218	5	4

E.G.Cantle
Mary F Luttrell } Churchwardens.

R. Lloyd Williams. Chairman.

Church Restoration of 1936

In 1929 Dr Francis Eeles[5] reported on Dunster Church. Writing from his holiday home 'Cross Meadows', Alcombe on 30 Dec 1929, he said he had examined the church with special reference to the damage done by the recent severe weather and found the following problems:

(1) Water has come through the lead valley gutter between the nave and the north aisle. This has apparently been due to one of the lead sheets being worn out; it has already been mended in some six places. The leadwork in this gutter has not enough fall, but owing to the western part being supported on an upper wall plate or beam it would seem doubtful if a sharper fall could be arranged

(2) Water has also entered the east end of the nave roof on the north side close to the tower. This is probably due to a defect in the short gutter on the south of the staircase turret which I could not reach.

(3) There has been penetration of water in the S. aisle roof, also apparently due to defective leadwork. Here there is insufficient fall in the gutter on the south side and the boxes at the heads of the downpipes are of bad construction and do not allow the water to escape quickly enough.

(4) The parapet on the south side requires repointing in places on the inside.

(5) The lead roof of the turret which contained the rood-loft staircase is in bad condition and has insufficient fall: there is no downpipe to keep the water clear of the wall and the pointing is bad.

(6) There is decay caused by damp at the base of the S. transept roof immediately beneath slates outside.

(7) At the base of the pinnacle on the W. side of the S. transept gable the lead flashing needs re-dressing.

(8) There is a hole in the slates in the roof of the N. aisle of the Priory Church caused by fall of the part of one of the tower pinnacles.

(9) The creeper should be removed from the gable coping of the N. transept.

(10) Better fall is required for the gutters on either side of the porch on the ground, and the dwarf walls should be set back on the outer corners of the porch so as to facilitate drying.

(11) There are slight cracks, probably not new, in the W. gable of the N. aisle and the tracery of the W. window is affected, though not seriously: a contributory cause seems to be the iron saddle bars. This is not a matter of such urgency as the others.

(12) The water drainage on the N. side of the church in the old cloister court is inadequate.

In the case of the tower I find the following:

(1) The position of the N.E pinnacle immediately below the finial has been split by the rust from the iron dowel and has fallen, leaving the finial in a very precarious condition and ready to fall. The finial should be removed without delay pending permanent repair of the pinnacle.

(2) The finial of the S.E. pinnacle is split; if it is in the least degree loose, it should be removed at once; if holding firm, it could be tied.

(3) The lightning conductor on the S. W. pinnacle has been blown down near the top and requires fixing.

All the pinnacles are held up by iron stays supporting iron collars; although the security of the pinnacle depends on these supports they are of a kind which the Bath and Wells Advisory Committee has been obliged to condemn in the case of many of our finest towers, owing to danger from rust and wind pressure. All these pinnacles appear to have been shaken by the recent gales and there are signs of weakness in the joints at their bases. I fear the time has come when these pinnacles ought to be rebuilt in accordance with modern methods eliminating iron supports and substituting a non-rusting metal. This is a matter which requires special skill and experience.

(4) Repair is required at the top of the staircase turret, fortunately very slight. The flat top requires protection from wet and might be covered with a damp-resisting preparation.

(5) The upper surfaces of practically all the string courses, battlements and off-sets throughout the tower are badly honey-combed with surface decay and rapid deterioration is inevitable if measures are not taken to

counteract this either by coating with mortar or synthetic stone. These string courses and off-sets have great practical value in throwing off water quickly and the increasing ineffectiveness of them is bad for the tower.

(6) There are some iron cramps which need very careful examination if not removal because of danger from rust, notably in the joint for the Window of the ringing chamber immediately above the nave roof.

Generally there are good many places in the church where minor repairs are required, such as very small pieces of pointing, and it is very noticeable that the "fatter" current pointing with fine sand is not so effective as the more old-fashioned style with coarser sand and a smaller proportion of cement. I am inclined to think that there is much to be said here in West Somerset for the view held by the architects, Central Council, Ecclesiastical Commissioners, H.M Office of Works and the National Trust that a good lias lime mortar is better for use where ancient buildings are concerned.

F.C. Eeles.

This report of Dr Francis Eeles in 1929 led eventually to the restoration of 1936. This was by no means a restoration on the scale of the great 1874-6 restoration but one which became the central issue during the Vicarate of Rev. A.B. Burney (1935-38).

Only item (1) was addressed during the Rev. Reeder's last years at Dunster, for the P.P.C. Minutes (23.2.1931) refer to the fact that 'repairs to the wall plate in the north aisle were discussed' and the Rural Dean's Report of 2.9.1931 recommended that 'the wall plate of the north aisle should be examined'. (The chimes were repaired in 1931 but the vast subject of the bells, chimes or carillon etc. will be dealt with in another chapter.)

At the same meeting questions relating to the roofing of the Lych Gate were raised. It was three years later on 10 October 1934 that the Treasurer, Mr Simpson, agreed to arrange for a specification for its repair to be drawn up. On 25 February 1935, a discussion took place regarding the re-fixing of the gates and it was decided to approach the Parish Council over this matter, and also the placing of suitable notices at the entrance to the church-yard.

On 2 November 1932 the Rev. Reeder pointed out the necessity for a safe to accommodate the Church Registers and other documents. The motion was carried but the purchase was deferred 'for the present' by the vicar on 16 October 1933 A safe stands in the north transept to-day but I have yet to discover when it was finally purchased. It was repaired by Mr Steve Bowden in September 1947 and for security reasons, it holds nothing of value and only the current Registers are held in the church, the earlier ones being deposited in the Somerset Record Office.

By October 1934 the Rev. Reeder was unable to continue with his ministry for reasons of age and on 3 May 1935 the Rev. A.B. Burney was instituted. The Rev. Reeder had been vicar of Dunster for fifteen years and his resignation was received with expressions of sincere regret from the P.C.C.

At Rev. Burney's first Parochial Church Council Meeting on 27 June 1935 the subject under discussion was the levelling of the churchyard, but 'it was first necessary to do something with regard to the churchyard entrances, before any levelling was undertaken'. The Secretary was instructed to ascertain from the Parish Council whether the Church Council, if they replaced gates at the entrances, would be 'acting within their rights'.

By July 1935 it was decided, on the proposition of Messrs Simpson and Long, that the gates at the Lych Gate should be re-hung with a central moveable post. It was also agreed that estimates be obtained for the erection of gates at the two bottom entrances to the churchyard.[6]

That October Mr Simpson produced Messrs J. Hine and Sons' estimate for the erection of these two gates 'at the lower end of the Churchyard'. Repairs to the walls from these two points to the south door of the church was also included. The tender was £21.6.0. and was accepted on the proposition of Mr Hopwood and seconded by Miss M Luttrell (Vicar's Warden). The order for the work had been placed by 26 November 1935. In the church accounts for the year ending 1935 there is an entry for £50 2s 7d, for repairs, including the Lych Gate. We hear nothing more about levelling the churchyard during this period but on 22 February 1937 Mr William Court offered to keep it generally tidy and to cut the grass at least four times during the year for the sum of £6 and this was accepted.

The vicar, the Rev. A.B. Burney, had arranged for an inspection of the church fabric by the architect, Mr Blacking. At the P.C.C. Meeting held on 17 February 1936 the members learned that Mr Blacking's report revealed that the tower, windows and screen needed immediate attention. Mr F.C. Eeles, who was an eminent authority on these matters and had brought the need for repairs to the Council's attention in his letter of 1929, quoted earlier, attended the meeting at the vicar's invitation. He suggested that the Council consider the advisability of carrying out the whole of the work outlined in the report. Mr Eeles stated that the repairs to the tower might cost £200, the iron and stonework in the windows £10 and the screen £20; but added that these estimates should be accepted with reserve.

Mr Hopwood, sidesman and member of the P.C.C., proposed that the work of the restoration be undertaken in accordance with the architect's report with the exception of the roof, heating apparatus and monuments, and that a sub-committee be formed to arrange and supervise the work. Mr Griffiths, also a sidesman and member of the P.C.C., stated that if Mr Hopwood would include the repainting of the clock dials in the work to be done, he would second the resolution. Mr Hopwood agreed and the resolution was carried (17.2.1936).

A more detailed estimate was received from Mr Blacking after he had revisited the church. The tender was for £320. This was accepted (P.C.C. Minutes 16.3.1936). It seems that the Restoration Subcommittee, which wished first to consider the architect's report, requested an amendment to this effect, but the Committee was defeated and the resolution was carried.

(As early as November 1932 various minor repairs to the tower steps, the roof and the tower had been discussed and Messrs Long and Simpson had been asked to take action.)[7]

The lightning conductor, it was reported on 16 April 1936, would cost £21 to put in order according to Mr Blacking's estimate. No decision was taken on this matter and on 30 June 1936 Mr Blacking wrote and asked what was happening. Mr Simpson suggested that the architect be asked for a report on the matter especially pointing out in what way it was defective and asking for an estimate of the cost of putting it in proper order. Eventually, on 22 June 1936, a proposal by Mr Hopwood that the lightning conductor should be repaired in accordance with the specification they had received from Messrs Lynch, was seconded by Mr Simpson and carried. However, when Mr Lynch's account for the work done was presented to the P.C.C. they did not agree. Mr Lynch had charged an extra £6 for three new earth terminals and it was decided to send the account to Mr Blacking, the Architect, for his opinion. Mr Blacking was also asked for an explanation as to why copper had been used on the tower in a way not provided for in the specification. He was also asked to report on the cost of the work to date. This was all in June 1936.

With regard to the tower, as late as October 1935 the problem was still not dealt with, for we read 'that the pinnacles of the Tower required immediate attention', and that Miss M Luttrell had proposed that Messrs Hine and Sons be appointed to deal with the removal of the damaged portions as soon as possible. It was reported on 26 November 1935 that the pinnacles had finally received attention.

On 22 July 1936 the Rev. A. B. Burney, Chairman of the P.C.C., referred to the state of the louvres in the belfry; it was proposed by Mr Hopwood and seconded by Mr Griffiths that the broken ones should be replaced. Additionally, the down pipes should receive two coats of paint and the lead repaired where required. A year earlier (P.C.C. 19.7.1935) it had been proposed by Mr Simpson that Messrs Hine and Sons be instructed to clean the shoots and fall pipes of the church generally where needed.

The belfry windows came in for attention again on 7 September 1936 when it was decided at the P.C.C. Meeting that Messrs Hine be instructed to board and wire them under the supervision of Mr Long. This was proposed by Mr Griffiths and seconded by the secretary but we read that at their meeting held on 9 November 1936 'the question of the boarding up of the belfry window on the west side of the tower was raised; but from the discussion which followed nothing definite transpired'. In December 1937, Messrs Hine & Sons were instructed to build a new door and frame in the belfry. The clock dials were re-gilded in 1936.

The Secretary, Mr R.P. Day, tendered his resignation at the P.C.C. Meeting held on 8 May 1936, because he felt that 'some of the Council's work was becoming confused through an absence of proper procedure at its meetings and in carrying out decisions'. Eventually the Secretary was asked to reconsider his decision to resign, and the Chairman suggested that he and the Secretary should confer on the point at issue. The Secretary then offered to continue in office in the anticipation that the matter he had mentioned would be straightened out.

Fund-raising for the Restoration

There remained the task of raising money to pay for the restoration. There was at Dunster a scheme called the Free Will Offering Scheme. In 1923 the income was £56 16s 7d. When electricity was introduced in that year, the cost was met out of these funds. The secretary was Mrs Cantle who, together with her husband, churchwarden for twenty-three years, retired at the Easter Vestry of 1929. Mrs Cantle was succeeded by Mr Walter Long who served as People's Warden with the Vicar's Warden, Miss Mary Fownes Luttrell.

It was agreed that after the P.C.C. had had the opportunity of considering the Architect's Report on the Church, the management of the Free Will Offering Scheme, which had lapsed, should be reconsidered. The collections and the money from the alms box had provided an income which was up to average.

Mr Ross undertook to revise the F.W.O. Scheme at the P.C.C. Meeting held on 28 January 1936. These meetings were, incidentally, held at the school and on some rarer occasions in the vestry. The secretary was now Mr P.R. Day.

It was decided in March 1936 that ordinary church expenses should be met out of collections and the F.W.O. Scheme, and the following month the recommendation of the Finance Sub-Committee that the visitors' gifts collected from the church box should be placed solely to the Restoration Fund was adopted and carried. The Chairman suggested that a special appeal to visitors should be placed on the church box, calling their attention to the work of the restoration at present being carried out and commending their generosity.

In his efforts to revive the F.W.O. Scheme, Mr Ross was to be assisted by the Finance Committee and, as members of the council, the Misses Mary and Beatrice Luttrell were co-opted. The first meeting of the Restoration Committee was held by the P.C.C. on 18 May 1936. The Treasurer, Mr Simpson, reported that 'there were twelve members in 1935 and that the total sum in hand was £478'. It was decided that a circular publicising the scheme should be placed in the church pews.

A finance meeting was held on 6 October 1936 and again on 9 November 1936. The October minutes show that the restoration of the church was well under way:

> The Committee then received the state of the Council's finances to date. These showed that out of the accumulated fund of £478 in the original F.W.O. Account, £150 had been paid to Mr Fry for Restoration and £27 to Messrs Lynch and Sons for work done to the Lightning Conductor. Outstanding accounts included those for painting clock dials; repair of louvres; restoration of screen; architect's fees and the remainder of Mr Fry's accounts, the total cost of which would not be less than £250. The Treasurer

also stated that since the F.W.O. had been revived, £30 had been received by that fund, which would be devoted to Church Expenses, and Visitors' Gifts through the Alms Box had totalled over £130 this season and this would help to meet expenses in connection with the work of Restoration.

On 9 November 1936 the Treasurer was called to make a statement on the restoration accounts. This showed that the total expense increased was £499 11s 8d, made up as follows:

Messrs Fry.	£376	2s	11d
Clock painting and repairs.	£18	17s	6d
Hire of cradle and cost of moving same for clock painting.	£ 8	0s	0d
Treating of Screen.	£13	18s	6d
Messrs Lynch for repairing of Lightning Conductor.[8]	£ 27	0s	0d
Architect's fees and expenses.	£55	12s	9d

Mr Simpson stated that £177 had already been paid, leaving £322 11s 8d still to be met. The accounts were discussed at some length and various questions asked. It was eventually decided on the motion of Mr Hopwood, seconded by Colonel Carlisle, that the account be paid; it was further agreed that the secretary be instructed to ask Mr Blacking, the architect, to forward accounts and that the Finance Committee should decide how the work was to be paid for.

The financial situation as reported in the P.C.C. Minutes for 22 November 1936 was that in the General Fund there was £197 6s 6d which included the £130 given by visitors, £301 in the original F.W.O. Fund and about £30 in the revived F.W.O. Fund. £322 11s 8d remained to be paid for Restoration Accounts and the Church Expenses from Nov ember 1936 to 31 December would probably be another £100. It was decided that the balance of £301 in the original F.W.O. Fund should be used to meet the remaining charges for the Restoration; the difference, namely about £21 11s 8d, should be met from the Alms Box Fund.

Mary Fownes Luttrell, Vicar's Warden since before 1920, retired through ill-health at the 1936 Easter Vestry. The register shows that she died on 7 October 1936, aged 83 years and that she lived at 'The Hall' (now the 'Castle Hotel'). Her name is inscribed on the priory altar cross, with that of her younger brother Alexander, and the date, 1876. Mary Luttrell was succeeded by her nephew, Geoffrey Fownes Luttrell (1887-1957). Her sister Beatrice Fownes Luttrell (1862-1941) also served on the P.C.C. and died aged 79 years on 25 February 1941.[9]

By January 1937 the amount spent on the restoration of the church fabric was £464 10s 1d while £136 10s 7d had been contributed in the Visitors' Box. However, the revival of the F.W.O. had not fared too well. The result of the year's effort had only resulted in £33 16s 7d. During the discussion which followed, it transpired that Miss Bond, F.W.O. Secretary, was not a member of the Council. Messrs Sparks and Patfield moved that she be co-opted and this was carried (20.4.1937).

The collections were indeed discouraging. The Treasurer reported on 12 July 1937 that the receipts from the 8.15 am and 6.30 pm services and the F.W.O. totalled £116 17s 3d, while the payments had reached £191 1s 8d, leaving a deficit of £74 4s 5d.

By December 1937 there was £142 on the deposit account, £33 in the F.W.O. account and £70 in the current account. Collections had been above average but there were several heavy accounts to be paid before the end of the year. At the A.G.M. of the P.C.C. on 21 February 1938 Mr Simpson reported a deficit of £44 2s 11d. Collections for church expenses were considerably lower than for the previous year but the Alms Box had produced 6 guineas more. It was unanimously agreed after discussion to transfer money from the Fabric Fund to pay the account of Messrs Hine & Sons.

Cleaning of the Rood Screen

One of the major undertakings during the 1936 restoration was the cleaning of the 1499 screen. Dr F.C. Eeles suggested that the work advised by Mr Blacking, the architect, might cost £20 (P.C.C. Minutes 17.2.1936).

On 16 April 1936, Mr Tudball proposed and Mr Griffiths seconded that a definite figure of the cost be obtained from Miss Becker and that the Restoration Subcommittee be empowered to instruct how to proceed with the work. This proposal was carried.

The vicar, the Rev. A.B. Burney, had an interview with Miss Becker who stated that her charge for supervising the work necessary on the screen was one guinea per day. She said that the total cost would therefore depend to a very large extent on the voluntary work which might be forthcoming. Miss Becker's estimate was accepted (P.C.C. Minutes 3.5.1936).

At this same meeting of the Restoration Committee on 18 May 1936, the Chairman reported that the Hoover firm at Bristol would not undertake the responsibility of cleaning the screen but that they would lend machines for doing the work. In consequence he had arranged for Miss Becker to come again in the Autumn to do the required work.

The same committee met on 7 September 1936. The vicar reported on the removal of the dust from the screen and said that if beetle were found active, the architect should instruct Mr Fry to brush and spray where necessary. The hope was expressed at the meeting of the Finance Committee on 6 October 1936 that work at present being done on the screen by Miss Becker would be completed in a fortnight. A minor detail relevant to the main screen was the decision taken on 9 October 1939 that a ramp should be supplied at the screen door.

A summarised statement on the insurance of the church and its contents resulted in the proposal of Colonel Carlisle that the cover be increased to £20,000. This motion was seconded by Mr Long and carried unanimously.

This concludes the information available concerning the 1936 restoration.

Cleaning of the church; Vergers

The life of the church is made up of a myriad of tasks one of which is the cleaning of the building. When I first came to live in Dunster in 1985 the verger was Mr Perry who retired after his wife's death and emigrated to be near his family in Australia. In her lifetime Mrs Perry presented a rococo-style silvered flower stand to the church. The cleaning of the church then devolved on a devoted but increasingly ageing band drawn from the choir, the flower arrangers, the bell ringers and general congregation.

Back in the 1920s the cost of cleaning the church was £12 6s and the cleaning of the belfry cost 12s. These expenses appear in the accounts for 1922/23/24. However, in 1925, for some reason, the cleaning bill was £8.16s for the church and £3 2s 4d for the belfry. By 1926 it was decided that 'the whole work of the Church be placed in one person's hands and that Mr Sparks' offer as caretaker at the sum of £1 per week should be accepted'.

Mr Sparks seems to have coped with this for eight years, but by 1934 he was finding it increasingly difficult to carry out all the duties devolving on him. He tendered his resignation in a letter to the P.C.C. Meeting on 17 February 1936. As a result other arrangements were made for the cleaning of the church while Mr Sparks was elected solely to carry out the duties of verger at a salary of £73 per annum.

In January 1937 the bell-ringers suggested that the P.C.C. should pay £1 per annum for cleaning the belfry, bells and cage, which sum had previously been paid by the ringers from their own collection. The chairman agreed and they did far better, for they were allocated £2 10s for this purpose on 22 February 1937. In November 1938, when Mr Sparks became both verger and stoker, he received £26 per annum, no doubt an additional remuneration for his duties as stoker.

War-time bonuses of £10 each were paid to Mr Sparks and to Mrs Haydon, the cleaner in November 1941. When Mr Sparks died in 1944, Mrs Haydon was appointed verger in his stead at a salary of 17s 6d per week.

In October 1945 she was reported in the P.C.C. Minutes as 'probably relinquishing her duties at the end of the year', and the question of appointing a verger and cleaner on a whole-time basis arose. Mr Sidney Willis was to be offered the post at a salary not exceeding £4 per week as from 1 January 1946. In fact, Mr Willis settled for £3 10s per week and started his duties on Christmas Day 1945. One of his duties was the winding of the clock, which had been the task of Mr A. Tudball, who had resigned from the P.C.C. in October 1945.

Music in Church

In the large red volume entitled the *1920 Dunster Book* which is, in fact, the Minutes Book of the Parochial Church Council, there is a reference to a meeting held in January 1924 when a discussion took place concerning the improvement of music and singing in church services. The vicar at the time was the Rev. Preb. William T. Reeder, who retired in 1935. Mr E.G. Cantle was secretary of the P.C.C. and the members included the Misses Luttrell. Repairs were needed to the organ. This was repaired by Messrs Daniel & Mimms; the estimate was for £185.

In the 1920s, the organist was Captain Hook who in 1923 received £52 per annum for his services. (The organ-blower was paid £5 p.a. in 1926.) He was associated, not only with the church choir, but with the Sunday School, the bell-ringers, the British Legion and the Choral Society. Captain Hook relinquished the post of organist on 22 July 1936 and planned to leave Dunster in the following September. Mr Amherst succeeded him as organist in October 1936. Not only was Mr Amherst the choirmaster and organist but he was the auditor of the church, for he was a professional auditor and partner in the well-known local firm of Amherst and Shapland.

Mr Amherst and Church Music; Church Furnishings

On his appointment, Mr Amherst asked for information on the arrangements, if any, made by P.C.C. for the purchase of music for the choir and the payment of choir expenses in attending choir festivals. In fact the P.C.C. Meeting held on 9 November 1936 overflowed with matters concerning the requirements of the new organist. Mr Amherst displayed great enthusiasm to see everything done to the best of his ability and to make a real success of his appointment. He sought permission, which was granted, to place his own piano in the vestry for rehearsals and arrangements were made for additional lighting there. However, his request for new psalters and chant books was deferred. He also persuaded the P.C.C. that the pews occupied by the ladies of the choir should be raised on platforms so as to be on a level with the men.

The minutes of the Parochial Church Council dated 22 February 1937 record that an annual fee was paid to the School of English Church Music. On 20 April 1937 it was agreed that a grant of £100 a year, to be paid in quarterly instalments, should be made to Mr Amherst. This would include his salary of £52, and the purchase of sheet music to festivals and outings.

In July 1937 Mr Amherst reiterated the need for new psalters and chant books. So the church accounts for the year ending 31 December 1937 show two entries for new psalters which cost £3 17s. 0d and for new chant books which cost £2.

Earlier on 26 November 1935 the secretary had proposed and Miss Luttrell had seconded a request for the heating of the church for choir practices. Nothing appears to have happened because on 6 December 1937 Mr Amherst made a request for the heating to be on on Mondays and Wednesdays for the said choir practices. At the December meeting Mr Simpson gave a comprehensive report on the heating system and Mr Amherst outlined what he felt necessary to enable the choir practice to be carried out effectively. Several P.C.C members referred to the coldness of the church and the contributory causes, such as draughts, open doors and the need for repairs etc. It was agreed that the boiler should be lit continuously up to Christmas. Messrs Hine and Sons were instructed to put T-springs on the insides of the two south doors and that of the north door and were instructed to repair the windows on either side of the chancel. The P.C.C. on 28 March 1938 decided to light the fire from Thursday to Sunday for the remainder of the winter. This involved extra stoking and Mr Sparks would be asked to accept £3 for his trouble.

At the beginning of December 1937 Mr Amherst suggested holding occasional meetings of a combined social and business nature to which all church people should be invited and at which reports on various church activities should be given and discussion and interest aroused. This was thought to be a good idea and the proposal was seconded by Mrs Long and carried unanimously.

Earlier in 1937 the vicar had mentioned that improvements in the furnishings of the Priory Church would be carried out. This probably relates to a legacy left by Miss Griffiths, a member of the P.C.C., part of which was used to purchase furnishings, books etc., as a fitting memorial of her faithful services over a long period. The two carved figures in the sanctuary of the Priory Church may have been purchased with her money.

In September 1938 it was decided to purchase a dozen new chairs for the use of the choir, to replace those which were worm-eaten. Up to the end of the Rev. Doré's incumbency there were rush-seated chairs stacked in the north aisle.

Reignation of Rev. A.B. Burney

The Rev. A.B. Burney, who had replaced Rev. Reeder in 1935, was ill in December 1937, and at the P.C.C. A.G.M held on 21 February 1938 he tendered his resignation from the living, a decision at which he had arrived only after close consideration and his medical adviser.[10]

The vicar reiterated the reasons for his resignation at the Annual Vestry Meeting held in the school on 9 May 1938. He said:

> It is very lovely here. If only the people would back up their vicar better it would make an ideal job. I see in the future that the spirit, the real Spirit of God, will in some mysterious way move the men of Dunster to give up the sort of slack way in which they are going on at the present time and that they will come out and back us up.

He emphasised that he was not the only one who felt the lack of backing. He referred to Colonel Hartley Carlisle's similar experiences with the Boy Scouts and alluded to the little help which Miss Griffiths received in connection with missionary work. He also took the opportunity of thanking Mr C.E. Simpson for help so readily given in the Sunday-school.

At the same meeting, Mr J. Griffiths enquired as to whether anything could be done to make the living of Dunster more attractive to a potential vicar and the vicar pointed out that the living would be worth £42 per year less when he went, because of the Tithe Act. He said 'by the time [the vicar] has paid out all his dues he gets about enough out of it to pay a gardener'.

He added that the living was in private patronage and the Ecclesiastical Commissioners would not augment any living under such patronage. Mr Griffiths wondered whether any benefit might not come from a pooling of resources of various parishes and remarked that it was unfair that such a living should be put at such a low figure.

On the resignation of a vicar and during the interregnum prior to the appointment of a new incumbent, the living is administered by the church-wardens. Mr Geoffrey Luttrell was then the Vicar's Warden and Mr Walter Long was the People's Warden. The Rev. Burney's parting gift was a new St George's flag which he presented to the P.C.C.

Bishop Underhill's Visitation

The visitation by the newly-appointed Bishop of Bath and Wells to Dunster was planned to take place on 16 May. No such bishop had visited Dunster for sixteen years. The vicar hoped that the bells would be rung and that all the wardens and clergy in the deanery would come and that the choir also would attend, including the choir of Alcombe, along with the school children. Afterwards the churchwardens would have an old-fashioned lunch at the *Luttrell Arms*, over which the Bishop would preside and where they would get to know each other.

The day previous to the vestry meeting, on 8 May 1938, Dr Francis Eeles preached at Dunster about the approaching official visitation by Dr Francis Underhill, Bishop of Bath and Wells. His sermon was fully reported in the *West Somerset Free Press*. Although Bishop de Salis had repeatedly held visitations at Dunster, Dr Eeles explained, he had done this in his capacity of arch-deacon and not as a Bishop. (Bishop de Salis was soon to resign as arch-deacon of Taunton, but would remain an assistant bishop in the diocese.) [11]

Facsimile of Missale Anglicanum

I should add to this account of the visitation of Bishop Underhill an inter-esting detail. In 1991/2 the NADFAS Church Recorders found a missal in an oak chest in the south aisle. Inside this beautifully illustrated missal, there was a sheet of paper saying 'this missal belonged to Francis Underhill Lord Bishop of Bath and Wells (1937-42).' Although it was customary to exchange gifts on the occasion of a visitation, I found on making my researches in the Bishop's Register, that there was no evidence of such a gift. In September 1993, I was informed by the Church Recorders that in 1992 the Rev. Doré had presented this missal to the bishop's secretary to be displayed in the Henderson Rooms in the Bishop's Palace.[12] This missal is 'a facsimile of the 1512 Missale Anglicanum'[13] and was published in 1912 by W. Knott. Brooke St. Holborn. Its cover, in the opinion of Mrs Pat Robinson, Deputy Warden of the Henderson Rooms, may have been the work of Mrs Underhill.

Reverend Austen Balleine

The successor to Prebendary A.B. Burney was the Rev. Austen Balleine. He was inducted on Wednesday 5 October 1938, at 3pm. The Bishop of the Diocese and the Archdeacon of Taunton were present. At this time the Rev. E.H. Smith was the priest-in-charge at Alcombe and at Dunster; Dr F.C. Eeles was the honorary licensed lay-reader; the churchwardens were Mr Geoffrey Luttrell and Mr W. Long and the organist was Mr W.J. Amherst.

A practical detail recorded in the P.C.C minutes for 8 November 1938 was the removal of the defective boiler and its replacement by a new seven-section boiler installed by Messrs Hine and Sons.

The new vicar decided that Matins at 10 am on Sundays were to be followed by a Sung Eucharist at 11 am. (His predecessor, the Rev. Burney, following on a complaint concerning the length of the Sunday morning service, had decided to omit the Sermon.)

By February 1939, the Rev Balleine had arranged for a new supply of prayer and hymn books for the congregation. The same month it was decided that the care of the churchyard would in future be a charge on the Vicar's Fund.

On Sunday afternoons during the summer months the gardens at 'The Priory', the vicar's residence (now converted into flats and known as 'Priory Court'), was open and anyone who cared to could wander round and view 'such flowers as the slugs and their friends have not required'.

The Second World War (1939-45)

Already in March 1938 the threat of the imminent Second World War posed questions about the safety of the people of Dunster and the question of Air Raid Precautions was raised by Rev. Burney at the P.C.C. meeting. Mr Geoffrey Luttrell offered to arrange a public meeting at the Castle at which Colonel Carlisle would speak.

Now, with the outbreak of war in September 1939, the bishop sent a pastoral letter and the Rev. Balleine wrote in the Church magazine for October 1939:

> Now that the catastrophe of war has come, each of us has to adjust his mind and his daily life to meet this new situation. Living in a sheltered corner of England, it is hard for us to realise the appalling burden of misery, suffering, sorrow, injustice, and despair which already is darkening the world, and soon will be coming closer to the homes of our fellow-countrymen. But we have got to face this, and facing it, to ask ourselves what difference it is going to make to each of us.

The names of those serving in the Navy, Army or Air Force were listed:

Alec Kendall;	Cecil Hobbs;	Leonard Preskett
Leslie Bond	Gordon Huxtable	Charles Simpson
William Henry Champion	Jim Hole	William Simpson

Douglas Collas	Arthur Ladd	Leslie Swain
William Dibble	Alfred Lake	William Taylor
Cecil Dibble	Edgar Lamacraft	John Taylor
George Furse	Ronald Lee	Bert Tapp
William Furse	William James Norman[14]	Harold Thorn
George Gould	Horace Geoffrey	
Norman Humphrey Wilson		Henry Osgood
Robert Haydon	Leonard Hobbs	Jim Gould

To these names were added in the Church Magazine for November 1939 the following:

Edward Bloys	John Poole	Albert William Giles
Robert Caddy	Philip Pound	
Eric Dyer	Leslie Tom Prescott	

Maintaining the work of the church and paying for its upkeep was a duty which still remained in the difficult war years. Upkeep was covered by the Sunday Church Expenses Collections and by contributions, as were those at St Michael's Church at Alcombe. Victorian pennies (known as 'Bun pennies' because they depicted Queen Victoria wearing her hair up in a 'bun') were collected for the Freewill Offering Fund. In August 1940 the collection of these pennies amounted to 18s 6d.

The army was encamped on Dunster Beach and provision for the men's hospitable reception was made. The W.I. went into action at the Memorial Hall. The vicar reported in September 1940:

> ...the Canteen and Recreation Room at the Memorial Hall is proving itself a great blessing to our new visitors on Dunster Beach. ... The Memorial Hall Committee has been very helpful in putting the main room at the disposal of the men, and the Women's Institute has undertaken the running of the canteen with splendid energy; its aim is to provide cheap suppers at the lowest possible cost. ... Gifts of money for expenses should be sent to the Vicar; gifts of food direct to the canteen on any evening.

In November 1940 he was able to add:

> The men are really grateful, and their gratitude is our reward to those who have worked so well for them under the unavoidable of limitation of space, and in heat which sometimes must rival the equator.

Wartime Evacuees in Dunster

In December 1939 the vicar wrote a letter in the Church Magazine concerning the evacuees who had been sent to Dunster, in which he said:

> The war had brought many changes and problems to the quiet life of Dunster ... Probably, he felt, the greatest problem, up to that time, had

been the provision of housing for the evacuees. He wished to put on record his own admiration for those householders who had been willing, with obvious inconvenience, to take evacuated people into their homes.... He felt that in spite of the need of haste better brains could have produced a more sensible evacuation process than the pushing of mothers and children into trains and sending them anywhere.... it was impossible to introduce a mother with small children into another person's home with any real hope that this would be a success. Most of these first evacuated mothers had returned to London, a return which was inevitable because this part of the evacuation scheme had been bad, and a return had caused a sigh of relief to some hardly treated householders!

'In Dunster', the vicar continued, 'they still had some of these evacuated mothers and little ones, and they recognised that with varying success they had faced their difficulties and were trying to make the best of their unnatural life. They deserved all the sympathy which was the right of any who tried to help themselves. Some on Dunster Beach had found it possible to make themselves contented, and if they persevered on windy, rainy and cold days they would have their reward in the better weather'.

However, most places in Reception areas had found it had been quite possible to place unaccompanied children with householders who had been able to absorb two or three extra children into their own families. They were fortunate at Dunster to have been asked to receive London Polytechnic schoolboys. This family of seventy boys had won a good opinion so far in the village; in most cases the boys had behaved well and had fitted themselves into the home-life, and the parents had in nearly every case shown deep gratitude for the kindness shown to their son, and in except a few cases had proved their gratitude by making some extra contribution towards the cost in addition to the bare official billeting allowance.

The vicar added a postscript, deploring 'the opinion of those officials at the Ministry of Health who decreed that any healthy-appetited school boys could be fed and kept at 8s 6d each per week!'.

More evacuees were sent to Dunster in November 1940 and the vicar wrote in the Church Magazine for that month:

> The coming of more evacuees in our midst has been another emergency, which has tested the character of our people. Many have generously opened their homes to receive people evacuated from dangerous areas, or those who have fled from London where their houses have been destroyed or are in immediate danger. It is difficult for us to realise conditions of life under such air-raids as have wrecked so many homes.

The Rev. Balleine built the Priory Hut as a room in which the evacuees could have their meals made. They slept in the attic of the Priory and later the Hut became known as the Priory Bungalow; the large room was subdivided into rooms affording accommodation for Mr and Mrs Lloyd.[15]

Blackout and Other Precautions

The war imposed black-out restrictions on all householders, and of course, the church was not excepted.

The choir practiced in the vestry so this was blacked out first. At a cost of £6, the Luttrells' 'Priory Chapel' was to be enclosed so that it could be economically heated for day-time celebrations and confirmation classes etc. The formidable task of blacking out the entire church was considered in June 1940 but the cost of providing curtains and rods, if only for some of the windows, was so high that a less expensive way of tackling the problem had to be found. Someone thought of using paper and battens; estimates for this solution were sought while the vicar offered to donate the Easter Offering towards the cost.

In the end the scheme for blacking out the nave had to be abandoned but it still cost what was a large sum in 1940: £81.10.0, paid to Messrs Hine of Minehead, to black out and provide 'furniture' for the Priory Chapel where Evensong was to be held during the winter months. When the remnants of the blackout were finally removed, a unanimous vote of thanks was extended to Mrs Mead King who had helped to prepare and make curtains.

Although the scheme for blacking out the nave had been abandoned, in May 1941, the vicar was still concerned to do this whilst expressing the thanks of all for the use of the Priory Church during the preceding winter. In July 1941 an estimate for £23.10s from Messrs Hine was accepted.

Naturally the services were affected by the black-out. In the winter of 1939 an afternoon service had been held instead of the evening service. This proved to be unpopular and from autumn 1940 a 6.30 pm service was held in the Priory Church. The vicar writing in the Church Magazine said:

> To have blacked out the whole church with its many windows would have been very costly. People are asked to enter by the south transept door, or by the door from the Priory Garden and not by the main door, as there will be no light in the nave.

A humorous West Country story appeared in the January 1939 issue of the Church Magazine.

> Many must have appreciated too the Carol Service on the Sunday before the festival. As someone remarked afterwards "We've nice little boys in our choir, whose voices soared 'hoier and hoier', till they reached such a hoight, they passed out of soight, and we found them next day on the tower".

The Parish Church was used during the hours of daylight. Troops stationed nearby occupied the pews on the northern side of the nave and the parishioners those on the southern side. On 10 June 1940 congregational practices and the more frequent rendering of anthems was suggested and practices were to commence that autumn. Mr A. Tudball was disturbed about the length of the services such as the 11am service held on the first Sunday in the month. The Rev. Balleine suggested that as a complete separation of the Matins and Choral Communion seemed impractical, he would, for the time being, omit the sermon.

In January 1941 a scheme for Fire Watchers was discussed and various gifts were made. For example Mr Louis Bowden offered a ladder and stirrup-pump and Miss Emmerson offered what would to-day be regarded as a dangerous gift, an asbestos covering to protect the High Altar. A further gift was a sanctuary carpet from Mrs Weatherburn.

The bishop made an appeal for a Diocesan Fund to meet War Damage to Churches. The P.C.C. decided on 13 May 1941 to build up a Reserve Fund to cover any war damage to church contents and on 30 November 1941 a special collection was made for this fund to insure the church against damage.

Day-by-day maintenance included the path to the west door which needed to be tarred and gravelled. The vicar pointed out this need but the estimated cost was £9 15s, well above the £5-£6 agreed by the P.C.C.

Money was invested in War Bonds, for example £200 in 1941 and £100 later the same year. By September 1943 it was thought possible that £1,000 in bonds could be purchased by early 1944, and by December 1945 another £200 was purchased.

Notable Parishioners

Mr Frost was appointed a member of the P.C.C. on 3 Feb. 1941; he would serve the church of St George until his death in 1990. In 1941 the People's Warden was Mr Walter Long, appointed on 16 April 1941. (This was a position Mr Frost was later to fill.) On 26 March 1941 the P.C.C. members stood in silent tribute to the memory of Mr Patfield who had died recently.

By 1941 Mr Griffiths had completed fifty years service in the choir. When one considers that he had sung in the choir at the end of the nineteenth century and had nearly completed the first half of the twentieth century, one realises what an incredible contribution this record represents. To mark this auspicious occasion a subscription list raised 8 guineas (£8 8s) for Mr Griffiths.

In 1941 a marble plaque was erected on the south wall of the south aisle in memory of her son by Mrs Norman of 'The Green', Dunster. William James Norman M.C.R.E was a colonel in the Royal Engineers who served throughout the Great War (1914-1918) and afterwards was engaged for nineteen years on a survey of India. He died at Dehra Dun on 11 December 1940, aged 46 years. A Bible inscribed to his memory is to be found in the ambo.

The first Dunster casualty of the war, Flight Sergeant Leslie Bond, was remembered when a Memorial Service was held on 18 April 1943.

Also in 1943 the Rev. Weatherburn was thanked for his assistance at Sung Eucharist and Festivals, while Miss Bond was thanked for running the Free Will Offering. The P.C.C. treasurer and representative at the Rural Deanery Conference, Mr Simpson, retired after long service at the meeting held on 14 February 1944. He was succeeded as treasurer by Mr Fenning.

Charities Supported

In July 1941 the Rev. Balleine suggested that a Sunday collection should be devoted to a new charity and the R.A.F Benevolent Fund was chosen. The National Day of Prayer was held on 7 September and on 21 September a Day of Thanksgiving marked the Battle of Britain in the previous year. The collections at both these services were given to the R.A.F. Benevolent Fund, as were those on certain Sundays in August 1942, and August 1943. The Red Cross benefitted from other Sunday collections in 1942 and 1943, and from a Garden Fête in the garden of the Priory on 18 August 1943, when £206 was collected for the Red Cross and the St John's war organisation.

In February 1942 donations were made to the Organists Benevolent Fund who received £10, plus £5 in January 1943. In 1944 there were special collections for the Aid to China Fund on 26 March, and for the Aid to Russia Fund in August 1944. On 13 May 1945, Thanksgiving Sunday, the collections were devoted to the fund of the British Council of Churches for assisting churches liberated on the continent to recommence their work.

The first Sunday in May 1943 saw a change in the services. On every first Sunday in the month there was to be a Choral Communion Service at 9.30am followed by Matins at 11am. In February 1944, the vicar agreed that the Litany should be said occasionally.

The Village of Elst in Holland

During the war years, in response to a special appeal, the village of Elst in Holland was adopted by the little town of Dunster.

The first we hear about this is recorded in the P.C.C. minutes for 14 Februrary 1944 when the Rev. Balleine mentioned a scheme in which it was proposed that the church should adopt a Dutch village. A gift of money could be made when families returned to their homes after the German occupation ended. It was agreed to make an appeal to local residents to subscribe to a fund to provide a Christmas gift of £500. It was further agreed in October 1944 that the church should sponsor the fund with a grant of £100 from its Deposit Account. Correspondence passed between the Rev. Balleine and the Bishop and Netherlands Red Cross and it was finally agreed in November 1944 that the appeal should be circulated on behalf of the village of Elst.

A letter of thanks from the Secretary of the Netherlands Red Cross for the gift of over £500, collected by November 1944 for the village of Elst, was read by the vicar to the P.C.C. at their meeting held on 19 February 1945. The end of the Second World War in Europe was celebrated on V.E. day, 8 May 1945.

In the year 2000, the 55th anniversary of the liberation of the Netherlands was marked by a generous gift which was reported in the *West Somerset Free Press*:

> A thousand Dutch tulips planted in Dunster were this week providing a
> blaze of colour to help commemorate today's 55th anniversary of the liber-

ation of Holland. The red and white displays of blooms around the village were a reminder of Dunster's part in providing aid to the war-torn Netherlands. The bulbs were presented to the village during the last winter's Dunster by Candlelight weekend as a millennium gift from Haye Gallama, mayor of the Dutch town of Elst. He hoped they would flower in time for the May 5 liberation anniversary, an important celebration in Holland.

Residents of Dunster, themselves coping with rationing during the war, sent food parcels to the people of Elst after hearing of their plight under German occupation. It was a gesture which was never to be forgotten by the Dutch townsfolk, who have ever since maintained a relationship with the West Somerset village.

Pictured is Dunster war veteran Bill Dainton, aged 80 and believed to be the village's last surviving veteran who actually fought at Elst during the famous Operation Market Garden campaign to seize the bridges at Arnhem and Nimjegen.[16]

Elst was a strategically important target on the road between the two towns. Mr Dainton[17] was an intelligence sergeant to the Somerset Light Infantry, part of the 43rd Division sent to relieve airborne forces trying to take the bridges. Elst was taken by the 7th Battalion of the Somersets and Mr Dainton's regiment went in as relief and then saw fierce fighting for a week as the town was held against German counter-attacks.

ENDNOTES

1.   At the time of the church restoration in 1874-6.
2.   Exactly as it was when I wrote this account in 1989.
3.   Bettey: C & C.
4.   The 'Cottage Hospital', established in 1867 for reception of nine patients see Lyte: H.D. Part II 340.
5.   Lay Reader and a founder member of the Central Council for the Care of Churches. See Chapter Nine.
6.   In 1985 a new gate constructed of oak was made for the South Gate (P.C.C. Minutes for March 1985)
7.   Mr J. Tudball voiced appreciation of the ringers for work done on restoration of steps leading to the belfry (16.10.1933).
8.   The Rural Dean had as early as 2 Sept. 1931 recommended in his report that the lightning conductor should be tested. Also that the ironwork of the windows would need attention.
9.   She was also of Dunster but their brother Alexander lived at East Quantoxhead. He died on 6 December 1944 aged 89 years.
10.   P.C.C. Minutes
11.   W.S.F.P. 14 May 1938
12.   Mr J F Berry, the Diocesan Register, told the author that he had no record since 1990 of the necessary faculty for removing the missal from the church.
13.   See letter 5 Sept. 1995 from Christopher Edwards, Manager of the Palace Trustees (of Wells Cathedral).
14.   William James Norman served throughout the Great War 1914-18. See below.
15.   Information from Mrs Lloyd.
16.   W.S.F.P. May 2000
17.   The late Mr Dainton was the retired director of the accounts department of the former Luttrell Arms Garage. He was Treasurer of the P.C.C. for many years.

CHAPTER NINE

THE YEARS 1945-1955; THE PARISH of ALCOMBE

After the war the Rev. Balleine intimated his intention to leave Dunster and take a living at Pilton. He found his financial position unsatisfactory and one of his grievances appears to have been the cost of the upkeep of the Cloister Garden. There was uncertainty about the ownership of the garden and in 1944 negotiations had resulted in the church being asked to accept the garden as a gift of the Luttrells.[1]

Rates and dilapidation charges on the vicar's residence also presented a problem and it was suggested that the Council should consider making payments to cover these charges. Messrs Amherst and Day agreed to communicate with the archdeacon on the matter of a Table of Fees.

The new vicar was the Rev. G.D. Dunlop to whom I am deeply indebted as his *Yearly Notes* are a mine of information. At his first P.C.C. meeting it was decided that the Rev. Balleine's gift of the Priory Hut in the rectory grounds (used for evacuees), should be let to Mr and Mrs H. Lloyd at a rent of 7s per week. The hut was renamed the 'Priory Bungalow', and remained until the present rectory was built in 1985/6.

Church Finances

When the Rev. Dunlop came to Dunster the 'Vicar's Fund' (the sum of the offertories collected at the early celebrations) was renamed the 'Alms Fund'; and a sub-committee of himself, Miss Muir and Miss M. Bond was formed to advise on the allocations to charity to be made.

In 1946 the church finances devolved round a Central Fund which consisted of the gross receipts for the year but did not include the special collections. Out of every 6d contributed to the Church, 4d went to the Parish Church, 1d to the Diocese and 1d to the work of missions. In 1946 this represented £645 to the Parish Church.

In February 1946, Mr Fenning, the Treasurer, reported that the finances of the church were in a satisfactory condition; a further £200 3% Defence Bonds Stock had been purchased in December, the money coming from the Deposit Account. £1,200 stock was held. The premium for the Church Insurance Policy that year was £30. The cover was for £45,000 to cover the Parish Church and the Priory Church.

The balance in the Deposit and Current Accounts totalled £743 in July 1946, when Mr Fenning wished to retire. He agreed to continue until the end of 1946. In 1947 the Rev. Dunlop reported that 'the visitors make smaller offerings these days'. The Central Fund had provided £600 for the care and improvement of the Church and about £130 for Mission purposes. Charities supported included Home and Foreign Missions, the National Lifeboat Institution, the British and Foreign Bible Society and the Hospital. The general collections for 1947 amounted to £280, special collections to £85, visitors' donations to £232. On 19 May 1947, Mr Dainton was asked to accept the office of treasurer on the retirement of Mr Fenning.

In 1948, the Rev. Dunlop wrote that about £500 had been devoted to the upkeep of the Church, £102 paid into the Diocesan quota and about £300 had gone to Missions. In 1950 the alms-giving consisted of £592 for the Parish Church and the services, £177 for Diocesan purposes, £115 for Mission Societies and £95 for other purposes.

Miss D. Todd was re-elected as the Diocesan Conference Representative in March 1946. The Misses C. and D. Todd, descendants of the Rev. Richard Utten Todd and his brother James Utten Todd, were much involved in church matters and with the running of the Sunday-school.

In his *Yearly Notes* for 1946, the Rev. Dunlop recorded that it had been a troubled year to live through. He wrote of:

> ... one long chain of restrictions, coupons, rations and forms: a shortage of food and clothing and coal, almost everything, and the weather throughout the year has been miserable: all through the spring a succession of north-east winds followed in the summer by continuous south-west winds and endless rain – with such a poor harvest just when a good harvest was most necessary. Practically no summer at all.

In May 1946 we read in the P.C.C. minutes, 'Terrier and Inventory in process of preparation'. The Salisbury Report on the conduct of church services was discussed.

It was decided at the P.C.C. meeting held on 15 July 1946 that there should be a Committee representative of both Choir and Congregation to promote the worship and services of the church.

The war was over and there was a general feeling of wanting to get back to a happier way of life, so it was also decided that there should be Church Socials from time to time and that the first one should take place in October 1946 and a later one at Christmas-time.

The Priory Garden (1)

The garden on the north side of the church was variously known in the 1940s as the Priory Garden, the Cloister Garden or the Old Cloyster Garden. In the time of the monks there was a wooden cloister along the north wall of the church; the Prior could walk along this cloister from his garden to the north door of the church.

At the Parochial Church Meeting on 19 May 1947, a sub-committee was formed consisting of Mrs Geoffrey Luttrell, Miss Mainwaring, Mr Hardwick and the vicar, to consider converting the Cloister Garden into a 'Garden of Memory and War Memorial' to commemorate the men of Dunster who had died during the Second World War (1939-1945).

Mr H. Baganel, F.R.I.B.A., the church architect, submitted a design for the garden together with various other recommendations (see below) and by August 1947 it was agreed that Messrs Wood of Taplow should be called in to design and estimate for the construction of a well-head and well to serve as a screen at the south end of the garden.[2] Mr Luttrell would provide the turf for the garden (no turfed area exists to-day). Mrs Luttrell offered to provide the well-head and the Rev Dunlop assumed responsibility for the herb garden. The cost of the work was estimated at about £250 and it was agreed that a circular letter asking for donations should be sent to every householder in the parish.

In September it was decided that Messrs Wood should also be asked to submit a plan for the garden together with an estimate. The plan cost £25 but in the event the plan was not used, as being thought beyond the means of the church.

By 1948 the vicar was pleased to report that the year had brought a welcome approval of the plan to convert the Cloister Garden into a Garden of Memory but there was much difference of opinion as to detail and very few offers of help but that 'some of us had undertaken to do what they could by their own efforts'.

The west border was planted with 144 roses and edged with lavender, while the east border was prepared for planting as a herb border. However a curb was put on operations in May 1948 when it was thought advisable to arrange for the final transfer of the garden to the church before proceeding with further plans and for its final dedication as a War Memorial.

The idea of the garden as a War Memorial then lapsed, as the British Legion proposed that a bronze tablet should be erected in the church. In March 1949 it was reported to the P.C.C. that drawings were being made by the Rev. A.F. Wynow of Newlyn. However his scheme, discussed the following May, would cost double the amount previously anticipated. Rev. Wynow was asked to present another, simpler design.

The plan was to transfer the present bronze commemorating the First World War to the north wall of the transept, fixing a similar tablet for the men of the 1939-45 war by the side of it, with a stone vase or bracket between them.[3]

However, it was found at the July 1949 meeting that these arrangements would necessitate the sending of the existing (1914-18) bronze to the founders. This work could not be completed in time for the Remembrance Day Service to be held on 6 November. It was therefore decided that the names of the fallen of the 1939-45 war should instead be inscribed on vellum (an idea previously mooted) and framed by Miss Mary Wood of Exeter. This was done and Mr Geoffrey Frost affixed the vellum to the wall under the 1914-18 bronze.

The plan to make the garden a Garden of Remembrance was taken up again in the Fifties (see below).

The Organ 1945-1957

At the P.C.C. meeting held on 9 April 1945 the question of an electric blower for the organ had been raised. The organist, Mr Amherst, undertook to make the necessary enquiries of Mr Daniel. An estimate of £85 was duly submitted by his firm and this was accepted on 16 May. However the electric blower was not installed until 18 July 1949.

The first mention of moving the organ from the north transept to its present position is in the P.C.C. minutes for 16 May 1945. After consideration it was decided to postpone a decision until after Mr Daniel's visit. In November 1946 Mr H. Baganel recommended in the interests of better acoustics, that the organ should be moved into the archway in the north aisle facing down the church.

On 19 May 1947 at a P.C.C. meeting this proposition was carefully considered but it was eventually agreed that the matter should be deferred, perhaps owing to the absence of both the vicar and the vice-chairman, Mr Luttrell. On 22 September that year Mr Amherst resigned from the post of organist and choirmaster and was replaced by Mr J. Popplestone, Mus. B, F.R.C.O.

When the council met on 4 May 1948 the main business before the meeting was to consider a scheme for the re-building and extension of the organ. According to the Minutes:

> The Vicar in an opening statement referred to previous discussions the Council had had on this subject and stated that with the recent removal of Purchase Tax on Organs, it seemed desirable to decide without further delay to work for the fulfilment of the Scheme; and called on Mr Popplestone who was present by invitation to report on what was considered necessary for such a church as this.

Mr Popplestone pointed out that, while much of the work in the present instrument was extremely good, there were 'limitations which seriously militated against good playing and choral work. He stated that the main alterations called for were the placing of a new console in the choir, electrification of action and blowing, rebuilding of the organ in the archway on the north side of the sanctuary and the addition of many stops to give a more balanced and greater variety than is now possible'.

The scheme was fully discussed and on the proposition of Mr Bowden, seconded by Mr Maidment, it was decided that the rebuilding should be carried out and that the firms of Messrs Compton and Messrs Harrison should be approached with the purpose of ascertaining what work they would undertake for the sum of £3,000.

Although no developments regarding contracts with Messrs Harrison or Compton are reported in November 1948, the vicar had discovered that there was an organ for sale from the Percy Chapel in Bath. Mr Popplestone inspected and reported favourably on this instrument. It would probably cost about £1,750 of which £1,000 would be expended on the dismantling and re-erection of the organ. It was agreed that a party might visit Bath at some future date to see the said instrument. (In December 1948 the organist's salary was £25 p.a.)

On 14 March 1949 Preb. Dunlop made a report from the chair on the plans which had been brought forward during the past few years for the improvement of the organ. The 'difficulties of the present time' were mentioned and it was agreed to establish an Organ Fund by making a grant of £100.

Compromises were made and a modified scheme for the improvement of this instrument in the north transept was presented by Mr Popplestone. This had been submitted by Messrs Osmond of Taunton and provided for an electric blower, additional new stops and the re-voicing of certain existing stops.

The estimate for this work was £460. Mr Popplestone gave a detailed explanation of the work and the specification was unanimously approved. It was, however, pointed out that the restoration of certain woodwork and cleaning might be needed and therefore it was agreed to request an examination and report.

The result of this report is included in the 18 July 1949 P.C.C. minutes and is as follows:

> A report on the organ from Messrs Osmond of Taunton mentioned the presence of woodworm in the frame, swell box, pedal action, etc. This firm was prepared to make tonal improvements to the instrument provided they were not held responsible for any mechanical defects which might occur later. They would treat the woodworm wherever possible and pointed out that the money spent on tonal improvements would not be lost.

The Council unanimously agreed to instruct Messrs Osmond to carry out this work, in accordance with the estimate considered at the previous meeting. It was stated that the electric blower had already been installed and instructions given to Mr T.W. Baker to do the necessary wiring.

On 31 October 1949 the vicar reported that the work on the organ was proceeding and that it was hoped that it would be completed by the following Easter.

An Organ Screen, designed by a Mr Erridge, was to be erected at a cost of £27 to be paid for out of the Easter Offering. This information appears in the P.C.C. minutes for 3 July 1950. In 1950 the comfort of the organist sitting in the draughty North transept was dealt with in the true post-war spirit of inventive self sufficiency. As Preb. Dunlop said in his Yearly Notes, 'he has always had to sit in a draughty passage, exposed to public view. We had a pelmet constructed above and we stencilled some black-out material and the effect is not bad'. This stencilled organ curtain was hung on 7 December 1950.

In 1952 Preb Dunlop referred to the organ as 'a poor thing and badly placed'. Five years later this subject was still exercising his mind and he wrote in his Yearly Notes:

> Perhaps the greatest need of all is an organ placed rightly. The present organ is not very good and is out of sight of the choir and congregation ...
> In my opinion an organ should be built in the archway north of the sanctuary with a console near the choir. The roof of the sanctuary would act as a sounding board.

Report on the Church Fabric

Mr H.B. Baganel F.R.I.B.A., the church architect, made various recommendations after he had visited and examined the church in 1946.

Firstly he advocated the removal of the ancient cross (the top of the Churchyard Cross) from the apex of the west gable.

Secondly, as one of the leading authorities on acoustics, he recommended that the walls of the nave should be distempered (presumably he meant the north wall of the nave and the south wall of the south aisle). He also suggested that a tester should be placed over the pulpit and that the organ should be moved from the north transept into the archway in the north aisle facing down the church. Curtains should be provided to transept screens on either side of the altar and the font should be moved to the south transept.

The summer of 1947 was very hot. In the autumn it was agreed that a low wire door should be installed at the west end of the church so that the doors could be opened during the summer months. That year the church also became affiliated to the Royal Society of St George. Rev. Dunlop wrote in his *Yearly Notes* that he had received much help in the conduct of services from the Rev. T.G. Morris and Dr F.C. Eeles. The Archbishop of Canterbury attended the services for five Sundays during the late summer. In 1948 Rev. Dunlop was not at all well and the Rev. T.G. Morris took charge in his absence.

The Rev. Dunlop wished to move the organ from the north transept in accordance with Mr Baganel's recommendations of 1946, into the position it now occupies (since 1960). He also desired to see the font moved into the south transept, again as recommended, thus forming a baptistry. This and other suggestions made by Mr Baganel: that a tester should be placed over the pulpit to improve the acoustics and that the walls of the nave and aisles should be distempered, were also turned down or postponed by the P.CC. The colouring and gilding of the bosses was not agreed either but the plan to convert the Cloister Garden into a Garden of Memory was accepted, as we have seen.

Repairs to the Church Fabric

In January 1948 the vicar, along with local church experts Dr Francis Eeles and Miss Judith Scott, surveyed the exterior of the church. In March, a report on 'Goods, Ornaments and Fabric of the Church' was presented to the meeting of the P.C.C. and approved.

The report states that:

> Mr Barton of Messrs Gallannaught and Nicholls, architects of Bridgwater, had inspected the Church and had stated that it was in good and sound condition. Mr Barton recommended the erection of a new Flag Pole; repair of the North East Pinnacle of the Tower; the cleaning, repair and painting of all the guttering and downpipes; attention to any loose slates and the re-conditioning of the Lightning Conductor.

A new flagpole was provided and all the leadwork repaired; all the loose tiles were put right and all guttering and downpipes repaired and painted. Mr Barton was the architect; the work was carried out by N.J. Furze and Co. Ltd of Cotham, Bristol, who also tested and repaired the lightning conductor and repaired the north-east pinnacle of the tower which was in a dangerous condition; (elsewhere it was stated that two pinnacles were straightened). The total cost of this work was £250.

In May 1948 the main business put before the P.C.C. was the consideration of a scheme 'for the rebuilding and extension of the Organ'. The organ was improved in 1949 but not moved to its present position and re-built until 1959-60.

Throughout Preb. Dunlop's *Yearly Notes* he makes tireless attempts to record the life of the church and the institutions of Dunster. There are references to annual events such as 'the Bell-Ringers supper at the New Inn'; 'the Sunday-School outings to Burnham-on-Sea'; 'the Servers Day at Weston-super-Mare, Wells and Cheddar', and to the 'Choir Outings to Torquay', as well as news of organisations such as the Mother's Union, the Women's Institute and the Scouts.

The Mother's Union was re-formed in 1948 and the banner, selected by Mrs Dunlop, was purchased in the July and cost £28. That year the vicar recorded that 'the choir has improved considerably and the attendance has been high and the Church has been lovingly cared for and kept in beautiful order'.

Sale of Dunster Castle and the Estate

The most momentous happening of 1948 was the sale of Dunster Castle and the estate to the Ashdale Land and Property Co. In 1950 Geoffrey Fownes Luttrell would buy back the castle and the Crown would acquire the agricultural land.

In 1949 the vicar remarked of his work as Rural Dean:

> The work is heavy but full of interest. This last year apart from visits I have officiated at an Institution at Sampford Brett, the Jubilee of the Priesthood of the Rector of Withycombe, a Harvest-Thanksgiving at Williton, a Deanery Mother's Union Service at Porlock, another Mother's

Union Service at Wootton Courtenay, a Morning Service at Timberscombe, a Dedication at Roadwater, another Mother's Union Service at Cutcombe, a Teacher's Service at St Andrew's, Minehead and there have been meetings of the Chapter and the Deanery Conference and two meetings at the Palace at Wells. The correspondence is extensive.

The Church in the Early 1950s

In 1950 the Rev. Dunlop wrote in his *Yearly Notes* that Mr T.R. Day, Headmaster of the School and Secretary to the Church Council, had retired and left Dunster. In his place Mr Powles, a licensed Reader, was appointed Head Master and accepted the post of Secretary to the Church Council. The Reverend T.G. Moores, who had been an unofficial member of staff for 4 or 5 years, had also left Dunster.

The same year well-framed and well-written notes were fixed at convenient points around the church for the guidance and information of visitors. Regarding the choir, the vicar noted that:

> 'the girls have been robed and occupy the Decani stalls [*i.e. the south side of the choir*] and the effect is remarkably good both to hear and see. Also a new entry for the choir has been devised. ... Now the choir enters the short way through the side doors of the chancel and coming down towards the congregation. The boys followed by cantors passing the organ on the way and the girls followed by the Decani coming through the Luttrell chapel and entering on the opposite side. ... A most remarkable improvement and altogether more decent and dignified.

The flower decorations in the church in the 1950s were outstanding. We read in the December 1950 P.C.C. Minutes that Mr Tudball remarked on the beauty of the display of the flowers in the church and how indebted the church was to the vicar, as he grew all these flowers himself for this purpose.

In 1950, because of the earlier sale of Dunster Castle, people were anxious about the future of the advowson (the right to appoint the vicar) and the Priory Church and Cloister Garden.

In the event the advowson remained in the gift of the Luttrell family and it was decided that the Cloister Garden should be transferred to the church from the family.

In 1951, six years after the conclusion of the Second World War, fuel was scarce and economy was necessary. It was decided in the December to use the Priory Church for a spoken Evensong and address at 4.00 pm. The vicar remarked on the totally different atmosphere which he found more peaceful and quieter in the Priory Church.

Food rationing ceased this year. Meanwhile the Mother's Union flourished with forty members. The Sunday school numbered fifty-six pupils taught by seven teachers. In 1951 there were thirty-five choir members.

The path to the south door and the front step from Church Cottage were causes of concern. Mr Hine was to be asked to provide an estimate for the replacement of the step and provision of Westleigh chippngs for the path.

At the Easter Vestry Meeting 'the first issue of the year book of the Church of St George, Dunster was introduced by the vicar, the Rev. G. D. Dunlop'. This contained a comprehensive report of the year 1950. The meeting proposed that it should be published each year at the church's expense. The Rev. Dunlop notes that the 1951 issue has a record of what had happened during the previous five years.

At the same meeting, Dr Francis Eeles wrote concerning the weakness at the base of the pillar of the pulpit. Mr Vincent Barton inspected it and by 24 April 1952 'tell-tales' had been inserted.

Other improvements in the church included a new set of bell ropes while outside the church, a current of air was established in the boiler chamber, while the boiler itself was thoroughly overhauled.

At the 1951 A.G.M. in April, Mr Bowden took the place of Mr Wilson who had retired as a member of the P.C.C. Mr Peter Tudball, the son of the former churchwarden still serving at that time on the P.C.C., was elected as one of the sidesmen. Canon Swann of St Mary's Church, Redcliffe, Bristol, was to reside at Dunster as from July 1951. The Rev. Dunlop had been made a Prebendary. He was installed as Prebendary of Twerton in Wells Cathedral on 25 June.

There was a discussion concerning the purchase of Church Cottage (the cottage on the south-east corner of the churchyard in Church Street) as a residence for a curate. In the P.C.C. minutes for 21 June 1951 it was pointed out that in the plan of the property to be sold in the near future by the Eagle Star Company 'it was questionable whether the bungalow tenanted by Mr H. Lloyd stood on Church Property'.

At the same meeting the vicar pointed out that the Dovecote and Flower Garden had been purchased for £300. £100 of this was a gift from the Church Commissioners, £100 on loan to be charged to the benefice and the Church Council should be prepared to find £100. It was agreed that £75 accumulated rent from the bungalow plus the Easter Offering might be utilised to pay this loan. Mr Bowden suggested that the Dovecote should be handed over to the Church Council and the chairman undertook to look into the matter.

Festival of Britain 1951

The suggestion of a medieval fair in Dunster to celebrate the Festival of Britain received little support from the members of the P.C.C. at the meeting held on 7 December 1950. However, Preb. Dunlop's *Yearly Notes* reveal that this did take place and he writes about this celebration and the large and active part the little town of Dunster took in this happy event:

> The Medieval Fair and Fête was the main attraction and this dwarfed all the other activities. It aroused a great deal of interest in Dunster and abroad and the town was enlivened by characters in colourful costume, character

of Men-at-Arms, Monks, Pedlars, Beggars, Ladies of the Court, a Town Crier, a Juggler and many more. A packhorse train came over the Packhorse Bridge, bearing wool to the Yarn Market, where there was a display of spinning and weaving, which recalled Dunster's ancient craft. There were booths in the market place and Village stocks. Morality plays were enacted and there was a Recorder Band, a Maypole, Folk Songs and Glees were sung and Handbells rung. In the Castle Grounds there was a display of archery, tilting, Morris dancing and Country dancing. Even the Vicar wore period costume and he represented John Wycliffe but he ruefully remarked 'nobody knew it'. The B.B.C. attended in the person of Mr Johnny Morris who took the part of a Jester.

In the local school crafts and educational work were on display and on the last day of the festivities a Fête and Children's Sports took place on the cricket ground, with side shows and attractions of all sorts.

A Service of Blessing in St George's Church was attended by the Bishop of Bath and Wells. That summer of 1951 the Archbishop of Canterbury made his customary visit and stayed for four Sundays. During the festival the church was floodlit and on the Thursday a peal of bells was rung. During the week the Angelus was rung daily and four Benedictine monks said their offices in the Priory Church. There were 50,000 visitors to the church in 1951. The festivities ended with dancing in the Market Place to the strains of a Gypsy Band; and a grand shower of rockets from the Castle Bowling Green.

On 11 July 1951 the Dunster Castle estate was put up for sale by auction. This sale included a smithy on the Ball, a saddler's shop, a chemist's shop, a news and craft shop, a radio shop, a hardware store, a tailor's shop, a butcher's shop with a sausage-making room, an antiques' shop, all on the High Street, together with the post-office.

Many buildings were associated with the church, such as Church Cottage. 'Built of stone and tiled, part timbered and with leaded light windows', it was let on a weekly tenancy to Mrs A. Davis at a rent of £13 8s 8d per annum; the landlord paid the rates up to £3 0s 8d per annum. This cottage had mains gas, electricity, drainage and estate water. The Old Priory, originally the Prior's dwelling and, after the Reformation, a farmhouse, was described as 'a small period house close to the Church being part of the Old Priory. Built of stone with tiled roof'. This had mains gas, drainage and estate water but apparently no electricity. It was let on a weekly tenancy to Mrs B. Burge who paid the rates at a rent of £12 2s 8d per annum. The portion running at right angles to the Old Priory was described as 'the adjoining cottage of similar construction but outside having a lean-to Carpenter's shop and W.C.'. This was let to Mr F. Quick at a rent of £9 10s 8d per annum, the rates being paid by the landlord up to £2 9s 8d per annum. The Limehouse near the Lych Gate was offered for sale with vacant possession.

At the Annual General Meeting held after the Easter Vestry on 24 April 1952, the chairman explained that the bungalow, orchard and kitchen garden had been presented by the Eagle Star Company to him as vicar of

Dunster. It was unanimously agreed that the dovecote and garden be retained by the Parochial Parish Council. In the vicar's *Yearly Notes* he tells his readers that the Ashdale Company had made a free-will gift of the orchard, kitchen garden and a bungalow, a self-contained property with a ring-fence around it, and that thus the size of the benefice property was substantially increased. Only a part of the 'Wild Garden' was retained and sold to the British Legion to be used as a shooting range. Up to the July 1951 sale of the Dunster estate, this had been let on an annual Michaelmas tenancy to Preb. Dunlop, at a rent informally apportioned at £2 per annum.

The shooting range was eventually pulled down and a house, with a preservation order on the ancient oak tree, erected in its place. Preb. Dunlop commented on the free-will gift: 'this is altogether too much for a vicarage and the time must surely come when part or all of it will be sold'. He, in fact, gave a plot of land to the diocese for the erection of four bungalows, one of which was inhabited by Canon and Mrs Swann.

May 1952, the organist was awarded a ten guineas cost-of-living bonus; the situation was to be reviewed at the end of the year. The next year, 1953, Alcombe became a separate parish (see below).

In 1954 Preb. Dunlop wanted to re-robe the choir, preferring 'School of Church Music Blue' to the existing purple robes. The question of the choir's apparel re-occurs in November 1955 when the Council recommended that 'immediate attention and repairs be made to the choir vestments'. The matter was shelved once again.

No small detail was omitted from the Parochial Church Council minutes and so we read that in July 1952 a vacuum cleaner was bought for the church.The same month, lead having been stolen from the church roof, it was decided to write to the Ecclesiastical Insurance Co. for advice on insuring against theft. The chairman also outlined the newly proposed Parish Boundaries. The Bath and Wells Dilapidations Board was in correspondence with the Parochial Parish Council regarding the purchase of the Dovecote.

The next year necessary repairs pointed out by Major Marsden, the Church Architect, were to be carried out on the roof at a cost of £80, employing a local village firm if possible.

Preb. Dunlop's *Yearly Notes* for 1952 recorded that the weather had been grey and cold from early autumn, so he had repeated his experiment of saying Evensong in the Priory Church on the first three Sundays in December and last three Sundays in January. He reckoned that there were 60,000 visitors to the church during the year.

Preb. Dunlop had been Rural Dean for six years in 1952. He found the work hard and that it took him away from Dunster too much and so he asked the bishop to accept his resignation but was bidden to carry on. He was, however, greatly appreciated at Dunster and the year before, at the A.G.M. held on 2 April 1951, Mr Bowden had thanked him 'for inspiring services that had taken place in St George's Church during past years'.

At this meeting Preb. Dunlop expressed the hope that, by offering the plot of ground presented to him as Vicar of Dunster by the Eagle Star Insurance Company to the Diocese, who wished to build four bungalows for retired priests, he would be able to revive the services of the Prior and monks, and that the retired priests would join him in saying their Hours in the Priory Church.

The Coronation of Queen Elizabeth II

King George VI died in February 1952 and his elder daughter, Elizabeth, was crowned on 2 June 1953 in Westminster Abbey.

In his *Yearly Notes* for 1952, Preb. Dunlop made reference to the proper celebration of the Coronation, to the special Service on the Sunday before, and to a Dancing Festival on the day itself. His account of the festivities records that they had special services and a Special Peal of Bells, which synchronised exactly with the peal from Westminster Abbey. 'We had teas for the old folk and for the children and a display of Dancing in the Market Square and a Procession and Barbecue and Community Singing and Fireworks. It was all planned very carefully in every detail but the performance was not quite equal to the plan.'

Luttrell Hatchments

The Luttrell hatchments have already been described, together with their heraldry. In 1953, in his *Yearly Notes*, Preb. Dunlop wrote:

> In the autumn a series of hatchments was erected in the Priory Church as a gift of Mr and Mrs [Geoffrey] Luttrell. They had been hidden away in the Tithe Barn for many years but were discovered by Dr Eeles and me – taken out and restored by an expert. They now form one of the finest series in the County from the time of Queen Anne to Queen Victoria.

According to Colonel Sir Walter Luttrell this is not quite accurate: the hatchments were not, in fact, 'hidden away in the Tithe Barn' nor were they 'a gift of Mr and Mrs Luttrell'. It was always known that they were in the Tithe Barn. At the time, the Tithe Barn was the Estate workshop. As a small boy, Colonel Luttrell often saw them stacked alongside the old family coach behind the piles of sawn timber. He was told by his mother that they came out of 'their church' (i.e. the Priory Church) and were 'the coats of arms of ancestors who had been hung up after their respective burials'. As Colonel Luttrell remarked in his letter to the author of 13 July 1989, 'the hatchments not the ancestors!'. The nine hatchments were beautifully restored, by the kindness of Mr and Mrs Geoffrey Luttrell, before being placed in the Priory Church. In 1988 Mr Julian Luttrell told me that, prior to having been stored in the Tithe Barn, the hatchments had been kept in the Outer Bailey tower on the Tor. They were moved when this tower fell into ruin.

The head of the 13th-14th century cross was removed from the west gable in 1953 and placed within the church.

In February 1954, the Vicar noted that it had been renovated by Mr Sparks. This was done in cement, which was viewed with disapproval by

Mr Hugh Harrison of Herbert Read and Co in 1991. In 1994 it was decided to place the cross in the south transept at the side of the old font but it is to be found now on the stone altar of the same date in the de Mohun chapel.

Quinquennial Scheme

In February 1954 Major Marsden was formally appointed as the first consulting architect. This was necessary because of the new requirement that all churches must appoint a consulting architect and have a quinquennial inspection and report. A Fabric Fund would have to be set up.

The church was to be inspected in 1956 and in the meantime directives were given to the members of the P.C.C. to watch for damp, insects and wind effects. Gutters and pipes should receive regular inspection; a log book was to be kept of work done to the church fabric. The Council agreed to have a Fabric Fund to prepare for any future necessary work, and £100 was put in this Fund.

Dr Francis Eeles

The year 1954 also saw the death on 17 August of Dr Francis Eeles O.B.E., D. Litt (Oxon). A tribute appeared in the annual review of the church:

> It was an honour to have such a man as Lay Reader in Dunster Church; and many of us will carry affectionate memories of that small figure with the hood of his degree reading the lessons and preaching from the pulpit of Dunster Church; and always humble-minded, in spite of his learning and attainments. Anything that such a man said was a contribution to the subject. Rapidly failing health forced him to resign from his office on the 18th of May, to take effect on the 18th of August. But on the 17th of August he died, still holding the office which he had valued and adorned so highly. By his own direction he was buried in Selworthy Churchyard.[4] A Memorial Service was held at St James's, Piccadilly, on the 19th November, at which the Deans of Gloucester and Chichester, with Bishop Dunlop, Dean of Lincoln, were the officiants and the Dean of York paid eloquent tribute to the life and work of Francis Eeles.

Dr Eeles (b. 1876) was founder and first secretary of the body then known as the Central Council for the Care of Churches. His association with Dunster began when he acquired a holiday house 'Cross Meadow', at Alcombe. (It was Dr Eeles who had sent in a report of the state of the fabric of the church in 1929, prior to the church restoration of 1936.) Just before the Second World War he moved his holiday home to 'Earlham' in St George's St., Dunster, where Council offices were set up with a skeleton staff. During the war years 'Earlham' became an influential nucleus which extended its influence to every part of the Church of England. The Council returned to London only after Francis Eeles' death.

Dr Eeles enjoyed a vast knowledge of church architecture and was consulted by the clergy and architects all over England, so his 1940 guide, *The Church of St George, Dunster*, is a noteworthy publication. He was also one of the leading authorities on liturgy and was consulted on important occasions including that of the Coronation of Queen Elizabeth II.

Miss Judith Scott O.B.E., F.S.A., who had been Dr Eeles's assistant at 'Earlham' and was on the Parochial Church Council at Dunster from April 1947 to April 1955, while living at Spear's Cross, later became Dr Eeles's successor at the Council. She assisted Alec Clifton-Taylor in the production of the second volume of his book '*English Parish Churches as Works of Art*' and it is to her that I am greatly indebted for the above information.

On 31 March 1955 a faculty was obtained for the removal of the Victorian brass pulpit desk installed during the church restoration, and its replacement with a new oak pulpit reader with brass fittings and a hooded lamp. In his *Yearly Notes* 1954-5, the vicar wrote:

> One small improvement has been made to the pulpit. The arrangements were about as ugly and unserviceable as human ingenuity and Church craftsmen could make them. Now, at least, there is adequate lighting and room for a Bible and for a watch. But the pulpit still needs alteration.

The Living at Dunster

In March 1955 Bishop Hornby retired and came to live in Dunster and was present, in an advisory capacity, at the P.C.C. meeting held in the school. In the absence of the vicar the chair was taken by Mr Dainton, because the position of the living at Dunster was under discussion. It depended on endowments which were inadequate, only amounting to £360. Most parishes had raised the benefice income to £550, exclusive of rates and dilapidations. The plan for raising the living at Dunster was for the Parish to contribute £100, and the Diocesan Board of Finance to raise £100, bringing the living up to £550. The motion was voted upon and carried unanimously.

The Preservation of Churches Act had come into being and Dunster was due for an exhaustive survey and inspection in 1956. The vicar thought that the church was in good repair to all appearances but that there must be an inspection of the roof against death watch beetles. £200 had been put into the Fabric Fund against such eventualities.

The meeting held on 21 November 1955 also dealt with the choir vestments; the handrail to facilitate ascent to the Tower: the bell-ringers would make one of piping; the lime tree in the church grounds (it was removed under the supervision of Mr Haydon) and the Verger's bonus. It was decided to grant the verger an annual bonus instead of a rise in wages.

The effects of television were also a concern of Preb. Dunlop in 1955. Many Dunster people had bought sets and the demand for the Sunday Evening Young People's Club at the Vicarage (ie. the Priory now Priory Court) no longer existed. and the vicar thought that it might become necessary to reconsider the hours of the service.

In his invaluable *Yearly Notes,* Preb. Dunlop mentioned Bishop Hornby and Canon Swann, both recently retired to Dunster, who had said Matins with him in the Priory Church daily. During 1955 four bungalows had been erected in the old kitchen garden of the Priory for retired clergy, under the direction of a Manchester architect. They were sited on a rather pinched space which the vicar maintained was quite unnecessary, as he had offered the whole of the orchard. At his suggestion the name of 'St George's Close' was chosen. Visitors in 1955 were still coming at the rate of fifty or sixty thousand a year and the Visitor's Book was full of kindly comments concerned with the peace of the church and the beauty of the flowers.

The year concludes with the news that Preb. Dunlop had resigned his office of Rural Dean after nine years service. He had, he said, assisted at the Induction of fifteen incumbents and had held forty meetings and he had undertaken as many journeys to Wells. He regarded his resignation as a real blessing and an opportunity to stay and work quietly at Dunster.

The Priory Garden (2)

The plan to convert the Cloister garden into a Garden of Remembrance was taken up again in the early Fifties. In July 1950 the P.C.C. were reluctant to grant money for its maintenance until its ownership was proved. But by December 1950 the garden had been officially transferred to the Parochial Church Council Committee, the living still being in the hands of Mr Luttrell.

The Rev. Dunlop, whose own garden, as we have seen, furnished the flowers for decorating the church, set to work, planting more beds with a backbone of carefully-chosen flowering shrubs to reduce the work. Low-growing shrubs were purchased and these formed a background for the mixed border; carefully selected rock plants such as pinks, campanulas and helianthemums graced the borders.

In March 1951 Mr Dainton, representing the sub-committee, reported its findings. It was decided to investigate the suggestion that a tablet of Portland stone be erected in the porch of the church; the cost of this to be met from the church's Reserve Fund.

The solution we see to-day was arrived at on 28 May 1952 when three suggestions were made by the sub-committee. They were (a) a tablet in the church, (b) a stone tablet in the porch, or (c) the dedication of the Priory Garden with a tablet bearing appropriate words. The last suggestion met with the Council's approval.

Mrs Luttrell promised to help with the designing of the well-head which would be built in front of the recess of the wall. An iron-work grille given by Colonel Garton would be built into the door.

The Foreword to the Church Review for 1952 informed its readers that the Church Garden had been 'handed over to the Church and People of Dunster by the kindness of Mr Geoffrey Luttrell, to be dedicated as a Garden of Remembrance'. Preb Dunlop wrote 'it is ideally suited for this purpose; there is peace there and fragrance and quiet memories'. He continued:

The garden carries associations of eight hundred years for it was at first the Cloister of the Benedictine Monks of Dunster Priory, and we can picture them at their work and meditation there on a summer day. Perhaps the sloping desk in the Priory church is one of the desks actually used by the Monks in their writing and illumination hundreds of years ago.

In 1953 Preb. Dunlop, having cared for and planted the garden for a number of years, thought it would be better to hand it over to the Church Council. He noted that there were necessary improvements to be made to the garden especially at the southern end.

That year the Cloister Garden was formally handed over to the church by Mr Geoffrey Luttrell and in July the newly named 'Garden of Remembrance' was dedicated by the Bishop of Bath and Wells at a special service. It was the year of Her Majesty Queen Elizabeth II's coronation.

The well-head, the gift of Mrs Luttrell, had been constructed by local craftsmen under the guidance of Colonel Garton, who later designed the Ambo for the church. The commemorative stone, from the Lincoln Cathedral quarry, was presented by the Dean and Chapter of this Cathedral and had been suitably inscribed. It was placed in the wall near the north door.

When the P.C.C. met on 16 February 1954 'the deed of Mr Luttrell's gift of the Priory Garden was signed and witnessed' and it was moved that a sub-committee consisting of Preb. Dunlop, Mr Pelton (later replaced by Mrs Bowden), Mr Frost and Mrs Williams should inspect the garden and advise the Council on its care, upkeep and improvement. As a result of the first inspection:

> The Council considered the building at the south end of the garden and it was decided to thatch the existing shed with brushwood and to arrange a soundly constructed pergola for roses to grow up to screen the building already there.

Major Marsden, now the church architect, was asked to advise on any questions concerning alterations in this south end of the garden. Permission to erect a tool shed and to effect minor operations in the garden was granted to the P.C.C. by Williton Rural District Council on 28 September.

The commemorative tablet in the garden was also discussed. As the existing wording on the tablet incorporated all the fallen of Dunster in all wars it was thought unnecessary to record the names of those who gave their lives in more recent wars. The tablet was renewed in the 1990s.

In August 1954 Major Marsden presented a plan for the improvement of the Remembrance Garden with particular reference to the approach to the north door of the church. The cost would be in the region of £160. The vicar pointed out that the garden was a village memorial and that the people of Dunster should be invited to contribute towards the cost. As the Council had insufficient money it was decided to do the work piece by piece, rather than carry out the whole plan at once. However, by dint of voluntary labour the path near the north door was reconstructed.

In December, the Fabric Committee was asked to plan out a grill for the well. The matter does not appear to have been resolved by the time the A.G.M. took place on 29 April 1957. The garden had been planted with shrubs and roses, herbs and rock plants. Preb. Dunlop remarked:

> ...it certainly makes a true Garden of Memory but upkeep is difficult. There seem to be no offers of help and it is right that the Garden should be better cared for. I fear that it may be largely my own fault and that my style of gardening does not appeal to local gardeners'.

In the May help was at hand as Mr Caddy offered his services. In October Mr Dainton and Mr Frost were appointed to direct him on matters concerning the garden. On 19 November it was decided that the garden would be cared for by Mr Williams under the direction by the new vicar, the Rev. McCormick. On 8 March 1971 Miss Withycombe, who now cared for the garden, presented a plan for a new arrangement of the Remembrance Garden and Mr Luttrell offered to replace some of the shrubs. The rough paths were a subject of concern, but as the Memorial Garden was consecrated ground, a faculty would have to be applied for if it was to be altered.

In 1972 a memorial light was erected at the entrance to the garden in memory of Mr J Tudball, churchwarden, who died in 1970. A teak garden seat was also added. Many roses were planted in 1973.

In 1986-7 Mrs Stella Calder, assisted by Mrs Bond, Miss Barber and Miss Withycombe, replanted the garden in accordance with a plan Miss Withycombe had discovered. How delighted Preb. Dunlop would have been had he visited the garden in the hot summer of 1986/7 when the garden was full of aromatic scents, colour, bees and birds, a joy to residents and visitors alike.

In 1990, the Walter Boyes Legacy provided over £7,000 for the Memorial Garden.[5] In 1995 this produced an annual income of £150, used for improvements when a water tank was removed, and the area beside the north wall was turfed and a stone seat erected.

A bird bath was placed in the garden in 1994, in memory of Freddie Royall (1920-1993), by his widow Edna and seven named roses were planted round this delightful commemorative gift. The late Mrs Calder, helped by various friends, but principally through her own endeavours, boundless energy and deep knowledge of plants, made the garden a place of constant delight. She was also responsible for the herbaceous border in the Village Garden. The latest addition to the Garden at the time of writing is a seat placed along the west wall of the garden in memory of Peter Horatio Sheppard, 1915- 1999.

Church Affairs During the Later Fifties

At the P.C.C. meeting of 7 February 1956 a sub-committee was set up to advise the vicar on minor repairs required in the church. The elected members were Messrs Frost, Haydon, Maidment and P. and J. Tudball. At the Annual Meeting held after the Easter Vestry, in April 1956, it was agreed that because of rising costs the printing of the invaluable *Year Book* would be discontinued.

Gifts to the church the previous year, listed in the vicar's report, included a plaque bought by Sir Henry Maxwell Lyte in Florence and presented in 1956 by his sister, Miss Maxwell Lyte, as a memorial to him. This tondo (round plaque) on the north wall of the south-east chapel represents the Annunciation, with the Angel Gabriel presenting the Christ Child to the Virgin Mary. This very fine 16-17c painted terracotta plaque has a partial surround of wood and the group of figures is sculpturally excellent. The work is very much in the spirit of the della Robbia family's work. Sir Henry Maxwell Lyte was Deputy Keeper of the Public Records Office 1886-1926, and the grandson of Henry Francis Lyte, author of many well-known hymns including 'Abide with me'.

A very fine Lectern Bible had also been presented to the church by Ruby, Countess of Cromer in memory of her husband Rowland Thomas Baring, 2nd Earl of Cromer P.C; G.C.B; G.C.I.E; G.C.V.O. The family had worshipped at Dunster together from 1921 to 1953. The bible is a replica of the Coronation Bible presented to the Queen at her coronation. It bears the family crest on the outer cover: *A mullet erminois between two wings Arg.* The Bible dedicated to his memory together with the Bible given in memory of William James Norman (see earlier) were both, at the time of writing, on the Ambo.

On 14 July 1956 it was recorded in the P.C.C. minutes that the repair of the north wall and the garden wall had cost £21. A window, which I suspect was the east window, which bears evidence of repair, was broken. The final meeting of the year on 17 December 1956 was told the winding jack for the clock had been installed, a relief to the verger Mr Haydon. The churchyard wall had been repointed. The vicar pointed out that careful planning for the intended levelling of the graves was required, so a sub-committee was appointed, consisting of Messrs Bowden (Louis), Haydon, Lloyd and Frost.

A hut erected at Dunster Marsh was given to the Church by a Miss Petersen for use by the Guides in 1956.

In 1957, at Preb. Dunlop's suggestion, his *Yearly Notes* were replaced by a published report on church activities over the last ten years. At the same time he was recording the Electoral Roll.

At the April A.G.M, Preb. Dunlop was presented with an illuminated address to mark the fiftieth anniversary of his ordination. He outlined his objectives for 1958: the heating system (actually completed in 1957); the Churchyard, and the gilding of the bosses in the roof.

The levelling of the graves in the churchyard was deferred in June. The vicar's dream of gilding the bosses in the south aisle was then also finally dropped by the Council. But by July 1957 Preb. Dunlop had decided to resign from the living and to leave Dunster by Michaelmas. He and Mrs Dunlop went to live at Woolston Grange, Williton. It is evident from the foregoing concerning Preb. Dunlop's activities that the many expressions of appreciation of the care he and his household bestowed upon the church during his term of office were indeed merited. Of the fifty years of ministry, eleven of them had been spent in Dunster.

In his final *Yearly Notes* he made a final plea for the removal of the Font to the south transept, thus forming a Baptistry, and he reiterated his concern over the gloominess of the church. He was also concerned with the acoustics and the absorbent nature of the stonework. Dr Eeles also thought it should be whitened. (We know he strongly decried the removal of the plaster by the Victorians in the south transept which revealed inferior stonework.) Mr Hope Baganel, who had earlier advocated a tester over the pulpit and was an authority on acoustics, said that the walls in their present condition absorbed sound like a sponge.

Following on Preb. Dunlop's letter of resignation read to the Council on 1 July 1957 it was proposed by Mr Bowden that a letter should be sent to Mr Luttrell indicating the type of man the Council would like to see as Preb. Dunlop's successor. On 8 August 1957, a letter from the Bishop of Bath and Wells was read to the Council. It was proposed to transfer the advowson to Geoffrey Fownes Luttrell, to which proposal the Council raised no objection. However, Mr Luttrell died that September.

The vicar told the Council that his successor would be the Rev. McCormick and he suggested that the P.C.C. might agree to be responsible for the dilapidations to the living quarters. This was agreed. The vicar then pointed out that technically the incumbent was responsible for the chancel of the church, an impossible burden, and he asked the Council to accept the liability. It was agreed to consult the insurance authorities and that the Council would support the incumbent in any action he cared to take in the matter. (I believe that the responsibility for the chancel is a reference to the chancel of the Priory Church since the first Lay Rector after the Dissolution of the Monasteries was Hugh Stewkley who was responsible for the Priory Chancel.)

On 9 September 1957 the cremation of Geoffrey Fownes Luttrell (b. 1887) took place and floral tributes were sent by the Parochial Church Council. In place of Mr Luttrell, Mr Dainton was appointed sequestrator. On her husband's death Mrs Luttrell agreed to become Vicar's Warden. She continued in this office until 1969 when she was succeeded by her second son, Julian Fownes Luttrell. She lived on until 1974 when she died at Dunster Castle aged 86 years.

At a P.C.C. meeting the same day, it was decided, among other things, that a Ladies Committee should be asked to look after the flower arrangements of the church. Mrs Bowden agreed to organize such a committee and this appears to have been a most successful enterprise. (Previously Miss White had been, in the main, responsible for floral decorations and when she gave up her duties it was regarded as a great loss.) The P.C.C. minutes also record the gift of the model of the church executed in cork by Mr Ford. This was installed in the south aisle.

At the same meeting, Preb. Dunlop asked if the Council would agree to the planting of a Glastonbury Thorn by the Guide Association in honour of Lord Baden Powell, as the year 1957 was the centenary of the birth of the founder of the Boy Scout and Girl Guide movements. Later that year, the Minehead Division Girl Guides planted a Holy Thorn from Glastonbury, with a commemorative plaque to mark it, near the south door of the church. To this place they and the Scouts come every year on St George's Day, for their annual Service of Thanksgiving.

Heating

Back in April 1957 one of the objectives for 1958 was consideration of the heating of the church. The estimate of £423 for the installation of an oil burner submitted by Garten and King of Exeter was accepted, together with the Shell Mex estimate of £78 for supplying a tank. It was hoped that the work would be completed by the Autumn of 1957. Major Marsden had stated that there was no need to apply for a faculty but the ever-present problem of raising money for the endeavour was addressed.

The Monk's chest was placed in the south porch as a collecting box for money towards the Fabric Fund. A fête also took place by kind permission of Mr and Mrs Luttrell and a profit of £320 was made.

The heating system was to be tested on the 24 October 1957. It was hoped that it would be functioning on the Day of Induction of the new vicar, the Rev. Michael McCormick, on 26 October 1957. The final cost, as quoted from the Receipts and Payment Accounts for the year ended 31 December 1957, was £591 16s 7d, of which the Crown Commissioners contributed £100.

Preb. Dunlop Retires; Rev. McCormick Becomes Vicar of Dunster

Preb. Dunlop had been vicar of Dunster from 1946 to 1957. On his retirement a presentation was made to him and Mrs Dunlop, along with an illuminated address to mark the fiftieth anniversary of his ordination which occurred at the same time.

The new vicar was the Rev. Michael McCormick M.A. (Cantab), R.N., whose induction took place on 26 October 1957.

The Ambo

The history of the Ambo (Lectern) spans the incumbencies of Preb. Dunlop and Rev. McCormick. In 1955 Preb. Dunlop had written in his *Yearly Notes* that 'the present lectern is altogether too low and the lighting is very poor'.[6] He noted that Colonel Garton had a design of a suitable 'pulpit lectern' in hand, with a figure of St George on the front panel and Mrs Luttrell had offered to present it to the Church if the Church Council and the advisory committee approved it.

After Geoffrey Luttrell's death in Sptember 1957, Mrs Alys Luttrell now desired to give the lectern not only in memory of her parents, Anne Caroline Bridges and Walter Bogue Bridges, but also in memory of her late husband.

Colonel Garton, the designer, came from East Pennard, near Glastonbury. His design was carried out by the Somerset Guild of Craftsmen. The figure of St George carved on the front is the work of Mr Hunt of Henlade, while the leaves and the acorns in the iron-work railings were made by Colonel Garton himself by a special process which he invented.

Preaching for the first time from the ambo on 12 October 1958, the new Vicar, the Rev. M.E. McCormick, said that it was best to think of an ambo as an article of church furniture which has a dual purpose. This ambo being a raised lectern or a small pulpit could be used both for reading the Word of God and for expounding it. The ambo, which was at the Somerset Guild of Craftsmen's recent exhibition at Bristol, had been dedicated by the Bishop of the Diocese the previous day,[7] and the first reading from it was given by the Vicar's predecessor Preb. G.D. Dunlop, who had a large share in its conception and design.[8]

ALCOMBE PARISH AND ITS CHURCH

As Alcombe became a separate parish in 1953 a short history of its ancient association with Dunster is appropriate at this point.

At the time of the Domesday Survey of 1086, Alcombe was in the possession of William de Mohun. This survey was taken as a basis for tax assessment: commissioners sent out by William the Conquerer were directed to collect precise details of land and equipment, ploughs, mills, livestock etc. These details in the case of Alcombe showed that:

> The desmesne then comprised three virgates for the cultivation of which the lord had one plough and four serfs. The remaining virgate was in the hands of three villeins and four bordars, who had two ploughs. Mention is also made of eight acres of meadow and three furlongs of pasture. The live stock comprised a riding- horse, five beasts animalia and two hundred sheep. The yearly value of the estate was 20s, as in the previous reign.[9]

Before the Norman Conquest and in the reign of Edward, the Confessor (1042 – 66), this manor of great antiquity had its only known resident lord, one Algar, whose estate was assessed as one hide.[10]

In an undated charter of William de Mohun I, written between 1088 and 1100, William granted to the church of St Peter of Bath, and to John de Villula, bishop of its Benedictine monastery, and to the monks both present and future, the church of St George at Dunster, the tithes of the town of Dunster, and 'the whole town of Alcume and all things belonging to it, free and quit of all service, that is to say a hide of land...'.[11]

So Alcombe became part of the endowment of the Benedictine monks cell of Dunster and remained so until the Dissolution of the Monasteries in 1539, when it continued to be part of the parish of Dunster until 1953.

The manorial rolls have disappeared but through the Chartularies of Bath we know something about the chapel at Alcombe dedicated to St Michael, the Archangel. According to these Chartularies, there was a chapel there in the second half of the fourteenth century but when it was built is unknown to us. Hancock quotes from No 40 :

> In ... 1357, the prior, and monks of Bath ... assign to Humphrey Stafford, lord of Stafford, in Southwyck, kt., one close of land in Dunster called le Lynche, lying next the chapel of St Michael the Archangel at Alcombe on the east.[12]

Lyte, referring to Chartulary L940 and additionally from the Calendar of Patent Rolls, 1467-1477, says:

> Two incidental notices show that there was a chapel there near 'le Lynch' dedicated to St Michael. As part of the pre-Norman Hundred of Minehead and Cutcombe, Alcombe was exempt from suit to the hundred court of Carhampton, but its tithing-man was required to appear at the half-yearly 'law days' at Minehead.[13]

After the Dissolution of the Monasteries in 1539, John Luttrell (d. 1558), the younger brother of Sir Andrew Luttrell (1525-71), and the lessee of the Priory and Rectories of Dunster and Kilton, had to render annual accounts as Henry VIII's agent, showing the profits of the manor of Alcombe. He showed these under sub-headings:

(1) The rent of three freeholders.
    (i) John Sydenham of Brympton who was liable for 10s in respect of land called Wyneard and Pytte.
    (ii) Nicholas Bratton of Bratton who was liable for 8s in respect of land at Sparkhayes in Porlock.
    (iii) The heirs of Bythemore who were liable for 4s in respect of land called Wilaller in Wythycombe.
(2) The rents of 'customary tenants', or copyholders, of houses and cottages in Alcombe.
(3) The rents from Budcombe [sic], Keynsham [near Bath], Cowbridge, Frackford and Marsh.
(4) The rents of 'conventionary tenants', or leaseholders, in Alcombe.
(5) The rents from lands and tenements in Dunster.
(6) The rents from land in Carhampton.
(7) The proceeds of the manorial courts.[14]

In 1540 John Luttrell claimed an allowance of 32s 10d spent by him on the repair of ruinous cottages at Alcombe and of 'the chancel of the church of that place, which was in the parish of Dunster'.[15]

In the memorandum of George Luttrell (1560-1629) about the Rogation week procession which proceeded from Dunster to Alcombe, we read that gospels were said at 'Alcombe Crosse' and at 'the chapelle of Alcombe'.[16]

In 1561 the manor of Alcombe was sold by the Crown to Sir George Speke of Whitelackington, whose first wife was Elizabeth, the youngest daughter of Sir Andrew and Lady Margaret Luttrell. (Elizabeth had previously been married to Richard Malet of Currypool in Charlinch.) Sir George died in 1584 in possession of the manor of Alcombe and lands in and near Alcombe which had, before the Reformation, belonged to the Benedictine monks of Dunster.

In 1640 Sir George's grandson, George Speke, died and the same estate is mentioned in the inquisition taken after his death. A John Speke is known to have been one of the principal landowners in Dunster in the second decade of the eighteenth century. In the early eighteenth century, Alcombe held its own courts which met about once in three years. There was no sworn jury and homage was not paid. The Spekes sold out in 1722 and the entire Alcombe estate and lands thereabouts were disposed of in small lots. We read:

> The 'royalty' of the manor, with various small 'chief rents' from freeholders, was bought for about 20*l* by Aldred Escott, whose family already owned property there.[17]

This manor was therefore in possession of the Crown after the Dissolution of the Monasteries and the 'royalty' refers to the fact that it was a district held directly by the monarch, George I.

In 1830 the manor belonged to the Rev. T. Sweet-Escott of Hartrow and around 1909 it belonged to his grandson, the Rev. W. Sweet-Escott.

Lyte remarks:

> On the sale of the Speke estate, most of the tenants purchased their respective holdings, but in the course of time many of these had been acquired by the Luttrells of Dunster Castle. Until the disfranchisement of Minehead, the votes of the householders of Alcombe, which was within that parliamentary borough, were of some importance.[18]

In the 1870s Dorothy Luttrell's eighteenth-century chapel at Dunster was demolished to make room for the present drawing-room. Mr George Fownes Luttrell (1826-1910) is reported by both Hancock and Lyte to have presented the silver communion set belonging to this chapel to the new chapel built at Alcombe in 1903.[19]

Preb. Hancock also refers to a processional cross at Alcombe:

> Preserved at Alcombe is a very beautiful cross of English work, once silver gilt, and perhaps of not later date than the beginning of the fifteenth century.... there is probably little doubt but that it was the processional cross of either the prior or a vicar of Dunster.[20]

However, according to the Rev. Alan Mills, vicar of Alcombe in 1990, 'there is no processional cross here even remotely of the kind you describe'.[21]

An eighteenth-century pulpit was also sent to St Michael the Archangel, Alcombe from St George's Church, Dunster. The Rev Mills told me that this was moved under Faculty by his predecessor. It has now been returned.

It is obvious how closely Alcombe worked with Dunster for in the Parish Magazines between 1874 and 1884 the hymns for the month are given under the heading of Dunster and Alcombe on the same page as are details of the offertories which appear one above the other.

In the spring of 1880 the Rev. R. Utten Todd, vicar of Dunster, wrote in the Parish Magazine that 'during the past month reverent and loving hands have been at work in the little Chapel of Alcombe, with a view to make it a more beautiful place of worship':

> The work had consisted in the painting of three Frescoes on the walls, repre-senting the Adoration of the Magi, the Flight into Egypt, and the Finding of Our Saviour in the Temple; and along with this, a Dado of colour, surmounted by a border, has been put round the Chapel, and Texts have been placed in different parts of it. The Frescoes have been executed solely by Miss Kate May, and reflect the greatest credit on her skill as a draughtswoman and artist. Her fellow-helpers in the other details have been Miss Orford and Miss Stadden....

In November 1880 Alcombe Chapel was again the subject of a short article by the vicar in the parish magazine, under which was printed the list of subscribers to the new organ. The Rev. R. Utten Todd's subscription of £2. 2s, two guineas, was matched by that of his brother the Rev. J. Utten Todd who was the Priest-in-charge at Alcombe and assistant priest at Dunster (and at Minehead) from 1873 to 1887. Mrs Elkington and Miss Kate May had asked for subscriptions to replace the existing harmonium. With the sum raised of £40, it was proposed to erect a small organ, to be installed by Mr Sparks of Williton. It was hoped that the new organ would be ready by Christmas.

The Siderfin Family

On 19 December 1916 Robert Siderfin of Alcombe died aged 79 years. The Siderfin family was pre-eminent in the history of the area.

Hancock writes about the 'first civil marriage entry at Dunster', when Hopkin Williams of Dunster, glovier, and Anne Webber of the same, single woman, were married on 29 December 1653, in the presence of Richard Blackford, John Giles, Andrew Hobbs and others, 'according to the Acte of Pliament in that case made and provided, by Tho. Siderfin, esq., one of ye justices of ye peace within ye sayd county, the day and year above said'.[22] Thomas Siderfin was a Justice of the Peace during the Civil War. A Robert Siderfin was High Sheriff for the year 1693.[23] Another Thomas was a J.P. in 1702.

Alcombe Church in the Twentieth Century

In 1903 the new church at Alcombe was erected. It was dedicated again to St Michael the Archangel by the Priest-in-Charge, Rev. James Utten Todd, who held that office between 1903 and 1911. The Perpendicular doorway which was within the great Norman doorway of St George's Church Dunster, (discovered in 1876) was sent to Alcombe. It was incorporated into the building of the new church there.

Trouble arose in 1917 at Alcombe concerning the way in which the Rev. Lockyer, the Priest-in-Charge, conducted the services. Apparently he was departing from the set order of services, had introduced a weekly Choral Celebration, and was encouraging his congregation to use a 'Green Book'.

On 22 May 1917 the Bishop of Bath and Wells wrote from the Palace at Wells to Preb. Hancock, who had become vicar of Dunster in 1898, and informed him that he had received a good many letters concerning the Alcombe question, including one from the Rev. Lockyer. The Bishop proposed to take the following line and I quote:

1. I propose to draw a great distinction between the sermon which has upset certain people and the practices (notably the Green Book) which are to my mind of greater importance.
2. I should be willing to consent to Mr Lockyer staying on and continuing to work as Curate-in Charge provided that he is willing to act in obedience to my directions. ...
3. I think at the present stage it is better that the whole matter should be determined, if possible, between yourself and Lockyer rather than between him and his bishop ...
4. The requirements are these:—
   Mr Lockyer must undertake:
   (a) to keep rigidly within the covers of the Prayer Book.
   (b) to give the customary Services on Sundays of a plain celebration at 8, full matins at 11, Children's service in the afternoon and full evensong at 6.30 to make no interpolation whatever in the Communion and other Services ... (I see no objection whatsoever to Lockyer having a later Choral Celebration of the Holy Communion on one Sunday in the month if he and the people of Alcombe desire it). ... I must require that the Green Book be altogether withdrawn from circulation...

A Mr Vernon of 'Inglese de Alcombe' wrote to Preb. Hancock on 24 May 1917 to inform him that after a further talk with him he had sent a letter to the bishop which 'he thought might strengthen your hands in the matter'.

Perhaps coincidentally, a letter dated 5 June 1917 to the bishop from one Rev. Cecil J. Heughan, says that he ventures to write concerning the possibility of a curacy in the bishop's diocese. After giving the bishop details of his qualifications and experience, he said he sought a Curacy in charge if possible and that he could promise loyal service to the utmost of his powers. A glowing testimony was attached.

In the meantime the Rev. Lockyer wrote to Preb. Hancock from the Presbytery, Alcombe on 18 June 1917, claiming that 'the storm has subsided'. He then gave details of the numbers of communicants and the collections, and said 'The collection and congregation at the 10 o'clock Choral Celebration is always the best of the day'. He then claimed that 'Messrs Thorne, ? Penning [*indecipherable*], Hine and Hitchcock' [*presumably the people who had complained about him*] are by no means confined to the ranks of 'High' Churchmen.

He concluded:

> I would do anything to please you which was not against my conscience, but my conscience will not allow me to resign under these circumstances.

Unfortunately Prebendary Hancock's correspondence is not among the letters made available to me but Mr J.M. Alcock wrote to him on 13 June 1917 from the Palace, Wells, to inform him that the Bishop desired him to say that he quite approved of him sending Mr Lockyer the letter which he had drafted, which he now returned together with Mr Lockyer's letter to Prebendary Hancock.

This letter was duly sent to Mr Lockyer who replied, very upset, on 20 June 1917. He said he had that afternoon received Prebendary Hancock's letter asking him to leave the Curacy. He continued: 'If the Bishop and you knew the awful campaign of lying and slandering that has gone on, I think the decision would have been otherwise'. He asked for the usual three months' notice (later extended to six months, as he was being dismissed rather than resigning), and concluded: 'I pray that God may bring good out of evil. I do not care twopence about myself but I do about my flock'.

By 27 June 1917, 221 adult Parishioners of Alcombe had signed a petition which was sent to the bishop.

Rev Lockyer sent Preb. Hancock a copy, with a letter saying 'I think it only fair to inform you that feeling here is running high on the matter... As you are aware, ever since Easter 1914 I have had the customary services on Sundays as you mention them. You told me that you thought I was wise in making the change, i.e. you gave it your approval. I am puzzled, and I think you would be too, my dear Vicar, if you were in my place'.

The vicar had already been apprised of the petition by a Mr W.H.A. Thomas of The Terrace, Alcombe, who claimed that the petition was being signed 'not only by Church of England people, but by Non-Conformists and, I am informed, by a Roman Catholic family!'.

A very neat and carefully written letter appears in the correspondence. The writing is laborious but the sentiment, even to-day, makes the reader aware of the deep anguish that the Reverend Lockyer's plight had caused. The letter dated just 'Saturday' was sent from 'The Pines', Alcombe by one Miriam Martin. She asks pardon for her presumption in writing 'but the thought of losing our beautiful Eucharistic service is such an anguish to me – I felt I *must*'. 'We thought', she continued,

> 'how wise you were to have a Service to suit Churchmen of one school of thought in **one** of your churches, and those of another, in the other, so that within a mile and a half we could *all* have a service that appealed to us all

... In any other case. you see, those who loved the Eucharistic Service would have to go to St Michaels-on-the-Hill, out of our dear little parish altogether'.

... To all of us who have men dear to us fighting in France ... Mr Lockyer has been a source of untold strength and comfort. Every day he brought our boys' names before the Altar; even those who have fought the good fight and passed on, he keeps daily in our remembrance, that their sacrifice, like their Lord's, should never be forgotten. He spares himself nothing.

She concluded in the hope that the vicar would use his influence with the Bishop.

There appears to have been a climb-down at this point for on 2 July 1917 Mr Alcock wrote to Prebendary Hancock from the Palace, Wells:

The Bishop wishes me to say that Mr Lockyer seems to have entirely given up the practices which caused the Bishop to say he might have to withdraw Lockyer's licence. There is evidently a very strong feeling In Alcombe in his favour, and the Bishop thinks it would now be the best plan if you and Lockyer and the Bishop all met together and consulted over the Alcombe question from its different points of view.

The suggested meeting, at Taunton, never took place. Prebendary Hancock seems to have been determined that Rev. Lockyer should leave, and had already offered his position to Rev. T. Hawkes of the Vicarage at Watchet, who had not yet decided whether to accept.

Further correspondence followed, but the bishop finally succumbed to the pressure and Prebendary Hancock's obdurate position. On 14 July, the vicar heard from the bishop's representative, Mr Alcock, that '[*the bishop*] quite sees your point of view, and the difficulty of keeping Mr Lockyer, and the Bishop equally approves of your engaging Mr Heughan'.

The final letter directly mentioning Mr Lockyer is dated 30 July and is addressed from 'Newlyn', Alcombe. One Isabel F. Davy writes to Prebendary Hancock expressing her 'great grief and regret' at the departure of Mr Lockyer:

... I am over 80 and in all these years I have never met a man who has given me the spiritual help that he has. My Sister Mrs West was, as you probably know, a considerable benefactress to Alcombe Church and much as lies in my power, I have endeavoured to follow in her footsteps, and have done so gladly for the sake of the beautiful services and religious priviledges which Mr Lockyer has given us ...A good many of Minehead people too have been attracted to this Church chiefly by the Choral Communion which so many of us love. They have however, supported Alcombe Church liberally, but they also will cease to attend if alterations are made in the Services. You may be able to find a *good* man to take Mr Lockyer's place, but you will never find his equal as an earnest and hard worker.

By December 1917 a house in Alcombe Terrace was being prepared for Rev. Lockyer's replacement, the same Rev. Cecil J.Heughan who had enquired about a possible curacy post in June.

The Rev. Heughan did become the Priest-in-Charge at Alcombe, but only briefly, for we know from a letter written on 12 February 1919 by a would-be applicant, Rev. Pitt-Johnson, that the post was vacant.

Performance of Marriages at Alcombe Church

Harris and Harris, Solicitors of Wells, wrote from the Diocesan Registry on 20 June 1919 to Prebendary Hancock concerning the performance of marriages and the licensing of the Church for that purpose. Apparently the bishop 'has power with the consent of the Patron and the Incumbent, to Licence Chapels for the solemnization of Marriages in populous places if he shall think it necessary for due accommodation and convenience of the inhabitants, notwithstanding that the Chapel, is not consecrated...'.

A letter to Preb. Hancock dated 4 July 1919 from the Palace of Wells stated that 'the Bishop will raise no objection whatever to licensing Alcombe Church for marriages, if you yourself desire it. The matter therefore rests entirely with you'. It was not until January 1939 that St Michael's Church was licensed for marriages.

In the P.C.C. Minutes for 25 January 1937, the vicar of Dunster, the Reverend A.B. Burney, recorded the successful completion of the extensions at Alcombe church, including a chapel paid for by Colonel Maud, who had also provided beautiful fittings for the Reservation and a screen (and who later left the church a generous legacy). All were invited to the Service of Dedication by the Bishop on 2 February.

In November, Mr and the Misses Ford, residents and worshippers for forty years, gave four silver candlesticks for the High Altar when they left Alcombe.

In December 1938 we read in the Church Magazine under the section devoted to St Michael's Alcombe, 'the working party are very happy on Wednesday afternoon working for the Building Fund. They would welcome anyone who is a Church woman at the Hut at 3.00 pm. There is a cup of tea at 1d a cup'.

Alcombe held a Fête in July 1939 in an endeavour to pay off the last £100 debt on its building fund. The vicar of Dunster and Alcombe, the Rev. Austen Balleine, adjured the Dunster people to support the Fête. He reminded Dunster that it had an obligation to see that the Alcombe end of the parish was provided with all that was required in the way of a church, a vicarage and an endowment so that 'in a few years time it may be separated from Dunster and become a separate Parish'. Further he said:

> Here at Dunster we have problems and duties of our own. But we are not faced with the problem of building a Vicarage, that has been done for us; we are not faced with the necessity of providing the Vicar's stipend, that duty has not been required of us. St Michael's, however, has all three

problems to face [*i.e. also the building fund*], and, though it is still in its very early days, it has been steadily contributing to all these essential needs, while at the same time paying the ordinary Church expenses, which absorb most of the income from our Sunday services.

Dunster did, in the event, provide two stalls at the Fête, which was a success; the debt of £127 was extinguished with a little to spare. The vicar gave a green frontal and curtains to the new church and one of the St Michael's communicants gave a pair of silver candlesticks for the High Altar.

That September the Rev. Balleine announced that the bishop had given directions that the Blessed Sacrament could be reserved in the chapel at Alcombe, 'with the understanding that the Sacrament shall be reserved to meet the needs of those in the parish and neighbourhood for whom a separate celebration would be impracticable'.

The Rev Balleine reported to the P.C.C. on 13 October 1942 on a meeting he had attended at the Alcombe Church Council at which plans for the increase of a fund to sustain that district were discussed. The present financial state of St Michael's, it was stated, would not suffice to maintain it as a separate parish whenever that change might be effected. It was therefore agreed that the Alcombe portion of the Diocesan Quota should be reduced in 1942 to £5, on the understanding that the £20 saved should be placed to the 'Sustentation' Fund of St Michael's. This was repeated in September 1943. In September 1947 the following comments occur in the P.C.C. minutes:

It was agreed to support any step that the congregation at St Michael's might take to constitute themselves into a separate parish and to inform them of this Council's opinion that such an arrangement was very desirable.

However, on 29 January 1948, the following entry appears:

The Chairman also stated that following the Archdeacon's visit to Alcombe the congregation had expressed a definite wish to remain part of Dunster parish.

In his *Yearly Notes*, dated Christmas 1949, Preb. Dunlop wrote as follows:

The late Colonel Hartley-Maude of Periton left a legacy of £10,000 to Alcombe Church for the payment of a Priest-in-charge. Up to date, £8,000 has been paid in and the whole legacy may or may not be paid up eventually. This should make it possible to establish Alcombe as a separate parish and the possibilities are being examined by the Bishop and the Church Commissioners. On the whole it would be better so. The ancient connection could be kept up by appointment to the Vicarage of Alcombe serving with the Vicar of Dunster. Then the position of Dunster would become clearer and more compact. This should be settled during the course of the year 1950.

However, it was not until 1953 that Alcombe became a separate parish. An Order in Council made at Windsor Castle on 19 June 1953, and published in the London Gazette on 23 June, constituted Alcombe as a separate Ecclesiastical Parish.

The Annual Review headed *The Church of Saint George, Dunster, 1953* records the close connection and friendship between Dunster and Alcombe over many centuries and refers to that history in the following words:

> We certainly must not altogether lose such a long and historic connection and must do our best to contrive some means of continuing ancient friendship between Dunster and Alcombe. Meanwhile we can be assured the Church in Alcombe of our very sincere good wishes, and every blessing throughout the future.

The new Vicar, the Rev. John Leslie from Curry Mallet and Alcombe, was instituted in Alcombe on 10 December 1954. During the interregnum Bishop Hornby took charge of Alcombe.

Preb. Dunlop writes of the new boundaries in his *Year Book*:

> This Year Book mentions something about the new boundaries between some of the Parishes and now an Order in Council[24] has been issued defining these boundaries precisely. But for working purposes it is enough to record that the Boundary between Dunster and Carhampton is now Saltry Lane and a line in continuation across the Park. This brings Dunster Beach, Dunster station and Lower Marsh into Dunster Parish. The boundary between Dunster and Timberscombe is more difficult to define but it is in effect, Avill Farm and Houses are the last houses in Dunster along the Timberscombe Road — Burnells goes to Timberscombe, Broadwood Farm and Wind Whistle come to Dunster. The boundary between Dunster and Alcombe is Ellicombe Lane.

On 25 July 1978 Alcombe celebrated twenty-five years of independence with a service at which the Bishop of Taunton officiated.

ENDNOTES

1. It seems that the Council was unaware that Dame Margaret Luttrell had bought the Priory, which would have included the monk's Cloister/Cloyster garden, after the Reformation.
2. The well was not placed at the south end of the garden but on the east wall.
3. Mr and Mrs Blofeld kindly consented to the removal of their son's memorial brass to the west wall of the north aisle, to make way for the new plaque.
4. Where there is a window dedicated to his memory.
5. Special Fund Accounts for 1991
6. The eighteenth-century lectern was given to Alcombe church but was later returned.
7. At a small family service on October 11[st]1958
8. *West Somerset Free Press*, 12 Oct. 1958
9. Lyte: H.D. Part II 455.
10. Ibid.
11. Ibid. 383
12. Hancock: D.C.P. 58
13. Lyte: H.D. Part II 456 (Notes 2 and 3)
14. Ibid. (Note 4)
15. Ibid. 421
16. Ibid. 346/7
17. Ibid. 457 (Note 5)
18. Ibid.
19. Hancock: D.C.P. 116; Lyte H.D. Part II 373 and Note I
20. Hancock: D.C.P. 116. See also Volume One, p. 84
21. Letter dated 27/9/1990 from A. Mills to the author.
22. Hancock: D.C.P. 109-10
23. Information supplied by David Bromwich, Somerset Local Studies Library, Taunton. The office was renewed annually, unlike that of the Lord Lieutenant's whose term of office is of longer duration.
24. Given in full in the 1954 Yearbook, *The Church of Saint George, Dunster*.

CHAPTER TEN

DUNSTER CHURCH and PARISH in the SECOND HALF of the TWENTIETH CENTURY

At the first Parochial Church Council meeting which the new vicar, the Rev. Michael McCormick, chaired in October 1957, various matters such as the Remembrance Garden, the floral decorations, the social evening and the £100 donated by the Crown Commissioners towards the newly-installed heating system were discussed. The new vicar also pointed out the need for a new organ (see below.) Dilapidations on the Priory Benefice were also covered and the vicar pointed out that the benefice included the bungalow tenanted by Mr H. Lloyd, who had agreed to pay £8 per annum to the P.C.C. to cover dilapidations.

In view of the vicar's wish that the house and grounds should not be a financial liability to him, it was agreed that the P.C.C. should be responsible for the dilapidations (£48 per annum); for rates of £35, and the maintenance and repairs of the garden by contributing the cost of half a day's labour (£30 per annum).[1]

In January 1958, Mr Dainton told the other P.C.C. members that Mr Marsden, the Consulting Church Architect, would soon submit his report on all of the fabric of the church. The architect's inspection of the roof had revealed slates missing, which should receive immediate attention and 'some dry rot into which beetle had become established'. He advised that treatment should be left until the spring. The Fabric Committee was asked to arrange an inspection of the roof each Spring and Autumn.

In February the organist and choirmaster, Mr Popplestone F.R.C.O., Mus. Bac., applied for a £60 rise. The matter was left to the A.G.M. on 14 April 1958 in the Priory Church following on the Easter Vestry held in the Priory. At this meeting the vicar announced the resignation of Mr Popplestone; he would be succeeded by Mr David Oliver M.A. (Cantab).[2] Over sixty people attended this annual meeting at which the vicar made his annual report and the Electoral Roll was presented for inspection. The treasurer's report showed the income of the year as £1,795 12s 0d and the expenditure as £1,797 12s 5d, showing an excess of payments over receipts to be £2 0s 5d.

All the church councillors were re-elected and Mr R. Revell Johnson, Mr P. Toogood, Mr Donald, Mrs Atkinson and Mrs Haydon were elected. The sidesmen (Dr Atkinson and Mr P. Toogood) were re-elected and in addition Mr R. Revell Johnson, Mr Taylor and Mr F. Seager.

A few days later an article appeared in the *West Somerset Free Press* written by the Rev. McCormick, giving his first impressions of Dunster. 'Dunster must be amongst the most genuine parish churches in England,' he wrote and continued:

> Whether one considers its worship or singing, or bell-ringing or ancient treasures, or the way in which the flowers are arranged and the church kept spotlessly clean, nothing is done just for show, but out of a genuine love of Christ and His Church. The attendance of the choir (children and adults) at practices and services is, I would have thought, quite remarkable, and there cannot be many churches in which the bells are rung before morning and evening service every Sunday without fail by ringers who are themselves regular members of the congregation.[3]

He also also drew attention to the good work done by Mr Powles, Secretary of the Church Council and Headmaster of the local school, and his helpers.

In May 1958, the consulting church architect, Major Marsden, was asked to prepare a specification for all the work necessary to repair the church. This was done in order that an appeal might be made to the Diocese, the Historic Churches Trust and the Incorporated Church Building Society. However, some of the work was undertaken voluntarily by members of the Council: Mr A. Griffiths, Mr Bowden, Mr Nichols, Mr Lloyd, Mr Haydon and Mr Bowden.

At the P.C.C. meeting on 11 November the vicar stated that Major Marsden was just about to complete the specification for the 1958 repairs. It was hoped to commence the cleaning and spraying of the woodwork in a few days time.

The entire waggon roof over the nave and chancel and the roofs of the north and south aisles and the north and south transepts were cleaned and sprayed and where necessary they were injected with insecticide. The Rev. McCormick adds to this information in the Annual Review for Easter 1959:

> ...except in the North Aisle, where the roof will have to be renewed, no death watch beetle or dry rot was found and the sections of rotten wood which had to be chipped away from the beams are nowhere large enough to need replacing. The belfry has also been cleaned and treated, the cracked glass louvres bound with copper strips and the east window of the belfry supplied with a fitted copper cage to keep the birds out. All this has been done by Dawson and Sons for a sum of some £30 less than had been estimated.

It remained to repair where necessary the lead guttering and down pipes, and renew the North Aisle roof timbers which are above the site of the new organ. The vicar hoped that the expense would be covered by the money still left in the Fabric Fund, into which £100 was put every year and the grants they hoped to get from the diocese, the Historic Churches Preservation Trust and other sources.

When the results of this, the first Quinquennial Survey of the fabric of the church, were explained to the P.C.C. by Major Marsden, the Church Architect, he said that there were no emergency repairs to be done, and at least half of the urgent repairs could be done in three or four years time. He described the fabric as being 'generally in a very good state of preservation' and commended the Church Council for their untiring care over the past fifty years or so.

By August 1959 authorisation for the undertaking of further repairs was required. A letter from Major Marsden was read to the P.C.C. which referred to the work Messrs Dawsons had carried out on the tower; he was authorised to proceed with up to £350 worth of work (Part 4 of the Survey) as contained in his letter and to accept their offer of credit for three years. Further discussions covered dilapidations and the chimes.

With regard to the vicar's residence it was decided in November 1959 that for the year ending 1 June 1960 and the four following years the P.C.C. should pay for the dilapidations, administration and insurance rates and repair rates on the Priory and stable block, and the rates, including water rates. They would also pay half the deficit on the dilapidations account for the five years period which ended on 1 January 1960.

Dilapidations on the Priory were also mentioned under the heading of Financial Position in the Annual Review for Easter 1959 when the Rev. McCormick reported as follows:

> Considering all that we have undertaken, we have done very well to end the year with only £14 less in the Bank than we had at the end of last year. ... The two principal factors affecting our finances were (1) the obligation which the Church Council has, quite rightly, accepted of bringing the Vicar's salary up to the diocesan minimum of £650 plus the payment of the rates and dilapidations on the Priory (but not schedule A Income Tax!) – an obligation which costs them in all some £180 a year, and (2) the raising of the quota or share of Diocesan and Church Assembly expenses from £112 to £212 a year.

The quota of £212 (Nov. 1958) was the subject of a protest expressed by Mr Geoffrey Frost, People's Warden. It was agreed as a result of this that 75% of the quota should be paid and that it should be accompanied by a letter of protest. This motion was carried. However, in January 1959, the Rev. McCormick recommended that the full payment of the quota should be made that year but that the cheque should be accompanied by a similar letter.

In 1959 the Lay Reader and Secretary to the P.C.C was the Headmaster of Dunster school, Mr John Powles. Mr William Dainton was the Treasurer. Mrs Alys Luttrell and Mr Walter Frost were Churchwardens. The organist and choirmaster was Mr David Oliver, M.A., (Cantab); the Tower Steward, Arthur Tudball and the Sacristan, Aubrey Gould. The Robe Mistress was

Alice Haydon. Officials for the Mother's Union were the vicar's wife, Mrs Rachael McCormick, and Mrs Mabel Bowden. The P.C.C. members in 1959 were:

Joan Atkinson	Harry Lloyd
Frank Bennett	Dorothy Lowe
Richard Bolwell[4]	George Maidment
Louis Bowden[5]	Valerie Piper-Smith
Mabel Bowden	Ronald Revell Johnson
Kenneth Donald	Brian Rowe
Aubrey Gould	Philip Toogood
Alvan Griffiths	Arthur Tudball
Alice Haydon	Jack Tudball
Jack Haydon	Jane Withycombe
Ron Heywood	

In 1960 Jim Bennett joined the P.C.C.

The eight flower arrangers in 1959 were: Joan Atkinson, Barbara Nicolls, Mabel Bowden, Patricia Phillips, Olive Dainton, Alice Haydon, Jane Withycombe and Sydney Williams. They were joined by Gwyneth Powles and Cecily Rawlings in 1960. From 1961, some parishioners from Minehead arranged the flowers in the Priory Church.

The St George's Hut is mentioned in the Easter 1959 Annual Review and the Rev McCormick recorded his congratulations to the Committee and all concerned with the erection of the hut and on establishing it as a financially solvent community centre so quickly. He said that the Committee was already planning improvements to make it even more useful, and that as soon as they found that they were solvent they voted for a donation of £50 to be made to the Organ Fund.[6]

At the Easter Vestry for 1960 Mrs Alys Luttrell was re-appointed Vicar's Warden and Mr J. Tudball became the People's Warden.

Rev. McCormick wrote in the Annual Review for Easter 1960:

> We have now completed all the structural repairs we need to for some years, considerably more than we can pay for with what we have in hand. The roof timbers have been cleaned, sprayed, injected with insecticide and, where necessary, as in the North Aisle, renewed. The lead guttering, down pipes and roof tiles have been mended and replaced and much of the stonework of the tower repointed.

However the Diocesan Advisory Committee for the Care of Churches, had decided that Dunster's need was not as great as that of other Churches. 'We must therefore face the fact that no further grants are likely to be forthcoming, and shoulder the burden of maintaining in good repair our large and ancient church unaided', wrote the vicar. A Church Fair would be held at the Priory on Wednesday 10August in aid of the Restoration Fund.

The Rev. McCormick enlarged on the financial position: it was really less satisfactory than it appeared from the accounts. 'The income for the year was in fact £1,469. 13.10 and expenses £1,563. In 1959 they spent £100 more than they received, their expenses and commitments being much higher and their total income only slightly higher. ... To meet extra expenses they had relied entirely upon the Sunday collections and the visitors' boxes, but these were altogether haphazard and too dependent upon the incidence of sickness and the weather'.

The vicar suggested asking people to give half what they intended as a donation paid direct to the Treasurer monthly, quarterly or annually, leaving the other half to be given in the collections. He himself would make a donation of £10 a year under Covenant for the Fabric Fund which is an ordinary Church expense, in addition to the £5 already covenanted for the Organ Fund. The Treasurer would be pleased to receive donations, covenanted or not, which are part of some self-imposed planned giving.

The Church Fair in aid of the Fabric Fund was held for the first time on the Priory lawns. It made £300 profit. The setting was found to be so perfect that it was resolved to make it an annual event. In 1960 the Fair was opened by the youngest member of the choir and in 1962 by the oldest member of the congregation – Mr Billy Hobbs, who at ninety never missed a Sunday.

At the P.C.C. meeting on 13 December 1960, the vicar stated that the Crown Commissioners had again contributed £100 to the Fabric Fund and the appeal for covenants had netted up to £150 a year. It was agreed that Mr Powles should be presented with a new Lay Reader's scarf as a token of appreciation of his services over ten years. Major Marsden, the Church Architect, was asked about damp walling; a repair to the screen and to the plaster on the north wall; the replacement of curtains on the west door; the need for more radiators, and a circulatory pump in the heating systems. The result was that it was thought that these matters could be left until the following year.

The first P.C.C. meeting in 1961 took place on 13 March. The vicar stated that the Historic Churches Fund Committee would be meeting on the 18th of the month and he hoped for a favourable decision. (However, it would be reported to the P.C.C. on 4 December 1961 that the H.C.F. Committee had decided that they could make no contribution to the fabric of the church.)

In 1961 the Rev. McCormick wrote in the Annual Review about the illuminated cross.[7] The verger, Mr Williams, sets up the Cross of Moss on the Rood Loft for Good Friday and 'causes it to blossom forth into flower on Easter Day'. The Easter Garden in the South Transept was the responsibility of the ladies known as the Merry Wives.

At the Easter Vestry held on 20 March 1961 Mrs Alys Luttrell and Mr Jack Tudball were re-elected as Churchwardens. Mrs Bowden was elected as the Lay representative on the Rural Decanal Conference; Mr A Tudball resigned from the Church Council and the remainder were re-elected. Kathleen Donald joined the Parochial Church Council. Gwyneth Powles and Cecily Rawlings had joined the team of flower-arrangers.

The Treasurer, Mr Dainton, presented his accounts for the year. In the General Fund Account the income was £1,639 13s 5d and expenditure

£1,593. 5s 5d, showing an excess over payments of £46. Collections were £101 up, covenants yielded £82, the visitors' box £43 less. A vote of thanks was made to the organist for his donation of £100 in lieu of salary and to the auditors for their special concessionary fee. The Electoral Roll was revised. The Parish Council was to be informed that the Gas Company, when removing a lamp standard, had disturbed a wall.

In his Annual Review that Easter of 1961, the Rev. McCormick mentioned the choir of thirteen children and twenty-three adults; the nineteen bell-ringers; the ten servers and the twenty-three sidesmen, along with the six Sunday School teachers.[8] The Whit-Sunday Evening Service in 1960 had been broadcast by the B.B.C. from Dunster. The Rev. McCormick was able to report that ' we actually ended the year 1960 with a small surplus, large enough to wipe out the deficit incurred in *one* of those years. Moreover, we achieved this in spite of a considerable drop in the Visitors' Boxes last summer owing, no doubt, to the appalling weather'. Basic expenses in 1960 had remained much the same, apart from a rise in wages of 5s 9d a week for the Vicar. A circulating pump costing about £100 was needed to improve the Church heating system (this was soon generously provided). The Fabric Fund, like the Organ Fund, needed £600 after allowing for money that could reasonably be expected over the following 5-6 years.

In September 1964, the vicar reported that Saunders and Allen had been selected to wire the tower and the Priory Church. In the Annual Review produced at Easter 1965, he noted that '£221 was needed to replace old and dangerous wiring in the Sanctuary, the Tower and the Priory Church'.

Mr Peter Tudball was congratulated by the Council on 15 August 1966 on the excellent and spectacular way in which the tower was floodlit. He and Mr Gould were also thanked in October 1967 for their work in installing the lights in the clock-room and in the tower.

Vergers from 1952 to 1983

In May 1952 the verger's wages had been increased to £4 10s per week. Mr Sidney Willis resigned in 1958 owing to ill-health and advancing years. He had taken up his duties on Christmas Day 1945; two gifts were presented to the church in his memory: a communion flagon, by Mr C. Willis, and a curtain to hang behind the altar, made by the Ladies Working Party.

Mr Sydney Williams was taken on in February 1958 as a part-time cleaner whose duties would include opening the church daily and winding the clock. For two and a half days a week he was paid £3 12s 0d. On Sundays the vicar would open the church and the verging would be done by sidesmen. This saved the church £50 and Mr Heretage locked up the church daily. By May 1958, Mr Willis, now retired, agreed to lock up the church and Mr Williams was employed for four days a week, the half-day being spent on tending the Cloister Garden (now called the Remembrance Garden) and the Dovecote garden.

In November 1958 it was decided to apply for a faculty to remove the gravestones to the boundary walls. However, on March 1959 the P.C.C.

minutes record that 'the question of the removal of the headstones was discussed and the matter was left to the new Council'.

Mr Williams's duties in the churchyard did not include the cutting of the grass in the spring and summer, though a new rotary scythe had been purchased. So in April 1959 he was awarded a £5 bonus for doing this job. However, by July it was agreed that instead of paying a bonus the wages of the Church cleaner and gardener be increased by 10/- a week for the six summer months and that his duties be as follows: to open the Church and wind the clock and carillon every day except Sunday (when the bell ringers wind the clock); from Tuesday afternoon to Saturday morning inclusive to clean the Church, including the ringing and clock chambers; to keep the drain channels and gully traps clean; to tend the Cloister Garden and the Dovecote Garden up to the Priory wall and to keep the Churchyard paths clear of weeds and the grass cut. After further discussion it was decided to extend this offer if necessary to £20 per annum.

In 1962 the vicar pointed out that the verger's wages would have to be increased to comply with the rise in agricultural wages, which he found some difficulty in meeting. He therefore asked the Church Council to allow the gardener (i.e. the verger) to work another half-day at the Priory (the Rectory), at their expense, thus allowing the vicar £40 per annum. After some discussion and with consultation with the treasurer, it was felt that owing to the financial situation the Council could not comply with this request but would be prepared to review the situation the next year.

In 1971 it was announced at the A.G.M held on 17 April that the verger's post had not been filled, but Mr Clark, the former verger, was thanked for his work. At the next year's A.G.M, held on 29 March 1972, the vicar remarked on 'the fortunate replacement of Mr Clark, the verger, by Mr Grant who had done a great deal of work in the garden'.

On Sunday 1 August 1983, Mr Hubert Perry became verger. The gift of a verge had been received and a verger's gown procured so that he could be suitably equipped and apparelled on that day.

A Facsimile of Handel's Messiah

During the incumbency of the Rev. McCormick, Dunster Church acquired a facsimile of Handel's 'Messiah' through the generosity of Mr H.R. Barry of Worcester.

Mr Barry wrote to the vicar with this offer on 8 December 1961. He knew Dunster extremely well as he visited every autumn, and desired to give this facsimile (which had belonged to his late brother, a church organist for at least sixty years) to the church. In addition he would meet the cost of a suitable showcase, provided it was made by a local cabinet maker. The original manuscript was in the library of Buckingham Palace and there were only a few copies in the country, including one on view in a display case in Chester Cathedral.

William Hunt Ltd submitted a design on 10 February 1962. The case was to be made of oak throughout and the inside base was to be covered with green felt cloth. The cost would be £15 16s 6d plus 13s 4d tax and could be delivered in three weeks from the date of the letter.

However there were bureaucratic difficulties with the Diocesan Faculty Advisory Committee, who asked: 'Was it something rare? Was there any particular reason for wanting to exhibit it at Dunster? Was there some connection with Dunster church?' On 24 April 1962 the authorisation was not recommended 'there being no known connection between Handel, or the original score of the 'Messiah' with Dunster Church. Further correspondence ensued. Mr Barry, writing to the Rev. McCormick on 4 June 1962, said he was 'in no way surprised at your having a rough passage in the getting of the necessary faculty'. He expressed regret that so much bother had been caused and also admitted being a strong supporter of the strictest supervision by the diocesan surveyors in general though as he said, 'this can at times be carried too far'. He paid for the case 'with pleasure'. The facsimile is now displayed in its case in the north aisle.

This prompts me to wonder why music of such universal appeal could have caused such a storm in the Diocesan teacup and why Mr Barry's gift could not have been accepted graciously without causing possible hurt to his generous spirit.

Needlework

Back in February 1939 the ladies serving on the Parochial Church Council agreed to examine the hassocks and seat coverings in the church and to report back. However, war broke out that September. In 1956 kneelers were made for the Priory Church; they are to be found before the altar rails and they bear the initials M.J.W., G.W., D.C.H., C.T., R.T. and P.M.B. These initials represent the names of Mary (or Margaret) Jane Withycombe, Gladys Withycombe, Dora Hay, Catherine Todd, Ruth Todd and Phyllis Mary Bachelor. The only initials not identified are those of W.D.J.

At the A.G.M. held on 29 April 1957, Mrs Mabel Bowden exhibited hassocks which had been made by the Dunster Branch of the Women's Institute. By July 1957 'kneelers for the Choir are almost completed'. The church agreed to be responsible for the making up of the hassocks, cushions, etc. up to £20.

In the Annual Review of 1959, the Rev McCormick, writing about the Victorian Altar Frontal and Super Frontal of 1876 says, 'the somewhat dilapidated altar hangings have also gone and it is now possible to see the old stone altar'.[9] Later, before the crimson altar frontal in the Priory Church was made under the direction of Mrs Nora Bennett, a blue altar frontal, the gift of Canon Swann, was in place. The Rev. McCormick added that the Litany Desk now had a kneeler, worked by Mrs Reckitt.[10]

At Easter 1965 the Rev. McCormick recorded that 'the ladies of the Priory Group and the stitchers, besides completing some beautiful cushions for the choir stalls have produced a remarkable curtain to shield the Organist, worked principally by Mrs Reckitt'. The cushions for the choir stalls of the Parish Church are indeed beautiful and are worked in petit point.

The work was undertaken, like the 1957 work, by the W.I. under the supervision of their President, Mrs Hay. The Alcombe W.I. and the Priory Group also assisted. Mrs Helen Waddell came from Winchester and demonstrated how her work was to be carried out in Winchester Cathedral colours. (Appropriately, as the guardian of the young heir of John de Mohun III (1269-1330) was Richard, Bishop of Winchester.)

In 1976/7 hassocks in gros-point canvas work were made for the Parish Church. They have a blue background with a gold cross and I am told that one of the workers, the daughter of Mrs Norah Bennett, wrote in ball-point on the linings details of every-day expenses at the time.

The Organ 1957 – 1985

When the new vicar, the Rev M.E. McCormick, was inducted in October 1957, he had indicated at his first P.C.C. meeting the need for a new organ. He pointed out that the present organ was in a parlous state and could not be tuned. It was proposed by Mr Bolwell that a new organ be installed and an organ sub-committee, consisting of Mr and Mrs Bowden, Miss Sangar, Mr Lloyd, the Vicar, the Secretary and the Treasurer.

The Rev. McCormick announced the opening of the Organ Fund in an article in the *West Somerset Free Press* in April 1958:

> It was calculated that the new organ, using as many pipes from the old organ as possible might cost over a period of five years, £5,000 but that £3,000 would be needed anyhow and as soon as possible. This is a large sum and that is why the help is being asked of all those who know and love Dunster, but do not necessarily live there.

A fête in aid of the Organ Fund was to be held in the Castle Grounds on 9th August, thanks to the kindness of Mr Luttrell. Mr Popplestone, the Organist, was in the process of getting tenders from organ builders.

On 20 May 1958 the vicar announced that Mr Popplestone had resigned and that the new organist and choirmaster would be Mr David Oliver. He also provided an interim report on the organ, noting that 'three things that are wrong with our present Organ: The position of the pipes; the position of the console, or keyboard at which the organist sits, the hopelessly worm-eaten condition of the action'.

He then outlined the options, in a very detailed report, only part of which can be reproduced here:

> ... A new organ, using as many of our new pipes as possible, could be produced by Willis for £6,750, by Walker for £6,500 and by Hill, Norman and Beard for £6,375. None of these schemes would solve one of our major problems, the position of the pipes.
>
> For this reason serious attention has been given to the product of the only firm which makes an electronic organ which sounds like a good Church organ — Miller's. Their Martin Electric Organ consists of (1) a

console (keyboard) ... (2) Two generator racks which take the place of pipes ... (3) At least two sound cabinets ...

A Martin Electric Organ equivalent to the £6,750 Willis one, would cost £3,500 allowing in both cases, for the sale or our use of our present pipes ...

Such an organ had been heard, examined and tested by the Vicar himself, by Mr David Oliver, (the organist), and also Dr Bernard Robinson, Head of the Physics Division of the National Physical Laboratory at Teddington and responsible for its acoustic measurements. As a result of this report, the council approved a closer investigation of a Miller Electric Organ.

However, at the P.C.C. meeting held on 12 November 1958, the vicar said that it was now thought that a Miller electronic organ might not be suitable for the church but that Hill, Norman and Beard had evolved an imaginative plan for the new siting of an organ at a cost of £4,800. David Oliver, the organist, enlarged on the subject. The following resolutions were made and carried: (1) that the P.C.C. would make an effort to raise the Organ Fund to £3,000 by May 1959 and that a Gift Day would be held for this purpose on the Patronal Festival next year; (2) that a Faculty be applied for at once (see below); (3) that the architect be asked to present estimates for the necessary beams to support the organ and to include in the first year's work repairs to the three most easterly bays of the North Aisle roof.

The vicar proposed to the P.C.C. on 7 January 1959 that the application be made for a Faculty for the following works:

> The dismantling and re-erection of the present organ and a new detached console placed in the North choir Aisle behind the Choir and just inside the Rood Screen and facing south (*in fact it faces east*); the pipes being re-arranged, re-sited and re-voiced in an Organ Case on a bridge 10 feet above the ground across the East end of the North aisle; all in accordance with a plan submitted by Hill, Norman and Beard.
> The boarding in with oak panels of the three roof bays above the organ.
> The removal and re-erection of two memorial tablets on the Tower Wall and one brass memorial tablet on the North Wall to positions nearby, if necessary.

At the same meeting, the Rev. McCormick introduced a new plan for raising the Organ Fund. A subscription of one guinea over a period of ten years was suggested and in order to assist the treasurer, Mr Westcott was opted. There appears to have been some anxiety about the Monk's chest at this time. It had been placed in the south porch to attract funds towards the fabric of the church. The P.C.C. minutes for 1 July 1959 record that the Monk's chest was properly secured and that the Jacobean chest in the vestry was to be repaired.

The final decision was taken the P.C.C. on 15 April 1959. It was proposed by Mrs Atkinson and seconded by Mr Revell Johnson that:

The Chairman be authorised to sign an agreement with Wm Hill and Son, Norman Beard Ltd, on behalf of the P.C.C. for the reconstruction of the organ in accordance with the plans and specifications set out in the Organ Builder's report of Nov. 5 1958 and for the installation of stages "A" and "B", for the sum of £5,460 to be paid in four instalments of £250 on signing the contract on May 1st, 1959; £1,115 on Nov 1st 1959; £2,730 on completion of the organ and £1,365 six months later.

This proposition was put to the meeting and carried by 14 votes to 5. It was unanimously agreed that a loan of £500 be accepted from the Diocesan Board of Finance and that the P.C.C. guarantee to repay it by five annual instalments of £100 together with interest due as agreed. At the Patronal Festival on 23 April, offerings for the Organ Fund would be presented at the altar.

In the Annual Review (Easter 1959), the Rev. McCormick wrote:

If all goes well the new organ will be in position before Lent next year. The organ builders require at least eight months to prepare the various parts in their factory and they have agreed that, if the organ is ordered by May 1st, they will be able to start the final dismantling of our present organ and its re-erection on the bridge across the North Aisle in January 1966.[11]

He explained that the new organ would not be large or particularly powerful, but it would be well-balanced with clear, distinctive and contrasting stops. The organ would stand on a 10-foot-high bridge across the North Aisle, and possess a row of pipes, set horizontally instead of vertically, and flanked by two wings of the tallest of the metal pipes.

In his 1959 Easter Review, the Rev McCormick was able to report that 'we are within sight of our target of £5,000 by April 23rd, St George's Day'. Over 90% of the £3,500 given or promised so far had come from the parishioners of Dunster. few as they are. Nevertheless, they were still £1,500 short of what was needed.

With the sum given or promised, they would be able to order the greater part of the organ. He continued, 'We would, of course, be able to complete the organ all the sooner and at the original price, if we could find a donor for the £500 console or keyboard, the £350 row of horizontal trumpets and the £200 bridge, or even a surtax payer willing to make us an interest-free loan for five or six years of £500 or so. The organ case ... is being given in memory of someone who worshipped in this church for 52 years'.

At the P.C.C. meeting on the 1 July 1959, it was decided that the date of the dedication of the organ would be 24 April 1960, at Evensong. In the event, the date of the dedication was brought forward to 27 March.

It was agreed in November 1959 that £186 10s 0d should be paid out of the Organ Fund to replace the 8-foot pedal pipes on the east side of the bridge; the existing oak casework (part of the original Bryceson organ casework) was retained and adapted to form the eastern face of the new organ.

The newly reconstructed organ was dedicated by the Bishop of Bath and Wells (Dr H.W. Bradfield) on Sunday 27 March 1960. The *West Somerset Free Press* reported on 2 April 1960 that:

> A very large congregation was present to take their part in a simple and impressive service at which the right note was struck in more senses than one. It had been decided to dedicate the organ as soon as it was sufficiently ready to accompany an ordinary Sunday service in Lent, and this it did well and truly, although the organist [*Mr David Oliver*] had only five stops available instead of the 35 he will have at his command when it is completed.

On Saturday 23 April the Opening Recital on the Dunster Organ was held at 5.15 pm. The organ was played by Garth Benson, the distinguished organist of St Mary Redcliffe, Bristol. The programme (costing 2s, or 2s 6d with photo) noted that when the Organ had stood in the north transept, the Organist could neither see nor hear the choir. The removal of the organ from the north transept opened up the view along the north aisle towards the east but the case to hold the pipes which was erected on a bridge over the aisle destroyed the view to the west and obscured the arch. 'The problem has been solved by putting the console just behind the choir and setting up the pipes on a bridge across the North Aisle from where they can speak directly into the Nave.... Only the larger pipes of the Pedal Organ, with their grave pervading tone remain in the North Transept.'

The same day at 7.30 pm. the Patronal Festival Evensong was held. All the Organ Fund donations so far received were presented; messages from the Archbishop of Canterbury and the Bishop of Bath and Wells were read, and the name of the donor of the Organ Case was announced (see below).

A report on this Patronal Evensong also appeared in the *West Somerset Free Press* and was headed 'Congratulations from Archbishop for Organ Scheme'.

> The fund, which was opened less than eighteen months ago now stood at £4,000, announced the Vicar, and half of that was cash in hand. About another £1,000 was needed to enable the essentials of the organ to be fitted.... The organ itself would serve as a memorial to a number of people. The case was being given by Mr Henry Eames, in memory of his wife Lilly who for 52 years worshipped at the church. Another generous donation had been made by her husband in memory of Mrs Elsie Maidment, a member of the congregation and the church choir for many years; Richard Cook, before his death, had expressed the wish that his friends make a contribution to the fund instead of sending flowers to the funeral The lesson was read by Preb. G.D. Dunlop and Col. Walter Luttrell and the organist was Mr David Oliver.

The rebuilding scheme, the report continued, was drawn up in consultation with the organist and choirmaster and the Vicar. An enthusiastic review of the recital followed.

In his Easter Review for 1960 the Rev McCormick wrote that 'the organist at his separate console is now able to see and hear the choir and has an instrument of great variety, interest and beauty which, with its most unusual feature (a triple row of horizontal trumpets) is proving a real aid and inspiration to our worship'. He continued:

> It has 1,538 pipes, nearly twice as many as the old one, three different wind pressures instead of one, and electro-pneumatic action. The organ was dedicated on Sunday March 27th by the Bishop of Bath and Wells [*Dr H. W. Bradfield*] before Mattins at a time when it was being used for its principal purpose — to accompany our ordinary Sunday worship. The opening recital given by Garth Benson, the organist of St Mary Redcliffe, was held on Saturday, 23rd (St George's Day) and was attended by the Somerset Organists' Association, which is some indication of the interest which this organ has aroused amongst those who know. Of the £6,700 needed at this stage we have so far collected £5,300 ... including two major gifts of the console and organ case given in memory of former worshippers in this Church ...

The question of the erection of a screen to the organ on the entrance to the North Aisle was discussed at the P.C.C. meeting held on 15 June 1960. The next we hear of this is from the P.C.C. minutes for 13 December, when it was reported the screen of the organ 'had been painted in accordance with Mr Norman's ideas'. The vicar pointed out that, 'the organ may need further alterations to give absolute satisfaction so that the council should wait before tidying up the North Aisle'. At this same meeting it was agreed that £100 be transferred from the Fabric Fund to the Organ Fund as a loan until April.

On 13 March 1961, a vote of thanks was made to the organist David Oliver for his donation of £100 in lieu of salary. The work of boarding the three roof bays above the organ with oak panels was not completed until 31 March 1961.

In the Easter Annual Review for 1961 Rev. McCormick wrote:

> ...both the Fabric and Organ Funds are more healthy than we could have dared hope three years ago ... Both funds still need about £600 each, after allowing for money that we can reasonably expect over the next five or six years. ... Both funds benefited from the sale of the two leaflets about the church (6d) and the Dovecote (1/-) which were again sold out.

There is an entry in the P.C.C. minutes for December 1961 which reads:

> ...after some discussion concerning the organ the following resolutions were proposed and carried, a) that Messrs Hill, Norman and Beard be authorised to fit the Trombone pipes already prepared for a cost of £370; b) that the Treasurer be authorised to lend to the Organ Fund from the General Fund such sums as are needed provided that neither of these two funds are allowed to become overdrawn.

In the Annual Review for 1962 there is more concerning the Trombone pipes. The Rev McCormick writes:

>...at a saving of £205 we have managed to secure a rank of good quality Trombone Pipes from an organ that is being reconstructed in Glasgow University and these will be set up in front of the 32ft wooden pipes in the North Transept shortly after Easter, which is as soon as the organ builders can manage it. We will then be able to screen that part of that organ altogether and, when we can afford it, make a really good entrance by the North door, perhaps with inner glass doors. To do this properly may well cost £250 or more. We shall then only need to put in the 61 pipes of the Swell 'Twelfth' Stop for a further £225 and the organ will be complete. We should be able to do this by St George's Day which, that year falls on the Tuesday, after Low Sunday, but to do so, the order will have to be placed this summer. These two sums are the only ones not yet covered.

At the AGM of the P.C.C. held on 16 April 1962 it was decided to send a letter of appreciation to Mr Oliver who had again donated his salary of £100 p.a. to the Organ Fund.

A very short recital, lasting only 10 minutes, was held on 19 May 1962, when 80 people stayed after matins and evensong to hear Mr Oliver demonstrate that, as a result of the addition of the trombone pipes, the organ was now much better balanced. The organist pointed out that the trombone pipes on an organ were included not as a solo stop but to provide a fundamental pedal note powerful enough to support the bass line, even when the full organ was being used.

It was decided that in order to enable others to hear this really fine instrument, David Oliver would give a series of ten-minute organ recitals after matins and evensong on the second and fourth Sundays in June, July, August and September, beginning on Whit Sunday. On 19 May his programme included the Prelude and Fugue in E Minor by Bach and Prelude in D by Healey Willan.

The organ screen, a screen to hide the pipes in the North Transept, was mentioned by the Rev. McCormick in his Easter 1962 Review. There is further reference to this in December 1963, and in March 1964 'some decision followed about the screening of the organ and plans made by Mr Gould and Mr Wakeley were examined'. However, it was decided to defer any discussion until the AGM. On 2 June 1964 a gift of £200 towards the work was made known to the P.C.C. by the vicar and thereupon it was proposed by Mr Lloyd and seconded by Mr Tudball that Messrs Lloyd, Haydon, Gould, Dainton and Toogood should form a sub-committee to investigate the said screen.

To revert to 1962 and the financial situation regarding the organ. On 20 November the vicar, at a meeting at the Priory, stated that the position for the year was that the instrument would be paid for by 1964. The Fabric Fund stood at £57, £825 having been paid for work done. The revenue from the boxes was up to £600 from the Visitor's box and £540 from the

Organ Fund box, the increase possibly being due to the influx of visitors staying at Butlins Holiday Camp. In January it was agreed that the floor round the organ should be re-tiled and tidied up. Loose tiles in the church would be fixed in position at the same time, the work to be done by Mr Hawkes. By 1963 the Organ Fund had a surplus of £309 but another organ stop was still required.

Thanks were expressed in September 1964 'to those who had voluntarily cleaned the church during this time and to the ladies who made curtains for the organ console and to Mr Gould for their erection'. In March 1965 the Organ Fund stood at £536 and the possibility of the expenses of tuning the organ out of this fund were investigated also. The vicar agreed to the erection of the organ screen.

By May 1965 he had communicated with Norman, Hill and Beard about this, but Mr Norman was for the time being away in Canada. There was also an adjustment to be made to the organ which came under the guarantee (P.C.C. Minutes, 18.1.1966).

The news that Mr David Oliver was resigning because he was leaving the district was received with regret at the P.C.C. meeting held on 17 November 1965. It was decided to make a gift to Mr Oliver, possibly from the Organ Fund, which was to be used for the maintenance of the instrument. Later, in January 1966, it was decided that the presentation of a cheque for £100 to Mr Oliver should take place on the first Sunday in February after the service. He had been an organist and choirmaster since 1958 but now his work took him to Westbury.

Mr Langdon succeeded Mr Oliver and started his duties on 1 March 1966. He also, like Mr Oliver, agreed not to charge a fee.

At that time the Organ Fund stood at £863 and it was decided to ask the Choirmaster to pay the child choristers monthly from this source which was also used to provide for the maintenance of the instrument.

In March 1966, Mr Norman, having returned from Canada, proffered advice on the type of screening for the organ but it was known by June that the vicar did not think the plan provided by Hill, Norman and Beard was sufficiently detailed for local estimates to be made. He therefore promised to contact an Exeter firm, expert in the making of screens. This was the notable firm of Whipples, who included in their estimate not only the screen but an estimate for a porch-covered way at the North door. The sum involved was £965 if the screen was of oak or £865 for a softwood screen.

However the vicar told the P.C.C. on 25 October 1966 that Norman, Hill and Beard had sent an acceptable estimate of £700 for a screen which would be pre-fabricated at their factory and assembled on site. The screen was delivered by March 1967 and erected after Easter that year. In the P.C.C. minutes for 23 May 1967 we read that the screen actually cost £540 plus labour costs which presumably came to the estimated total of £700.

The Rev. McCormick resigned on 15 March 1967 and the Rev. Christopher Alderson was inducted on 2 April 1967.

On 9 October 1967 the Rev. Alderson reported to the P.C.C. that Mr Pritchard, the organ tuner, had pointed out that some deterioration in the organ had resulted from the door being constantly opened and that a glass door would obviate that. However, the council felt that as Norman, Hill and Beard had designed the casing the responsibility was theirs.

Again at the P.C.C. meeting held on 12 November 1968, the Rev Alderson reported further misgivings which the organ tuner had voiced and said that he was concerned about the deterioration of the organ because of dampness and the lack of circulation of air. As a result of this it was decided to bore holes in the casing to allow air to circulate.

On 7 May 1969 the Rev Alderson, reporting on the organ, pointed out that the firm concerned with its maintenance were persistent in their advice that a weather door was essential. The possibility of a porch to the door was to be investigated. At the P.C.C. meeting held on 29 September 1969 the secretary, Mr Powles, was instructed to write to Mr Torrens (the Church Architect in Taunton) asking advice concerning this porch.

At the AGM held on 29 March 1972 Mr Langdon, the organist intimated his intention to retire. In July arrangements were made to advertise the post of organist. In February 1973, Mr Dainton, the treasurer, suggested that Mr Langdon should be prevailed upon to accept £100 to cover his travelling expenses over the years he had given his services. In April 1973 Mr Langdon was still the organist and apparently was content to continue for a while.

At the P.C.C. meeting held on 10 December 1973, the Rev. Alderson reported that the organ had been tuned but was badly in need of a major overhaul. It was agreed that the Standing Joint Committee should have power to organise this with the organ builders. Mr Toogood asked about the paint on the organ case and it was decided to incorporate this with the overhaul.

It was reported on 11 February 1974 that the organ project had been held up because of the three-day working week (brought in because of the miners' strike and the need to conserve coal). In June 1974 the Rev. Alderson reported that he had received a quotation of £3,495 + VAT and expenses for cleaning and renovation of the organ. It was decided to leave this matter over.

In January 1976 the Organ Fund stood at £1,444, according to the P.C.C. minutes.

At the P.C.C. meeting held on 20 June 1977, the Rev. Alderson read out a letter from Norman, Hill and Beard estimating the cost of repairs to the organ at £352. It was agreed to proceed and at the P.C.C meeting held on 17 October 1977 it was reported that the repairs were completed.

On 2 April 1979 the Organ Fund stood at £1,362. 92. In November thefollowing year the organist's expenses were raised to £200 p.a. Mr Langdon was still the organist.

The vicar, at the P.C.C. meeting held on 9 July 1984, reported on the progress of the organ repair. Tenders had been received from George Osmond and Co Ltd, who were associated with the original organ builders Hill, Norman and Beard, and a staged programme of overhaul and repair had been costed. (Deane Organ Builders currently tuning the organ were ex-employees of Osmonds.) A decision was made on priorities in the repair stages; a faculty would be required before any work could begin. The Diocesan Board of Finance was to be advised by the Cathedral Organist. The cost of a staged and fully comprehensive restoration to efficient working order would be £8,000 - £10,000, and an overhaul by Deane, £2,000.

Following on the Organ Builders' repair specifications outlined at the July meeting, the anticipated visit of the Cathedral Organist to verify the faults had not taken place owing to his absence abroad and an illness. However, an equally qualified colleague was appointed to give his advice.

On 10 December 1984, the P.C.C was told that tests by Mr Martin, a competent organist recommended by the Cathedral, had now taken place. He had confirmed that the repairs detailed by the organ builders were necessary. A faculty would now have to be sought. A decision had also now to be made as to whether Messrs Osmond or Deane should be engaged to carry out the necessary work. The tenders from these firms had been discussed at previous meetings and the relative competence, reliability and financial stability of these firms had now to be considered. Messrs Deane were prepared to carry out an overhaul at a lower figure.

It was agreed, with one abstention, that Deane should be engaged. This firm of organ builders was to be paid the sum of £1,595 including VAT and it was hoped that the work would start after Easter. The faculty for the repair of the organ was in the Chancellor's Court awaiting the Registrar's completion of the documents. By 13 June 1985 the faculty for the repair work had been received and was shown to the council before exhibition in the church porch.

It was in September 1985 that Messrs Deane wrote to the rector, now the Rev. Doré, and suggested that work on the pedals was badly needed. The rector said that this had been confirmed by Mr Keith Jones and another organist, but the Council wished to have this referred to the Organ Adviser. The sum of £180 was at issue.

The organ builders, Messrs Deane, revised their tender to tune the organ and agreed to do the work for £45 + VAT per visit and suggested that the organ be tuned three times a year. It was agreed that this should be discussed with the Diocesan Organ Adviser.

In July 1991, Dr Roy Massey returned to Dunster during the incumbency of the Rev. Robert Doré, formerly a prebend of Hereford cathedral. Dr Massey had five times been conductor-in-chief of the Three Choirs Festival and ran the Hereford Choral Society. Known world-wide as an organ recitalist, he premiered several important works by modern English composers and had appeared on several occasions on television – most notably as solo organist at a Henry Wood Promenade Concert at the Royal Albert Hall. He gave a lecture recital which was much appreciated by a delighted audience.

ENDNOTES

1. Today, in 2002, this would cost a minimum of £25 per day. In 1962 it cost £10 to cut the hedge around the Priory grounds.

2. As late as 1961 when Mr Dainton the Treasurer presented his accounts, a vote of thanks was made to Mr Popplestone who received a donation of £100 in lieu of salary.

3. 19 April 1958

4. Mr Bolwell ran the Willow Café.

5. The owner of the former Luttrell Garage

6. By 1962 it was also being used for the Sunday School

7. The work of Margaret Tudball

8. At the A.G.M. in June 1962, the vicar paid tribute to the late Miss Ruth Vincent, Sunday-school teacher.

9. Later these were professionally restored (see earlier chapter).

10. Mrs Reckitt was the mother of Rachael Reckitt, a notable local artist whose metalwork may be seen in the chapel at Rodhuish, Old Cleeve Church and Withycombe, and on local inn signs.

11. In fact, owing to active wood-worm, the organ was dismantled on 6 July 1959 and a small organ on loan was installed in its place.

CHAPTER ELEVEN

THE BELLS of ST GEORGE'S CHURCH, DUNSTER; THE DOVECOTE

This chapter takes up the history of the bells, the clock and the carillon.

At least as early as the 1920s, a bell was rung at 6.00 a.m. and again at 8.15 a.m. by the person who also wound the clock daily. In 1936 Mr Tudball, whose duty this was, observed to the P.C.C. that the item costing £13 for ringing the bell should really be called 'Ringing Bell and Winding Clock' since the latter entailed far greater time and labour. The 6 a.m. bell was finally abolished in March 1939, and Mr Tudball was appointed to wind the clock for the same £13 p.a. When the Rev. G.D. Dunlop became Vicar of Dunster in 1946, the ringing of the five-minute bell before matins and evensong was discontinued.

A Junior Band of Bell-ringers had been set up by Mr James Griffiths in March 1923. In 1926 Mr Thrush completed fifty years as a bell-ringer, and this record was also achieved by Mr Elliot in 1937, who was presented with a Westminster Chiming Clock.

After the long enforced silence of the war years, the bells rang out again in February 1944 when the final victory of 1945 seemed assured. There was a desire to return to happier times after the privations of the war years.

The bells had been repaired in 1929 by Messrs Mears & Stainbank at a cost of £178 4s 0d. In September 1947 the bells were again examined and the Tenor Bell found to be in need of repair. That December it was agreed that £20 should be spent on the clock and bells. The set of handbells needed repair the following year.

A remarkable achievement by the Dunster Guild of Change Ringers was recorded in the Rev. Dunlop's notes for 1945-56:

> ...the Dunster Church bells have never failed on Sundays... it was a fine achievement when a peal of 5,040 Stedman Triples was rung in thre hours and nine minutes ... on 9th March 1950. This was the first Peal of Stedman by all the Band, the first Peal of Stedman to be conducted by a Dunster Ringer and the first Peal of Stedman since the rehanging of the Bells and it deserves to be put on record.

To commemorate this achievement, the council approved the erection in the bell-chamber of a board, made by Mr Tudball. In 1962, Mr Geoffrey Frost would ring a tenor bell to a peal of Grandsire Triples in two hours two minutes, thus breaking the 1883 record of the first time this peal was rung in Dunster Church, on 23 August 1883, of 5,040 Grandsire Triple changes in three hours eight minutes.

Bell-ringing and floodlighting played their parts in the 1951 Festival of Britain, as we have already seen. A special peal was rung on the Thursday evening of Festival Week. (There were nineteen bell-ringers that year; their names are given in the vicar's *Yearly Notes*.)

In April 1952 the bell-clappers were all re-bushed on the advice of Mears & Stainbank; the Bell Frame was overhauled and a new set of ropes provided. The ringers' New Year festivities included their annual supper and social, and the annual outing to other churches to ring their bells.

The following April the ringers reported that the bells were again showing signs of wear, and this was reported to the same firm. In the accounts for August 1956 was a bill from Mears & Stainbank, sent that April, for £3 16s 10d, plus carriage costs, for 'gorging and welding a new top to the clapper of the Tenor Bell'. Another firm, Whitechapel Bell Foundry AD 1570, had been responsible for repairing the clapper of the Tenor Bell, for £2 3s 0d. They had also checked, oiled and adjusted the Treble wheel. Together with carriage costs, their bill came to £7 15s 11d.

On 1 February 1961 a further bill (for £4 18s 0d) was received from Mears & Stainbank for fitting and welding on a new top, etc. for the No. 6 bell.

Mr Arthur Tudball completed fifty years of ringing in 1964; he was presented with an inscribed cigarette case. He was presumable still ringing in January 1966, when at his request a heater was bought to heat the ringing chamber.

In the mid-Sixties it became clear that the bells would have to be recast and retuned. As this major undertaking would also include repairs to the clock and the chiming mechanism (the carillon), we will leave the history of the bells for a while in order to bring the history of the clock and carillon up to this point.

The Clock and Carillon

In 1936 all the clock dials were regilded. Mr Blacking, the church architect, arranged for this to be done at a cost of £4 per dial. However, it was agreed that a local firm should be invited to tender, and the work was given to Messrs W.T. & A.R. Tudball, whose estimate was for £18, only a little more. The statement of accounts for 9 November 1936 shows that £18 11s 6d was spent on 'clock painting' and £8 on the hire of a cradle from Mr Fry.

The winding of the clock, a daily and laborious task, had been carried out by Mr A. Tudball. But when he retired from this job in October 1945, it was decided to investigate using electricity to wind the clock. Mr Bowden obtained an estimate for £300 by February 1946. In the meantime the clock continued to be wound by hand.

Mr Tudball had reported that the flagstaff socket had become so worn that rain had leaked through to the workings of the clock. Messrs Hine and Sons were called in to rectify this. He also reported that parts of the mechanism connected with the carillon had become unsafe through wear.

It had been necessary to carry out repairs to the carillon in 1931, during the incumbency of Rev. Reeder. These were done by Mr Hartley of Oxford, whose estimate of £5 10s was accepted, provided the sum was only exceeded if further work was required. Now, in July 1946, both clock and carillon were inspected by representatives of the Synchronome Clock Co. of Abbey Electric Clock Works, Alperton, Middlesex. They provided a report costing £17 10s and an estimate of £117 for the repairs.[1]

The Rev. Dunlop's *Yearly Notes* for 1946 relate that the clock and carillon had been found to be in a dangerous condition. They were silenced for two months in the summer while being repaired at a cost of £175.

In 1947 a further £20 was spent on the clock and bells. The suggestion by the Synchronome Clock Co. that they should make an annual visit, at a cost of 10 guineas, to keep the mechanism in order, was adopted at the Parish Church Council meeting on 31 October 1949.

In 1954 Mr Bowden suggested (again) an electric clock, but this was not followed up. Instead in May 1956 the vicar enquired of Mr Fincham, making his annual checkup on behalf of Synchronome Clock Co., whether the weight of the winding mechanism could be reduced. The answer was that a removable 'independent reduction gear' could be provided, to be refitted each time the clock was wound up. The estimate for providing this 'winding jack mechanism' came to £64.13s 6d.

More correspondence followed. On 19 July, the company wrote that their representative Mr Fincham had inspected the clock and carillon on 25 June, and come to the conclusion that he could not recommend fitting any motor-driven winding gear, either automatic or hand-controlled. He suggested his previous idea of the winding jack would be a more satisfactory solution.

A similar letter to Mr Dainton of the P.C.C. explained that the clock was not suitable for motor winding as special apparatus would have to be fitted to keep the clock going while it was being wound up. Both letters stressed the 'unfailing good performance' of the clock.

The idea of the winding jack was adopted and it was delivered on 4 October 1956. The cost was £67 16s 3d plus £3 for the packing case and 10s 6d carriage.

During the incumbency of Rev. E.M. McCormick, further enquiries were made about the possibility of winding the clock electrically. A letter to the vicar dated 14 July 1959, from 'Smith of Derby Clocks', following a visit of inspection by Mr J.E. Howard Smith, noted that the clock and carillon, both made in 1876, are in very good mechanical order: 'we have rarely seen an installation so well maintained'.

With regard to the clock, standard-geared electric motors could be introduced and provide power to operate the hours and the quarters. The very heavy weights of these chimes, probably weighing 12 or 13 cwts together, would be completely eliminated. 'Manual winding of the weights would then be a thing of the past.' Mr Smith's letter went on to explain the advantages of this improvement. He also explained that, as the time part of the clock already works for one week with one winding, that could still be hand-wound. But if they wanted the whole clock electrically operated, he recommended one of the firm's latest 'synchronous-electric units'.

The carillon machine, incorporating very heavy weights, could be dealt with in the same way as the hours and the quarters. An estimate was also offered to redecorate two clock dials and thoroughly clean all four motion works, since building work was being carried out on the tower at the time. This would cost an estimated £65.

Estimates for the cost of all the work were enclosed, but these were not taken up.

In November the same year, 1959, the P.C.C. agreed to pay up to £20 to regild the southern and western faces of the clock with gold leaf. The weather-vane was also regilded.

In his Annual Review for Easter 1960, the vicar thanked Arthur and Jack Tudball of the Luttrell Arms Garage, for repairing 'more than once' the striking mechanism of the clock and carillon without charge, thus saving the annual fee of £16 made by the London makers.

By March 1963 the vicar warned the P.C.C. that they should be preparing for the installation of an electric winder for both clock and carillon. (A Clock-and-Chimes Fund had been set up the previous year.)

Thwaites and Reed Ltd, of Clerkenwell, submitted estimates for converting the clock and carillon in July. It would cost £26 for a preliminary inspection by Mr Fincham (who also worked for the Synchronome Clock Co.). He duly arrived, and reported to Thwaites and Reed that Dunster intended having the tower completely re-wired in the near future.

Following a misunderstanding about the need for dismantling the clock for cleaning etc. when according to Mr Fincham's report, it was in perfect condition, the firm explained in April 1964 that it was the pulleys, wire lines, etc. that would cost £116 to repair before converting the clock to electric wiring. They explained the difference between their method of automatic winding and that of using geared electric motors, which, they understood, were far more costly to install than their own.

A subcommittee of the P.C.C. was formed in June to look into the whole matter of electrification. It consisted of Messrs Bowden, Tudball, Gould, Lloyd, Powles and Dainton.

The vicar, Rev. McCormick, wrote once more to the John Smith company regarding the system they had described back in 1959, and asking for a new estimate. Their 1964 estimate proved to be £755, £135 more than the 1959 one. In response to a letter from the vicar on 23 July 1964, Mr Howard Smith wrote back with more explanations and details. The firm's representative visited Dunster on 18 November and offered favourable and delayed terms.

However, the whole project had to be postponed in 1965 because masonry, roofs, guttering and drainage channels had continued to need urgent repairs. These cost £530, with a further £221 for replacing wiring in the sanctuary, tower and Priory Church.

The caretaker, Mr Sydney Williams, had been ill for six months and died this year. Mr Aubrey Gould had voluntarily wound up the clock during his illness. The new caretaker was Mr Clark.

Another firm now came on the scene. Gillet & Bland, of the Steam Clock Factory, Croydon, had installed the clock and carillon in 1876. Now the firm, now called Gillett and Johnston, wrote in July 1965 wishing to offer their own estimate for converting the clock and carillon to automatic winding. In their method, the winding was carried out 'by means of mercury tube type switches' – in this way 'the clock would not be subjected to undue stresses and strains, as would be the case in direct motor driving, and the original escapement and pendulum would be retained, thus keeping accurate timekeeping independent of the main supply'. After an inspection, they sent in an estimate of £722.10s 0d for the whole work. They also sent pulley and weight lines in August, presumably for urgent repairs.

Fund-raising began in earnest in November 1965. The Fund was to be called the Dunster Chimes Fund. Nearly one hundred people attended the second meeting of the Fund Campaign held in the School Hall on 2 February 1966. Mr Bucknell was co-opted to act as co-treasurer with Mr Dainton, the P.C.C. treasurer. The principal function was to be a Fête, to be held on 30 July 1966 in the forecourt of Dunster Castle, by kind permission of Mrs. Alys Luttrell. The vicar wrote a pamphlet for sale, *Dunster Clock and Chimes*.

Another scheme was to have a vegetable stall at the Yarn Market, but the Ministry of Public Buildings and Works refused permission for this and for a collecting box to be attached to the building. This was the idea of Mrs P. Barber of Dunster Café; however she was allowed to have a skittle board outside the Tithe Barn for a Skittle Week. After the Garden Party, the Chimes Fund stood at £1,808.

Bells, clock and chimes

Meanwhile it had become clear that the bells themselves should be recast and retuned. A Faculty would be required, as the No. 2 and No. 4 bells were cast in the late seventeenth century. The Petition for the Faculty was sent in August 1966.

The same month Mr H.J. Sanger, Tower and Belfry Adviser for the Bath & Wells Association of Church Bell Ringers,[2] visited Dunster at the invitation of Mr Tudball, to go over the proposed restoration of the bells programme set out by Mears & Stainbank of London. In his opinion, the recommendation to recast the whole ring was a wise one, likewise the replacement of the ring fittings, as the present wheels would need attention in a few years. But Mr Sanger drew attention to points of weakness in the frame, which were not addressed in the estimate.

In September 1966 the vicar received a letter form a Mr T.R. Robinson of Bristol, about the clock at Bideford which was being repaired. He said it was almost a duplicate of the Dunster one, two years older. 'I am so glad that you are planning to have automatic winding gear', he continued, 'and not this "synchronous mains drive".' He mentioned that Gillett and Johnston had just done a fine job on the bells at Alveston Church, and he offered to be a kind of technical 'watchdog' for Dunster, as he had been for Salisbury, Dorchester, etc.

Also in September Rev. McCormick received a letter from Mr C.H. Coombes, director of Gillett and Johnston, subsequent to a report from their Mr Sanger. In this letter Mr Coombes pointed out the desirability of co-ordinating the clock and bell-work, particularly in the kind of carillon machine which they had at Dunster. As his firm had installed the original machinery, they would be happy to accept responsibility for the entire instal-lation, including the re-casting and re-hanging of the bells.

In this connection his firm had contacted the bell-founder Mears & Stainbank, who had already been in touch with him, as had John Taylor and Co, Bell-founders of Loughborough.[3]

Smiths of Derby was still hoping for the contract, and asked leave to visit for an up-to-date inspection. This resulted in an estimate of £880 for modifying the clock and the carillon. The conversion of the clock to synchronous electric drive etc. was now £500, only £80 less than converting the clock to automatic-electric winding and motor drive. However an additional £690 would now be needed to deal with the bells, as the whole framework would be changed, requiring new hammers etc. When preparing the earlier quotations, as Mr Smith explained, the firm had no knowledge of any work connected with the bells and frame. He could not reduce the estimate further.

On 27 September Gillett and Johnston submitted to the vicar their comprehensive estimate for carrying out all the necessary work to put the bells, tower clock and carillon machine in perfect working order. Further inspection had shown that the carillon and clock hammers were in need of overhauling. The timber bell-frame appeared to be moving bodily and they suggested re-positioning the two existing rolled steel joists (RSJs) to support the new frame. The cost of all the work to be done, including re-casting the bells, was estimated at £4,987.

The bells themselves were to be re-cast by John Taylor & Co. of Loughborough. Their estimates for re-casting and re-hanging the bells arrived in November. Of the four options offered, the fourth was considered the best. This provided for entirely new fittings throughout, apart from retaining the present headstock and wheel of the tenor bell. Rather than simply repositioning the old frame, they now, after further inspection, advocated removing the floor and the old timbers beneath it. This would allow new girders carrying a new cast-iron frame to be placed directly on the existing RSJs, to which the new girders would be bolted. These would be cross-braced and grouted into the tower walls, which would not only make a strong foundation for the bell-frame but also lessen the degree of movement noticeable in the tower itself at present when the bells are rung.

Taylor & Co. would be able to start the work in October 1967. Rev. McCormick replied thanking them for the estimates and asking for a copy to forward to the Diocesan authorities.

As Rev. McCormick had left the parish by February 1967, it was Mr J.H. Powles, the school headmaster and also secretary to the P.C.C., who contacted the Diocesan Registry about the progress of the Faculty. In further correspondence, it appeared that the Faculty included no reference to the installation of an electric winding apparatus for the clock and carillon. A specification of the winding gear and a copy of the relevant resolution at the P.C.C. meeting had to be sent to the Diocesan solicitors, Messrs Harris & Harris, thus further delaying the granting of the Faculty. It was finally granted on 10 April 1967.

Mr Powles also wrote to the Central Council of Church Bell Ringers concerning the proposal to put the floor at a lower level. Mr Sanger replied that this job could probably be done by local labour at a cost of about £500. But Mr Sanger stressed that it was very important that all the work set out in Messrs Taylors estimate number Four (the one favoured) should be done.

At the request of the P.C.C., Major Marsden, the church architect had, on 6 April 1967, examined the proposals, especially those relating to the structural alterations in the tower, and discussed them in detail with P.C.C. members, giving advice on the builders' work entailed.

No decision had yet been taken on which firm's estimate to accept, though the P.C.C. 'favoured asking Taylors to see to the bells', as Mr Powles wrote on 6 April to Mr Coombes of Gillett & Johnston. The Council was also interested in Gillett & Johnston's method of automatic winding of the clock and carillon. Mr Powles enquired whether, when giving the estimates sent in July 1965, they realised that the bells would be recast and hung in a new frame.

A sub-committee consisting of Messrs Tudball, Lloyd, Meddick, Gould and Mr Powles, met Taylors' representative the following day. Major Marsden and Mr Sanger were invited to attend.

Mr Powles also wrote to John Smith & Son, asking whether their last estimate for £1,575 ('which caused us a good deal of concern')would be affected by the knowledge that Taylors now proposed installing the new metal frame for the re-cast bells on RSJs resting on the existing floor level.

The firm replied that much of the increased cost regarding the clock and carillon was related to the precise positioning of the re-hung bells. It might now be possible to make some reductions in their estimate; they were in contact with John Taylor & Co., who would send them the relevant plan and measurements.

Gillett & Johnston replied on 11 April: their director, Mr Coombes, would visit Dunster in the near future.

John Smith & Son sent revised quotations on 18 April; their representative would visit Dunster on 27 April. This was the firm offering the option of 'synchronous-electric timing' for the clock, as well as electric winding. They had lowered the price of this by £25, and the cost of modifying the carillon by £20. The total cost was now estimated to be £1,290 for electric winding or £1,185 for the synchronous-electric timing for the clock.

Mr Powles wrote on 3 May 1967 to the Clerk of Williton Rural District Council, asking if the Council would give a grant towards the cost of the recasting of the church bells and the other improvements planned. The cost was likely to be around £5,000.

Mr Coombes of Gillett & Johnston duly visited Dunster. He said he had been in touch with John Taylors, asking them to pre-drill the bell-frame or fit the hammers at their works, but they felt that the work on the hammers was the responsibility of the clock-maker. However, fitting the hammers in the tower might mean some awkward drilling.

Gillett & Johnston then submitted an estimate of £1,292 for installing automatic winding of the clock, and a motor drive to the carillon. Electricity would be used only to automatically wind the weights. They suggested Mr Powles contact Ashford Parish Church, which had an identical installation.

The new vicar, Rev. Christopher Alderson, and his wife welcomed the P.C.C. to the Priory on 23 May 1967. It was agreed at this meeting that the Council should approve the start of the work of re-casting of the bells and installing electric winding of the clock and carillon that October, subject to the support of the village committee. It was left to the sub-committee to decide on which firm should be employed to install the conversion to electricity.

Gillett & Johnston wrote again to Mr Powles on 26 July. Mr Coombes wrote that he understood the sub-committee had now decided to electrify the clock rather than automatically wind it, as previously supposed. He referred to a photograph of a mechanism manufactured only by his company and included with their estimate of August 1965. This photograph had apparently been used to publicise the appeal fund, and had perhaps encouraged horologists (those interested in clocks) to contribute, when they would not have given money towards a system using a synchronous motor. He continued to rehearse the arguments against this latter method (offered as an option by Smith of Derby) and concluded that for an independent view, the sub-committee should contact their local branch of the Bristol Horological Institute.

Mr Coombes's firm may have won the argument, but it did not win the contract, for we learn from a letter sent by John Smith & Son, sent to the Rev. Alderson on 6 September 1968, that they were waiting for their account outstanding for electrification of the Clock and Carillon, completed on 4 April (1968), to be paid: £1,290. They believed the clock had given no trouble since installation, and the carillon had now received its final adjustments. It seems from the final sum that the slightly more expensive option of electric winding was the system adopted, rather than a synchronous-electric unit.

Recasting of the Bells

In October 1967, Mr Arthur Taylor was in charge of the operation to remove the bells for re-casting. He was assisted the vicar, and by many willing villagers. Once the bells were removed, the silence was unnerving, as Peter Hesp wrote in the *Somerset County Gazette*:

"We miss 'em terrible", declared one Dunster old man, and a lady who has lived in the village for close on 80 years told me they kept waking her up at night.

"But they've gone. There aren't any to ring night or day", I said.

"Yes", she replied. "That's just what I mean, me dear. They've gone and I miss 'em – especially at night".[4]

That November, Taylors also repaired the ten smallest handbells, at a cost of £9 6s 6d. They wrote the same month about the inscriptions on the bells: the estimate included reproducing the existing inscriptions but was any new inscription to be added? The cost of such lettering would be 1s 6d, but they needed to know soon, before the moulds were made.

Major Marsden, the church architect, suggested in November that with the bells away it would be a good time to inspect the roof timbers, and he offered to do so. Later Mr Powles, secretary to the P.C.C., received a letter from Taunton, dated 5 December, from Mr Michael Torrens, M.B.E., F.R.I.B.A., offering his services as architect responsible for work arising under the 'Inspection of Church Measure', and adding that it was kind of Mr Marsden to suggest his name. If appointed, he would undertake the work for the minimum charges laid down by the R.I.B.A.

Mr Torrens met the vicar and Mr Powles on 14 October 1967 and undertook a brief inspection of the church. He reported back on 28 December regarding the work that had to be done in the tower before the bells were re-hung. As regards whether this was a good time to reconstruct the tower roof, he had seen much defective timber, in the wall plates and central beams in particular. This could be a problem unless the timbers had been treated thoroughly with insecticide in recent years, and he asked to see Major Marsden's report. The possibility of a 'lantern' to enable sound to escape through the roof, and the provision of sound deadening in the existing belfry windows could be considered, but this could not be completed, he thought, by Easter. He would also prefer to have the foundation beams at a lower level where they could bear into thicker walls, and where the mouths of the bells would be below the belfry windows. Then a simple reinforced-concrete roof would be enough and this would strengthen the top of the tower. An absorbent lining under the roof could reduce downward reflection of sound.

Mr Torrens was officially appointed as the church architect the following January. He corresponded with the bell-founders, John Taylor & Co., and made a detailed inspection of the tower. By February he had prepared the specification of the relevant builders' work in the tower, and he made sure it was carried out as agreed that spring. His fee was £49 18s 0d.

Regarding new inscriptions for the bells, Taylors informed Rev. Alderson on 12 January 1968 that their chosen additional inscription would be put on the largest bell, the Tenor, as this was the custom. The No. 2 bell had no inscription, while the Treble bell and the No. 5 bell merely had the name of the bell-founders, so they proposed also adding this inscription to the two latter bells, with the addition of their own mark and the inscription 'RE-CAST 1968'.

The inscription was:

THIS RING OF BELLS WAS RECAST IN 1968
CHRISTOPHER ALDERSON. VICAR
ALYS LUTTRELL ⎫
JOHN TUDBALL ⎬ CHURCHWARDENS

On 25 January, Mr Sanger wrote to Mr Powles in his capacity of Diocesan Tower Adviser for the Care of Church Bells. He remembered having suggested to Mr Tudball and his brother that a sound lantern might be of great benefit in improving the sound of the bells outside. If Mr Powles was interested, he could discuss the layout with the church architect, Mr Torrens.

In February 1968 the bells were re-cast at Loughborough by John Taylor & Co.: the tenor and bell No. 6 on 1 February and the remaining bells on 9 February.

The builders who undertook the work on the tower under the direction of Mr Torrens were Anderson & Marchant, of Poundfield Road, Minehead. The steel foundation beams were to be delivered from Loughborough on 26 February, by which time the holes and padstones for the ends of the beams had to be in place. Other necessary work included repairs to the inner faces of the belfry walls, and strengthening work to the roof, where the main beam had suffered insect damage (it was to be thoroughly doused with Cuprinol Special Grade Beetle Fluid). The builders were also to fix in position the steel girders supplied by the bell-founders. Their estimate of £129 12s 0d for the fixing of the girders, etc. and the one for supports to the timber roof structure, for £134 8s 6d, were recommended for acceptance by the church architect.

The Certificate of Completion was dated 31 December 1968. Mr Geoffrey Frost (d. 1990), the same bell-ringer who in 1962 had rung a tenor bell to a peal of Grandsire Triples in two hours two minutes, raised much money for the Fund by his skilful ringing this year of the re-cast Tenor bell, which weighed 21 cwt. The Dunster bells also figured in the April 1969 edition of the magazine *Ringers World*.

The Clock and Carillon after 1968

The firm which had installed the electric winding mechanism in the clock, John Smith of Derby, wrote in June 1969 offering to service the clock. However Mr Harwood of Dunster did the inspection and was thanked by the P.C.C. for his help and continual attention to the church clock.

In May 1972 the clock and carillon were damaged by vandals, who also attacked a window. Gillett and Johnson wrote to offer their services and spare parts for, as they pointed out, it was their firm (then Gillett & Bland) which had installed the original machinery for both. After their representative had visited Dunster to inspect the damage, they sent, on 5 June 1972, an estimate of repairing the carillon for £74. This did not include replacing a roller crank that was found to be broken. 'The electrical engineer who maintains the installation agreed to have this repaired locally'.

The work was carried out, and paid for on 9 August 1972. Several contributions to the cost of repairs were received, notably from the Girl Guides, whose Commissioner, Mrs Joyce Martin, sent a cheque on behalf of the Division Executive on 16 May, because 'they were all very fond of Dunster Church...'. On hearing of the damage from Mrs Martin, the Somerset Girl Guides Association also sent a cheque, 'with the good wishes of Somerset Guiding'. A cheque even arrived from a lady in Birmingham, who had happy memories of holidays in Dunster.

At the P.C.C. meeting on 9 April 1973, Rev. Alderson paid tribute to Mr P. Tudball and Mr Frost, whose work on the carillon had saved a great deal of money. Back in Arthur and Jack Tudball's time, too, they and the Luttrell Arms Garage had rendered valuable service, having repaired, without charge, the striking mechanism of the clock and carillon..

A further small repair to the bells was made in March 1977. John Taylor & Co. repaired the clapper of bell No. 6 for a total cost of £34 0s 34d. By October 1982 a new clapper was required for this bell, supplied by the same firm at a cost of £109 0s 23d.

J. Dawson & Son, Church Tower Spire Restorers offered in April 1976 to clean and gild the south face of the clock tower (which had not been gilded with the others in 1959). This would cost £89.

The final item regarding the clock and bells, etc. which has been made available to me is dated 21 September 1981. Mr Tudball reported that the electrical work necessary on the church clock had been completed.

THE DOVECOTE

A momentous event for the church took place in the beautiful summer of 1989 with the complete restoration of the medieval dovecote which is such a feature of the village of Dunster. It was built to supply the priory monks with a constant supply of pigeon meat. An ingenious revolving ladder with platforms attached allowed the monks to reach the nesting holes in the walls.

The dovecote had been purchased for £300 when the Luttrells' Dunster estate was sold by the Eagle Star Insurance Company in 1951. On 24 April that year the Minutes record a unanimous decision that the dovecote and its garden be retained by the Parochial Church Council. This was confirmed at the meeting on 28 May, when it was proposed by Mr Fenning, seconded by Mr Bowden, that the dovecote and garden be purchased by the church and the secretary was instructed to communicate this intention to the Bath & Wells (i.e. Diocesan) Dilapidation Board on the matter. The P.C.C. Minutes for 21 June record that £100 of the price was offered by the Church Commisssioners (a grant recommended by the Diocesan Dilapidations Board from the funds supplied to them by Westminster); £100 would be on loan to be charged to the benefice, and the Church Council should be prepared to pay £100. The Diocesan Board pointed out that as purchasers the P.C.C. would be responsible for repairs.

On 28 July it was proposed by Mr Fenning, seconded by Mr Maidment, that the purchase be made, subject to a right of way to the dovecote being guaranteed. This motion was carried. By the time of the Easter Vestry on 20 April 1953 the Chairman was able to report that 'the Dovecote and Church garden now was the property of the church', though legal formalities would not be complete until May 1956.

In September 1954 the Dovecote was insured for £400. It is clear from a letter dated 1 October 1954 from the Principal Officer of the Church Commissioners that by then the Church council had paid both their share of the purchase price, £100, and also discharged the loan from the Diocesan Board, a further £100. In November 1954, the vicar, Preb. Dunlop, received a letter from the diocesan solicitor Mr C.W. Harris stating that as he understood it, only the Dovecote building was to be transferred (to the P.C.C.), leaving the adjoining garden as a benefice property.[5] He suggested a form of words which would keep a right of way over the garden.

On 18 April 1955, the vicar pointed out that the dovecote needed some repairs, but the matter was left until the financial and legal situation was clear. The conditions of the conveyance of the dovecote to the Church Council were read and discussed by the P.C.C. on 21 November 1955. Mr Walter Frost proposed, seconded by Mr Tudball, that the draft be accepted. The conveyance was finally executed on 7 February 1956, and the purchase completed by May that year.

In March 1963 repairs were necessary and an estimate of £165 for the work was received. The vicar, now Rev. M. McCormick, informed the P.C.C., that the expense would be met by outside bodies: the County Council, the Ministry of Works (who carried out the repairs), and Mr Butlin.

In March 1964, a Dilapidation Fund was started. By November 1965, this fund stood at £386, but £114 of this was the cost of producing leaflets for sale.

By March 1966 there was £308 15s 0d in the Fund. The vicar wrote to the Ministry of Works again, telling them further repairs appeared to be necessary to the roof and the floor of the dovecote. The Ministry sought the advice of the Historic Buildings Council for England, and in June 1966 agreed to make a grant of £450 towards the cost of the repairs, subject to certain conditions. As in 1963, the Ancient Monuments staff based at Cleeve Abbey could do the work on a repayment basis. It was suggested that Rev. McCormick try to get a grant from his local authority.

The Ministry Architect had reported on 30 June 1966 that the condition of the walls appeared to be satisfactory, following the repairs carried out in 1963-4. However, the roof had deteriorated and the lantern on top appeared to be unsafe. The weathervane had collapsed through the lantern; many of the stone slates were missing and areas of the roof had settled, suggesting that the wood laths had decayed. Beetle damage was suspected in the collar and at the ends of some of the main rafters.

The work would include replacing defective or missing slates with similar ones from the quarries at Delabole, Cornwall; new laths should be used under the slates and main timbers repaired as necessary. The lantern and weathervane would be repaired at Cleeve Abbey.

The vicar agreed to the work being done on a repayment basis, and asked local authorities for grants. However the full sum necessary, in spite of the help from the Ministry of Works, could not be met, and this was a precondition of the Ministry before it would start work. The vicar wrote to the Ministry on 12 September 1966 that the whole project should be postponed for a year, with only necessary patching undertaken.

That September, the vicar also had a scale working model made of the dovecote for Dunster School (and perhaps another for himself); he thought it would be educational and perhaps a commercial proposition. The idea was to have a removable roof and a way of lifting up the central, revolving, post to reveal the ingenuity of the bearings.

By the spring of 1967, the Rev. Christopher Alderson had become the new vicar. At the P.C.C. meeting on 23 May, arrangements were made to open the Dovecote to the public, for a fee. By 9 October, almost £170 had been collected this way. Messrs H. Owen, A. Tudball, Cottrell and Bolwell were thanked for showing visitors around. However the potence (the base of the revolving ladder) was showing signs of wear. The vicar contacted the Ministry of Works, whose architect estimated in November 1968 that repairs would cost £1,500.

In May 1969, the vicar wrote that the church would be prepared to pay £150 towards the sum needed. That June, Williton R.D.C informed the P.C.C. that the dovecote was now registered as a building of special Architectural and Historic interest. The following January the Ministry of Housing and Local Government asked the P.C.C. to invite tenders.

In November 1972, in response to a letter from the church architect, Mr Torrens, that their contribution to repairs was expected to be about £1,700, the P.C.C. secretary replied that this was not possible.

In February 1973, the amount earned from visitors to the dovecote was £232. The vicar had acquainted the Chancellor of the Diocese with the need for repairs; the legal situation, he was told, was not yet clear.

Winters came and winters went, and winds and gales took their toll of the ancient dovecote. In the winter of 1987, weather conditions were particularly violent. Questions about damage to the dovecote were asked in the local press. In February 1988, the rector, Rev. Doré, set out the situation in the Parish Newsletter. He had started making enquiries four years ago about repairs to the dovecote. Clearly the Parish Church Council, which owned it, could not find all the money itself. Before these winter gales, repairs had not been seen by the relevant bodies as of high priority, even though visits had been made by the Shire Hall (i.e. the County Council) officers and by those from English Heritage. All had agreed that the dovecote was of national importance and that public funds must meet the cost of repair. During this period the dovecote had to be closed twice because of internal damage by vandals.

However the 1987 gales, the rector continued, with the loss of about one sixth of the slate roof, had now altered the priority situation entirely:

drawings had been prepared; tenders had been obtained, and funding sought. English Heritage would offer £4,000 towards a total cost of £10,000. Shire Hall hoped the Exmoor National Park would match this offer. On 14 March 1988 the P.C.C. learnt that the National Park would match the English Heritage grant of £4,000. This left £2,000 to be found. The P.C.C., it was agreed, should give £500 and underwrite the remaining £1,500 in the hope that this could be raised by an appeal to the public. By 13 June just over £300 had already been received.

Tenders went out in June 1988. The cost of repairs had been estimated at between £6,500 and £10,000, plus VAT, but due to inflation, the estimates now received ranged from £11,300 to £16,155, plus VAT. Two other firms would be approached. Both English Heritage and the Exmoor National Park agreed to meet 40%, as before, of the increased sums. New tenders were sent out in September. The specification for the repairs was drawn up by the County Architect's Office in November.

By the same month £400 of the sum for which the church was responsible for had been raised. The following February it was agreed that a joint appeal for the church restoration and the dovecote should be launched with an exhibition. The fund-raising would have three objectives; repair of the dovecote; the re-roofing, re-wiring and internal re-ordering of the church, and church house-keeping (that is, the payment of insurance, diocesan quota, etc. which was to be put on a sounder basis).

By March 1989, work on the dovecote had finally begun. The firm employed was St Cuthbert Builders of Porlock Weir. Tiling was completed on Friday 28 July, when the rector, Rev. Doré, placed the last tile in position. The repaired lantern, or 'glover', was erected on his birthday, 31 July 1989.

That July the P.C.C. was told that the Exmoor National Park had contributed £5,880 towards the repairs to the Dovecote. The people of Dunster had already given £1,410, and it was expected that the P.C.C.'s contribution would be £2,800, which, with the promised funding from English Heritage, would give a total of £14,000. (£11,727 had by now been expended on the dovecote.) In fact, English Heritage added £2,350 to the original grant of £4,000, making a total of £6,350. The rector estimated the final cost of repairs at about £16,500, depending on the cost of the gates.

There was some doubt about who owned the gate between the dovecote and the road. A photocopy of the sale document which was obtained from the Church Commissioners showed that the gate belonged to the P.C.C. but the wall and the gate dividing the dovecote garden from the Priory garden belonged to the Diocese. The P.C.C. agreed to renew the gates and rebuild the wall where necessary. Neither gate exists today.

On 10 July 1989 two alternatives faced the P.C.C. Either a grill could be installed from which the interior of the dovecote could be viewed, or the ladder could be removed and the platforms anchored, in which case the public would still be able to enter the dovecote. From fear of futher vandalism, it was agreed to instate a grill according to a design from the Somerset County Council.

During the repairs it was discovered that much of the timberwork had been replaced during the nineteenth century, probably at the time of the restoration work at the castle and the church. The ladder which revolved at the touch of a finger, the iron fittings and supports on the upper part of the base (the potence), were all now thought to be Victorian. However the central pivot of the ladder was possibly of medieval origin and the Field Archaeologist of the County Planning Authority, Mr Bob Croft, agreed it could have been re-used.

A coin of 1971 was found underneath one of the flagstones. This probably dated from an excavation at that time for an x-ray of the iron fittings and the central pivoting iron pin. Mr Croft concluded from his investigations that the current floor level is very close to the original floor level of the dovecote, suggesting the floor was flagged for many years.

The roof was repaired using sweet chestnut lathes, known to have been employed for roofs in Dunster in the thirteenth century. (Medieval carpenters used it because spiders will not fasten their webs to sweet chestnut.) There was no attempt to renew or straighten old or crooked timbers unless they were unsound. The main crossbeam had dropped 90 – 100 mm and had to be jacked into its original position.

Each pre-drilled slate was precisely cut on site and hung from hand-made graduated pegs. The curvature of the conical roof was taken into consideration. The slates had to be laid 'spalled' edges uppermost and closely jointed in straight horizontal courses, diminishing from eaves to ridge, with the width of the slates selected to the centre of the vertical joints over the slate below. Thicker slates were used on the lower courses, and the eaves were laid with a double course, with the undercourse fixed over the bottom batten.

At 8.20 a.m. on 1 August 1989 the weather vane was placed on top of the glover, and the beautiful gilded pennant, paid for by Mrs Deakin in memory of her late husband George, a local artist, and made by Mr Poirier of Roadwater, followed the dictates of the wind. With repairs complete, the next decision was whether to finish off the exterior in lime mortar or not. As the dovecote roof could not have guttering, water inevitably had to trickle down the walls. Lime mortar was the traditional way of finishing off a building to make it weatherproof, and there was evidence that it had been used on the dovecote in medieval times and again in the 1700s.

The disadvantage of lime mortar was a) the cost and b) the smooth appearance that would result – so unlike its former appearance as a stone building. After hearing advice from the experts, the P.C.C. decided that because the final cost of the repairs had risen by £2,000 over the original estimate, the further cost of using lime mortar could not be justified. Instead, the building would be re-pointed in such a way that a lime-mortar finish could be applied in future if desired.

The restoration work on the dovecote, completed that summer of 1989, attracted a Civic Award, for 'The Dovecote' and for 'Enhancement Works to Priory Green'. After the presentation ceremony, held on 11 March 1991 in the Inner Hall of Dunster Castle, Lady Gass, Chairman of the Exmoor National Park, unveiled the Interpretation Board in Priory Green.

ENDNOTES

[1] The full versions of the letters and estimates referred to in this chapter are in the Benefice files

[2] Who also worked for Gillett and Johnston, Croydon

[3] Estimate dated 28 July 1964; letters of the same date and 13 & 15 September 1966. John Taylor and Co., had written on 7 September 1966.

[4] 27 October 1967

[5] P.C.C. meeting on 30 March.

THE LUTTRELLS

The name of Luttrell does not appear in the Domesday Book and it seems likely that the first Luttrells came to England in the wake of the Norman invasion rather than in the van of the Conqueror. The idea of their Norman ancestry is given credence by various references in French records For example, an Osbert Lotrell had the farm of Arques in Normandy in 1180 and 1198 (*Rotuli Scaccarii Normanniae* (ed. Stapleton) vol i, pb5, vol 11, p422) Also, a certain John Loutrel of Dieppe is mentioned as a subject of the French King in 1419, while in 1422 a Robert Loterel was presented to a church near Bayeux [*Norman Rolls*, 6 Henr V, part 2, mm 40; 9 Henr V, m 5).

Towards the end of the twelfth century Sir Geoffrey Luttrell (d 1216/17) had a small property at Gamston and Bridgeford in Nottinghamshire The foundation of the Luttrell fortune was laid when Sir Geoffrey married Frethesant, the daughter of William Paynell a younger son of the powerful Paynell family from whom, together with her sister Isabel Bastard, she inherited fifteen knights' fees, situated principally in Yorkshire (*Pedes Finium Ebor* (Surtees Society) pp87, 88; *Rotuli de Oblatis*, etc, p205; *Red Book of the Exchequer*, pp77, 430, 490, 569; *Pipe Rolls*, 13 John, York,).

It was Andrew Luttrell, the son of Sir Geoffrey and Frethesant, who consolidated the Luttrell fortunes. On the death, in 1230 in Brittany, of his third cousin Maurice of Gaunt, the heir of the elder branch of the Paynell family, Andrew claimed certain properties; his representations being made to Henry III in Poitou. Eventually, following litigation, he obtained the manor of Irnham (Lincs) in April 1231, and those of Stockland, Quantoxhead and Huish in May 1232. From his grandfather, William Paynell of Hooton, he obtained fifteen knights' fees and from his cousin, Maurice of Gaunt, twelve and a half fees (see Lyte H D, Part I, pp62/65).

The Tables

The Luttrell genealogy which follows has been divided, for convenience, into three tables, namely:

- The Luttrell Genealogy 1: 1200 to 1461
- The Luttrell Genealogy 2: 1461 to 1711
- The Luttrell Genealogy 3: 1711 to the present day

Key to Abbreviations

(a) Letters in brackets associated with dates

- b = born
- bd = buried
- c = circa
- d = died
- dy = died young
- sp = sine prole = without issue

(b) Other letters

- a: Appears in the Luttrell Psalter commissioned by Sir Geoffrey (1276-1345).
- b: Armorial tile (mediaeval or Victorian) in the priory church.
- c: Bought Dunster castle and its estates from Lady Joan de Mohun.
- d: Armorial window (Victorian) in the priory church.
- e: Sir John was created KB at the coronation of Henry IV. On Sir John's death in 1403 Sir Hugh Luttrell (d1428), the first lord of Dunster, inherited East Quantoxhead Sir Geoffrey (? 1348-1419) accompanied Sir Hugh to the French Wars in 1417.
- f: Appear in effigy on monuments in the priory church.
- g: Buried at Dunster.
- h: Memorial brass.
- i: Purchased the priory after the Dissolution of the Monasteries in 1539
- j: Portrait/allegorical painting at Dunster castle. In the cases of Mary and Charlotte Drewe their portraits are at East Quantoxhead.
- k: Mural monument.
- l Hatchment.
- m: Windows in the parish church, with the exception of the east window in the priory church to Lt Col Francis Luttrell (1792-1862) and the window at the east end of the south-east aisle to Thomas Luttrell (1794-1871) and his sisters Margaret and Harriett, also in the priory church.
- n: Armorial pew in the parish church.

Note: KB signifies a Knight of the Bath. This Order of Chivalry had only one class until 1815.

The Luttrell Genealogy: Table 1

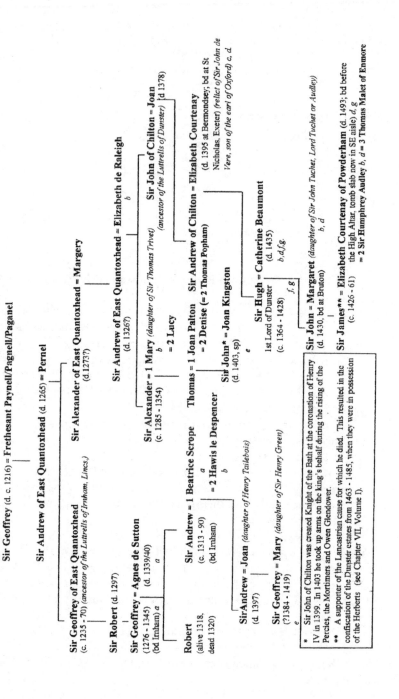

Sir Geoffrey (d. c. 1216) = Frethesant Paynell/Paygnell/Paganel

Sir Andrew of East Quantoxhead (d. 1265) = Pernel

Sir Alexander of East Quantoxhead = Margery
(d. 1273?)

Sir Andrew of East Quantoxhead = Elizabeth de Raleigh
(d. 1267)
b

Sir John of Chilton = Joan
(ancestor of the Luttrells of Dunster) (d 1378)

Sir Geoffrey of East Quantoxhead
(c. 1235 - 70) (ancestor of the Luttrells of Irnham, Lincs.)

Sir Robert (d. 1297)

Sir Geoffrey = Agnes de Sutton
(1276 - 1345)   (d. 1339/40)
(bd Irnham) a   a

Sir Alexander = 1 Mary (daughter of Sir Thomas Trivet)
(c. 1285 - 1354)   b
          = 2 Lucy

Thomas = 1 Joan Palton   Sir Andrew of Chilton = Elizabeth Courtenay
          = 2 Denise (= 2 Thomas Popham)   (d. 1435)
                                    (d. 1395 at Bermondsey; bd at St
                                    Nicholas, Exeter) (relict of Sir John de
                                    Vere, son of the earl of Oxford) c, d.

Robert
(alive 1318,
dead 1320)

Sir Andrew = 1 Beatrice Scrope
(c. 1313 - 90)   a
(bd Irnham)   = 2 Hawis le Despencer
                          b

Sir John* = Joan Kingston
(d. 1403, sp)
e

Sir Hugh = Catherine Beaumont
1st Lord of Dunster   (d. 1435)
(c. 1364 - 1428)   b,d,f,g.
          f, g

SirAndrew = Joan (daughter of Henry Tailebois)
(d. 1397)

Sir Geoffrey = Mary (daughter of Sir Henry Green)
(?1384 - 1419)
e

Sir John = Margaret (daughter of Sir John Tuchet, Lord Tuchet or Audley)
(d. 1430, bd at Bruton)   b, d

Sir James** = Elizabeth Courtenay of Powderham (d. 1493; bd before
(c. 1426 - 61)   the High Altar, tomb slab now in SE aisle) d, g
                          = 2 Sir Humphrey Audley b, d = 3 Thomas Malet of Enmore

* Sir John of Chilton was created Knight of the Bath at the coronation of Henry
IV in 1399. In 1403 he took up arms on the king's behalf during the rising of the
Percies, the Mortimers and Owen Glendower.

** A supporter of the Lancastrian cause for which he died. This resulted in the
confiscation of the Dunster estates from 1463 - 1485, when they were in possession
of the Herberts (see Chapter VII, Volume I).

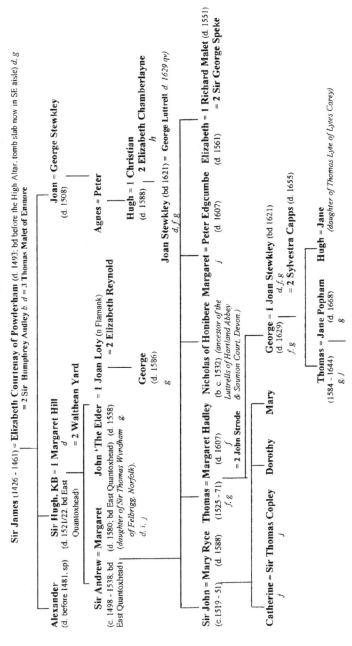

The Luttrell Genealogy: Table 2

The Luttrell Genealogy: Table 3

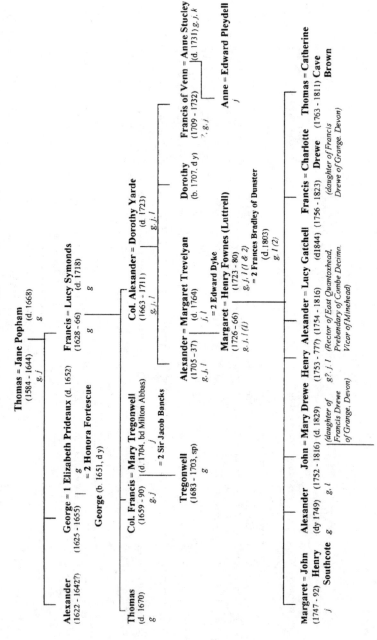

The Luttrell Genealogy: Table 4

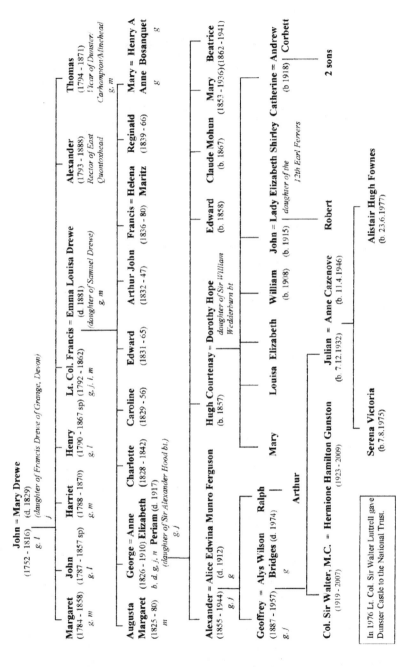

Thomas
(1794 - 1871)
Vicar of Dunster,
Carhampton/Almethead
g, m

Mary = Henry A
Anne Bosanquet
g   g

Alexander
(1793 - 1888)
Rector of East
Quantoxhead

Reginald
(1839 - 66)

Mary   Beatrice
(1853 - 1936)(1862 - 1941)

Catherine = Andrew
(b 1918)   Corbett

2 sons

John = Mary Drewe
(1752 - 1816) │ (d. 1829)
g, l │ *(daughter of Francis Drewe of Grange, Devon)*

Lt. Col. Francis = Emma Louisa Drewe
(1792 - 1862)   (d. 1881)
g, j, l, m   *(daughter of Samuel Drewe)*
                           g, m

Helena
Maritz

Claude Mohun
(1867)

Shirley
daughter of the
12th Earl Ferrers

Henry
(1790 - 1867 sp)
g, l

Francis
(1836 - 80)

Edward
(1858)

John = Lady Elizabeth
(b 1915) │

Robert

Harriet
(1788 - 1870)
g, m

Arthur John
(1832 - 47)

Hugh Courtenay = Dorothy Hope
(b. 1857)   *daughter of Sir William*
                      Wedderburn bt

William
(b. 1908)

Alexander = Alice Edwina Munro Ferguson
(1855 - 1944)
g, j   *g*

John
(1787 - 1857 sp)
g, l

Caroline
(1829 - 56)

Edward
(1831 - 65)

Mary   Louisa Elizabeth

Julian = Anne Cazenove
(b. 7.12.1932) (b. 11.4.1946)

Serena Victoria
(b. 7.8.1975)

Charlotte
(1828 - 1842)

George = Anne   Elizabeth
(1826 - 1910) **Pertam** (d. 1917)
b, d, g, j, n *(daughter of Sir Alexander Hood bt.)*
                  g, j

Ralph
Geoffrey = Alys Wilson
(1887 - 1957) Bridges (d. 1974)
g, j   *g*

Arthur

Margaret
(1784 - 1858)
g, m

Augusta
Margaret
(1825 - 80)
m

Col. Sir Walter, M.C. = Hermione Hamilton Gunston
(1919 - 2007)   (1923 - 2009)

Alistair Hugh Fownes
(b 23.6.1977)

In 1976 Lt. Col. Sir Walter Luttrell gave
Dunster Castle to the National Trust.

GLOSSARY

amercements	Infliction of a penalty left to the 'mercy' of the inflictor, hence the imposition of an arbitrary mulet or fine. Originally, lighter than appropriate fixed penalty.
apparitor	Ecclesiastical servant.
armed	Having teeth, talons, horns or claws (beasts), or wearing armour (cap-à-pie: fully armed). Heraldry.
bixgay/	A tool for rooting, consisting of a combination of a heavy bisgay/mattock and a small axe, called also a Visgay, two-tailed.
bisgy/ bisgee	Somersetshire name for a double-axe, having two faces, opposite and transverse to each other. Variant of besague, 15c.
buckram	(Then) costly and delicate fabric made from cotton or linen; (later) coarse fabric, often gummed for lining.
broadpiece	A twenty-shilling piece of the reign of James I and Charles I, broader and thinner than succeeding coinage.
camlett	A light stuff, formerly much used for female apparel, made of long wool, hard spun, sometimes mixed in the loom with cotton or linen yarn. Originally, beautiful and costly Eastern fabric. In the sixteenth and seventeenth centuries it was made from the hair of an angora goat.
cadenas	Knives and forks in a box.
caster	[= castor] fur hat: rabbit, rather than beaver.
court baron	Court of the baron (*court de baroun*). Usually annual court for dealing with small civil disputes, consisting of the freehold tenants of a manor under the presidency of the steward.
crape	Thin, transparent, gauze-like fabric, plain-woven, without any twill, of highly twisted raw silk or other staple, and mechanically embossed so as to have a crisp or minutely wrinkled surface. Originally comprising fine worsted fabrics; latterly usually referring to black silk etc.
crined	Having hair or a mane. Heraldry.
damask(e)	(From Damascus.) Here: rich silk fabric woven with elaborate designs, often of various colours.
drabdebery	(Drap-de-Berry.) Woollen cloth, originally from Berry region of France.
drong/drang	Variation of drong: a narrow passage or lane.
drugget	Material of wool, or wool mixed with silk or linen, used for clothing.

empryse	Enterprise.
etui	A term covering a number of small items, small boxes, scent bottles, sheaths holding scissors etc. Often bejewelled.
frieze	A coarse hairy material.
galloon	Narrow, close-woven, ribbon or braid, of gold, silver or silk thread – used for trimming articles of apparel; a trimming of such material.
gorged	Encircled about the throat with, e.g. a crown. Heraldry.
holland	A smooth hard-wearing linen fabric, orig. of a kind produced in the Netherlands (Holland).
hoops	Bullfinches.
impropriate	Annex (an ecclesiastical benefice) to a corporation or person as corporate or private property; *esp.* place tithes or ecclesiastical property in lay hands.
jessimy/jessamy	Typical of a dandy; a fop. From jasmine-scented gloves.
kersey	A kind of coarse cloth woven from short-stapled wool. Probably originally from Kersey in Suffolk.
mazarine	A deep plate, usually of metal, esp. one placed as a strainer inside a serving dish. Late 17th century.
moyders/moidore	A Portuguese gold coin current in England in the first half of the 18th cent., then worth about 27 shillings.
orace, orrice	(Orris) Lace of various patterns, of gold or silver; embroidery made of gold lace.
padoway	Strong corded or gros-grain silk fabric, now known as *poult-de-soi*. (Also 'paduasoy', 'pattiskiay', 'poudesy': from Padua.)
parclose	A screen enclosing a chapel or shrine and separating it from the main body of the church so as to exclude non-worshippers.
paten	plate for Eucharistic bread.
pattison	(Partisan) Military weapon used by infantrymen in the 16th and 17th centuries, consisting of a long-handled spear, with a blade having one or more lateral cutting projections.
periwig	Var. of peruke: wig.
pinnions	The short refuse-wool left in the comb after the long-stapled sliver has been drawn off. The word, which is evidently from the French *perignons*, is purely West Country (Hancock, *Dunster Church and Priory*, p. 159, note I).
pipe	A large cask, now esp. for wine; this as a measure of two hogsheads, usu. equivalent to 105 gallons; the quantity of wine held by such a cask.
predial tithes	Tithes produced from land or farms.
present	To lay before a court, magistrate, etc., a formal statement of a matter requiring legal action.
procurations	Management, superintendence; attention, care stewardship. The action of appointing a person with legal authority to act on one's behalf, the authority to delegate, the function or action of one's agent.
quarrell	A small usually diamond-shaped pane of glass.

rasdejane	Rash: a cloth of combing and carding wool mixed; twill-woven (from French meaning 'smooth').
ratteene	Thick twilled woollen cloth, usually friezed or with a curled nap, but sometimes dressed.
sack	Also (earlier) seck, ie. dry from French *sec*. A white wine formerly imported from Spain and the Canaries.
sad	Dark (of colour etc.).
sarcenet	A thin transparent silk of plain weave. The name is derived from the Latin *Saracenus*, from first having been woven by 'Saracens', probably in Spain. In the 17th century it could be 'clouded'(i.e. diversified with colours of indistnct outline), florence, persian or striped
scantling	Architecturally a timber beam of small cross-section, esp. one less than 5" square; timber or stone cut to such a size. Also a block of stone of a fixed size. 17c.
solidus	(pl. 'solidi') In Medieval England, a shilling. Earlier a gold coin of the later Roman Empire.
Spanish cloth	In the 17th century it was well-known that the really superfine cloth everywhere must be entirely of Spanish wool, and it was therefore often called Spanish cloth. Finer and more expensive than broadcloth, Spanish cloths were a West of England speciality in the 17th and 18th centuries.
suitor	In feudal law, a person who owed suit to a court, and acting as an assessor.
tabby	Silk taffeta, originally striped.
tearce	A third of a pipe (q.v.).
tippet	A long narrow piece of cloth or fur; a stole or short cape worn around the neck or shoulders.
tithing/tything	Originally a company of ten householders in the system of frank-pledge (i.e. mutually responsible); later, a rural division originally regarded as one tenth of a hundred.
trentall/trental	A set of thirty Requiem Masses for the repose of the soul, whether said on a single or on successive days. The word was formerly in occasional use for a Mass or other service (also Month's Mind) on the thirtieth day after death or burial.
unguled	Describing the hooves of animals. Heraldry.
virgate	Variable measure of land: on average 30 acres.
water bouget	A yoke with two pouches of leather. Heraldry.
watered	(or 'waved') having a lustrous damask-like pattern or finish; moiré.
worstede	woollen fabric made from well-twisted yarn spun of long-staple wool combed to lay the fibres parallel.

BIBLIOGRAPHY

I.C.P. BATES, E.H., 'An Inventory of Church Plate', *Proceedings of the Somerset Archaeological and Natural History Society*, Vol. XLVI (1900) Part 2

C. & C. BETTEY, J.H., *Church And Community* (London, 1979)

C.T. 19c. BEAULAH, K., *Church Tiles Of The Nineteenth Century* (Shire Publications Ltd.)

G.B.S. BARRINGTON SIMEON, Rev. G. *The Registers* 1670-1847

B.G.A. BURKE, Sir BERNARD, Ulster King Of Arms, *Burke's General Armory 1882*, 4th edition (*Heraldry Today*, Ramsbury, Wilts., 1989)

S.C. BYFORD, ENID, *Somerset Curiosities....* (Dovecote Press, 1987)

E.C.C. CAMDEN SOCIETY, *The Ecclesiologist* (The Cambridge Camden Society)

CHURCHWARDENS' ACCOUNTS 1847 – 1861, Somerset Record Office D/P/DU.4/1/1

L.S CLARK, Sir GEORGE, *The Later Stuarts 1660-1714*, 2nd Edition (Oxford History of England, 1956)

E.P.C CLIFTON-TAYLOR, A., *English Parish Churches*, 2nd ed. (Batsford, 1986)

H.C.S. COLLINSON, Rev. J., *A History Of The County Of Somerset.* 1791 (Bath: Cruttwell, R.)

M.B.S. CONNOR, A.B., *Monumental Brasses In Somerset* (Bath: Kingsmead Reprints, 1970)

O.D.C.C. CROSS, F.L., *Oxford Dictionary Of The Christian Church* (London, 1958)

E.S. DAVIES, G., *The Early Stuarts. 1603-1660*, 2nd ed. (Oxford History Of England, ed. Sir George Clark,1989)

D.C.G. DODD, DUDLEY, *Dunster Castle Guide* (National Trust, 1990)

S.D.G. DODD, DUDLEY, *The National Trust Year Book 1976 –77* (London, 1977)

D.P.B. DUNSTER PARISH BOOK, 1920 *Minutes Of The Parochial Church Council* (1920-1989)

C. of St.G. EELES. F.C., *The Church Of St George:Guide* (Westminster, 1940)

D.J.E. EVELYN, JOHN, *Diary*, ed. Bédoyère, Guy de (Woodbridge: Boydell Press, 1995)

D.J.E. EVELYN, JOHN, *Diary*, ed. Bray, William (London & New York: Dutton)

G.D. of D.   FOREMAN, A. *Georgiana Duchess Of Devonshire* (Harper Collins)

D.P.C.   FREEMAN, E.A., 'Dunster Priory Church', *Proceedings of the Somerset Archæological and Natural History Society*, Vol VI (1855) Part 2, 1-16.

E.T.D.   FREEMAN, E.A., *English Towns And Districts* (London, 1883)

N.D.H.   FRIAR, STEPHEN, Editor, *A New Dictionary Of Heraldry* (London)

V.E.S.G.   GALICKI, M., *Victorian And Edwardian Stained Glass* (English Heritage)

L.G.   GRIMWADE, A.G., *London Goldsmiths 1697-1837 — Their Marks And Lives*

D of A   GROVE'S DICTIONARY OF ART (NY,1996)

D.B.S.   GUNNIS, ROBERT, *The Dictionary Of British Sculptors 1660-1851* (London, 1953)

H.A.D.   HAMPER, WILLIAM , 'History And Antiquities Of Dunster', *Gentleman's Magazine* Vol. LXXVIII, Part II, 1808

D.C.P   HANCOCK, Rev. Preb.F., *Dunster Church and Priory* (Taunton, 1905)

E.G.   JACKSON, Sir CHARLES, *English Goldsmiths And Their Marks* (Antique Collectors' Club, 1989)

M.M.   LAWRENCE, C.H., *Medieval Monasticism* (London & New York, 1984/8)

H.D.   LYTE, Sir H.C. MAXWELL, *A History Of Dunster Parts I And II* (London,1909)

D.L.   LYTE, Sir H.C. MAXWELL, *Dunster And Its Lords* (1882)

L.H.D.   MERCHANT, H.F., 'The Luttrell Hatchments At Dunster', *The Coat Of Arms* (The Heraldry Society, Autumn 1985-Winter 1985/6)

H.G.B.   MOWAT, R.B., *The History Of Great Britain 1688-1924* (Oxford, 1931)

D.A.A.   MURRAY, P. and L., *A Dictionary Of Art And Artists* (Penguin Books, 1959)

O.B.A.   PAPWORTH, JOHN, *An Ordinary Of British Armorials.* (1961, reprinted from 1874)

G.T.E.H   PARKER, J. H.,   A Glossary Of Terms Used In English Heraldry (Oxford, 1847)

D.S.P.   PEPYS, SAMUEL, *The Diary Of Samuel Pepys* (Collins Library Of Classics)

S and WS   PEVSNER, NIKOLAUS, *South And West Somerset* (Buildings Of England Series, Penguin Books, 1958)

H.M.St S.   SAINT-SIMON, DUC de, *Historical Memoirs 1691-1709*, edited and translated by Lucy Norton, vol I (London, 1974)

H.H.C.   SAVAGE, JAMES, *The History Of The Hundred Of Carhampton in The County Of Somerset* (Bristol:William Strong and others, 1830)

H of.C.   SEDGWICK, ROMNEY, *The History Of Parliament. The House Of Commons 1715-1754* (London: H.M. Stationery Office, 1970)

T.L.   SIRAUT, MARY, Ed. *The Trevelyan Letters to 1840*

H.T.   STEINBERG, S.H. , *Historical Tables* (London,1964)

H.T.H.   STEVENS, DOUGLAS, *Back Through The Centuries: A History Of Townsend House* (Winsford: Nether Halse Books, 1986)

M.G.E.S.   STREET, G.E., *Memoirs Of George Edmund Street.R.A. (1824 -1881) by his son A.E. Street* (John Murray, 1888)

H.E.   THORNE, J., LOCKYER, R. and SMITH, D, *A History Of England* (London: Benn)

V.D   VIVIAN, J.L., *The Visitations Of The County Of Devon* (Privately printed by Henry S. Eland, Exeter, 1895)

G.III   WATSON, J. STEVEN, *The Reign Of George III 1760-1815*, Oxford History Of England, ed. Sir George Clark (Oxford, 1997 (1962))

C of S   WICKHAM, A.K., *Churches of Somerset* (David and Charles; Macdonald,1965)

W.S.   WILLIAMS, BASIL, *The Whig Supremacy 1714-1760,* Oxford History of England, ed. Sir George Clark, revised C.H. Stuart (Oxford, 1997 (1960))

A.R.   WOODWARD, Sir Llewellyn, *The Age Of Reform (1815 -1870)*, Oxford History of England, ed. Sir George Clark (Oxford, 1997 (1962))

PLEASE ACCEPT ACKNOWLEDGEMENTS FOR ANY PUBLICATIONS ERRONEOUSLY OMITTED

INDEX